Jewish Emancipation in a German City

Stanford Studies in Jewish History and Culture
Edited by Aron Rodrigue and Steven J. Zipperstein

Jewish
Emancipation
in a German City

Cologne, 1798–1871

Shulamit S. Magnus   '72

Stanford University Press
Stanford, California 1997

Stanford University Press
Stanford, California
© 1997 by the Board of Trustees of the
Leland Stanford Junior University
Printed in the United States of America

CIP data are at the end of the book

Stanford University Press publications are distributed
exclusively by Stanford University Press within the United
States, Canada, Mexico, and Central America; they are
distributed exclusively by Cambridge University Press
throughout the rest of the world.

This work is dedicated to the memory
of my grandparents,
Salomon Grossman
and Leah Juda Grossman,
my uncles,
Yidl,
Berl,
Nissn Yitzchok,
my aunt
Brandl,
killed in the War Against the Jews,
and my uncle
Simcha,
killed in the Siege of Jerusalem, 1948.
It is also in honor of my mother,
Libby Grossman Magnus,
who survived and gave life.

לזכר נשמות
סבא וסבתא
שלום בן משה וחנה שרה
ולאה בת ישעי־הו הירש וחנה
דודי
ידל
בערל
נתן יצחק
דודתי
בראנדל
שנספו בשואת יהודי אירופה
ודודי
שמחה
שנפל בירושלים, תש̈ח.
ולכבוד אימי מורתי, שתבדל לחיים
ליבה גרוסמן מגנוס
שקדשה את החיים בחייה.

Acknowledgments

This work began as a doctoral dissertation, completed at Columbia University under the guidance of Professors Fritz Stern and Paula Hyman. Professor Stern suggested Cologne when I first proposed the idea for a case study of Jewish emancipation in Germany. He and Professor Hyman read my dissertation drafts with great scrutiny and both contributed immensely to whatever clarity and perspective I bring to this subject. Paula Hyman has been a mentor and friend, generously taking time from a crowded schedule to comment on the revised manuscript and steadfastly supporting my intellectual efforts. For all this, she has my sincere thanks.

Michael Stanislawski, Hillel Kieval, Roger Kohn, Vicki Caron, Jack Wertheimer, Steven M. Cohen, Robert Liberles, Allan Silver, and Herbert Gans gave feedback on the dissertation that helped tremendously in its revision. Stephanie McCurry made important suggestions about the Introduction. Steven Zipperstein commented astutely on drafts of the revision, gave generously of his time, and was enormously encouraging of this entire project. I also want to thank Professor Carol Berkin for first encouraging an incredulous and timid undergraduate to indulge the love of learning and Professor Zvi Ankori for directing my path to the study of Jewish history at Columbia.

The staffs of several archives facilitated my work: the Historisches Archiv der Stadt Köln, Cologne; the Rheinisches Bildarchiv, Cologne which kindly made available to me the images reproduced in this book; the Hauptstaatsarchiv, Düsseldorf; the Staatsarchiv, Koblenz; the Stadtarchiv Bonn; the Central Archives of the Jewish People, Jerusalem; the Jewish Theological Seminary of America, New York. Dr. Gabriele Teichmann of the Hausarchiv Oppenheim, Cologne, was extraordinarily helpful and made my time in the archive a pleasure. She also generously helped clarify some archival and secondary source citations after my return to the United States. Oberarchivrat Waldmann of the Zentrales Staatsarchiv, Merseburg, was kind enough to locate and send me an important document I had long tried to find.

I am grateful to the National Foundation for Jewish Culture, the Memorial Foundation for Jewish Culture, and the German Academic Exchange Service for dissertation grants and to the National Endowment for the Humanities and the German Academic Exchange Service for grants that allowed me to do additional archival research in Germany.

This work has been a challenge to the spirit as well as the intellect. Toby Brandriss, Ken Karlin, Esther Halem, Rob Staples, Katharina von Kellenbach, Phyllis Klein, Nancy Fuchs, Sarah Luria, Ace Leveen, and Ruth and Al Sporer gave wisdom and emotional support that helped sustain me. Several people made a difficult time in Germany bearable. Lioba Theis was the first non-Jewish German I knew. Her honest declaration at our first encounter — "I am not responsible for Beethoven and Goethe either, but I claim them. You can't pick" — instantly won my trust. Her friendship and assistance in clarifying some of the more illegible documents were invaluable. The Levinger family, then of Cologne, made me a member of their household for the months I did my major research. Dorly Levinger, in particular, has been a wise and constant friend. Agnes Peterson of the Hoover Institution, Stanford University, graciously helped me unravel the meaning of one crucial source and cheerfully helped me find the best translation for several obscure German terms. Pamela MacFarland Holway of Stanford University Press gave me the precious gift of an editor with humor. She has my particular thanks for answering my many worried queries.

Ida Goodman, ע"ה, saved my mother from the fate that engulfed the rest of her family. She and her husband, Morris, ע"ה, were like grandparents to me. Ida's love has sustained me all my life. All that is mine is hers.

My father, Irving Magnus, ע"ה, had only a few years of parenting, yet left a child's memory of loving involvement, artistic creativity, and love of books.

My mother, Libby Grossman Magnus, has been a model of courage and endurance. Despite great tragedy and difficulties, she has held onto her love of life and family and to human decency. She has always taken pride in my endeavors and offered quiet but proud support.

My husband, Roger Kohn, helped me track down obscure books, articles, and archival sources, gave much helpful advice about research and writing, and generously helped with the index. He saw me through some terrible moments with near-saintly patience and gentleness. He has borne the burden of this work, and I am grateful to be able to share with him its fruition.

My son, Natan, helped by ever so sweetly tapping on the keys of my computer, reminding me of the line between sense and gibberish. Sunshine, even in California, he helped in many other ways as well.

Contents

(*Twelve pages of illustrations follow p. 190*)

Maps and Tables

Jewish Emancipation in a German City

Introduction

In the process of redefining themselves in the modern, industrial era, European states of necessity redefined the civic status of their Jewish populations. Premodern society in Europe was organized by Estate, with nobility, clergy, townspeople, and peasants each having different and legally defined privileges, duties, and disabilities. In such a social structure, Jews could also exist as a distinct group, governing themselves — at the behest of the authorities — according to their own legal system (*halakha*, rabbinic law), with their own communal and social institutions.

Unlike other legally distinct groups, Jews were also religiously separate from European Christendom. Because of this, even though they were as indigenous a European population as the Christian majority, Jews were seen, and saw themselves, as aliens — a body in, but not of, larger society. Indubitably present, Jews nonetheless did not belong. Although Jews labored under a heavy burden of anti-Jewish legislation, structurally legal disabilities were not an exclusively Jewish affliction in a society built on inequalities. Alienness, by contrast, allowed for expulsion.

Believing themselves alien, Jews awaited redemption and renewed sovereignty in Palestine. Believing Jews alien, non-Jews ordained eternal suffering for them for having rejected Christianity. At best, Christians awaited an apocalyptic Jewish acceptance of Christianity — mass conversion — as the herald of the Second Coming and the solution to the irritant of Jewish Otherness.

Beginning as early as the voyages of discovery and the Scientific Revolution, fundamental changes began in the economy and politics, in philosophy and religion, which undermined the feudal structures of society and, with them, the sense that the peculiar arrangements that had governed Jewish life for centuries were either necessary or beneficial. This is when the modern debate over the "Jewish problem" began. The discomfort with Jewish status and the struggle to fashion a new system, ranging from lessened discrimination to complete equality and integration, constituted the essence of the "problem," which preoccupied statesmen and philosophers, churchmen and bureaucrats, in England and on the Continent from the eighteenth century onward. The debate about the Jews was part of the process of constructing a secularized state, to be composed not of Estates but of individuals. It was prompted not by philosemitism but, in the words of Reinhard Rürup, by the perception that "the condition of the Jews and their position in the state were . . . unbearable; unbearable not only, not even primarily, for the Jews but for the state and the Christian population."[1]

Scientific rationalism, the weakening of religious authority in the larger society, and the awareness that a debate about Jewish status had begun encouraged small groups of alert, articulate, and influential Jews in France and Germany not just to chafe at their disabilities — Jews had always lamented the "bitterness of Exile" — but to hope for significantly improved lives in Exile. Once actual reforms began to be made during the waning years of the old regime in France, Austria, and Prussia, average Jews experienced the promise of improved circumstances, and the desire for betterment soon typified most of European Jewry, a minority of ultra-Orthodox rejectionists in eastern Europe notwithstanding. For Jews, this was as much a historical turning point as the rejection of feudalism in the larger society. From the beginning, then, the general and the specifically Jewish processes of rejecting received beliefs and social realities and redefining new ones were inextricably tied.

Of all the places where a debate over the Jewish place in non-Jewish society occurred, the most prolonged and agonized struggle was in German-speaking lands, where, to cite Rürup once more, "hardly any other question . . . exercised both practical politics and public opinion to the same extent for scores of years."[2] France resolved the issue relatively quickly and cleanly, if not easily, during the Revolution, which granted Jews full legal equality and abolished their separate religious and cultural institutions; resolution was similar in Holland. In England, vast areas of equality in residence, education, and occupation were established de facto, despite pockets of discrimination in elite university education and parliamentary service; Jews having been expelled from the country in 1290, there was no medieval, autonomous community to abolish. In tsarist Russia, which acquired a large Jewish population from the partitions of Poland at the end of the eighteenth century, there was some significant expansion of Jewish educational, occupational, and residential privileges during the nineteenth century. Russia, however, was a rigid autocracy with a backward, agrarian economy, while Jewish emancipation was the creation of liberalizing, industrializing states. This and the cruelty and overt Jew-hatred of many tsarist policies made it difficult for Jews to imagine a sweeter Exile under the tsars.

The states of central Europe were neither democracies nor, after Napoleon and the revolutions of 1848, pure autocracies; after a late start, compared to England, France, and Belgium, they began serious industrialization in the middle third of the nineteenth century. In contrast to the situation in England, France, Holland, Belgium, or tsarist Russia, there was no single German national state until 1871 capable of a uniform Jewish policy, one way or the other. After a century of furious debate, spurts of reform followed by "reaction" and renewed discrimination, popular riots against the Jews, and quiet bureaucratic machinations designed to deny them even those rights already conferred by law, Jews were granted civic equality in Austria-Hungary in 1867 and in Germany in 1869–71. Even then, significant areas of discrimination remained in the German civil service and the army.

In Germany, then, there was a seeming inability, or perhaps an unwillingness, to let go of the Jewish issue by resolving it. This prolonged torment was a function of the unresolved nature of modern German society and identity as a whole. For Jews, the recurring turns of Jewish policy meant living in a state of perpetual, wavering uncertainty about their place in society, or even their basic rights. Yet it is important to realize that the irresolution of Jewish civic status plagued Germans as well as Jews, for it was a constant reminder of the inchoate nature of the Germans' own civic identity.

This irresolution and the pressures it put on Jews, who were forever trying to read the climate to determine which of their actions or pronouncements would further the extension of rights and acceptance, has always seemed particularly poignant to me and drew me to study Jewish emancipation in Germany. The frustrations and ultimate catastrophe of German Jewish accommodation seemed better documented than cases where fundamental social change was successfully negotiated. I especially wanted to study the dynamics of such change, to see what worked, and why.

In this book, I focus on one major German city to see how Jews and non-Jews rewrote the rules of their relationship and shaped and experienced the process of Jewish emancipation. *Emancipation* is the term commonly used for the process in which Jews were freed from ancient discriminatory laws and, over the course of decades, became citizens.[3] That process was surely a complex human drama, yet it appeared as an abstraction in most works on German Jewish emancipation, which focus on the legal and ideological aspects of the struggle over Jewish rights and on the elite of non-Jews and Jews who took positions on this issue.[4] I wanted a more tangible understanding of how so fundamental and dramatic a transformation in the relations of Jews and non-Jews was experienced by people who lived it, how economic, social, political, and ideological forces interacted to bring about change, and how accommodation actually occurred.[5]

The scope of this inquiry necessitated study of one location where the dynamics of change were particularly illustrative. In many ways, Cologne was the perfect site.

As an autonomous city, Cologne expelled its Jews in 1424 and excluded Jews from residence or trade for nearly 400 years, until French Revolutionary forces annexed it and the rest of the left bank of the Rhine in 1797 and granted Jews legal equality. City leaders saw this as an abrogation of Cologne's historic privileges and an insult to its dignity. Discriminatory legislation introduced by Napoleon in 1808 and retained on the books until 1845 gave them the opening to reassert local control of Jewish status once Cologne returned to German rule, under Prussian hegemony, in 1815. For more than a decade, city fathers waged a tenacious, bitter, losing battle with Berlin for control of Jewish status.

Cologne was in a class of major German cities — Frankfurt am Main, Lübeck — that resisted Jewish rights in the post-Napoleonic years, but the peace Cologne eventually made with the new realities was remarkable. Cologne was the Rhineland's most populous and economically important city, a chief entrepôt for the Rhine river trade. After centuries of decline, its economy revived, and, from the mid-1830's on, Cologne became a center for innovative business and financial initiatives, especially railroad development. The changes revolutionized city politics, and, by the 1840's, official Cologne's stance toward the Jews was as liberal as it had previously been regressive.

Some of the Rhineland's most famous liberals, men who would leave their mark on Prussian and national politics — Ludolf Camphausen, Gustav Mevissen, David Hansemann — came from Cologne or had extensive business dealings there. In stark contrast to their liberal counterparts in south and southwest Germany, all these men championed Jewish equality in the Rhineland and Prussia as a whole. This advocacy had manifold, complex origins, including previously unexplored ties by these men, entrepreneurs all, to the powerful Jewish banking house of Oppenheim in Cologne. The Oppenheims, pioneers in investment banking, were also tireless campaigners for Jewish rights who fervently mixed business with politics.

Well before the revolution of 1848, then, Cologne was in the vanguard of Rhenish liberal advocacy of Jewish emancipation. In the decades following the failed revolution, for the most part years of retrenchment on Jewish rights in Germany, the city's policy toward the civil rights of its own Jewish community far surpassed in liberality anything in place on the state level in Prussia.

Freedom of movement was one of the chief benefits emancipation conferred on Jews, and internal migration, particularly to cities, was one of its chief results. While the height of German Jewish urbanization occurred only in the last third of the nineteenth century (only 9 percent of Rhenish Jews lived in the region's six largest cities in 1815), Jews came to Cologne in relatively large numbers from the beginning.[6] The growth rate of the city's Jewish community was the fastest in Germany; by midcentury, Cologne's Jewish population was the fifth largest in the country. Cologne's Jews thus anticipated an important development in German Jewry. Members of a limited big-city elite for much of the period under study, they are the more interesting for that adumbration and provide an opportunity to study Jewish urbanization and its economic, social, and communal effects in the age of emancipation.

As Cologne's economy improved, Jews made remarkable strides into middle-class standing despite the persistence of discriminatory legislation: by the 1860's, Jews, who made up 2.2 percent of the population, bore 7 percent of the tax burden. They made disproportionately great use of the city's *Realgymnasium* (secondary school), indicating a desire both for economic betterment and acculturation. At the same time, the 1850's and 1860's saw a vigorous expression of communal vitality and a determination, without the organized religious reform that emerged in other major German cities, to confront the prime challenge of Jewish modernity: creating viable structures for continued group existence while also seeking integration into non-Jewish society.

All the major themes of the emancipation era were thus encompassed in the experience of this city: the move from exclusion to integration of Jews; the Jewish rush to take advantage of new opportunities; and, finally, an organized Jewish response to the challenge that entry into the non-Jewish world posed to Jewish continuity. In less than a century, Cologne had gone from being a provincial bastion of xenophobia to an economically modern and politically forward-looking metropolis, with a relatively wealthy and well-integrated Jewish community. It was a great success story in the troubled history of Germans and Jews. Why and how this came about is instructive, I believe, for the larger study of German-Jewish relations in modernity.

The goal of this work is not a narrative in the classic genre of German Jewish communal histories, written in the age of emancipation to establish

the antiquity and chronology of those communities and, since the Holocaust, to memorialize them. Several such histories of Cologne exist, and
there is no need of another.[7] Rather, my goal is a study of Jewish emancipation in Germany from both the Jewish and non-Jewish perspectives, as
experienced in one locale.

I define *emancipation* broadly, as the societal change that occurred in
order for Jews to be granted partial or full equality, and as the further
changes that occurred in both Jewish and non-Jewish society as equality was
extended. I treat emancipation as a process of dynamic, mutual accommodation between Jews and non-Jews — not as a fixed event, however important laws and decrees were, but as a fluid, interactive process in which
Jewish behavior affected the attitudes and policies of non-Jews. Although
this approach required close study of one site, Cologne was as much lens as
subject.

Aside from making this project manageable, a local approach to German
Jewish emancipation seemed particularly suited to the fractured political
conditions in nineteenth-century Germany, where localism remained a potent political force, and provided a window on a central constitutional question in German history. The different states in pre-unification Germany
each had their own Jewish policies. The largest, Prussia, lacked even an
internally coherent policy, with different Jewry laws in effect in the various
provinces well into the century. Within the states, different rights were
granted Jews by the state and by localities (*Staatsbürgerliche, Lokalbürgerliche Rechte*).[8] The line between the two, not always clear, was increasingly
disputed as states pressed for greater centralized control over economic and
political life, including Jewish affairs, and localities fought to retain jurisdiction. The battle over Jewish civic status in Germany was thus one of procedure as well as substance. At issue was not just the rights that would be
granted or withheld but who — which level of government — would decide.
I am convinced that Cologne's battle with Prussia for control over the city's
Jews was an instance of the locality-state conflict that wracked Germany in
the early decades of the century and that the struggle over Jews in Cologne
is part of the larger history of German localism.

Rather like Mack Walker's description of German home towns — "What
was common to all of them derived from the individuality of each of
them"[9] — what was common to the course of Jewish emancipation in German localities was the peculiarities of the process in each of them: Jews
became German Jews in particular local contexts, and non-Jews absorbed
the new realities against a particular historical background. Thus, while it
would be impossible to write a local case study *representative* of German
Jewish emancipation (Cologne, if anything, was more singular than typical), I hope to have written one *characteristic* of it, to have illuminated the

essential dynamics of the struggle over Jewish emancipation in one "small world" within the macrocosm of modern Germany. Although personal documents are rare, I hope this approach also evokes some of the human reality of emancipation.

I study Jewish emancipation as a chapter in German history and the German context as an integral part of the Jewish story, not as mere backdrop. These might seem obvious premises, yet this is not how existing histories of modern Cologne or its Jews have been written.

Events in Jewish and non-Jewish history appear in histories of Cologne and its Jews like trains on parallel tracks, casting shadows on each other in passing but having no fundamental relationship. Jewish historians chronicle the city's hostility to the Jews and its metamorphosis on the Jewish question without analyzing these positions as part of broader processes in society. Oppenheim advocacy is treated hagiographically, as latter-day *shtadlanut* (the traditional pleading of powerful Jews before the authorities), when it was a distinctly modern phenomenon, inseparable from trends in broader society and expressive not of a desire for protection or privilege, as was the case with *shtadlanut*, but for integration and acceptance. Jewish immigration, occupational structure, economic mobility, educational patterns, and acculturation are not embedded in the social history of the city as a whole.[10]

Two major histories of the city of Cologne, one written before the Second World War, one since, all but ignore the city's Jews, reflecting a tendency that marks much historical writing about Germany: the perception of Jewish history as parochial and largely irrelevant. This ghettoization of Jewish history continues the marginalization of the Jewish experience that emancipation was supposed to end and (sometimes unconsciously) embodies the same bias that made it so difficult for many contemporaries to imagine Jews as members of German society.

Eberhard Gothein's masterly *Verfassungs- und Wirtschaftsgeschichte der Stadt Cöln vom Untergange der Reichsfreiheit bis zur Errichtung des Deutschen Reiches* (published in Cologne in 1916), makes the barest mention of the city's prolonged conflict with the Prussians over the Jews, the book's central focus on relations between city authorities and the Prussian state notwithstanding. Nor does it investigate the city's historic reversal on the Jewish question. Pierre Ayçoberry's equally impressive, two-volume "Histoire Sociale de la Ville de Cologne (1815–1875)" (dissertation, University of Paris I, 1977) makes a few very valuable references to Jews but does not consider them in any systematic way, despite the work's exquisite sensitivity to the different social classes in the city.[11]

Ignoring the Jewish case was a great missed opportunity for historians of Cologne. As I will show, consideration of the evidence about Jews refines the assessment of the city's political history while the story of Jewish economic and social mobility—the patterns of this quintessentially urban group—can provide an instructive comparative focus for trends in non-Jewish society.[12]

Cologne's historians are not alone in overlooking not just Jewish sources, but even German sources on the Jews, even when this material is in the same archival collections they heavily utilized, in this case, records of the municipal government. With the exceptions of Thomas Nipperdey and especially Reinhard Rürup, historians of modern Germany generally ignore the Jews.[13] Great Jewish spokesmen — Mendelssohn, Heine — may be mentioned; Jews may appear in treatments of broad reform programs, such as Stein's in Prussia. Primarily, however, Jews enter the pages of modern German historiography as objects of German hatred, and even this, except in specialized treatments, is more accepted as a given than investigated.

Reinhard Rürup is prominent in treating Jewish emancipation as a central event in modern German history, a bellwether of German liberalism and constitutionalism. But his focus, too, has fallen heavily on non-Jewish resistance to Jewish integration. Other major German historians who consider the Jewish question a central problem in German history have also emphasized the tensions and animosities between Jews and non-Jews, especially after 1871.[14]

When mentioned in histories of Germany, Jewish economic activities, petty or grand, are usually subsumed under treatments of antisemitism.[15] The phenomenal economic mobility of German Jewry during the emancipation era is generally not treated as part of modern German social change; Jewish embourgeoisement is not studied as part of the emergence of the German middle class.[16] Religious, cultural, and demographic developments in Jewish society are not recognized as part of trends in non-Jewish society.[17] As a result, Jews appear to lack a positive historical reality, existing only to the degree that someone objects to their existence. This puts the focus on non-Jews rather than Jews in treatments of "the Jewish question" and thereby distorts reality, since Jews were a vital part of the German social mosaic. Resistance to Jewish rights, although a basic part of the emancipation experience, was not its totality. Powerful forces in the economy and society promoted Jewish rights during the era of emancipation. The existence of German antisemitism and its grim outcome must not be allowed to efface the complex reality that Jews encountered in this period and the real gains they made.

Nor should the focus in both Jewish and German historiography remain so disproportionately on prominent intellectual figures, whether friends or foes of Jewish equality. We know remarkably little about how the majority of Jews and non-Jews experienced the transformations of this era and renegotiated their relations when ancient lines of demarcation blurred.[18] Most Germans and Jews were interested less in ideology than in living their lives uneventfully and comfortably. For Jews, emancipation promised vast new opportunities; the emancipation struggle was about access to them. Not all Germans saw this as a threat to their own interests, and much accommodation took place quietly. The upward mobility that Jews enjoyed in Cologne testifies to Jewish adaptiveness and striving for betterment, but also to the receptiveness of the environment. This part of the emancipation story also needs telling.

Only a social and economic study of the Jews can do that. Such analysis also highlights the gap between inferior Jewish legal status and solid material advancement — the distinction, in Ernest Hamburger's words, between "constitutional laws" and "the facts of life."[19] Here, too, Cologne is a good site for study of a broader phenomenon, because its Jews lived under discriminatory legislation — the Napoleonic decree of 1808, Prussian rulings — and prospered nonetheless. Given the city's history, its Jewish community was founded on immigration, which remained high despite anti-Jewish immigration controls in the French decree. The study of the origins and motivations of the immigration and of immigrant and overall Jewish occupational structure, wealth, and acculturation, is a basic element of this work. Marion Kaplan has established the crucial role that women played in the making of the German Jewish middle class in the era of emancipation.[20] Although the sources focus overwhelmingly on Jewish men, there are enough data on women to say something about the nature of their work and contributions to the Jewish ascent into middle-class standing in Cologne. Finally, I also investigate religious and communal developments — the Jewish institutional response to the challenges of modernity. These aspects of the book are part of a new social historical approach to Jewish modernity.[21]

As Avraham Barkai has shown, during the era of emancipation, German Jewry underwent significant social and economic changes that formed the basis for German Jewry's phenomenal "takeoff" after unification.[22] These changes directly affected the ability of Jews to integrate as citizens into the new German state and were also the basis for antisemitic stereotypes of Jews that emerged in the last third of the nineteenth century. Yet, in comparison with work on the Imperial and Weimar eras, this period has received curiously little attention from Jewish historians, a gap this study is meant in part to fill.[23]

German social historians commonly divide the German middle class into two major strands: the *Bildungsbürgertum*, comprising university educated men, members of the free professions, and high-ranking government officials, and the *Besitzbürgertum*, the "economic bourgeoisie" of wealth, comprising great merchants and manufacturers.[24] A significant branch of German Jewish historiography has stressed the importance of Jewish acquisition of *Bildung* — European education, culture, and values — as a means of Jewish entry into the German *Bürgertum* in the dual sense of this word as both "middle class" and "civil society."[25] While a radical intellectual circle did exist in Cologne (composed disproportionately of Jews or former Jews — Karl Marx, Moses Hess, Andreas Gottschalk, Dagobert Oppenheim), Cologne was not an important intellectual center but a thriving commercial and financial one. For the most part, Cologne's *Bürgertum*, non-Jewish and Jewish, was one of property more than culture. Study of Jewish success and acceptance here can shed light on the role of material factors in Jewish entry into German civil society. The distinctly middle-class context of emancipation in Cologne is an important focus in this book, which I hope will further our understanding of the close relationship between the emergence of bourgeois society in Germany and the process of Jewish civic integration.

There is a fair amount of writing by Jewish scholars, some of it extremely critical, about German Jewish attitudes to Germany and German culture. Hannah Arendt and Gershom Scholem, in particular, have charged that the lure of emancipation seduced German Jews into perilous self-delusion about German antisemitism and shameless abandonment of Jewish culture. By contrast, Ismar Schorsch and Marjorie Lamberti have stressed German Jewish political activism from the end of the nineteenth century onward, after German unification and legal emancipation had taken place.[26] The material from Cologne, coming from individual Jews and the organized community from the 1820's on, offers a perspective from the heyday of the emancipation struggle and can contribute to this significant debate about the perceptions and behavior of German Jews.

A chief source for this work is three large volumes of documents generated by enforcement of the Napoleonic decree of 1808, which mandated controls on Jewish businesses and immigration. Scribbled minutes of City Council sessions and records of correspondence to and from the Council, the so-called *Judenpatente*, are a rich source of information not only about the Jews but also about the city bureaucrats who oversaw them and about the relationship of these bureaucrats with their own, Prussian, overseers.[27] They are the basis for study of the Jews, German-Jewish relations, and German-German relations on the Jewish question.

The French-decreed consistorial synagogue system, also established in 1808, remained in force almost until the end of the period under study. It, too, produced records that furnished much of the basis for my analysis of Jewish class stratification and economic mobility.[28] Both the *Judenpatente* and the consistorial records sources contain precious documents in which ordinary Jews speak in their own voices. Other records, preserved in various government and private archives, filled out the story. The records of the Jewish community itself are no longer extant, consumed in the willful destruction of *Kristallnacht* and in the larger conflagration that followed. Because Jewish life came under so much official scrutiny, however, significant communal material has been preserved in city and state archives and could be used to reconstruct communal affairs. Under these circumstances, older histories of Cologne Jewry that utilize and sometimes cite *Gemeinde* records are particularly valuable. There are many studies of Cologne's political and economic history. I rely especially on those of Eberhard Gothein and Pierre Ayçoberry for putting developments in broader perspective.

Because the medieval legacy continued to play an important role in the sensibilities of city authorities well into the nineteenth century, Chapter 1 sketches the dynamics that determined Jewish status in the premodern period and the changes that came with French rule. Because most of Cologne's Jewry derived from the surrounding territory, it also traces the social profile of the Jews in Cologne's hinterland under the old regime. The main study begins with the French era, when Jews and Germans began to digest new realities, and ends in 1871, the year of German unification, when, on paper at least, Jews of the Second Reich attained civic equality. But 1871 seemed a clear demarcation on other grounds as well, given the dramatic developments in both German and Jewish societies during the *Gründerjahre*, the prolonged economic crisis that followed the crash of 1872, and the recrudescence of antisemitism in the latter decades of the century.

I have organized the work chronologically because formative developments clearly fell into periods: the French years; the initial decades of Prussian rule; the sea change of the 1840's; new strides toward acceptance of Jews as well as startling expressions of Jewish communal assertiveness in the 1850's and 1860's, the latter phenomenon clearly linked to Prussia's Jewry law of 1847 and to Cologne's political and cultural environment in these decades. While Jewish social and economic change is not datable so concretely, it was linked to, and itself influenced, larger trends and is accordingly studied with them. Where the volume of material warrants it, I devote separate chapters to the main themes of each period: the non-Jewish stance toward Jews, Jewish accommodation to the larger environment, and Jewish efforts to perpetuate Jewish culture and identity.

CHAPTER ONE

From Old Regime to Revolution

"We within our city may settle and uproot whomsoever
appears to us to be of use for our city."
The City of Cologne to Emperor Sigismund, 1431

The Medieval Period

On October 1, 1424, Cologne's City Council expelled the city's community
of some 100 Jews, ending a Jewish settlement dating back at least to the
early fourth century C.E. The expulsion culminated decades of wrangling
between municipal authorities and the archbishop-elector of Cologne,
both of whom claimed jurisdiction over the city's Jews. Both wanted control of the revenue Jews generated through taxes, commerce, and money
lending. But control also signified sovereignty and, for the city, autonomy
from its territorial overlord, over which city and archbishops had been
warring for centuries. The expulsion of the Jews, decades before Cologne
won official status as a free imperial city, marked the city's decisive victory in
this struggle.

The Jews of Cologne and elsewhere in Europe could be expelled because,
as a group outside the Christian fabric of medieval society, they had a
negotiated, not an inherent, right to toleration. Jewish status was fixed in
renewable accords called charters, which stated Jewish privileges (protection of life, limb, and property and the right of self-rule by rabbinic law), as
well as their financial obligations and permissible economic activities.[1] In
Cologne, the charters' duration was about ten years. Renewal was not
automatic, and if a charter lapsed without renewal, Jews were expelled.

Jurisdictional conflicts over Jews among levels of the feudal hierarchy
marked the medieval and early modern periods in Europe. The church

claimed ultimate control of the Jews on theological grounds. The Holy Roman Emperors, as purported heirs of Rome, erstwhile conqueror of Jerusalem, did so on political grounds, calling Jews "serfs of our chamber."[2] Actual control was increasingly decentralized as rulers mortgaged their prerogatives over the Jews to vassals in return for cash, troops, or support in power struggles. Such transfers of authority, intended as temporary expedients, tended to become permanent. While never formally renounced, the imperial prerogative gradually passed to the electors, who themselves were challenged for control of the Jews by cities growing in economic and political importance in the late Middle Ages and early modernity.[3]

This is what happened in Cologne. In the middle of the tenth century, Emperor Otto I invested the city's archbishop with temporal authority over the archbishopric, after which succeeding archbishops began to claim the Jews as an imperial fief.[4] Preoccupied with imperial politics, however, the archbishops exerted little presence in the city. In this vacuum, merchant elites began to expand their control over city affairs, including the Jews, who were an accepted part of the civic body. By the thirteenth century, when the archbishops tried to reassert control, they "ran up against the rights and privileges established" earlier and a major power struggle ensued, involving warfare and arbitration by popes and emperors.[5]

The ambiguous position of the Jews, "concives" in the city yet "serfs of the archbishop's chamber" by imperial fief, placed them in the direct path of this conflict, their predicament symbolized by the location of the Jewish quarter in the parish of Saint Lawrence, in the shadow of both the archbishop's palace and city hall.[6] Most German historiography has not recognized the Jewish element in the power dispute between the city and archbishops, while Jewish historiography has not linked the worsening status of the Jewish community to that dispute.[7] But the interrelatedness is clear in thirteenth-century developments.

Cologne's archbishops consistently sought to maintain a flourishing Jewish community in the city in order to benefit from Jewish economic activities. The city government also wanted a productive Jewry but, lacking formal claim to jurisdiction over the Jews, had to fight to win a share of Jewish revenue. The progress of the larger power struggle between the archbishops and the city intensified its peculiarly Jewish aspect as the cost of the conflict itself engendered a growing need for revenue and a sharper interest in keeping Jewish resources out of the hands of the adversary.

The charters granted the Jews in the thirteenth century reflect the dynamics of this conflict and its eventual resolution in the city's favor. In 1252, after his forces fared poorly in a battle against the city, Archbishop Conrad von Hochstaden issued the Jews a generous charter and asked that the city act as its guarantor. With this, the city had the beginnings of a legal claim over the Jews. Within six years of the "small arbitration" of 1252, as it is known in German historiography, when hostilities again broke out between municipal and archepiscopal forces and again came to arbitration (the "great arbitration" of 1258), the city charged the archbishop with infractions of his own Jewry charter and could reasonably allege that this constituted an invasion of the *city's* immunities. The archbishop, in turn, charged the city with taxing the Jews, which was his exclusive prerogative as their sovereign. The arbitrator, Albertus Magnus, upheld the archbishop's rights as legitimate overlord of the Jews but also ruled that the archbishop must abide by the formal prescriptions of that relationship, which now included a role for the city.

Within a year of this agreement, the city had won the archbishop's consent for a municipal tax on the Jews. This was a major compromise of the archepiscopal prerogative and vindication of the city's jurisdictional claim. The city also got confirmation of its role as guarantor of the archbishop's charter to the Jews, establishing a custom of dual protectorship of the Jews and a dual claim to the rights and benefits this conferred.

The city's power struggle with the archbishop led to war and decisive defeat for Archbishop Siegfried von Westerburg at the Battle of Worringen in 1288. Siegfried removed his seat from Cologne to Bonn, thereafter the archepiscopal residence, from which he and his successors continued to assert their historic privileges over all the territory's Jews (which were in dispute elsewhere in the electorate), including those of the city of Cologne.

From the fourteenth century on, then, the Jews had to come to terms with two masters and satisfy the financial demands of both. The archbishops and the city, now led by the merchant patriciate, granted separate charters. Both authorities recognized the other's claims on the Jews: the archbishop conceded that his privileges were issued at the city's sufferance, while in 1321 the city for the first time received the archbishop's recognition of its charter to the Jews. In 1324, in return for a stiff fee, the City Council even worked to procure for the Jews renewal of the archbishop's privilege, which had been stalled for three years by a recalcitrant Cathedral Chapter.[8] For all its apparent contradiction, the city's intervention made sense: it raised revenue and exerted sovereignty.

The protection of Jews regularly promised by city and archepiscopal charters failed when anti-Jewish mob violence erupted in 1349, during the Black Death. Cologne's Jewry had escaped some of the worst excesses perpetrated elsewhere in the Rhineland in the thirteenth century; now, it shared in the anti-Jewish devastation that shook the territory.[9] The Jewish quarter was sacked and torched and the entire community perished. The debate over who had superior legal claim to the Jews continued in macabre fashion after their deaths, as suits commenced for distribution of Jewish assets. The archbishop's preeminent right to Jewish property was upheld in arbitration, but he made a generous settlement with the city, and both profited mightily in the end.[10]

For twenty years after the massacre, there was no Jewish community in Cologne. It was a period of turmoil as the guilds, led by the weavers, revolted against the rule of the patriciate and briefly established power in city government. The patriciate crushed this uprising in 1372 and for several decades succeeded in repressing outside political challenges.[11] Shortly after returning to power, the patriciate agreed with Archbishop Frederick III von Saarweden to reestablish a Jewish community; both were in dire need of money and had found no substitute for Jewish taxes and loans. Christian moneylenders had replaced Jews but, in the absence of competition, charged higher interest rates than the Jews had. The resulting money shortage was hurting trade, the city's lifeline. The archbishop's financial straits were desperate. Anarchy prevailed in much of his territory as robber bands preyed on road and river traffic, yet he lacked the cash to establish order. As before, both city and archbishop issued separate charters to attract Jewish settlement, thus reconstituting the dual protectorship of the Jews, with all its tensions.[12]

The Jewish community that gathered in Cologne in 1372, composed largely of survivors from the archbishopric and farther south on the Rhine, was smaller than the previous one, its population never exceeding more than 200 people.[13] Even so, it filled an important banking function as the city called on Jewish loans in decades of renewed urban unrest, clashes with the archbishop, and periodic depredations of marauders.[14] Between 1370 and 1392, and again from 1414 to 1424, the Jews of Cologne, individually and collectively, lent the city 22 to 29 percent of its total debt. The entry and protection fees that the city and archbishop required of prospective Jewish settlers ensured that only Jews of means could settle in the city. Only such a community could have met the tax and loan demands placed on it.

Political developments in the offing boded ill even for this community, however. In 1396 the guilds, the weavers again in the lead, took advantage of the intermittent civil war between clans of the ruling patriciate to stage another coup. Ominously for the Jews, the new artisan elite was implacably hostile to the money professions Jews practiced and was imbued, as well, with fanatical religious prejudice.

As Hermann Kellenbenz notes, Jewish economic activities had well suited the needs of the merchant elites of Rhine cities, whose long-distance trading activities required loans. Rather than competing with the business of this class, Jews facilitated it and were therefore granted a high degree of toleration. The artisan guilds, on the other hand, depended on a closed urban economy. They sought to limit long-distance commerce and to promote and monopolize trade with the local hinterland. Jews, whether engaged in petty trade (purveying agricultural produce to the urban market; peddling), handicrafts, or money lending, were their natural enemies.[15]

The guilds expressed their economic hostility in religious idiom, introducing distinguishing clothing for Jews in 1404. This sort of measure, first enacted by the Fourth Lateran Council in 1215 to segregate and degrade Jews, had been available for nearly two centuries, yet only now did a city government choose to enforce it.[16] Soon, the guild elite became unwilling to tolerate even a degraded Jewish community and balked at renewing Jewish charters of settlement. In this atmosphere, the old conflict between the archbishop and the city, which resumed early in the fifteenth century, became the more ominous for the Jews.

As before, the conflict centered on money and control over revenue sources such as tolls, courts of justice, and Jews. Archbishop Dietrich von Mörs (1414–63) was determined to regain his Jewish prerogative, while the city was determined to preserve all of its liberties, including control of the Jews.

While this competition had previously generated favorable charters, now the Jews were merely a weapon with which the feuding sides sought to provoke and injure each other. Dietrich precipitated a crisis in 1414 by summoning two city Jews before his court in Poppelsdorf. The act violated Jewish rights against such summons, which was one of the basic privileges of all charters, as well as explicit agreements with the city, which since 1258 had sought to limit the archbishops' administration of justice to Jews. In part, Dietrich's move was financially motivated, because dispensing justice was a means of raising revenue. But it was also an act of sovereignty and a conscious insult to the city's perceived immunities.

Despite protests by the City Council, Dietrich levied accusations and fines against several Jews three years later, and again rejected protests by the city and the Jewish community. The city now turned to Emperor Sigismund, who in 1414 had confirmed the customary privileges of his "beloved Jewish serfs of the chamber" in Cologne, specifically including the right against summons. The city's complaint was referred for adjudication to the archbishop of Trier, who upheld the fines levied by Dietrich's court and thus his claim to jurisdiction over the Jews.[17]

Jewish toleration in Cologne, as elsewhere, was extended only if perceived as beneficial to the granting authority. If Jews became unprofitable to their protectors because they became impoverished or because the burden of protecting Jews from popular passions or outside meddling became too great, the basis for toleration was undermined. Obviously, if Jews seemed a threat to the ruler's interests, no grounds for toleration existed.

By the second decade of the fifteenth century the Jewish presence no longer seemed beneficial to city authorities. Jews had been recruited to the city in 1372 for the revenues they were expected to produce, an expectation the guild government maintained; indeed, the single largest Jewish loan extended to the city was made in 1418, under the guild regime.[18] But the multiple levels of taxation to which the Jews were subject, the extraordinary levies they had to pay (as, for example, for the war against the Hussites), and, finally, Archbishop Dietrich's judicial exactions were consuming Jewish assets and destroying their ability to play the fiscal role required as the price for toleration. Even lawsuits to determine the disposition of their status drained their resources, because Jews had to contribute toward the expenses of both archbishop and city as they sought satisfaction of their claims before various courts of appeal.

Deteriorating conditions led to Jewish emigration, leaving a smaller group with less ability to shoulder the financial burden. At the same time, the effort required to protect Jews from mob attack increased. Cologne was a collecting point for Catholic armies headed south to fight the Hussite "heretics," with whom Jews were accused of being in league. A timely bribe to the City Council averted disaster for the community, but then a plague erupted in the city, which was blamed on Jewish well poisoning.

Popular passions were reaching uncontainable levels while municipal authorities lacked means or will to stem mob violence against the Jews. As the city's Jewish charter approached its expiration in 1424, the City Council resolved unanimously not to renew it. Shorn of legal toleration, the Jews were told to quit Cologne by October 1, 1424.

Archbishop Dietrich appealed to Emperor Sigismund against the city's alleged violation of his rights. The emperor agreed with the archbishop, but his support was ineffectual. The city took its case before Pope Martin, presenting itself as more zealous for the city's Christian purity than its spiritual shepherd, the archbishop. The pope's position is not clear. The city maintained its resolve to expel the Jews. As the City Council stated in a long justifying letter to the emperor in 1431, "We within our city may settle and uproot whomsoever appears to us to be of use. . . ."[19] It was a claim the city would maintain well into the nineteenth century.

By the time the expulsion order took effect, only eleven taxpaying Jewish families remained.[20] But the fact of the expulsion, not the size was significant, however. Cologne formally attained the status of a free imperial city, bound in homage to none but the emperor, only in 1475, but with the expulsion of the Jews in 1424 — over the objections of its archbishop and territorial lord — the city had won an important round in its battle for autonomy, because control over the Jews was the prerogative of a sovereign power.

For nearly 400 years thereafter, until it lost its independence to French revolutionary forces, the city of Cologne maintained its sovereign right to exclude Jews.

Jews in the Electorate of Cologne

The expulsion of the Jews from the city of Cologne was part of a broader pattern emerging in western and central Europe in early modernity. For complex economic, political, and religious reasons, expulsions became common in the fifteenth and sixteenth centuries, which in itself made them easier to rationalize. Thus, Cologne's letter of 1431 cited the precedent of Jewish expulsions from the archbishoprics of Trier in 1418 and Mainz in 1420. Many other Rhenish cities expelled their Jewish communities in the decades following. In some German localities, Jews were readmitted and re-expelled several times, subject as before to general taxation and special fees but also to economic and social restrictions unprecedented in severity.[21]

Scholars have often noted that there never could be a wholesale expulsion of Jews from German lands such as occurred in England (1290), France (1306 and 1394), Spain (1492), and Portugal (1497), because Germany was not a unified state with a single monarch capable of such action. But neither did Germany have a single ruler capable of preventing expulsions from territories nominally under his control. As many scholars have shown, the expulsions of the pre-Reformation period had a heavily urban character, guilds often taking the lead against the wishes of territorial lords or the emperor. Imperial free cities were particularly hostile to Jews; none of any importance, except Frankfurt, had a Jewish population after 1570.[22] The recurrent violence and expulsions and the decline of Jewish economic and legal status in central Europe in these centuries set off an eastward migration that left regions of Germany with no settled Jewish population for centuries. In only three German cities — Worms, Frankfurt am Main, and Regensburg — were there Jewish communities of any size until the eighteenth century.[23]

There was continuous Jewish settlement in south and west Germany, in the Rhine and Main river basins. Here, in the most politically fractured area of the empire, the multiplicity of political jurisdictions afforded Jews a measure of security since expulsion from one territory often meant absorption in another nearby state or city that needed Jewish economic services.

In the ecclesiastical states of the Rhine, Jews expelled from principal cities — Cologne, Mainz, Trier, Strasbourg — were absorbed into the hinterland under the protection of the ecclesiastical overlords. In Cologne, these were the archbishop-electors. Settling in smaller towns and villages, expelled urban Jews performed a host of small-scale but vital economic functions. They served as agents between rural and urban economies, selling agricultural produce in city markets (not Cologne's, however, whose fairs and weekly markets were barred to Jews), furnishing the peasant population with manufactured goods and with credit to meet feudal obligations. Jews supplied the territorial lords with taxes and special fees; the rich among them extended loans and obtained luxury goods and staples in times of peace and, especially, war.

Many of the Jews expelled from Cologne in 1424 settled just across the river in Deutz, a short ferry ride away. Some 40 years later, Jews expelled from Neuss, including some former residents of Cologne, also came to Deutz. Thus enlarged, Deutz's Jewish community was the foremost of the electorate, seat of the territory's *Landrabbinat* until this office moved to Bonn late in the sixteenth century.[24] Except for Cologne and Neuss, there were Jewish communities throughout the electorate, the most important in the sixteenth century being those of Deutz, Brühl, and Hersel, with Bonn assuming significance only in the eighteenth century through the activities of court Jews.[25] In 1765, the Jewish population of the territory numbered about 1,000, some 300 of whom lived in Bonn and 56 in Deutz.[26] The other Jewish communities consisted of as few as three families or even a lone individual. Such communities depended on larger ones in the towns for religious needs, earning their livelihoods from the non-Jewish environment.[27]

Cities and towns had a Jewish street (Deutz) or ghetto (Bonn). In villages with but a few Jewish families, no physical segregation existed, although Jews were distinguished by dress, speech, and occupation.[28] Over half the Jews of the electorate lived in such circumstances.

Toleration of Jews in electoral Cologne was influenced by complex and volatile factors. The archbishop-electors favored settlement of Jews with means because of the profit they derived from Jewish economic activities, which they hoped would give them a measure of financial, hence political, independence. For this same reason, the Estates and the Cathedral Chapters opposed Jewish settlement, as did the guilds, which saw Jews as competitors. In the sixteenth and seventeenth centuries, the Estates of Cologne pressed for expulsion of the Jews but did not succeed; instead, the Estates stood vigilant over their economic interests and worked to prevent the archbishop-electors from achieving fiscal independence.[29]

All of this spelled limited toleration for Jews, with areas of permitted economic activity defined to serve the territorial lord's interests without infringing on those of the guilds. Rulers, understandably, were less accommodating to the Estates, which, having failed to eliminate the Jews, would have liked at least to share in the benefits of their activities (and diminish the income of the archepiscopal treasury) by taxing them. For the most part, the Estates had to satisfy themselves with controls on the size of the

Jewish population, while the church was mollified by various discriminatory measures.

As was true elsewhere until emancipation, Jewry ordinances defined the conditions of Jewish toleration. First promulgated in electoral Cologne in 1599, they remained in effect until the dissolution of the electorate by French revolutionary armies.[30] The ordinances set Jewish population limits by requiring residence permits which were purchased corporatively by Jewish communities and, until 1700, by individuals as well.[31] Given the rulers' desire for financial benefit from Jewish settlement, prospective Jewish settlers had to demonstrate a minimum of assets even to purchase a permit. Thus, residence permits regulated the financial character as well as the size of the Jewish population. Since they had to be purchased and repurchased with the election of each new archbishop, they also raised revenue.

Jewish children reaching the age of majority had to establish financial independence or quit the territory. To reside in or even pass through it without proper certification was to risk confiscation of goods and property. Since emigration represented a loss to a treasury, it was taxed. In addition to regular tolls, foreign Jews passing through electoral Cologne had to pay a body tax (*Leibzoll*) as well as protection fees for each day of their sojourn, which could be limited.

These measures were not entirely successful. Many Jewish families secretly employed Jewish domestic workers who, of course, lacked residence permits, yet who married and, according to eighteenth-century sources, multiplied abundantly.[32] Thus, there also existed a Jewish subpopulation of undetermined size, performing menial jobs in Jewish homes and businesses, existing in legal limbo and outside the tax structure.

The Jews had to pay ordinary taxes to the elector and to their localities as well as special fees to the elector. The exactions were of such magnitude that by the end of the electorate's existence, its Jewish community owed a large collective debt to the archepiscopal treasury.

The Jewry ordinances minutely delineated the occupations Jews could practice. Only those areas of the economy underserviced or undesirable to Christians were open to Jews: wholesale trade in foodstuffs and, to a limited extent (so as not to clash with the weavers' guild), wool; in articles constructed of precious metals; in jewelry; and in old clothes. In recognition of Jewish ritual needs, trade in wine, cattle, sheep, poultry, and hides was also permitted. Slaughtering of meat was allowed in quantities sufficient only for Jewish consumption, not commercial sale, in order not to injure the butchers' guilds. Similarly, handicraft production was permitted for Jewish consumption but not on a scale that would compete with the guilds.

Of course, it was not for petty trade but for banking services that the archbishop-electors extended toleration, and these the Jewry ordinances regulated so as to prevent "usury." The ordinances set interest rates, stated items Jews were permitted and forbidden to take as pledges, fixed modes of contracting and collecting loans, and regulated Jewish pawnbroking.

Beginning in the seventeenth century, court Jews made their appearance in electoral Cologne, their activities no different in essence, though of lesser scale, than those in Berlin, Frankfurt, Vienna, and elsewhere.[33] Court Jews emerged in central Europe in response to economic needs created by chronic warfare and profligate princely spending, which existing credit and supply mechanisms were inadequate to meet. The same conditions existed in electoral Cologne during the rule of its last four archbishops, who were heavily embroiled in continental politics and dynastic wars yet who also sought to live as princely a lifestyle as French and Austrian subsidies, heavy taxation, and steep borrowing would allow.[34]

A number of factors brought Cologne into the thick of European political battles in the seventeenth and eighteenth centuries. It was the most powerful ecclesiastical state in north Germany, located close to the French border and to Austrian hereditary lands on the left bank of the Rhine, to Prussian and Bavarian possessions on the right. Its ruler was a prince of the Empire as well as the church, heavily involved in imperial politics. Because it was an ecclesiastical state, there was no dynastic succession and elections to its throne were often strife-ridden. Every interregnum opened the door to intrigues by Bavaria, Austria, Prussia, and France, as each sought to fill the electoral see with an obeisant candidate.

From 1583 until 1761, the archbishop-electors of Cologne were princes of the Bavarian house of Wittelsbach. The last elector, Max Franz, was the youngest son of Queen Maria Theresa of Austria and the brother of Emperor Joseph as well as Queen Marie Antoinette of France.[35] Given all this, the electorate's political center of gravity lay somewhere between Vienna, Versailles, Berlin, and Munich, and Cologne enjoyed little peace after the end of the Thirty Years' War. It was involved in Louis XIV's wars of expansion in the last third of the seventeenth century, its geographic position and alliances making it a thruway for troops of the various combatants. The existence of Wittelsbach princes on the throne during the two great wars of succession of the eighteenth century, the War of Spanish Succession (1701–14) and the War of Austrian Succession (1740–48), ensured Cologne's siding with Bavaria, ally of France.

It was during this period, when enormous outlays were necessary to feed, outfit, supply, and pay armies, that court Jews rose to prominence in the electorate. During a 44-year period of peace, until the wars of the French revolution, Jewish court factors served the peacetime demands of princely sumptuousness and on occasion, conducted diplomatic missions. The first Jewish court factors emerged during the reign of the Bavarian

Joseph Clemens (1688–1723), whose military alliance with Louis XIV and lavish tastes created a huge, permanent need for cash. In 1700, over the protests of the Estates, Joseph Clemens issued a Jewry ordinance sanctioning continued Jewish residence in the electorate and appointing Meyer zum Goldstein tax farmer for the fees Jews owed the treasury. During the War of Spanish Succession, Goldstein and several other Jewish businessmen furnished the electoral army with food, cloth, finished clothing, and animal fodder and extended sizable loans.

Their usefulness unquestionable, Court Jews became a fixture at court. Under free-spending Clemens August (1723–61), the united sees of Cologne, Münster, Paderborn, Hildesheim, and Osnabrück became a veritable "El Dorado of court factors."[36] Clemens August had relied on Jewish loans even before assuming office, dispensing bribes to secure his election by the Cathedral Chapter. He continued to lean heavily on the services of numerous local Jewish lenders, as well as the famous Financial Privy Counselor of Württemberg, Joseph Suss Oppenheimer. In 1745, the court Jew Hirsch Oppenheim asked him to intervene on behalf of the Jews of Prague and Bohemia, then threatened with expulsion by Maria Theresa. Clemens August complied, participating in a remarkable effort by Jewish financial notables and court factors from some of the leading capitals of Europe.[37]

By the time Max Friedrich (1761–84) ascended the throne, court Jews were an institution embedded in the bureaucracy, not just individuals bound in a personal relationship to the archbishop. With no heir apparent whose favor could be cultivated in advance, court Jews developed ties to leading officials in the bureaucracy through shared business transactions. Thus, one of the greatest court Jews of Cologne, Baruch Simon, developed a partnership with the most powerful minister of state; the two even collaborated in construction of a cloth factory in Poppelsdorf.[38] Despite a resolution to economize and an aversion to court Jews, Max Friedrich found them indispensable. Their influence was at its height during his reign and continued during that of the last elector, Max Franz of Austria (1784–1801), although the latter considered Jews "a plague." There were more court Jews in Bonn than in the capital of any other ecclesiastical state.

In the seventeenth and early eighteenth centuries, court Jews even made their way into the city of Cologne, which over the centuries had taken extraordinary measures to keep Jews out. Permanent residence was forbidden Jews and even temporary sojourns were severely circumscribed. Jews were admitted only for approved missions: Jewish doctors answering the summons of a wealthy burger; potential converts coming for religious instruction; communal leaders seeking an audience before the archepiscopal court.[39] All Jews who entered the city did so for a fee, by day only, wearing distinguishing clothing and accompanied by a red-cloaked guard who escorted them to approved destinations and saw to their departure. They were barred from conducting any business during their stay. Visits unauthorized by the City Council or violation of any of the conditions for entry were punished by arrest and confiscation of goods.[40]

Yet the city could not isolate itself from the continual warfare that engulfed the electorate or from its consequences. When troops of the elector or other combatants passed through the city or were stationed in it, the exigencies of wartime supply took priority over the wishes of the guilds and City Council. Between 1685 and 1715 alone, scores of Jewish court factors in the service of the elector, the Dutch Estates General, the emperor, and the rulers of Brandenburg, Prussia, electoral Pfalz, Saxony, Hesse-Kassel, and Bavaria, were admitted to the city, against its wishes, to stockpile and transport munitions and other supplies to various armies. At the insistence of their sovereigns, they were freed of the byzantine restrictions customarily imposed on Jewish visits.[41] They moved about freely, were not banished at night to Deutz, and, of course, conducted business. Sometimes they competed with resident merchants as, for instance, in the late seventeenth century, when several Jewish court agents contracted with the city itself to provide corn, grain, and wine at reduced prices. During the Seven Years' War, the French king overrode Cologne's sovereign rights in order to assure free activity by his Jewish army purveyors. It was a taste of things to come.

Court Jews came, broke the rules for a while, but then departed. Earlier, in the mid-sixteenth century, the city had welcomed Portuguese Marrano merchant-bankers from Antwerp who made Cologne a major transit point for their trade in spices, pearls, and jewels.[42] But these were outwardly Christians. The outcome was quite different when ordinary, unambiguously Jewish Jews sought to reside in Cologne. In 1583 Jews from Deutz, which had been burned twice during fighting between contenders for the archepiscopal throne, sought refuge and the possibility of an indefinite stay in Cologne.[43] They received partial backing from Christian refugees who had pawned property with them, which they wanted time to redeem. The Jews were given six months in Cologne to liquidate their businesses and were enjoined from contracting new loans. The City Council refused a further stay lest a temporary concession become the occasion for renewed Jewish settlement.

During the Thirty Years' War some 50 years later, when Deutz again came under attack, the Jewish community sought protection in Cologne only for its possessions, not its members, and had had difficulty achieving even this.[44] Jewish merchants transporting their wares from Mainz or Frankfurt in the seventeenth century were prevented from stepping onto Cologne's wharf while awaiting the ferry to take them to Deutz. Jews allotted escort passes were arrested anyway, their goods confiscated. "A very sick

Jew" (according to City Council records) was brought to a city hospital in 1679 and ordered removed to Deutz at the earliest opportunity.[45]

Most telling is the request of Jews from the electorate in 1784 for permission to pass through Cologne, with the customary police escort, rather than circumvent it on the way to business elsewhere. Employing the best Enlightenment idiom, they appealed to the members of the City Council in the name of a shared humanity. "For in common with Christians and all human beings, we have Adam, the first created man, as our ancestor and are therefore all of the same flesh and blood." The petition was denied, its authors counseled to patience and acceptance of age-old custom in these matters.[46]

Thus, unlike the situation in France, Austria, or Prussia, where significant reforms in Jewish civil status were enacted in the eighteenth century, in Cologne policy changed not a whit and the new era broke as a shock.[47] Ten years after the Jewish appeal for passage was rejected, troops of revolutionary France, which had recently granted its Jews legal equality, occupied Cologne and showed little sympathy for its ancient customs and sensibilities. The city government made strenuous efforts to spare the city the worst consequences of occupation and, above all, to salvage its autonomy, but succeeded only in delaying the inevitable.[48] With hindsight it is obvious how futile were its attempts to extract compromises from revolutionary regimes determined to give France its "natural boundary" on the Rhine and to absorb the left bank into the French Republic.[49]

It is true that in the first years of the French occupation, before the left bank was militarily secure and its political future decided, there was a possibility that Cologne might retain some degree of civic control. Advocates of a satellite Cisrhenish republic on the left bank favored the city as the site for a capital because of its history of stubborn resistance to the archbishop-electors. ("There has always been a master at Bonn. Never has there been one at Cologne," as one French official put it.)[50] But this did not come to pass, and the city eventually lost every round with the French. Troops were quartered within its walls, worthless *assignats* were imposed over the local currency, the population was forced to meet requisition demands of the invading army and to provide forced loans. The church was suppressed and its clergy (a "vulgar mob of monks") persecuted.[51] There was particular indignation at the city's intolerance toward its Protestant minority, which labored under serious disabilities. "You are intolerant, and I—I will be inexorable; I will be inflexible; I will not listen to, nor read, anything about your city," the French commanding general thundered at a city delegation. When offered ingenious excuses to explain the lack of a Protestant church in Cologne (public opinion had been violently opposed, he was told, and the popular will had been respected), he threatened to exempt Protestants from all taxes.[52]

It is interesting that there was at first no similarly unequivocal commitment to Jewish equality. The existence of court Jews at Bonn raised questions about Jewish loyalties, and the same general who was so incensed at anti-Protestant discrimination let the humiliating Jewish body tax stand until September 1797, because the "Jews have proved that they merited no part of the title or advantages of citizens."[53] With Cologne's autonomy insulted but still intact, and no firm declaration of Jewish equality, city policy toward Jews remained unchanged. Thus, at some point in the first few years of the French occupation, a young man "with a Jewish name" was denied residence in Cologne and was escorted from the city under armed guard, as ancient ordinances prescribed.[54]

But in 1797 the French dismantled the city government, abolishing the constitution forged in triumph over the archepiscopal overlord some 400 years earlier. In the same year, the Peace of Campo Formio was signed and Cologne was formally incorporated into the French Republic. The free imperial city was now but a municipality like others in the French state. Its relative importance made it seat of the second district of the new Roer department, fashioned after the left bank of the Rhine was ceded to France in the Peace of Lunéville (1801). But this only made it part of the most centralized state in Europe and, equally insulting, subordinate to a higher regional authority in Aachen.

With its incorporation into the French Republic, Cologne became subject to all the laws of France, including those which had made Jews equal citizens. Henceforth, Jewish status would be fixed in law according to the immutable dictates of universal reason.

On the twenty-first of Frimaire of the year VI (June 1798) government commissioner Rudler proclaimed the following to the inhabitants of the left bank: "Whatever smacks of slavery is abolished. To God alone will you give reckoning for your religious beliefs; your civic rights are no longer dependent on them. Opinions be what they may, they will be tolerated without distinction and enjoy equal protection."[55] Although not mentioning the Jews specifically, Rudler's words opened the door to their free migration. There was no longer any basis by which they might be excluded from Cologne or anywhere else under French rule, or have their rights circumscribed.

Some of the first Jews who came to Cologne were among the wealthiest of the communities of Bonn and Mülheim. One of these was Salomon Oppenheim the Younger, merchant, banker, and the last court Jew of the electorate. To a city forced against its will to accept Jews in its midst, these must have been the least objectionable. But French toleration, unlike that of the Jewry ordinances, was unconditional, and along with Jewish grandees came the far more typical Jews of the small towns and villages of the Rhineland: butchers, gut spinners, and hide dealers; religious teachers and synagogue functionaries; small-time money lenders and currency exchangers; peddlers, old clothes and rag dealers; transients, scoundrels, and criminals — precisely the kind of Jews the city had rigorously excluded for nearly 400 years. And they did not come alone but *en famille* — husbands and wives with children, servants, and other family members. They settled not in a special Jewish quarter or street but in all districts of the city according to what their incomes would bear, plying their usual trades. To a city accustomed to arresting bearded men on suspicion of being Jews,[56] the sight of such Jews moving freely in the streets must have been as jarring as that of the liberty tree erected in the center of town. Both symbolized the demise of the free imperial city and its conversion to a modern municipality. The tree, however, was only a symbol. The Jews were citizens.

In 1424 a higher authority had tried to keep Jews in the city but lacked the means to impose his will. The year 1798 marked the beginning of a new era. Jews were admitted by a higher authority of utterly superior force. Cologne would remain subject to the will of two of the greatest powers of Europe, France and Prussia. Both imposed their Jewish policies on the city as they did their trade and tariff policies. Thenceforth — in their view, at least — it would be the task of the city merely to administer the directives of Paris and Berlin.

CHAPTER TWO

The Genesis and Development of a Community in Emancipation, 1798–1814

Modern Jewish history in Cologne began on April 17, 1798, with the migration of a single Jewish family. "On the second day of the new month *Iyyar*, 5558, we, the undersigned, moved from Mülheim on the Rhine to Cologne," reads the memoir of Joseph, son of Isaac Stern, and his wife Sara. Pointedly recalling that the old city government had prevented Jews even from setting foot in Cologne, the Sterns continued that they had "applied to the French municipality for permission to reside here . . . obtained justice a few days ago and so moved here immediately."[1]

Freedom of movement was among the most tangible benefits emancipation conferred.[2] In territories like the former electorate of Cologne, which limited the size and location of Jewish settlement, emancipation meant unfettered internal migration as well as immigration. In cities like Bonn, which had segregated Jews in ghettos, it meant freedom to live anywhere in town. In cities like Cologne, which had barred Jewish settlement, or Aachen, which had restricted it severely, it meant the possibility of significant new settlement. Under the new regime, Jewish migration was to be determined by market forces, the lure of opportunity.

By the end of the French era in 1815, 211 Jewish men, women, and children lived in Cologne, more than in any other city in the French Roer department.[3] In a region where the typical Jewish community in 1808 numbered less than 50 and the important community of Bonn numbered just

TABLE I
Size of Left-bank Jewish Communities in the French Era
(Roer, Rhine-Moselle departments)

	Number of communities in	
Size of Jewish community	Roer Department (1806)	Rhine-Moselle Department (1808)
1–5	23	28
6–10	13	37
11–20	24	33
21–50	61	55
51–75	27	7
76–100	10	1
101–150	2	—
151–200	1	—
201–350	—	3
TOTAL number of communities	161	164
TOTAL Jewish population	5,484	4,063

SOURCES: Kober, "Aus der Geschichte," pp. 94-97; *HASK*, Französische Verwaltung, 2470.
    NOTE: The largest Jewish communities in these years were in Koblenz (342), Bonn (309), Kreuznach (286), Krefeld (160), Cologne (124), and Cleves (120).

over 300, this was a sizable Jewish population (see Table 1). The rapid development of a Jewish population suggests that Cologne held a special attraction for Jews. That it was Cologne, specifically, and not cities in general that drew Jews can be seen by comparing the growth of its Jewish population with that of others in the department, Aachen and Krefeld. Aachen's Jewish population grew from 60 to 114 between 1806 and 1816; Krefeld's declined from 160 in 1806 to 96 in 1812.[4] The Stern memoir and the whole record of Jewish immigration to Cologne, by contrast, suggest that Jews were poised for the first chance to move there.

Little wonder. Unlike Aachen or Krefeld, where manufacturing predominated, Cologne was the Rhineland's leading trading center.[5] The changing contours and depth of the Rhine, coupled with ancient river privileges, made it a necessary stopping point for ships traveling between the Low Countries and Basel. The city also sat astride main east-west land routes. A modernized manufacturing sector had never developed there because of guild opposition and the city's religious discrimination, which drove Protestant entrepreneurs to more hospitable locations.[6] At the time of the French takeover, its economy depended, as it had for centuries, on *Zwischenhandel* — the transshipment of Italian, south German, or Dutch colonial goods between Frankfurt and Dutch ports. Goods produced in Cologne and the middle Rhineland, wines especially, were also traded through the city. Cologne's great merchants were *Kommissionäre* (trading agents). It was activity Jews understood well.

The city's economy had stagnated in the eighteenth century because of rising river tolls and trade disruptions caused by the Seven Years' War. By 1794, it had long since lost its stature as a great Hansa town. Still, it remained a major entrepôt, making it a lure to Jewish brokers and financiers. With a population of 40,000 to 50,000, Cologne was the region's most populous city, with plenty of opportunity for lesser merchants, as well, down to the lowliest peddler and moneylender.

French policy had mixed effects on the city's economy, with some sectors spurred and others hurt, but the net effect was positive. The transformation of the Rhine into France's "natural frontier" cut traditional trading connections with the river's right bank, which had been made into a French satellite state, the Grand Duchy of Berg, but which was not part of France. The Continental system separated Cologne from Holland, historically its most important trading partner. But the city's losses were more than compensated by its inclusion in France's protected domestic market and by the creation of a new manufacturing sector after the guilds were abolished in 1804 and secularized church property was made available for industrial plants. Industrial production also stimulated trade by adding locally manufactured goods to the pool of wares marketed in, and through, Cologne.

Jews would surely have settled in Cologne under the far less favorable economic circumstances of the old regime had city policy been merely discriminatory and not exclusionary. Under the French, enhanced economic opportunities were suddenly accessible to Jews, and they responded immediately: the heaviest immigration occurred in the first years after annexation, with the yearly high for the period, nineteen new households, occurring in 1800 (see Table 2).[7]

Jewish migration was pulled by perceived opportunity rather than

TABLE 2
Jewish Immigration to Cologne by Household,
1798–1813

Period	Number of Households	Yearly Rate
1798–1802[a]	41	8.2
1803–7[b]	21	4.2
1808–13[c]	15	2.5
TOTAL	77	

SOURCES: *HASK,* Französische Verwaltung, 2466, 2467, 2468, 2469, 2470, 2471, 2472, 2473, 2474, 2475, 2476, 2478, 2479, 2480, 2481, 2793, 4293, 4884, 4888, 4923; Oberbürgermeisteramt, 400, II-13-C-10.
[a]Residence permitted, French law not fully in place.
[b]Full emancipation.
[c]Migration and occupations restricted.

pushed by negative forces. Discrimination was not a factor since most of the immigrants came from locations under French rule, within 100 kilometers of the city.[8] The immigrants' high degree of permanence further bears out that they were not simply refugees fleeing upheaval: although there were Jewish transients (some 30, according to my count, drop from the French records or fail to appear in early Prussian records), most of the Jews who came to Cologne stayed. Most also came in families rather than singly, another indication of intended permanence: of 71 immigrants between the ages of 20 and 79 in 1806, 48 were married, most with children.[9] The Jews were also fertile: between 1799 and 1809 alone, there were 43 births in a pool of some 60 couples with women in their childbearing years.[10]

This record is more impressive since the first immigrants must have felt considerable anxiety about living in Cologne, as we learn from a Stern family memoir dating from their earliest days in the city. One night, Stern heard the pealing of bells and a cry rising from the street, which he understood to be, in Cologne's dialect, "Juden eruhs!" — Jews out. Fearing an attack, he and his wife prepared to flee with their infant daughter, until they realized that the call was actually "Büdden eruhs" — a summons for water barrels to extinguish a fire.[11]

The city's historic hostility had left a tangible, as well as a psychological, legacy: there was no preexisting community to help absorb the newcomers (or deflect poor and undesirables elsewhere). No previous business contacts, no family already resident, could have drawn Jews or facilitated their adjustment. The very look of the city, beyond its shoreline facade, was completely unfamiliar.

Most of the immigrants were not used to life in a big city, 26 of 46 about whom the information is known having been born in towns of fewer than 5,000 inhabitants. Only five had experienced life in a city of comparable or greater population than Cologne's. Even Jews who had migrated previously, before moving to Cologne, had generally not moved from smaller to larger urban settlements. Most of the Jews with traceable migration histories had been born in large cities — Amsterdam, Rotterdam, Grodno, Lübeck, Fürth — but had migrated to much smaller locations before coming to Cologne. In eight of thirteen documented instances of intermediate migration, Jews had moved to locations of fewer than 2,000 inhabitants.[12] Thus, coming to Cologne was not on a continuum of movement from smaller to larger cities. Cologne's Jews were intent not on urbanization per se, but on Cologne, specifically.

Obviously, Cologne's lack of a Jewish community did not deter these immigrants, even though most of them (25 of 47 about whom we have information) were born in places with Jewish populations of between 51 and 500, larger than the Rhenish norm. An additional ten immigrants had been born in very large Jewish communities (between 501 and 35,000), including Grodno, the second largest Jewish community in Lithuania (4,000 Jews), Amsterdam (35,000), and Fürth (2,600). In such places, Jews had not only strong communal facilities but the inestimable psychological comfort of being a sizable minority — in Grodno, the majority — of the population.[13] In Cologne, Jews were a speck of the population. Only the immigrant from Lübeck, a city roughly Cologne's size with a similar history of anti-Jewish exclusion, would have found conditions in Cologne familiar.[14]

While poverty motivated the migration of some, it did not spur the migration as a whole and was not a factor in the immigration of the first Jews to pioneer settlement. Of eighteen men who gathered to found a synagogue in 1801, most (ten) paid a middle-range dues assessment and the rest were evenly divided between those paying the highest and lowest assessments.[15] While synagogue dues are not the best gauge of poverty, since the poorest were exempt from payment and often do not appear on communal membership lists, it is noteworthy that the synagogue's founding constitution makes no mention of poor relief, a need Jewish communities traditionally met if only to avert non-Jewish hostility.[16]

In fact, Jewish settlement in the city was pioneered to a disproportionate degree by wealthy Jews. Three of four men singled out by French authorities in 1808 as Cologne's "Négotians Juifs les plus notables" arrived in the first two years of Jewish settlement (one was our previously mentioned Joseph Stern); the fourth came in 1804.[17] What we know of these Jews, moreover, suggests a clear pattern of migration for betterment.

Stern, a wealthy grain merchant, came from Mülheim, a prosperous commercial town on the right bank of the Rhine not far from Cologne; it had been home to many of Cologne's Protestants fleeing oppression in the city under the old regime. Economic life in Mülheim was certainly tenable, but Cologne's much larger size and left bank location made it more attractive. Bonn, home of Salomon Oppenheim and Samuel Benjamin Cohen, suffered considerable loss of status and economic importance with the abolition of the electorate. For Oppenheim, formerly a court factor and by far the wealthiest Jew in Cologne ("recommendable sous tous les respects," the authorities said of him, compared to a simple "bon citoyen" about the other Jewish notables), and for Cohen, a metal dealer, Bonn was suddenly a backwater compared to Cologne; both moved by 1799. Heymann (soon to be called Henri) Cassel, a pawnbroker and cotton merchant, came from Mainz in 1804. Like Cologne, Mainz was an important Rhine port annexed by France. With a population half that of Cologne, however, it, too, probably seemed like a backwater.

The immigration of these Jews was one of choice, not necessity, their destination deliberate. There could be no more tangible proof of Jewish confidence in French rule than the willingness of such "haves" to move their businesses, fortunes, and families — all four men were married, with at least one young child or one on the way — so quickly to the new Cologne.[18]

Occupations, Economic Function, and Class

Six other wealthy Jews also migrated to the city by 1809.[19] Four were brokers; the others were a merchant who also lived on income, and a pawndealer. Thus contrary to the conclusions of Kober and Gothein, the well-to-do were a significant segment of the new community.[20] In 1808, when there were 174 Jews in the city, 55 individuals, or 32 percent of the total Jewish population (including Jewish servants and nonimmediate family), lived in wealthy households.

The rest of the Jewish group had the kind of occupational profile we would expect of a Jewish population derived largely from the Rhenish hinterland. The first citywide surveys of Jewish households, conducted in 1806 and 1808, listed merchants and brokers; money changers, lenders, and pawnbrokers; butchers; peddlers; secondhand clothes dealers; and teachers.[21] Correlation of occupations with generally low levels of synagogue dues assessments and addresses in unspectacular locations in the city, establishes that in 1806, 25 of 30 households were headed by people of modest means.

Still, most of these were not poor. The 1806 survey shows twelve Jewish households employing "servants." Eight of these households were on the lower economic stratum; three were headed by peddlers, two by butchers, two by schoolmasters (see Table 3). There is no doubt that "servants" in such households were not domestic employees engaged for personal service or child care (as Table 3 shows, poorer households also tended not to be especially large), but business assistants, apprentices. This means that two-thirds of the Jews on the lower economic stratum had enterprises large enough to require assistants and means enough to provide at least room and board in return (the teachers, obviously, had more than one occupation, a common pattern for Jews, as we shall see).

All the "servants" were female and, judging by their names, Jewish, yet not obviously related to either household head. All were also young, in their teens or twenties. For young, unmarried Jewish women without independent means, helping with business while living with a Jewish family may have been a means of immigration as well as livelihood.[22]

Cologne's Jews were all middle class in economic function, if not standard of living; agriculture within the city walls was a viable option in these years, yet, unsurprisingly, none of the Jews chose it.[23] One Jewish occupa-

TABLE 3
Address, Occupation, and Size of Jewish Households Employing Servants, 1806

Occupation	Address by city section	Number of children in household	Number of servants in household	Total in household[a]
Merchant[b]	I	6	1	9
Peddler	II	2	1	5
Peddler	II	1	1	4
Butcher	II	1	1	4
Schoolmaster	III	1	1	4
Schoolmaster	III	6	1	9
Peddler	III	3	1	6
Merchant	III	1	1	4
Butcher	III	1	1	4
Commissionaire[b]	IV	5	1	8
Pawn dealer[b]	IV	7	1	10
Merchant[b]	IV	3	1	6

SOURCES: *HASK*, Französische Verwaltung, 2470, 4884.
[a]Households sometimes included relatives other than parents and children.
[b]Address more than occupation title correlated with wealth. The four households with servants in sections I and IV were wealthy.

tional subgroup, butchers, draws notice for its relative size: 6 of 25 Jewish men in the lower economic stratum in 1806 were butchers, and they could not all have been serving the needs of the small Jewish population.

We might have expected some concentration in animal and meat dealing, one of the most common Jewish occupations in the Rhineland and central Europe in general. Yet meat provisioning had been one of the sectors of Cologne's economy most restricted by the guilds, to the point that meat shortages were common in the *Reichsstadt* era.[24] Whatever the legal status of the guilds under French rule, guild members and their interests did not simply disappear. There is evidence from the earliest years of Jewish settlement that the city's traditional meat suppliers did, in fact, resist the encroachments of Jewish meat dealers — who, the 1806 evidence attests, persisted nonetheless.[25] This attests not only to the viability of this occupational path, but to Jewish success in penetrating a formerly closed market. That success was to be permanent: butchering remained one of the most popular Jewish occupational choices in the city.

It would seem that Cologne's meat provisioning needs were to petty entrepreneurial Jews what the city's brokerage opportunities were to Jewish commissionaires: a specific lure. Even for less wealthy migrants, then, this was a conscious urban migration. For Jews with less specialized occupations — peddling, old clothes dealing — perhaps we can appropriate the words of Glückel of Hameln about the reasons her family decided to leave tiny Hameln for the great city of Hamburg, despite its anti-Jewish reputation: "Hameln," she wrote in her famous *Memoirs*, "was not a trade center and my husband did not wish to confine himself to money-lending among the country folk."[26] Whatever Jews had done in the countryside and small towns could be done on a larger scale in Cologne.

Although the Jews on the whole appear to have been a solid, upstanding group, there were some "undesirables." We know of two Jews with complaint or arrest records and of three who were guillotined.[27] The records also speak of an unmarried Jewish woman who lived in the city with her two illegitimate children and of a Jewish man accused of "swindling" and all kinds of dissimulation, including the use of an alias and abandonment of a starving wife and children elsewhere while he lived "with a Jewish prostitute" in Cologne.[28] But there was no Jewish crime problem, which is consistent with the class character of the migration. In 1808, the mayor wrote a warm endorsement of the Jews of the Roer department ("they have never given the slightest complaint . . . they do not indulge in any illicit business"), which he surely would not have done had he felt the Jews of his own locale were a problem.[29]

Group Cohesion, Integration, and Acculturation

Language and Culture

The regional derivation of Cologne's Jews meant that they were ethnically homogeneous, unlike the mixed Sephardi-Ashkenazi population of Hamburg, for instance, where cultural differences led to the creation of separate communities.[30] It also meant that there was no linguistic barrier to Jews making a living. While the Jews used *jüdisch-deutsch* for communication among themselves, wrote German poorly, and spoke in a manner that undoubtedly stood out against Cologne's dialect, their language difficulties were far from crippling.[31] Except for the few migrants from non–German-speaking lands, such difficulties would have been different neither in kind nor degree from those the Jews had experienced in their places of origin, where Jews lived among non-Jews in a symbiotic economic relationship and knew enough of the vernacular to do business.

A good proportion of the community in Cologne was eager to go beyond this minimum level of communication. In 1805, when there were 48 Jewish households in the city, ten Jews subscribed to Mendelssohn's German translation of Psalms.[32] That work, like Mendelssohn's translation of the Pentateuch, had been meant both to draw acculturating Jews back to their own sacred literature and to teach Jews "decorous and refined" German, a desideratum since Mendelssohn considered pure language (as opposed to *jüdisch-deutsch*) the path to morality.[33] As Mendelssohn had put it, "a better translation . . . of the holy scriptures . . . is the first step toward culture," for which reason he used idiomatic German phraseology and German syntax rather than mimicking Hebrew linguistic forms.[34] His subscribers in Cologne, we surmise, wished not merely to interact with the non-Jewish world for the sake of making a living, as Jews had always done, but also to approach non-Jewish society and culture on high ground. As Jacob Katz has shown, such behavior signals a profound attitudinal shift toward the non-Jewish world.[35] That this was true for some 20 percent of households at this early date suggests that material expectations alone did not motivate the migration, or at least that hopes for cultural improvement and acceptance arose soon after settlement. Three wealthy families, we also know, sent their sons — including the grandchildren of the entirely traditional rabbi of Bonn — to non-Jewish secondary schools and kept Christian tutors in permanent employ at home.[36]

Residential Patterns

Since there was no preexisting Jewish quarter in Cologne, there was nothing to draw Jewish settlement to a particular street or neighborhood. Assuming no de facto discrimination limited options, legal equality meant Jews were free to settle according to their inclinations and incomes. Under such circumstances, the residential choices Jews made would tell us much about their attitudes: would the immigrants create a Jewish street or disperse?

Study of Jewish residential distribution shows that Jews lived in all four sections of town, with a high correlation between wealth and address: 8 of 9 wealthy families whose addresses we know in 1808–9 lived in the two best sections, fronting the river, while 19 of 30 Jewish households in 1806 lived in the other two sections.[37] (See Map 1.) This tells us both that serious housing discrimination did not exist and that, under conditions of liberty, economic rather than religious factors determined where Jews lived. The purchase of a site for the synagogue in 1802, which could have set off residential concentration, had no such effect.

Indeed, the synagogue's founding constitution attests that Jewish residential dispersal created serious problems for communal life. Given the small pool of eligibles, it made gathering a *minyan*, the requisite prayer quorum of ten adult males, extremely difficult. Threats and fines were directed at *minyan* shirkers, but even the authors of the constitution had to concede that a *minyan* could realistically be expected only in mild weather. Members residing at a "great distance from the synagogue" were relieved of

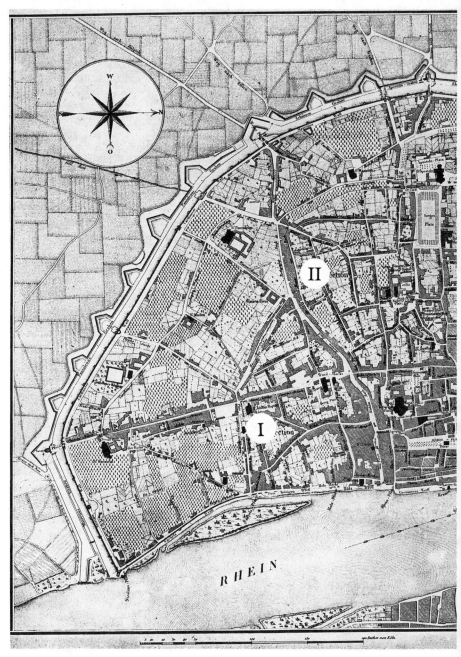

Map 1. Cologne in 1815, by city section, showing the location of the synagogue.

GRUNDRISS
der
Stadt Köln
1815
Zu haben bei C. F. Thiriatt.

Gezeichnet von und Gestochen von Proquet

III

IV

FLUSS

DUYTZ

fines for nonattendance but were enjoined on their honor as Israelites not to abuse the definition of "distant."[38]

Community Building

Cologne's history meant that there were no prior Jewish communal patterns, traditions or authorities, to bind or even influence the settlers' religious behavior. Similar circumstances in other communities forged in modernity (England, the United States) meant unprecedented license for Jews to disregard Jewish religious norms.[39] What effects did lack of an institutional past have on Jewish communal life in Cologne? How did the organized community function when affiliation was voluntary?

The clearest expression of the new reality is the voluntaristic solution to the problem of gathering a *minyan*, without which such crucial elements of worship as the Torah reading and remembrance of the dead (*kaddish*) could not proceed.

It is not surprising that eighteen Jewish men got together to found a *kehillah* (organized community) some four years after Jewish resettlement. As we have seen, most of Cologne's Jews came from places with relatively significant Jewish populations where at least rudimentary community services existed. Sixteen of 54 (30 percent) for whom we have information came from Deutz, Mülheim, and Bonn, where organized communities certainly existed. The *kehillah* traditionally fulfilled social as well as religious functions, and the need for this, we would imagine, was great for a group as small and newly arrived as this one. As its constitution testifies, the *kehillah* founders undertook their labors "for the welfare . . . the foundation and for the survival of our community."

The community in its formal sense was the work of a few wealthy and well-connected individuals, who came mostly from Bonn and had close personal ties to its rabbi. They bore a very disproportionate share of the *kehillah's* costs and were responsible for representing Jewish interests before the authorities, who, particularly from 1806 on, recognized, used, and thus confirmed, their leadership.[40] Their responsibilities, particularly when imposed from without, could be burdensome and unwelcome. Solomon Benjamin Cohen was charged with collecting the community's share of the costs charged to Roer department Jewry for representation at Napoleon's Assembly of Jewish Notables, a task he fulfilled with difficulty. The French drafted Salomon Oppenheim against his will to represent Roer department Jewry at that assembly. Oppenheim earnestly petitioned for exemption, offering many reasons: his poor knowledge of French, his position as "sole protector . . . of my large family," the losses his business would suffer in his absence. He suggested a better qualified (and apparently willing) candidate from Cleves, but this was rejected.[41]

As we would expect at this point in German-Jewish history, the *kehillah* constitution drafted in Cologne was traditional; rumblings of religious reform in these years were largely confined to a circle of long-urbanized and highly acculturated, but unemancipated, Jews in Berlin.[42] The community in Cologne was like dozens of others its size, which did not have full-fledged communal institutions relying instead on those of nearby communities. This alone would have predisposed its institutions to traditional forms, since there were no heterodox communities in the Rhineland at this early date.

The rabbi of Bonn, formerly *Landrabbiner* of the electorate, participated in the community's founding and was made Cologne's rabbi as well, a precedent that would last for much of the century and have far-reaching consequences. The constitution established that the rites in Cologne would be patterned after those of Deutz, whose cantor would adjudicate ceremonial questions. The fledgling *kehillah* was soon able to fill this office with an immigrant who also served as community teacher and general synagogue functionary.

The ancient *mikvah* (ritual bath) of the medieval community appears to have been rehabilitated, since there is no mention of the need to excavate a new one. The *mikvah* required a new cistern, however, as well as funding for ongoing upkeep. This and other costs to launch the community were considerable and financial concerns dominate the constitution. Torah scrolls and an ark had to be obtained; services, conducted in provisional quarters, required a permanent site. As was universal Jewish practice, membership dues varied according to means and rewarded wealth and generosity with increased synagogue honors. These could also be purchased by additional donations, which assured the giver "the blessings of heaven." New members were to pay initiation fees and users of the ritual bath, user fees (payable to the cantor's wife, hot water extra). Fines for disobedience of communal ordinances were set, although there was no way they could be enforced.

Finally, the community's founders held an auction for assigned seats in the synagogue, with bidders assured priority choice "whenever, sooner or later, our provisional synagogue is erected in another house, or if ever we build a permanent synagogue where more seats will be available." If the Jews of Cologne were not avid synagogue goers, once there they wanted their due, it seems, because the constitution has strong traces of actual or anticipated conflict over synagogue seats and honors, the second most prominent concerns of the document. Its framing appears to have capped considerable prior wrangling, which accounts, perhaps, for Rabbi Bunem's self-justifying lament, "For I have seen that the coming together of the entire community is a difficult matter here and that without supervision, confusion will result." Indeed, the entire tone of the document is one more of stoic self-sacrifice than hopeful anticipation about the vigor of religious life.

Still, the record of the actual seat sale shows that the constitution's goal of 200 Reichstaler was more than met, thanks in part to multiple bids by four of the wealthiest members.[43] In a vivid commentary on the possibilities of the new age, the site chosen for the synagogue was the recently nationalized monastery of St. Clarisse. In applying for title to the site, community leaders showed they were well aware of the historic significance of their choice, as well as of their rights as French citizens to make it. As they wrote to the Minister of Cults, Portalis,

[We express] our appreciation to the government for the great favor of liberty and civil and religious equality which we now enjoy in a city . . . from which fanaticism banished us several centuries ago, entry being forbidden to us until the coming of the French.

Until now, we have not had a fixed place for celebration of our services, but with rental of the monasteries of this city [now allowed], we have bid for the small monastery of Clarisse, situated on the [Glockengasse], which we consider a suitable location for our services. . . . The government, having granted the Protestants of this commune the vast edifice of [another church and monastery for their use], we believe we may claim the same opportunity, since the principles of the government protect each religion equally.[44]

The former monastery of St. Clarisse, consisting of two small buildings and a courtyard, did become the site of the Cologne synagogue and remained in use until 1861, although the community's request for formal title to the property apparently was never granted.[45] In France as a whole, Jewish purchase of nationalized property was seen as a sign of revolutionary enthusiasm and patriotism.[46] In Cologne, it must be seen as a sign of the commitment of a determined group of Jews to establish permanent Jewish presence in the city and to found religious and communal institutions despite the difficulties to organized Jewish life posed by the very freedom these Jews sought.

Emancipation Compromised: The Decrees of 1808

For ten years, unconditional emancipation was in force. Although life did not simply correspond to legal decree, Cologne's Jews had every reason to feel vindicated by history, the clear sentiment conveyed in the community leaders' letter to Portalis as well as the Stern family's memoir.

Legal equality had been tested several times, and Jewish trust in the French upheld in each instance. In 1801, "rabbis or ministers of the Jewish cult" appealed for permission to accompany a Jew condemned to death and prepare him for death "according to the principles of their cult." The president of the criminal court readily agreed, since the law "encourages religious freedom." Fearing, however, that "malevolent people" might mock the proceedings, he asked the mayor to provide police protection against any outbreak that "fanaticism might want to excite."[47]

In the same year, Samuel Benjamin Cohen of Cologne was charged the Jewish body tax (*Leibzoll*), prevalent under the old regime, in Deutz, which was in territory France had occupied but not annexed. Outraged, he insisted on his rights as a French citizen — and was told that it was precisely for this reason that the levy was being imposed. Cohen had no choice but to pay, but he immediately presented the receipt to the French police commissioner in Cologne, who referred the matter promptly to the prefect of the Roer department and to higher state authorities, because it concerned the treatment of French nationals on foreign soil. The wording of the official correspondence is telling, since the communications were internal and thus free of any propagandistic purposes. Cologne's police commissioner referred to "French citizens . . . who follow the Jewish rite," asserting the primacy of French citizenship and Jewish civic equality. Other officials expressed indignation at the body tax as a "humiliating," "disgusting" impost appropriate to the intolerance and ignorance of German princes; the incident at Deutz was an act of insolence offensive to all French citizens. We do not know what action, if any, was taken, but Cohen must at least have had the satisfaction of knowing the government was on his side.[48]

It is hard to imagine that there would have been no popular backlash to the radical changes in Jewish status in Cologne, and two incidents bear this out. In 1803, a rumor circulated that the Jews were to be expelled and the synagogue closed. The Jews were convinced that "evil intentioned and envious" business competitors were behind the rumor in a crude but effective effort to arouse uncertainty in their clients. (They had no doubt that the rumor itself was "absurd," because it was "contrary to the spirit of our [meaning French] law.") Precisely for this reason, however, the mayor saw no need for official action and matters, apparently, did sort out on their own.[49]

There was a potentially far more serious incident in 1808, when a lower French official accused a Jewish butcher of ritually murdering a Christian boy in the cellar of the Jew's house. The official's family rented rooms in the butcher's house and owed both back rent and loans. The butcher was arrested, tried, and imprisoned but was eventually acquitted, returning in triumph to Cologne, while his accusers were severely punished.[50]

The French had proven reliable. But matters began to change in 1806, when Napoleon ordered a temporary suspension of debt payments to Jews in Alsace, Metz, and three of four departments on the annexed left bank of the Rhine, including the Roer. Worse would follow. A decree issued on December 11, 1808, mandated the reorganization of Jewish religious and communal life under state auspices. Synagogues and educational and welfare institutions would be replaced by a highly centralized, governmentally controlled consistorial system, whose real function was to further Jewish assimilation. Having wrung from elite assemblies of Jewish "notables" and rabbis an official definition of Judaism as pure cult, without an ethnic component, the state made rabbis and religious teachers agents of enforcement. The synagogue was to be the forge of a new type of French Jew whose Jewishness would be nothing more than a "persuasion."[51]

Another decree, issued on March 17, 1808, and dubbed "monstrous" by Jewish contemporaries, struck at the mainstays of Jewish economic existence: trade and money lending. It annulled, opened the possibility of annulment, reduced, or delayed payment on all debts owed Jews, and it presumed Jewish businessmen guilty of unethical and illegal behavior unless they could prove otherwise. From then on, special licenses (*patents*) would be required for Jews to conduct legally recognized business. The licenses would have to be renewed yearly, so the authorities could closely monitor Jewish behavior. Departmental prefects would issue the licenses upon certification by the applicant's town council that the Jew had not engaged in usury or other illicit trade and upon assurance from the local consistorial synagogue that the Jew was generally upstanding.

The same decree also legislated severe restrictions on Jewish immigration into France as well as internal migration. All Jewish immigration to Alsace, a border region, was prohibited. Foreign Jews would be permitted to settle elsewhere in the country, and resident Jews to move across departmental boundaries, only if they purchased land and worked it themselves.

The "infamous decree" was the product of the personal prejudices of Napoleon and his chief advisers and of politics. Alsace was a traditional heartland of anti-Jewish sentiment. The Jewish economic profile there was much like that in the Rhineland: a predominantly rural and small-town folk barred from agriculture, Alsatian Jewry supported itself by peddling, animal dealing, and money lending.[52] Under the old regime, Jews had been a primary source of credit to peasants unable to pay their feudal obligations, and Jews continued to be indispensable under the new. In fact, Jewish money lending increased after the Revolution, as land-hungry but penniless peasants took out loans to purchase nationalized feudal property. There had been a rising clamor for the government to grant relief from Jewish "usury." It was answered in 1808.

The infamous decree was meant to be both punitive and educational, a brake on alleged abuses and a goad to occupational restratification; as Napoleon put it, "it is necessary to employ . . . two methods concurrently, one . . . to stop . . . the conflagration, . . . the other to extinguish it."[53] For this reason, the decree was enacted for ten years, in the hope that "at the end of this period and as a result of these . . . measures . . . there will no longer be any difference between them and the other citizens of the Empire." Should that hope be disappointed, however, the decree could be extended indefinitely, "until whatever time shall be judged convenient."[54]

The legislation did not revoke emancipation—ghettos were not re-established, nor were Jews re-expelled from places, like Strasbourg, from which all but a wealthy handful had been excluded. But it seriously compromised Jewish equality. In punishing precisely those activities to which Jews had previously been restricted, the decree differed fundamentally from the ordinances that governed Jews under the old regime, yet like those ordinances, it was exceptional legislation, conferring on Jews a degraded civil status. New and hopelessly confused was the demand that the same legislation that distinguished Jews somehow work their total integration into society. Similarly conflicted was the legislation creating the consistories, which perpetuated the very corporate separateness Napoleon found intolerable.[55]

Indeed, for all the ostensible physiocratic sentiment behind the "infamous" decree—the prejudice against commerce and money—and the pious outrage against Jews in particular ("The French government cannot stand by indifferently while a contemptible and degraded nation . . . assumes ownership of the two beautiful departments of old Alsace," Napoleon declared), careful reading of the law and its supporting documents reveals a more complicated set of attitudes.[56] Neither Jews per se nor money activities in themselves were objectionable, because the decree exempted the Jews of the city of Bordeaux and the departments of Gironde and Landes, who were capitalists par excellence. Descendants of Spanish and Portuguese crypto-Jews who had reverted to Judaism in France, the Sephardim made their living at large-scale colonial trade and banking. Thoroughly acculturated and on the whole a far wealthier (and less numerous) community than the Ashkenazim of northeastern France, the Sephardim had long been regarded as "model Jews" ("Faites commes ceux de Bordeaux, comme les Portugais," Napoleon exhorted the newly founded Central Consistory).[57]

Thus, where the Jews of Alsace were "hucksters" and "usurers," those of Bordeaux and Bayonne were "wholesalers" and "bankers." While the unacculturated Ashkenazim were considered superstitious and fanatical, the Sephardim were seen as enlightened.

They were the least objectionable of Jews. Their exemption from the 1808 decree tells us that for all the talk of "useful" (i.e., noncommercial) occupations for Jews, it was not so much the Ashkenazi preoccupation with trade and finance but their poverty and the pettiness of their enterprises that damned them. The real offense was not what these Jews did for a living but their failure to do it on a grand scale, since the larger business and banking operations of their Sephardi coreligionists were quite welcome and even exemplary.

Internal consistency is not a hallmark of prejudicial thinking, and the 1808 decree conveyed two contradictory messages to the Jews, one explicit, the other implicit.[58] The first told them to become peasants and artisans; the second told them to remain in their traditional mercantile occupations but to practice them more successfully, to "do as the Jews of Bordeaux."

Since most French peasants and artisans lived in poverty equal to that of the peddling and money-lending Ashkenazim, there was little to recommend the first option, which would also have required total occupational retraining and lifestyle change. Clearly, if Jews were to "earn" civic equality and acceptance, it would be via the second route. If, as Heine would note, baptism was the Jews' admission ticket to European culture, a degree of wealth and respectable position on the occupational ladder were the prerequisites for Jewish civil equality in Napoleonic France. Champagny, Minister of the Interior, said as much in a report to the Emperor while the 1808 decree was being drafted. Jewish peddlers, dealers in secondhand goods and coins, and in general, he said, "all those who are not bankers, wholesalers, large-scale merchants, owners of property or factory directors" would be subject to restriction.[59] Clearly, emancipation was for the bourgeois Jew. If the desire for material betterment was not enough to induce diligence in mercantile Jews, that message would have been another powerful incentive.

Champagny hoped that the spectacle of certain Jews being exempted from the decree would serve as a spur to the rest, and in one respect, at least, he was correct. Within days of the decree's promulgation Jewish communities began petitioning for exemption.[60] The appeals showed that the unspoken message of the infamous decree had been heard. Along with such proof of good citizenship as the number of local Jews in military service and in public and vocational schools, petitioning communities also cited the number of wealthy Jews in their midst. The Paris petition, composed by wealthy Sephardim, cited the progress toward embourgeoisement that the Ashkenazim of the capital had made since the Revolution and asked exemption at least for those Jews who practiced a trade or profession—not for Jewish artisans, much less farmers, but bourgeoisie.[61]

The Jews of the Roer department, represented by Salomon Oppenheim of Cologne, petitioned, too. The petition failed, although it was endorsed warmly by the mayor of Cologne and the deputy prefect of the *arrondissement* (district) of Cologne ("The conduct of the Jews is, in general . . . no different from that of [members of] other religions. I have nothing but praise . . . [for] them. . . . There are bad people in all religions. . . . I . . . wish that the Jews of this department be allowed to partake in favors [exemption] which His Majesty . . . has bestowed on several other departments").[62] In remaining under the strictures of the decree, Roer Jewry shared the fate of the majority of French Jewry, who regained only under the Bourbon restoration the civic equality originally granted by the Revolution.[63]

By an accident of history, the Jews of the Roer and of France's other left-bank departments remained under its strictures a good deal longer than that. When Napoleon's empire crumbled in late 1813, the left bank of the Rhine passed to Prussia, which retained the Napoleonic Jewry legislation until 1845 — almost three decades after it had lapsed in France, where the decree was dropped at the conclusion of its original tenure. The consistorial system lasted even longer, until 1863. Thus, the infamous decree governed the civic status of left-bank Jewry for much of the era of emancipation. It shaped both Jewish and non-Jewish perceptions of Jews as not-quite-citizens, and provided the reference point against which opponents and proponents of emancipation argued their cases. In communicating so clearly the bias in favor of middle-class over petty capitalist occupations for Jews, and in linking their civic status to the attainment of a certain standard of living, it could only have added an element of urgency to Jewish economic striving.

It also provided a point of entanglement for rivalrous city and state authorities, who would shortly begin a modern version of the ancient struggle for control of the Jews of Cologne.

CHAPTER THREE

Sinking Roots:
The Consolidation of Jewish
Settlement, 1814–35

On New Year's day, 1814, troops of the collapsing Napoleonic regime left Cologne. After years of warfare, levies, drafts, and quartering, the population was glad to see them go. "I passed the whole summer and autumn of 1815 and the winter of 1816 in Cologne," Ernst Moritz Arndt, a German nationalist writer, would later recall. "I found the old *Reichsstadt* and its inhabitants completely different than . . . almost twenty years previously . . . in the summer of 1799 [when they] . . . had an utterly dead and desolate appearance and made a gloomy and troubled impression."[1] While Arndt was not an objective observer, there is no reason to doubt that the city greeted the new year with relief.

Jews surely shared the sentiment. They suffered the same privations as the rest of the population as well as the special burdens of the 1808 decree. Prussia, by contrast, one of the powers that vanquished Napoleon, had issued an Edict of Emancipation in 1812 that had abolished much of the legal discrimination against Jews.[2] Although the city's political future was uncertain at first — disposition of France's former left-bank territories was not decided for another year — Prussia was sure to have a large part in shaping the peace, and that could only have boded well.

Jews clearly wanted relief from the 1808 decree. In 1811, when Napoleon had passed through Cologne, Salomon Oppenheim had repeated his appeal

for exemption of Roer Jewry.[3] Given Prussia's recent liberal Jewry edict and
its hatred of things French, it was reasonable to expect that this piece of
Napoleonic despotism would be cast aside. In France itself, the decree was
allowed to lapse in 1818, at the end of its original tenure.

It would not be so in the Rhineland. Yet, despite the intended blow to
Jewish commerce, money lending, and immigration, Jewish life in the city
continued, and Jewish numbers increased. Jewish fertility remained high, as
did immigration, with 83 new households established between 1814 and
1835.[4] Of these, 60 percent were permanent: records compiled in 1835
show that half of 86 Jewish households then present in the city had been
established since 1814 and were not headed by grown children of French-
era immigrants.[5] Estimating an average of five persons per household, we
arrive at a population of 430 Jews by 1835. But even lower official counts
show a substantial increase in the Jewish population. One source puts it at
354 in 1823; another cites 371 Jews in 1830.[6] By contemporary standards,
this was a substantial community. Only 41 cities in all of Prussia, and none
of them in the Rhineland, had Jewish populations exceeding 500 in 1817.
Locally, Cologne's community remained second in size only to Bonn,
whose community numbered 475 in 1823.[7]

All this raises obvious questions about enforcement of the decree, yet we
should remember that the decree did not bar Jewish migration completely,
only movement across departmental boundaries. Internal migration within
the former Roer department, including migration to cities, was legal. Since
the derivation of the immigration to Cologne continued to be regional,
even strict enforcement would not have precluded all immigration, and
enforcement was hardly foolproof.

As before, most of the immigrants came to Cologne with no prior experience of big city life. Sixty percent came from locations with fewer than
10,000 inhabitants, most from towns of fewer than 5,000 inhabitants. Only
3 immigrant households out of 42 with known places of origin stemmed
from cities with populations larger than Cologne's — Berlin, Hamburg, and
Warsaw — and only 10 came from cities of between 10,000 and 35,000. Far
from being a deterrent, Cologne's size again seems to have been a beacon to
Jews, whose move there was deliberate.

Cologne experienced heavy immigration in these years, its population
increasing by 34 percent between 1816 and 1834, from 46,500 to 62,200,
largely because of immigration.[8] Like the Jews, most of the non-Jewish
immigrants came from Cologne's immediate hinterland or elsewhere in the
Rhineland.

But there were important differences in the nature and motivations of
the Jewish and general migrations. There were several agrarian crises in

these years, the worst in 1816, another from the late twenties through 1831. Non-Jewish immigration to Cologne fluctuated directly with the price of food, rising as staples became dear, falling off when supplies became more bountiful. Emigration rose when economic conditions improved.[9] Non-Jewish immigration, then, was pushed by distress in the countryside rather than pulled by perceived opportunity in the city.

By contrast, Jewish immigration was low in bad economic years and increased in better ones.[10] Records of synagogue assessments show that most Jewish immigrants were not in desperate straits and that a good number were well-off. Nor were they fleeing antisemitism: none came from locations that experienced anti-Jewish riots in 1819.[11] Jews came to Cologne in search of opportunity. Better the risk of migration with the possibility of real gain than remaining in inherently limited situations in towns and smaller cities. The pattern in Cologne seems to fit Utz Jeggle's observation about Jewish emigration from German villages: "The wealthy went to cities; the . . . poor to America."[12]

The economic character of this immigration is striking because economic conditions in the region as a whole and in Cologne in particular were far worse in the first decades of Prussian rule than they had been under France.[13] The interregnum, when neither French nor Prussian trade or monetary policy was in place, was a time of tremendous dislocation. Bearing a huge war debt, Prussia soon slapped its new Rhenish territory with high taxes from which localities received no benefit and abolished levies on which local treasuries had depended. In 1816, the effects of unrestrained British and Dutch competition and a failed harvest began to be felt. The city's merchants, shorn of the protective embrace of Napoleon's Continental System and the boon of France's internal markets, were subjected instead to Prussia's free-trade policies. International river trade, the city's lifeline, was buffeted by Dutch tariffs the Prussians did nothing to counter, while overland trade in the Rhine region, as well as with "old Prussia," was stymied by abysmally poor roads. There was a severe shortage of credit, even specie, which the Prussians refused to treat aggressively. A multiplicity of coins — old Reichstaler from Cleves, French francs — continued in circulation long after Prussia made its taler the official currency. A local patriot boasted in 1828 that the declaration " 'I am a Bürger of Cologne' passes in London as 'civis Romanus sum' [did] in a proconsular province," but this was sheer bravado. The very mention of aggressive, enterprising London could only have sent shudders through a merchant from Cologne.[14]

Yet Cologne's problems were also structural. According to Pierre Ayçoberry, Cologne's great merchants brought stagnation on themselves by failure of nerve and by a mentality we might call economic morbidity — refusal to leave past patterns behind and enter new or risky ventures.[15]

Rather than accept dawning economic realities and seizing new opportunities, Cologne's magnates preferred to fight for the preservation of ancient, and obsolete, patterns.

It was a doomed course and one that made conflict with Berlin inevitable. Prussia was a commercially and industrially backward eastern German
state with no overseas colonies. Its postwar economic policy aimed at de-
veloping its newly enlarged internal market by loosening or abolishing
internal tariffs and allowing market forces to operate freely. Cologne's great
merchants remained wedded to the dream of their city as an intermediary
trading center, dominating international traffic on the Rhine in the way it
had from medieval times until the French era: through maritime tariffs and
a monopoly on transshipment of goods traveling the river (the *Stapel* and
Umschlagsrechte) — in short, through restraint of trade. France had abolished these medieval river privileges and free-trade Prussia was hardly about
to restore them.

Although trade in Rhine wines was one of the few healthy sectors of the
economy, Cologne's merchant elite refused to move into *Eigenhandel* —
the management of a commodity from producer to retailer, preferring to
squeeze what floated by on the river. When their vision collided with that of
Berlin, they chose to fight rather than adapt. In the end, in Ayçoberry's
words, all that Cologne's elites accomplished was "the situation of their city
in the center of a purely imaginary [economic] space" of a bygone era.[16]

Cologne's banking houses contributed to the city's economic lassitude
by investing their funds almost exclusively in manufacturing outside the
city. Prussia did nothing to help, valuing Cologne more for its strategic
importance as a garrison city and Rhine fortress than for its economic
promise.[17] This neglect, coupled with the "fundamentally anti-industrialist
mentality" of the city's commercial elite, led to near extinction of a small but
significant industrial sector that had begun to develop under French rule.
There were 30 bankruptcies in large-scale manufacturing between 1817 and
1825 alone.[18]

There were a few important economic developments in this period,
spearheaded by Cologne's Chamber of Commerce under the leadership of
Peter Heinrich Merkens: the beginnings of a maritime insurance industry
and the founding of a steamship company. Cologne's blossoming as an
insurance and financial center, with particular investment in mechanized
transport, lay in the future, however. The city would ride out of the dol-
drums on iron rails only after 1835.

Jews seeking betterment came to Cologne despite all this because the
whole regional economy was depressed and opportunities for a mercantile
group were still better in the big city than elsewhere. As we shall see,
moreover, aside from general trading, Jews entered sectors of the economy

TABLE 4
Jewish Occupational Structure, 1825, 1835

| | Number of Jews engaged | |
Occupation	1825	1835
Trade and Commerce		
Type of Activity		
Commission and forwarding,	4	5
Business ownership	2	1
Trading, selling	21	26
Petty trading	6	2
Butchering	6	13
TOTAL (% of all occupations)	39 (62)	47 (53)
Banking, credit		
Banking	5	5
Currency changing	6	3
Lottery collecting	1	9
TOTAL (% of all occupations)	12 (19)	17 (19)
Manufacturing		
Writing materials	1	1
% of all occupations	1.5	1
Crafts		
Embroidery in gold, silver, silk	1	1
Hat making	1	1
Gold- and silversmithing	—	2
Saddlery	—	1
Oil and gypsum or rock milling	—	2
Metal and stone engraving	—	1
TOTAL (% of all occupations)	2 (3)	8 (9)
Manual Labor		
Wagoning	1	—
% of all occupations	1.5	—
Salaried Employment	—	2
% of all occupations	—	2
Service		
Rental of Horses; Books	—	3
Innkeeping	1	3
TOTAL (% of all occupations)	1 (1.5)	6 (7)
Professions		
Teaching		
Hebrew, Judaica	3	2
Non-Jewish languages	1	1
Music	—	1
Medicine	1	2
TOTAL (% of all occupations)	5 (8)	6 (7)
Pensioner	2	1
% of all occupations	3	1
Unemployed	0	1
% of all occupations	—	1
TOTAL occupations	63	89
TOTAL individuals	60	81

SOURCE: *HASK*, Oberbürgermeisteramt, 400, II-4-13-2, 400, II-13-C-10, 400-4-C-1, 400, II-4-D-1, *Adress-Buch oder Verzeichniss der Einwohner der Stadt Cöln,* 1822, 1828, 1835.

(*notes continued on facing page*)

that were specialized in Cologne (commission and forwarding of Rhine cargoes, trade in colonial wares) as well as created by circumstance (money changing and financing the municipal debt).

Jewish Occupational Structure and Change

The 1808 decree was a form of educational legislation intended to wean Jews away from trade and into "useful" (noncommercial) occupations.[19] It did not bar Jews from commerce; in theory, even urbanizing migrants could do legal business if they had not moved across a departmental border and had procured the requisite "Jew" license (*Judenpatent*).

As we shall see, most Jews who applied for these licenses got them. In effect, this meant that Jews were free to continue practicing traditionally Jewish occupations, and it is not surprising that, for the most part, they did. Still, some occupational change, significant in kind if not numbers, did occur.

Table 4 illustrates the range of economic activities Jews practiced and the group's occupational structure in 1825 and 1835, ten and twenty years into Prussian rule. Commerce clearly predominated, accounting for 65 percent of all occupations practiced by Jews in the earlier year, and 60 percent in the latter. Most of this was petty trade, with the tendency toward small commerce growing more pronounced with time, doubtless the result of overall economic conditions.

Jewish traders dealt in local, regional, and foreign wares. They often practiced more than one occupation, combining several related business activities, such as innkeeping with horse rental or wine selling. They also combined trade and banking activities (such as the sale of luxury goods or food with lottery collecting) and trade and a craft (such as horse dealing and oil milling).[20] Since Jews at both ends of the commercial spectrum diversified, this pattern indicates both economic success and failure, activity from surplus capital amassed in profitable ventures and an expedient when no single occupation sufficed for a livelihood. Both the lofty Oppenheims (as well as their non-Jewish counterparts) and lowly Jewish innkeepers engaged in activities other than banking and room rentals.[21]

NOTE: Because most of the Jewish group was engaged in commerce of some kind, this occupational category is the most subdivided. The evaluation and ranking of occupational titles is notoriously difficult. Among the problems, such as deciding if a butcher or jeweler engaged primarily in crafts or retail, is the question of multiple occupations listed for one individual. This table reflects the totality of occupations practiced by Cologne's Jews, which is somewhat greater than the number of Jews with recorded occupational histories. Occupations are grouped according to function and scale of activity rather than wealth of practitioner; cf. Table 6.

Commodities traded in these years were cloth and fabrics; rags and old clothes; writing supplies; jewelry; art; pipes and whistles; wine; fruit; agricultural produce; food; cattle; horses; animal hides; fats; colonial goods; and spices.

Jewish financial activities ranged from petty lottery collecting and money changing to the dealings of the Oppenheim bank, which was the second largest in the city by 1810.[22] Oppenheim wealth derived originally from purveying luxury goods to the last archbishop-elector of Cologne. After the bank's founder, Salomon Oppenheim, Jr., moved to Cologne from Bonn, he continued to combine banking with commodity brokering, primarily in grain, practicing the forwarding and commission activities upon which Cologne's great merchant houses were built and which, until the French, had been reserved for Catholics.[23] The house also traded in Rhine wines. Merchant banking was the norm among Cologne houses, so there was nothing extraordinary about Oppenheim's diversification. On the contrary, the house set the trend in the other direction; it was among the earliest to specialize in banking, which it began to do by the second decade of the century. By 1830, under the leadership of Salomon's sons Abraham and Simon, it had made the transition to pure banking.

The proportion of Jews engaged in some type of banking — 20 percent — remained constant from 1825 to 1835, but some significant changes occurred in the type of banking activity.[24] Money changing, a private, largely unregulated enterprise, declined, while lottery collecting, a form of tax collection subject to standards and some supervision, increased substantially.[25] Judging by the tendency for lottery collecting to appear as a side occupation alongside other small-scale business and by the low amounts lottery collectors were assessed for synagogue membership, the nine Jewish *Lotterie Einnehmer* of 1835 were petty agents.[26] But it is significant that Jews had been made part of the city's revenue collecting apparatus. One Jewish lottery collector even served as a low-level employee of the municipal loan office.[27]

And Jews were not confined only to minor responsibilities in the municipal financial establishment. When the city's poor relief office opened a loan and pawn operation in 1819, a Jewish pawnbroker, Joseph Stern (the first Jewish man to settle in the city), was entrusted with running it. Several years later, when a city-sponsored savings association for servants and craftsmen was established, Stern was placed in charge of that, too. His association with both institutions continued into the mid-1830's and his son-in-law, Abraham Ochse-Stern, who succeeded him, turned the municipal savings and loan institution into a family business.[28] It was an ironic outcome for a program meant, in part at least, as a latter-day *monte di pietà*: the institutions had been established because (according to the provincial government), before 1819, Cologne's lower classes had only Jews (those of Deutz) to turn to for pawnbroking services.[29] The municipal government's willingness to use Jewish financial expertise belied its assertions, oft-repeated in enforcement of the 1808 decree, that this expertise was unwholesome and unwelcome.

While Cologne's Jews concentrated overwhelmingly in commerce and banking activities, a small artisanal sector did arise, a development in line with what we know of German (and French) Jewry in this period: 7 of 81 Jews (8.5 percent) with recorded occupations in 1835 practiced some form of manual craft.[30] Two of these Jews were trained by non-Jewish masters, and several worked in crafts that were not traditionally Jewish (i.e., involved in making ritual objects): oil, gypsum and rock milling, and saddle making.[31] This means that at least some Jews were responding to the expressed demand of the 1808 decree for radical occupational reorientation. We do not know why these Jews entered crafts. There was in Cologne no "society for the promotion of crafts among Jews," such as existed elsewhere, to encourage them.[32] Poor Jews often found a route to upward mobility through artisanship, although if that was the hope of these new craftsmen, synagogue dues records indicate it was not realized.[33]

The Jewish professional sector remained tiny, yet underwent some noteworthy changes. By 1835 there were two Jewish doctors, whose clientele must have been largely non-Jewish, since both could not have made a living from the Jewish community.[34] Although in 1825 three of four teachers served the Jewish community and taught Judaica, in 1835 two of four Jewish teachers had no known affiliation with the Jewish community's school and specialized in secular subjects: languages and music.[35] Education was not compulsory in Cologne until 1825, when existing church-run and private institutions came under state supervision. Even then, many children were tutored privately, and it is quite possible that the Jewish teachers were employed by non-Jews. Even if they taught only Jewish children, however, their secular expertise — and the secular interests of their students — are important indications of changing attitudes.

It is significant too, that both the veteran director of the synagogue's school and his replacement left Jewish education entirely in these years. The first became a small-scale trader, apparently less demanding work than education for a man advancing in years. The second opened a lending library and did lottery collecting on the side.[36] Since, as we shall see, the synagogue leadership demonstrated a singular lack of commitment to the Jewish school, it is not surprising that these men left the field. Whatever the causes, the clear trend of Jewish professionals was toward greater integration with the non-Jewish environment.

Wealth, Stratification, and Mobility

Jews came to Cologne in hopes of betterment. Were their hopes realized?

Occupational titles are only partially indicative of material standing. A "petty trader" may justly be assumed to have a lower standard of living than

TABLE 5
Jewish Income Stratification as Reflected in Synagogue Membership Assessments,
1825/26, 1835
(by head of household)

Assessment bracket	1825/26			1835		
	Amount (in talers)	Number of households	Percentage of households	Amount (in talers)	Number of households	Percentage of households
High	5–7	8	14	3–13	13	23
Middle	2–3.10	21	36	1.25–2.20	11	20
Low[a]	0–1.20	29	50	0.10–1.20	32	57
TOTAL		58	100		56	100

SOURCE: *HASK,* Oberbürgermeisteramt, 400, II-4-D-1.
[a] In 1825/26, the low assessment bracket included nine Jews listed as *unvermögend* (penniless), who were assessed no dues.

a "wholesaler," but, as the evidence from the French years showed, we cannot conclude that even those whom the records term "peddlers" were necessarily poor. Moreover, a Jew who was a petty dealer in a small town and who remained one in Cologne may still have experienced improved circumstances.

The best measure of the wealth of Cologne's Jews is the records of synagogue membership assessments, extant from 1825/26 on. Since there was considerable external pressure on Jews to join the synagogue (they needed its character endorsement to receive a *Judenpatent*), the lists can be considered fairly inclusive and representative. The *Cultus Kosten* lists also provide a way to relate income to occupation and to evaluate the material significance of occupational change among the Jews.[37]

Analysis of these data shows that 14 percent of the community was in the highest assessment bracket in 1825/26 and that by 1835, nearly 25 percent of it was (see Table 5). The relative wealth of the Jewish community is corroborated by other sources. A survey of the Jewish population in 1820 listed 23 of 43 male householders as possessing "wealth" (*Wohlstand*).[38] In 1836, the rabbi of Krefeld, impressed by the 108 taler in yearly dues that the Cologne community paid the consistory of Bonn, asked that Cologne be redistricted under his supervision.[39] The wealth of Cologne's Jewish community stands out especially against the poverty of the Jews of the immediately surrounding territory (*Landkreis Köln*). While only 60 percent of Jews in the *Landkreis* as a whole were able to pay some amount of trade tax (*Gewerbesteuer*) in 1818, 80 percent of the city's Jews could, and they were assessed significantly higher amounts than their rural co-religionists.[40]

Yet the *Cultus Kosten* records also depict a community with a large and growing class of members able to pay only the most minimal assessments and a group of moderate wealth halved in size between the mid-1820's and the 1830's. In the absence of figures on the number of poor Jews who turned to the community for support, it is difficult to evaluate what degree of poverty is indicated by a minimal synagogue-dues assessment, but it would appear to have been something short of outright destitution. This group probably corresponds to what Pierre Ayçoberry calls "les gens gênés" of Cologne's larger society: those living in chronic economic distress but not dire poverty.[41] In 1825/26, however the lists contained a category for the destitute (*unvermögend*), in which a considerable 16 percent of adult male Jews were classed. The overall trend in Jewish economic standing was downward, with increasingly sharp stratification between wealthy and poor Jews. The picture even in 1825/26 is a far cry from that presented by the first synagogue dues assessments in 1801, and it worsened with time.

Unfortunately, the data are not available for a similar analysis of the non-Jewish population.[42] Ayçoberry estimates that a very substantial 40 percent of the overall population was on the economy's lower rungs in "ordinary" (that is, noncrisis) years and that 16 percent of these were utterly destitute — the same percentage as for Jews. Any comparison must be cautious however, because inability to pay a form of tax and inability to pay the market price of bread (Ayçoberry's criterion) probably reflect very different levels of poverty. We can safely say that many Jews were not enjoying a markedly better standard of living than non-Jews.

Assessing occupational mobility is another way to measure how well Jews were doing in the city, but we can only evaluate their ability to move up and do better when we know what *up* and *better* meant in occupational terms. The fiscal data on the synagogue membership lists make it possible to rank Jewish occupations and obtain a picture of the contemporary value of various occupational titles.[43] With such a ranking, we can more accurately assess which occupational paths were more and less lucrative and meaningfully evaluate Jewish occupational choices.

Table 6 shows that money trades predominated among wealthy Jews in both 1825 and 1835 but that by 1835 large-scale trade in food, colonial wares, and dry goods had replaced the commission and forwarding business as the second most common occupation of the well-to-do. Assuming there was a real distinction between these activities — the difference between acting as a brokerage agent for goods owned by others and owning the shipments themselves — the shift may signal deeper Jewish involvement with an array of importers and producers as well as wholesalers. If the level of financial return remained the same, the degree of economic integration was greater. This change would also mean that wealthy Jews were leaving the more traditional, declining sectors of Cologne's economy for newer, expanding ones.

Banking activities were also the most common occupation of Jews in the

TABLE 6
Occupational Ranking of Cologne Jews as Reflected in Synagogue Membership Assessments, 1825, 1835
(by head of household)

Synagogue membership assessment level[a]	1825		1835	
	Percentage of Jewish households	Occupations	Percentage of Jewish households	Occupations
High	15	Banking, currency changing Commission and forwarding	24	Banking Wholesale trade in textiles, colonial wares, agricultural produce
Middle	42	Banking, currency changing Wine trade Food provisioning Stationery manufacture Miscellaneous trade, peddling	20	Trade Money changing Stationery manufacture Teaching Horse dealing and oil milling Innkeeping and horse rental
Low	44	Butchering, trade in livestock and animal-products Teaching Trade Wagoning	55	Butchering, trade in livestock and animal-products Lottery collecting Teaching Jewelry making and trading Petty trade Salaried work

SOURCE: See Tables 4 and 5.
[a]See Table 5 for the amounts of the assessment levels.

middle-range synagogue-assessment category, followed by trade in every commodity except colonial wares. We should note that two peddlers were in the middle-level wealth category in 1825, supporting the finding for the French period that petty dealers were not necessarily poor.

If practicing a profession brought Jews enhanced status, it did not boost their earnings. All but one of the professionals in the Jewish community — between three and four teachers and two doctors — were in the lowest dues categories, along with almost all the butchers, livestock and animal product dealers, and two of three Jewish artisans in 1835. The lesson of all this was that the road to upward mobility for Jews lay in commerce and banking. The fact that, despite this, butchering and animal trade increased (from 10 percent of Jewish occupations in 1825 to 15 percent in 1835) and that a small Jewish artisanal group developed in these years (see Table 4) suggests an inability of Jews to move into more lucrative, but also more capital-intensive, activities. This is, once again, a sign of economic stress.

No evaluation of Jewish occupational choices and wealth stratification can be accurate without assessment of the impact of ongoing Jewish immigration. The influx was very substantial relative to the size of the resident Jewish population, and any reckoning of overall group mobility must separate the records of newcomers from those of resident Jews and their children who were born or came of age in Cologne. Separate consideration allows us to judge the economic character of the immigration as well as to isolate patterns that emerged in Cologne itself.

There was, indeed, an immigrant differential (see Table 7). The records of synagogue assessments, with data on some 60 male heads of household, show that in two sample years, 1825 and 1835, recent immigrants were relatively underrepresented in the highest income stratum, proportionately overrepresented in the middle category, and were about the same proportion in the lowest range as resident Jews. By 1835, however, when immigrant households established in this period constituted half of the total population, a higher percentage of immigrant Jews was in the high wealth category, while immigrants were a smaller element in the lowest stratum. Since the bulk of the immigration of this period took place between 1825 and 1835 (57 of 83 new Jewish households were established in this decade), upward mobility in the city cannot account for this differential. A large proportion of the immigrants must have come to Cologne with significant means.

As we have seen, there had been a large proportion of wealthy Jewish immigrants from the beginning, a tendency perhaps bolstered by the immigration controls of the 1808 decree — or the way they were enforced. Strictly applied, the law would have barred Jewish migrants even from such nearby and important sources of immigrants as Bonn, Deutz, and Mülheim, which had not been in the French Roer department. In fact, however, Jews stemming from outside the borders of Cologne's former department (later its government district, *Regierungsbezirk*), were allowed to settle in the city without abandoning commerce if they could prove probity and economic self-sufficiency. This economic loophole obviously favored the immigration of successful Jews. While the means of enforcement were not effective enough to bar poor Jews completely, they may have acted as a sieve, filtering out the poorest and helping to fashion a particular kind of immigration.

If Jewish wealth was relatively concentrated among recent arrivals, this can only mean that the general decline in economic standing of the Jewish group was caused by the downward mobility of longer-settled Jews. Table 7 shows that the segment of this group assessed a middle-range tax did decline, while the proportion of its members ranked in the lowest assessment category increased. Jews assessed several taler in 1825/26 were assessed a

TABLE 7

Income Stratification of Jewish Immigrants as Reflected in Synagogue Membership Assessments, 1825/26, 1835
(by head of household)[a]

Synagogue assessment level	Amount (in talers)	Long-settled		Recent		Overall	Amount (in talers)	Long-settled		Recent		Overall
	1825/26	No.	%	No.	%	No.	1835	No.	%	No.	%	No.
High	5–7	6	17	2	9	14	3–13	5	16	8	28	21
Middle	2–3.10	12	34	9	39	36	1.25–2.20	9	28	7	24	18
Low	0–1.20	17	49	12	52	50	0.10–1.20	18	56	14	48	61
TOTAL		35	100	23	100	58		32	100	29	100	61

SOURCE: See Tables 4 and 5.

[a]Numbers indicate male heads of household assessed at that level.

few groschen in 1835. While this decline was not, for the most part, accompanied by occupational changes, there were a few cases of dramatic shifts: Jews listed on the assessment records as commodities brokers and currency exchangers in 1825 who appear as unemployed or as petty dealers in 1835.[44] Even the upper income elite of long-settled Jews, which remained the same in proportionate size, was buffeted by change and decline: four of six Jews in the highest assessment brackets in 1825/26 had either dropped into lower brackets by 1835 or left the city. Their places were taken not by new, rising individuals but by members of the Oppenheim family, come to maturity and taxed separately and at by far the highest rates of anyone on the membership lists.[45] Were it not for this, the size of the upper-income group would have shrunk drastically.

Cologne in the twenties and early thirties was clearly not a land of opportunity for the immigrants of the French period. This was not because of the "lack of [occupational] qualification and instability" that was the root cause of poverty in the general population.[46] Nor was it because of discrimination. The occupational record attests to a remarkable degree of Jewish integration into a wide range of economic activities. There was strong official support for the decree of 1808 and opposition to Jewish economic integration, but the record suggests that resistance was, in part at least, a reaction to substantial integration taking place. As we shall see, that opposition was ineffective. Not discriminatory legislation, not Jewish exclusion from the economy, but their participation in it, caused the economic regression of the long-settled Jews.

There were no striking success stories among either the immigrants of this period or the long-settled Jews and their children. Whatever Jewish wealth existed was either made elsewhere and brought to Cologne, or amassed during the French years, or both. In this the Jews resembled non-Jewish society in this period, when old wealth endured but new wealth was generally not created or was not able to persevere.[47]

Jewish Integration and Attitudes to the Non-Jewish Environment

Residential Patterns

Jewish residential patterns can be a clear indication of Jewish attitudes toward non-Jewish society as well as the receptivity of that society to Jews. The evidence about Jewish attitudes in this period is less clear-cut than in the French years. While Jews continued to disperse geographically, they showed a clear and growing preference for the third section of the city

TABLE 8
Location of Jewish Households by City Section, 1825/26, 1835

Section	1825/26		1835	
	Number of households	Percentage of households	Number of households	Percentage of households
I	8	16	12	21
II	10	20	10	17
III	22	43	25	43
IV	11	21	11	19
TOTAL	51	100	58	100

SOURCE: See Tables 4 and 5.
NOTE: See Map 1 for city sections.

(see Table 8 and Map 1). This is where the synagogue but also some of the city's major trade and traffic thoroughfares were located: the Schildergasse, Streitzeuggasse, Breitestrasse, and Hohestrasse.[48] Since it was normal for occupational groups to cluster residentially in Cologne, this pattern may have been motivated by occupational factors as well as religious or ethnic solidarity.[49] There was also a growing housing shortage in the city, which was physically quite small and undergoing a population boom. This, too, may have contributed to the Jewish concentration, with family members living with each other rather than establishing independent residences.

There is no reason to think that housing discrimination was a factor. We know of 33 city properties bought or rented by Jews of average and above-average wealth between 1815 and 1830.[50] Jews of moderate means seem to have benefited from the predicament of non-Jewish craftsmen, generally an economically stressed group, who sold their properties in order to obtain cash and rid themselves of mortgages; most of these sales were transacted between these principals. But there is no sign that restrictions existed in the best sections of town either, where we would most expect them. Cologne's wealthiest Jews had addresses commensurate with their economic stature. They resided among wealthy non-Jews on the best streets of the first and especially the fourth sections of town, some of them a door or two from the most powerful business and financial figures in the city.[51]

Economic Function and Patterns

Seen in the aggregate, Cologne's Jews had a distinct economic function, serving the business and consumer needs of Cologne's middle class, to which they themselves for the most part belonged. In particular, they extended credit to people who could not otherwise easily obtain it in Cologne's credit-tight and economically stratified circumstances.[52] But there was no "Jewish economy" in the sense of a sector dominated either by Jewish entrepreneurs or a Jewish clientele.[53] As had been true during the French period, even such a traditional Jewish business as butchering did not have only a Jewish clientele, since there were too many Jewish butchers for this to have been the case.

Judenpatente records show that a good number of Jews formed business partnerships with or employed other Jews.[54] Members of the Jewish elite certainly collaborated with each other on such ventures as debt financing and management of private obligations as well as the public debt. Yet they also joined with non-Jews in financing credit deals to the municipality. Such associations declined after 1826, but for purely economic reasons.[55]

Jews were economically distinct from the population at large, 37 percent of which practiced crafts in 1818/21 and 53 percent of which did in 1834/35.[56] But they were well integrated into the city's trading and banking sector. That says as much about the receptivity of the environment as it does about Jewish initiative. Since exceptions were often made for wealthy Jews even in the most hostile environments, it is the evidence about Cologne's middle- and lower-income Jews that is particularly significant.

Education

The most striking evidence we have of the importance Cologne's Jews placed on economic advancement are the statistics on Jewish attendance in non-Jewish schools.

German Jewish historians have emphasized the crucial role that Jewish educational reform and utilization of non-Jewish schools plays in the Europeanization of the Jews and their remarkable rise from generalized poverty to predominantly middle-class status during the nineteenth century.[57] Indeed, the opening of state or privately run schools to Jews, and Jewish willingness to use such institutions, are hallmarks of the emancipation era.[58] Prior to the late eighteenth century, traditional Jewish attitudes as much as external restrictions made Jewish attendance in Christian educational institutions extremely rare.[59] Yet less than a century later there were proportionately five times as many Jewish students in Prussian secondary schools (*Gymnasien*) as Jews in the population at large.[60] While there were considerable regional and class variations in the pace of this trend, which grew particularly pronounced in the second half of the nineteenth century, there were proportionately twice as many Jews in the German student population as Jews in Germany even before 1850.[61]

Even by this standard, Cologne's Jews were precocious in sending their children to non-Jewish schools. In 1820, four years before elementary education in Cologne became compulsory under Prussian law, 18 of 32 Jewish families with children sent their youngsters to such schools — and these figures probably understate the case, because some of the families listed as not sending children to "public" schools in 1820 may have had underage or grown children in that year.[62] By the time education was made compulsory in 1824, about half of approximately 60 school-age Jewish children attended non-Jewish institutions of one kind of another. Within a few years of the founding of a government-licensed *Realgymnasium* (secondary school) in 1828, 4 to 6 percent of enrolled students were Jewish, although Jews then constituted only 0.7 percent of the total population.[63]

This type of school was a departure from the usual *Gymnasium* with its humanities- and classics-based curriculum and university orientation, and Jews not only utilized it to a disproportionate degree, they also used it differently than did non-Jews. The *Realgymnasium*, as the name implied, was designed to meet the needs of male students who would enter the hard world of business. Although non-Jewish petty traders and artisans rarely sent their sons to this (or any other) kind of secondary school, the sons of Jewish "provisions dealers," "horse traders," "innkeepers, coal, ribbon, clothing, leather and fruit merchants," attended in relative abundance. If the *Realgymnasium* was the creation of Cologne's middle-class merchants, and both mirrored and perpetuated the class distinctions of larger society, this was not the case in Jewish society. Sons of the wealthy Oppenheim, Gompertz, and Ochse-Stern merchant and banking families attended the Kreutzgasse *Gymnasium* alongside sons of Jewish butchers and lottery collectors.[64] Jews of little or moderate wealth clearly saw education in the *Realgymnasium* as a means for their sons to attain success; wealthy Jews, as a means for them to sustain it. Both were ready to jettison the tradition of separate Jewish schooling in the pursuit of material progress. Even the community's religious teachers sent their sons to the *Realgymnasium*.[65]

While German Jewish communities elsewhere in this era continued to fund and utilize separate Jewish schools when permitted, Jewish education in Cologne languished despite not just permission but pressure from the government to operate such a school.[66] The community did run a school in which Talmud, Hebrew, and German were taught; private instruction in Judaica was also available. Yet less than half the Jewish school-age population availed itself of either option, a situation that apparently caused the community leadership no great concern.[67]

It was the Prussian government, pursuing an aggressive policy of educational reform in the city as a whole, that insisted in 1826 that the community set up an improved, separate Jewish primary school, to which the synagogue board, composed of Salomon Oppenheim and one other member, replied that the community lacked the means. Motivation was clearly lacking as well, since the board expressed the opinion that it was preferable for

Jewish children to attend Christian rather than separate Jewish schools "in order that the members of both religions be less alien to each other and that mutual affection and trust be furthered thereby."[68] Prussian authorities did not relent, however, and finally pressured the community to open a Jewish elementary school worthy of official recognition in 1831. Yet, despite a modernized curriculum including arithmetic, geography, German history, and enhanced German language study in addition to religious subjects, the school succeeded in attracting only 28 students by 1834, when the total Jewish population numbered over 350 according to official statistics and 430 according to my count.[69] With the Jewish educational system in a state of "profound vegetation," no wonder several Judaica instructors quit the field, as we have seen.[70]

If the scale of occupation and level of wealth of most Cologne Jews resembled that of the city's middle classes, their mentality resembled that of Cologne's upper-class *Bürger* merchants, whose ranks, as we shall see, they strove mightily to join.[71] The discrepancy between the material circumstances of most and their aspirations, the failure of the hoped-for upward mobility, is attributable to the strained economic circumstances of the era. The end of the period studied here found the Jews of Cologne not enjoying upward mobility, but poised for it. An improving economy in subsequent decades would bring the promise to fruition.

CHAPTER FOUR

Jewish Integration and the Politics of Resistance, 1814–35

"I passed my youth in an old republic, the free imperial city of Cologne, in pride about whose freedom, the citizen would say, 'I am as free in my house as the Emperor is in his castle.'"   Peter Heinrich Merkens, 1847[1]

The Prussian Rhineland

In early January 1814, allied troops under the command of a Prussian general forged the Rhine from the right bank, ending French rule. Napoleon's troops had fought hard to hold onto the left bank, which the French considered a natural and rightful part of France. It was clear that a revanchist France would try to regain the territory — French troops departed Cologne proclaiming, "Till spring!"[2]

The allies knew that securing the Rhine as "Germany's river, not its border," would require effective vigilance.[3] Of the four powers that defeated Napoleon — Russia, Prussia, England, and Austria — Prussia was deemed the logical candidate for the job. It had Rhenish territories that would now revert to its control, and so in any case would have to take measures to contain France.[4] Berlin did not at first welcome this role, preferring to acquire Saxony, so much closer to the Prussian heartland, and a simple return of its former Rhenish enclaves. But Austria and England were determined to see both a strong German presence confronting France and a Prussia divided into eastern and western halves. It was this vision that ultimately shaped Prussia's postwar configuration, drawn at the Congress of Vienna.[5] On February 8, 1815, the former French Rhineland north of the Palatinate was joined to Prussia.[6]

Securing the territory militarily turned out to be the least of Prussia's problems. A more formidable challenge lay in its integration into Prussia's legal and political structure. French legal, economic, and political institutions had sunk deep roots in the Rhineland. If Napoleonic despotism was detested, important segments of Rhenish society were determined that French laws and institutions — tellingly, now called *Rheinisches Recht* (Rhenish law) — endure. Equality before the law, an independent judiciary, open trials and a jury system, merchants' committees and Chambers of Commerce to represent the interests of business before government, had come to suit Rhenish tastes well.[7]

Prussia's notion of integration was total absorption. The Rhineland was to assume Prussian forms of governmental organization, replace the *Code Civil* with Prussia's *Allgemeines Landrecht*, and adopt Prussian trade and tariff priorities and the Prussian taxation system.[8] In the end, neither King Frederick William III nor Rhenish patriots — representatives of its urban business class, in particular — won a pure victory. Prussia's integration of the Rhineland proceeded as a compromise between the extremes of total assimilation on the one hand and regional autonomism on the other.[9]

Shortly after annexing the territory, Prussia organized it into two provinces, which were united in 1822 and eventually called the Rhine Province.[10] Berlin's free-trade policies, suitable to old Prussia's agrarian, semifeudal economy, were imposed on the far more urbanized, industrialized west despite fierce opposition from Rhenish merchants and manufacturers.[11] At the recommendation, however, of the *Immediat Justiz Kommission*, a consultative body created by royal cabinet order in June 1816, most of French law was retained.[12] The *Kommission* had been conceived as a shoehorn to introduce Prussian ways into the Rhineland. But its members, Rhenish jurists as well as Prussians now posted in the west, understood their mission more broadly as securing the best interests of the region, as defined by its inhabitants. They solicited "public opinion" and were deluged by position papers from private individuals, officeholders, newspapers, merchants' associations, and city governments, the vast majority of which strongly supported retaining "Rhenish institutions."[13]

Among the discrepant areas of Prussian law that the *Kommission* was to adjudicate was the status of the Rhineland's Jews. The "infamous decree" was set to expire in 1818, but the law provided for its own renewal should the Jews be found persisting in degenerate economic practices, thus demonstrating the need for continued state tutelage. The question was whether Prussia, archenemy of Napoleon, would perpetuate this legislation or extend to the Rhine territories its own far-reaching Edict of Emancipation, proclaimed in 1812.[14]

The *Kommission*, which met in Cologne, received diverse assessments of the "moral character" of Rhenish Jewry and the wisdom of the Napoleonic decree. The Consistories of Krefeld and Bonn condemned the law as unwarranted and immoral and protested the arbitrary discrimination Jews were suffering while its fate was under review. Individual Jews protested the law as well.[15] Significantly, several high-ranking provincial officials, including some from old Prussia serving in the Rhine territory, expressed similar views. They rejected the term *usury* to describe Jewish economic activities in rural areas, denied that rural poverty was caused by Jews, and condemned anti-Jewish restrictions as counterproductive. Equal rights and obligations, not discrimination, would bring about the "moral improvement" of the Jews. The "great progress" made by urban Jews — those of Cologne and Düsseldorf were cited specifically — was proof of the possibility of Jewish reform and regeneration.[16]

But there were negative affidavits as well. Period pieces of antisemitic thinking, they illustrate the depth of anti-Jewish sentiment and the argumentation used to rationalize continued discrimination. Any effort on behalf of Jewish rights, by Jews or non-Jews, by the most prominent banker or the lowliest peddler seeking a business license, had to confront and counter such images and arguments and they therefore merit some attention.

The ancient charge of usury is a fixture in the critical reports, the profits of which, according to one source, "German Jews drag off to Jerusalem."[17] One lengthy report, which I believe was written by a member of the *Kommission* and influenced its ultimate recommendations, condemns all Jews and, especially, Judaism.[18] Drawing, apparently, on several anti-emancipation tracts circulating in Germany during the Restoration, it is a full rejoinder to arguments made on behalf of Jewish rights since C. W. Dohm's epoch-making essay of 1781, *Concerning the Civic Improvement of the Jews.*[19]

The report opens by rejecting Dohm's central thesis, shared by all advocates of emancipation, that persecution caused the Jews' concentration in trade and money professions and their separate existence on the margins of Christian society. Far from being oppressed, the report insisted, Jews had enjoyed privileged status and great liberties in Poland, Spain, France, and Germany. They had not been forced into trade and usury but had chosen these activities out of inveterate misanthropy. Their hatred for Christians was not a reaction to oppression but the fruit of the Jews' xenophobic "religious and political constitution," which enjoined exploitation and ruination of non-Jews through corrupt business practices. This law was the basis for their "isolated, hostile existence." Having claimed the one God of the universe as their exclusive national deity and excluded non-Jews from their law, "opposition to the entire human race was inevitable."

Anti-Jewish feeling and policies, the report argues, were the normal reaction of the Jews' victims; the advocates of emancipation, in other words, had fundamentally misconstrued cause and effect in assessing the Jewish situation. Flawed perceptions led to dangerous proposals — lessening or abolishing anti-Jewish discrimination — which would leave Christians unprotected against the Jewish peril. Not ghetto walls but *"Jewish consciousness"* [*Judensinn*], the *"spirit of Judaism"* [*Judengeist*], *"Jewry"* [*das Judentum*], and *"Jewishness"* [*die Judischheit*] made Jews "Jewish" — that is, misanthropic (emphasis in the original). It was Judaism, not Christian society, that needed reform. Since hatred of non-Jews was a central tenet of Judaism, however, even a reformed sort of Jew could not be granted more than limited toleration (*Schutzgenossenschaft*). Full citizenship could be enjoyed only by adherents of one of the Christian denominations. To be full members of society, in other words, Jews would have to convert.

Because the 1808 decree created a form of limited citizenship for Jews, this report endorsed its retention. Had not France itself retreated to this more cautious position less than twenty years after granting Jews full citizenship? Had not the free city of Frankfurt, after being forced by France to emancipate its Jews, also reinstated the old restrictions? Reflecting the (accurate) perception that substantial Jewish immigration to the region had occurred since French times,[20] the report warned that continuation of a liberal policy would only invite an influx of this most fecund of peoples. The glory of Germany would one day perish in the hands of the Jews, who would make of the country "a second Poland."[21]

Because expulsion and repatriation to Palestine were unfeasible, the only alternative was the program Napoleon had instituted: restrictions on Jewish immigration and economic activities to contain the present danger, combined with long-term measures to wean Jews away from trade and direct them into agriculture.[22] Given the basic source of Jewish depravity, however (and the apparent expectation that most Jews would not convert in order to attain full citizenship), most important were measures to remake Judaism.

The *Kommission* issued its own report on January 30, 1818, sending it to the Prussian Minister of State. A masterpiece of bureaucratic malevolence, it not only supported Berlin's decision in 1818 to renew the 1808 decree but, as we shall see, informed the provincial Prussian approach to implementing the law in subsequent decades.[23] Thus, the report remained of singular importance to all those affected, however differently, by the decree: the provincial and local authorities who executed it, as well, of course, as the Jews.

The report opened with a review of the circumstances that occasioned the 1808 decree — complaints about Jewish "oppression" — observing that the French "finally" realized that the full equality the Revolution granted Jews "had not changed [Jewish] customs and habits" and that a return to "significant restrictions on their civil freedoms" was necessary. Turning on its head Dohm's use of the term, the report stated that the 1808 "Jewry ordinance" (*Judenordnung*) was intended for the "civic improvement" of the Jewish "nation" — meaning not, as Dohm had, a lessening of discrimination but its continuation.

After the Prussian conquest of the Rhineland, the report continued, Jews assumed they no longer needed the special business patents the law mandated, but they "were . . . roused from their hallucination" when Jews lacking them were unable to press commercial claims in court. The Consistory of Krefeld had asked the *Kommission* to instruct the courts that article seven of the decree, establishing the patent requirement, had lapsed in 1814 and that the lack of a patent should not prejudice a Jew's commercial transactions. It asked further that the "detested decree" be abolished altogether, a request the Consistory of Bonn soon seconded.

That the *Kommission* would not issue any such orders to the courts, the report said, was "self-evident." The decree remained in force as much as any other law unless a higher authority abolished it. The Consistories' claim, however, that no grounds existed for the decree's persistence constituted grounds for investigation of the behavior of the Jews, whom "public opinion" continued to accuse of usury. At the *Kommission*'s behest, district governments gathered intelligence.

The resulting inquiry, the *Kommission* said, was damning.

Almost all reports agreed that . . . [the Jews] still devote themselves exclusively to trade and dealings in secondhand goods and not at all to agriculture; that for the most part, especially on the plains, they practice the most pernicious usury and almost everywhere employ the same means and tricks to entice the credulous peasant needing money into a net, and keep him there. For this reason, all regional branches of the Prussian government [*Königliche Regierungen*], without exception, have moved for a continuation of the decree. Even in places where, because of the small number of Jews, no particular complaints had been lodged, people still want [the decree] to remain in force, so that [the Jews would stay under close surveillance] without which they would all too easily yield to their deeply rooted tendency to usury.

The regional governments of Düsseldorf, Trier, and Koblenz had even gone so far as to ask for more sweeping measures than those the 1808 decree provided, and it was the *Kommission*'s sense that several district magistrates elsewhere felt similarly.

Given these reports, other expert opinions, "and our own observations, which several of us have had the opportunity to make," the *Kommission* favored renewal of the 1808 decree. "A true, lasting improvement" (*Verbesserung* — again, using this term in the opposite sense Dohm had) would only come about through an "assault" on the "innermost roots" of the evil.

It was this evil — Jewish behavior, not discrimination — that kept the Jews apart from civic life (*vom Staate*).

The matter being so important and its own grasp of the problem so thorough, the *Kommission* felt duty bound to offer further suggestions. There should be no time limit to the 1808 decree; it should stay on the books until the German Confederation devised a policy for all Germany.[24] Prussia's Emancipation Edict of 1812 should certainly not be extended to the Rhine territory; "more effective measures are required here" than had been in Prussia's old provinces. On the contrary, the decree should be introduced into the right-bank Duchy of Berg and, when renewed, should be made more stringent by denying Jewish leaders recourse to courts of arbitration, because cunning Jews had abused this right to "persecut[e] . . . deluded debtors," ruining them.

The other major provision of the decree — severe restriction of Jewish immigration — was "very wise." It would not only hinder the "all too copious" immigration of foreign Jews who became a burden to the state but would be "one of the most beneficial means of . . . improving" those immigrants who would choose to abide by the requirement to practice agriculture. Neither the immigration proscription nor the forced occupational reform had been enforced strongly enough, with the result that the number of "indolent [Jews], who produce nothing and live only off captured loot, with which they can abscond at any moment . . . has so greatly increased." Enforcement of this provision, therefore, should be sharpened. Immigrants who had not complied with the decree's demand for occupational change should be allowed to remain on the left bank only if they complied now, unless they could prove that they had obtained special exemption and exceptional residence permission.

The *Immediat Justiz Kommission*'s report on the Jews did not determine Berlin's decision on March 3, 1818, to renew the 1808 decree. The era of reform was over in the capital, and the *Kommission*'s recommendations only sustained the prevailing mood.[25] Ironic as it appears for Prussia to have breathed life into a Napoleonic decree that was allowed to lapse in France itself, that decision contradicted neither general Prussian policy in the Rhineland, where most of French law was retained, nor broader Jewish policy, which was regressive in the monarchy as a whole. Berlin did not enforce the 1812 Edict of Emancipation even in the province for which it had originally been proclaimed.[26] While not revoked, the liberal edict was effectively nullified by royal orders and bureaucratic actions.[27] Post-Napoleonic Prussia was a hodgepodge of territories and legal systems that were not fully integrated until well after midcentury, and this was true of Jewry law as well. Over 30 Jewry ordinances were in force for a population of less than 125,000.[28]

Still, Prussian willingness to retain the Napoleonic decree in the Rhine Province contrasts sharply with its determination to impose the *Allgemeines Landrecht* and Baron Stein's reformed system of municipal government on the territory. These, obviously, were seen as intrinsic, essential Prussian *Wesen*, while the liberal Jewry Edict of 1812 was considered an aberration.

Far less consistent with *its* overall ideals were the recommendations of the *Immediat Justiz Kommission* on Jewish policy. Much of the work of the *Kommission* concerned the nature of citizenship, the rights of citizens, and the limits of government power, issues necessarily raised in any discussion of Jewish status. The *Kommission* had endorsed French over Prussian law because it upheld the principle of *Gleichheit*, civic equality, yet this is what the *Kommission* recommended denying to Jews. The ability to distinguish between citizens and Jews and to withhold application of universal principle to the question of Jewish rights was to become a fundamental problem in German liberalism; the *Kommission*'s report is one of the earliest examples of this problem.[29] The liberal spirit was generally moribund in Berlin but its demise on the Rhine was highly specific — of the two, the more interesting and troubling death.

The *Kommission*'s analysis of the Jewish "evil" lacks any understanding of the economic symbiosis between Jewish traders and moneylenders and their clients, especially in the countryside. Despite the urban backgrounds of the *Kommission* members and their constituency, the report shows no awareness that Jewish society was composed of different classes. The whole report is framed in terms of haggling rural crooks whose behavior is inborn rather than socially conditioned. Finally, in stark contrast to the *Kommission*'s generally enlightened approach to issues of criminal justice, it criminalized all Jews rather than targeting criminal behavior.

The report made odd bedfellows of officials on the Rhine and in Berlin: denying emancipation to the Jews was the only major area of policy on which the *Kommission* and Berlin agreed. The report buttressed the crown's determination to slow the course of Jewish emancipation in Prussia at a critical historical juncture, and it was quoted by similarly minded officials for more than two decades.[30] One can only speculate about the possible outcome had the *Kommission* resisted Berlin on this issue, as it did with remarkable success on so many others.[31] As it was, the decisions of 1818 left the non-Jewish population of the Rhine provinces with some of the most progressive civil legislation in the monarchy and the Jewish population with what the *Kommission* itself rightly called a *Judenordnung* — a premodern Jewry ordinance.

This contradiction persisted until 1845, when the 1808 decree was substantially modified, then abolished in 1847. The decree's restriction of the rate of interest Jewish lenders could charge, its mandate of special patents for Jewish businesses, and its controls on Jewish migration made for a great deal of government presence in Jewish lives. Since Prussia also retained the Consistory, the government-supervised synagogue and community structure instituted under Napoleon, Jewish communal life also remained under close official supervision.

In this chapter, we will look closely at the effects of this presence on Jewish lives but also at the impact of the decree on the government agencies that enforced it. For if the 1808 decree made government an inescapable reality in Jewish life, it also made Jews a perennial item on the agenda of government.

It also made Jews the subjects of bitter bureaucratic contention. The legislation involved several levels of government in its execution, charging the municipality with granting or withholding the testimonials required for Jewish patents but leaving the grant of the actual licenses to the provincial government. This created ample opportunity for city-state conflict over interpretation and enforcement of the law. The right to ultimate determination of Jewish status — the medieval power struggle between state and local authorities — resumed in modern garb.

Cologne had passed but a few years without its sovereign right to exclude Jews. It suffered the loss of autonomy poorly, and the fact that it did not regain it upon returning to a German realm was an even greater outrage. City authorities resisted being simply absorbed into Prussia and fought over a host of economic, political, and administrative questions, including control of Jewish status in the city. Prussia, facing a serious challenge to its administrative integrity, was not about to relinquish jurisdiction over Jewish status to any competing authority. In such circumstances, whatever Jews were as a social, economic, religious, ethnic, or mythic entity, they also symbolized the all-important question of control. Or the lack of it.

"We Have Married into a Poor Family": Cologne under Prussian Rule

Cologne's stance on the Jewish question must be placed in the context of the city's larger political ambitions and its exceedingly tense relations with Prussia. We have already seen that the city government fought for ancient economic patterns that contradicted postwar Prussia's economic policies. This was but part of a broader pattern of hoped-for restoration and consistent rebuff, of which the battle over the Jewish question was a part.

Cologne's city fathers took the initial uncertainty about the political disposition of the left bank as an opening to assert claims for privileged status for Cologne. Most ambitious and quixotic was their advocacy of

Cologne's return to free imperial status — which presumed the reestablishment of the Holy Roman Empire. Bewigged, outfitted in their traditional costumes, Cologne's erstwhile *Bürgermeister* paraded through the streets with the heads of now-abolished guilds, asking for restoration of ancient ranks and titles, the former Rector of the University of Cologne dreaming about the configuration the new *Freistaat* (independent city-state) would take.[32]

For these men, salvation loomed in the hoped-for ascendancy of Catholic, imperial Austria in the peace negotiations. With Prussia's acquisition of the left bank and the realization that "Prussia was serious about the Rhineland," any such hopes were dashed.[33] Berlin was no more favorably disposed to Cologne's requests for autonomy than Paris had been and Frederick William III less receptive than Napoleon even to suffering the city's petitions. The disparity between the city's grandiose expectations and Prussia's niggardly intentions received tangible expression when Prussia denied the city's request even for permission to expand beyond the increasingly cramped girdle of its ancient walls. To policy makers in Berlin, Cologne was first and foremost a fortress city; its broader ambitions would simply have to be contained. The disappointment of Cologne's patriciate with the reality of the Prussian connection received expression in the lament of one of its more prominent members: "We have married into a poor family."[34]

Barring autonomy, the city argued for a privileged position in any future assembly of the Rhenish provincial estates. With a population of 50,000, it was, after all, the region's most populous city. Unique economic interests lay behind this move since, with manufacturing moribund, Cologne was the only Rhenish city whose economy relied completely on trade and that wanted no import duties on the Rhine. The effort failed.

Obsessed with restoring Cologne's preeminence as a Rhine port, the city government and merchant community, organized under the French into a Chamber of Commerce, fought for restoration of the medieval river privileges that had sustained the city's merchant houses and dock economy: the staple and transshipment rights.[35] These privileges had allowed Cologne to tax passing boats and to require cargoes being transferred to smaller or larger ships (necessary because of the Rhine's configuration) to be handled in Cologne's port. They also gave Cologne's shipping agents a monopoly on forwarding transactions.

Cologne's Chamber of Commerce argued for restoration of these privileges, which had been abolished by France, before the provisional Prussian government in Aachen. The city also made unsuccessful efforts before the Congress of Vienna. But in 1818, Berlin promulgated a new tariff law, which abolished internal trade barriers in the Prussian kingdom and established import duties on most commodities — except colonial wares, which were among the most important commodities traded through Cologne and which Cologne did not want taxed. The law also struck a body blow to the city's traditional trading patterns by setting high tariffs on goods being traded by non-Prussians and transshipped on Prussian roads or rivers, which now, of course, included the Rhine. The city and Chamber of Commerce fought all the harder for Cologne's erstwhile river privileges, pressing the campaign until the late 1820's. But ultimately the city obtained no more than indemnification.

The city also suffered defeat and rebuff — sometimes incidental, sometimes deliberate — as Berlin decided the shape of government and administration on the Rhine. Prussia had originally made Cologne the seat for the governor of one of the two new left bank provinces, but when that governor died in 1822, rather than appoint a successor, Berlin unified the provinces into a single Rhine Province and made Koblenz, an economic backwater compared to Cologne, its capital. It was Chancellor Hardenberg's unmistakable slap at the city's political pretensions.[36] Cologne *was* made seat of the government district (*Regierungsbezirk*) in which it was located, but this only placed it under the close watch of the district governor (*Regierungspräsident*), a Prussian official with extensive power over local affairs and a direct line to Berlin.[37]

The city fared no better at the most local level of provincial organization. Because of its size, Cologne was allowed to constitute its own county (*Kreis*) rather than being joined to neighboring towns and villages. But the Prussians kept the county of Cologne and the municipality administratively separate. Thus, the mayor's office was not given jurisdiction over county affairs, which included military security and public order, executing state economic policy, and overseeing revenues. As in all counties, these duties were entrusted to a royally appointed district magistrate (*Landrat*), who was seen in Cologne as an interloper on traditional municipal functions.[38]

The old city elite was most unhappy, too, when Prussia decided to retain the French system of municipal government, under which cities were tightly controlled by the central government. The state would appoint mayors who would preside over town councils, which had only advisory functions and lacked police power.[39] The new Prussian-appointed mayor of Cologne, Karl Joseph Freiherr von Mylius, scion of one of Cologne's old families, pressed for a series of modifications to amplify the mayor's powers, but here too, Cologne's dreams collided with reality.[40] Insult was added to injury when the new Police President turned out to be a foreigner, a Protestant, and a Prussian patriot, one Georg Karl Philipp von Struensee.[41] Von Mylius tried desperately to convince provincial authorities and Berlin to abolish Struensee's position, especially because the latter had also been named district magistrate — in effect, the mayor's overseer. He failed. When in 1819 von Mylius was also unable to prevent the Prussians from abolishing the city's indirect tax, a mainstay of its revenue base, he quit his office in disgust.

Two deputies discharged the mayor's duties until 1823, when the Prussians appointed a new mayor, Adolf Steinberger. Steinberger was as accommodating as von Mylius had been cantankerous; he suited the new realities well. A quintessential bureaucrat, this wealthy, "much-occupied notary" was the ideal officeholder — from Berlin's perspective. The archbishop, who would have preferred a more assertive character in the mayor's chair, called him the "imbecile *Oberbürgermeister*" and wished him a short career.[42] It was not to be. Steinberger served until 1848.

Von Mylius's departure from office has been seen as a watershed in the city's history, the end of Cologne's era of grand challenges to Prussian will. This is a view particularly stressed by city historian Eberhard Gothein. Steinberger, Gothein says, was no match for Struensee, a tough, determined administrator, while the hamstrung, demoralized (and, according to Gothein, spineless) City Council continually lost ground to the more vigorous Chamber of Commerce in pressing the city's interests before the Prussians.[43]

The Chamber of Commerce had, indeed, become an institution of considerable political significance. The French had given its members, founders and scions of Cologne's greatest trade and banking houses, an important consultative role in administering economic policy in the Roer Department. This precedent persisted in the Prussian period.[44] While the mayor's office and the entire apparatus of city government were absorbed into the Prussian bureaucracy and thus, according to Gothein, robbed of independence, the Chamber, as a "semiofficial" institution, retained far greater freedom of action as a kind of "loyal opposition."[45]

From the outset of Prussian rule, the Chamber vigorously championed the city's business community, whose interests it identified with those of the city as a whole, challenging a host of Prussian policies. As it increasingly took on the role of city defender, it became the competitor of the City Council, whose mantle in this area it had largely inherited by the midtwenties. A bitter power struggle between the two institutions marked the period. Even after the Chamber won official recognition as a Royal Chamber of Commerce, Mayor Steinberger pointedly refused to address the body as such, referring merely to the "Members of the Chamber of Commerce."

There is no challenging this basic presentation of the city's history. Yet there is evidence, ignored by Gothein and other city historians, in which the City Council emerges as anything but submissive toward the Prussians. That evidence is contained in the documents recording implementation of the 1808 decree.[46] On the basis of these records, we might say that if the era of grand municipal campaigns against Prussian authority ceased with von Mylius, an era of determined and audacious rearguard actions was only just beginning.

What I would call the city government's "war of attrition" with Prussia for control of Jewish status in Cologne was motivated by genuine fear and abhorrence of Jews and not simply, as Gothein would have it, by a (to him, admirable) "meticulous accuracy" in administering Napoleonic law.[47] As Gothein himself notes, similar exactitude was lacking on other issues. Moreover, as we shall see, the city's punctiliousness in applying the 1808 decree was of a very peculiar nature. The Jews were not mere targets of municipal bookkeeping.

Taking a position, any position, against the Prussians on implementation of the 1808 decree was a means of resisting the encroachments of Prussian rule, since the Prussians were posing as the ultimate arbiters of Jewish status. Yet the Jews were also not just a hammerhead. Their newness in Cologne's rigidly stratified society and the abhorrence with which the elite viewed them made Jews outsiders par excellence, while the 1808 law touched on the most sensitive of a community's prerogatives: the power to decide who might live in its midst and enjoy access to its resources and opportunities.[48] A *Judenpatent*, moreover, was a passport not only to discrete economic rights but to privileged social standing. With it, lowly *Juden* suddenly became *Kaufmänner*, members of the most respected social group in Cologne: the business class. As such, they were subject to the same regulations, privileges, and status as other members of this class — pariahs with equality.[49] As we shall see, Cologne's merchants zealously guarded entry into their ranks, and what was in general a highly restrictionist admissions policy became particularly so with regard to the Jews.

The struggle over the Jews concerned identity and power, economic interests and communal ego. It was supercharged. In this joust, Jews were both genuine and strategic targets.

Coming to Terms with the Jewish Presence: The Battle of the Bureaucracies

Given the bitter contention between city and state authorities over the Jews of Cologne, it is striking that there was no disagreement on fundamentals: all upheld the 1808 decree. As soon as Prussia took over the left bank, the provincial administration declared the law binding. As we know, Berlin renewed the decree in 1818, ultimately retaining it until 1847.[50] The French-appointed mayor of Cologne as well as Mayor von Mylius endorsed it.[51]

When the Chamber of Commerce was consulted, it took an even more restrictionist line regarding the Jews than did the City Council.

What, then, was the problem?

Article 16 of the law, barring Jews from moving from one administrative district (*département*) to another unless they purchased and worked land, was not being implemented strictly. Many Jews were moving, much of the immigration was to cities, and virtually all of it was for trade. This certainly was the case in Cologne. The article provided the possibility of exemption, but what was to be done with immigrants who had slipped in without permission? And who, city or state, was responsible for enforcement? Moreover, with the French gone, there were no more *départements*. Across what boundary lines was Jewish migration to be measured?

Article 7, which mandated the special licenses Jews had to obtain, was even more problematic.[52] The patents could be granted only after the city council of a Jew's municipality testified that he or she had engaged in neither usury nor other illicit business and after the local consistorial synagogue endorsed the candidate's conduct. But how, precisely, was a Jew's "patent worthiness" to be established? Was each applicant to undergo thorough investigation, and, if so, which bureaucracy was to have the burden of executing it? An early French ordinance stated that a city council was to issue or deny endorsements by simple majority vote, stating its grounds in case of denial.[53] But what kind of, and how much, justification was necessary? Or would municipal judgments be accepted readily by the provincial authorities who issued the actual patents? Who, in short — city or state — was to make the real decision about a Jew's worthiness for acceptance into the business community, who to be the mere ticket stamper?

The city and the Prussians fought over many details of the law, but underlying it all was this basic question of hegemony. The struggle began under Mayor von Mylius, heated up during the interregnum of the deputies (1819–23), and reached its apex under the supposedly quiescent tenure of Mayor Steinberger. Throughout, the city rejected the burden of meticulously documenting implementation of the decree while insisting on the right to make ultimate decisions about Jews. For the Prussians, it was the same.

The City's Position

Disagreements between the city and the Prussians emerged as soon as the provincial government began to administer the 1808 decree. The first step was to get a count of the Jewish population and enough background data on individual Jews to allow judgments about immigration status and *Judenpatente* to be made. On April 10, 1817, the First Division of the Royal

Government in Cologne, a branch office of the district president's office responsible for religious minorities, ordered Police President Struensee to compile such data in detail.[54] Name, birthplace, age, date of settlement on the left bank and in Cologne, occupation, and date of most recent patent were all to be noted. Struensee was then to send his findings to Mayor von Mylius and the City Council, who would deliberate issuance of testimonials.

Struensee responded with alacrity; the data were ready for delivery to the city nine days later.[55] But this and subsequent intelligence on the Jews only raised eyebrows at First Division and led to its most persistent complaint: the city was derelict in enforcing the 1808 law. None of the Jews on Struensee's list had been issued patents since 1813 and, although 14 of 42 heads of household had come to the city since 1808, not one of them practiced agriculture.[56] First Division would soon claim that Cologne's Jewish population had doubled since 1813 because the city ignored the law's provisions against Jewish immigration. The city, moreover, was doing nothing to police Jewish trading activities. Unpatented Jews whose business agreements should have had no legal standing were even using the courts! Jewish affairs were in complete disarray, First Division charged, because the city administration had recklessly disregarded a law provincial authorities had confirmed since 1814.[57]

Curiously, the city did not voice the obvious rejoinder: why had the provincial government waited over three years to begin enforcing the 1808 law? The City Council expressed unequivocal support for the immigration restrictions in Article 16 of the decree, on the strict enforcement of which, it said, the welfare of Cologne's citizenry depended. But it also suggested that state authorities take measures to keep Jews from coming to Cologne and trading there in the first place. The city also returned another of First Division's accusations: why were Jews who had settled in violation of Article 16 not being expelled? The city thought this an excellent idea — but left it to the Prussians to execute.[58]

There can be no doubt about the sincerity and depth of official Cologne's antipathy for Jews, expressions of which permeate its dealings on the subject. If the city had been (and would continue to be) sloppy with the 1808 law, it was not for lack of sympathy with the decree's goals, since, whenever ambiguities arose, the city consistently took the restrictionist interpretation. This, however, simultaneously served another purpose: asserting Cologne's historic and grievously wounded pride. The city had its own interpretation of the law, which it felt it had a right to enforce, particularly when doing so would jab at the insulting reality of Prussian annexation.

Thus, for instance, the Council for years denied patent endorsements to Jews who had migrated from locations outside the former French Roer *département*, although the left bank was now divided into Prussian *Regierungsbezirke*, not French departments. Did not the 1808 law specifically restrict migration between *départements*, the Council pointedly asked? The Council was of the opinion, von Mylius informed First Division in a communication bristling with resistance, that Prussia's redivision of the territory into *Regierungsbezirke* had no bearing on the "political status of the inhabitants."[59]

Accordingly, Jews coming from nearby Bonn, which was now located in the same *Regierungsbezirk* as Cologne but had previously been in a different *département*, were deemed migrants from a "foreign region," subject to Article 16 of the 1808 law and ineligible for patent consideration in Cologne.[60] Not surprisingly, provincial authorities as well as the Ministry of Interior found this reasoning outrageous and rejected it.[61] On this point, the city acquiesced. There were other ways to deny Jews patents.[62]

The city received considerable help toward this goal from the police inspectors of Cologne's four sections and especially from the Chamber of Commerce, to which it turned for "expert advice" in evaluating the business reputations of Jews on Struensee's list.[63] Both went well beyond simple comments about the Jews' guilt or innocence of usury or illicit business to create other grounds for denial of patents.[64] Several of the police inspectors expressed prejudices about Jewish petty trade, which was not a crime under the 1808 law. One of them recommended, to good effect, that a testimonial be denied a Jew whose occupation, old clothes trading, lacked social standing but who otherwise enjoyed a good reputation.[65]

The Chamber of Commerce warned in dire tones about the dangers of Jewish immigration and the need for vigilant enforcement of Article 16 of the decree — about which its opinions had not been asked. In line with its quasi-governmental pretensions, however, the Chamber clearly felt a mandate to advise on general welfare. To its mind, the requirement of *Judenpatente* was a wholly inadequate expedient against a dire threat: the possible influx of mightily prolific Jews who, through their fertility, would "everywhere gain footing like a voluptuous, snaring weed."[66]

The Chamber of Commerce divided the city's Jews into three categories. In the first were long-settled Jews with solid reputations, who were to be granted patents for "unconditional" (business) rights. In the second were Jews whose "reputations were not entirely blameless," although they had committed no actual crime, and who were to be given patents for "limited" rights. In the third were Jews who made their living in "any and all manner" and who in the Chamber's view "had earned no trust," although they too were not necessarily charged with specific misdeeds. These were to be denied all (merchants') rights.[67]

The Chamber did not define its terms, but we can deduce its intentions from a look at which Jews it placed in the various categories. Not surprisingly, Cologne's wealthiest Jews were in the first. In the third were one Jew with a genuinely suspect record as well as fifteen others whose only offense appears to have been practicing petty trade or recent arrival in the city. The Jews in the second class lay somewhere between these poles. Of 42 Jews on Struensee's list, the Chamber classified 15 in the first category, 11 in the second, and 16 (38 percent) in the third.

Von Mylius and the Council adopted the Chamber's innovation (without crediting its source), revising upward the number of Jews recommended for patents — assigning nineteen Jews to the first class, thirteen to the second, and denying testimonials to nine applicants (22 percent).[68] Most important, the municipality defined what caused Jews with questionable reputations to be placed in the second, "limited" patent category: having previously been granted a patent and having given no legal cause to be denied one. This liberal-sounding provision was actually a device to broaden the Council's scope for denying patents, because prior receipt of a patent could now be made a precondition for receiving one in the future. Applied strictly, this would have frozen patent distribution at its 1813 level, the last year patents had been issued.[69]

While children of patented Jews reaching maturity were generally favored when they applied for their own patents, previously unpatented Jews, whether recent immigrants or long-term residents, could always be denied on these grounds.[70] In this manner the city could not only diminish the resident Jewish population, not all of whom had patents, but more important sabotage the immigration of Jews who, since 1818, had been able to obtain Prussian exemption from Article 16 and special permission to settle as merchants.[71] In 1821, when the Council was headed by deputies, nonmembership in the Jewish community was added as grounds for denying patent testimonial to recent immigrants who *had* previously been patented.[72]

None of this — the three-class division, the creation of first- and second-degree patents, the contrivance of prerequisites for patent consideration, grounds other than criminal business activity for the denial of patents — had any basis in the 1808 law, as First Division began informing the Council. But the city, egged on by the Chamber of Commerce, was adamant about its right to judge who was an acceptable member of its business class, which both bodies consistently identified with society as a whole.[73]

The city was particularly insistent about its rights regarding Jewish immigration. As it repeatedly told First Division, "no . . . city, including this one, can be obliged to accept all Israelites born in the kingdom and to permit them to settle and practice trade without further ado. . . . The Council believes it to be most necessary to abide by the most exact legal limitations on Jewish residence because the opportunities are more abundant and the ways and means of practicing usury are far more readily available in a large city than elsewhere."[74] (Even in victimization, Cologne wanted special status.) The city had already stated that inhibiting general Jewish population movement was the state's responsibility. Limiting Jewish immigration to Cologne by manipulating *Judenpatent* requirements was a city prerogative.

While the Chamber of Commerce and the City Council shared a special horror of Jewish immigration, that is, a fear of "new" Jews, they did not necessarily trust "old" Jews either. Analysis of the cases in which the Council denied its endorsement in 1820 and 1821 shows that long-settled Jews, including people who had immigrated before the 1808 decree, were denied endorsements without being charged with any particular misdeed.[75] The Chamber of Commerce expressed dire concern about the activities of Jews already in the city, even those with patents. "The public," it alleged, was convinced that such Jews would secretly begin practicing usury and other illegal activities at the first opportunity, a view, it said, there was no need to substantiate.[76] Several years later, however, the Council triumphantly produced proof: three patented Jews accused of practicing usury and fraud. The case against these three, it said, only bolstered the "public's view" that legal restrictions ought to be scrupulously applied "against all Jews, without exception."[77]

For all the rhetoric, the Council's record of patent recommendations shows that it was willing to have a small Jewish population. As Table 9 shows, the Council granted most requests for endorsements. The same was true even for the Chamber of Commerce, which, despite its vitriol, had judged most Jews on Struensee's initial list worthy of patenting. Faced with the evidence on the Jews actually in the city, the authorities obviously concluded that some Jews were acceptable, as long as their practices were carefully controlled. But they were not willing to face an uncontrolled influx.

Ultimately, the power to decide the issue was more important than actual number of patents granted or denied. To make its claim perfectly clear to the Prussians, the city opposed new Jewish immigration categorically and the integration of already-resident Jews only slightly less absolutely. As we shall see, not even wealth guaranteed a Jew favorable treatment. In a history of bitter strife with the Prussians over many issues, the city's particular recalcitrance on the Jewish question is attributable to two crucial realities. First, unlike trade or tariff policy, in which the city had no recognized voice, the 1808 decree gave municipalities some say over local Jewish affairs. Second, unlike other areas of disputed policy, state and city supported the same law when it came to the Jews.

The city's restrictive interpretation of the 1808 law was meant to defy Prussian rule, yet it also bespoke genuine abhorrence for Jews. The city

TABLE 9
City Council Judenpatent *Recommendations, 1817–35*

Year	Recommendation requested	Recommendation denied	Recommendation granted
1817	41	9	32
1818	44	7	37
1819	42	8	34
1820	43	8	35
1821	48	15	33
1822	47	14	33
1825	35	3	32
1827	40	0	40
1828	44	0	44
1832	43	3	40
1833	50	1	49
1835	51	—[a]	—[a]

SOURCE: *HASK,* Oberbürgermeisteramt, 400, II-C-1.

NOTES: These figures reflect only the patent recommendations granted by the City Council. The number of actual *Judenpatente* issued was often higher, because the Prussians would overturn denials or because some applications held in abeyance at the time of a Council vote later received Council approval; cf. the figures in Kober, *Cologne,* p. 199.

Note the figure for 1821; it was this City Council patent deliberation that First Division completely rejected, setting off the "showdown" of 1825. In 1822, while the Council was still refractory, the number of rejections was again unusually high; from 1825 on, rejections were rare.

[a]There were no data on the dispensation of patent requests in 1835.

could have manifested resistance to the Prussians by granting character endorsements indiscriminately had Jews not been seen as a true menace. Instead, the city denied them with only the vaguest justification or none at all. The specifics of the 1808 decree forced the Council and the Chamber to cite some pretext for denying Jews patents, but both obviously viewed the legalities as formalities. Faced with the threat they perceived in the Jewish presence, city authorities felt justified in taking whatever interpretive liberties seemed necessary.

Prussian Attitudes and Policy

This is where the city collided with Prussian authorities at the provincial level (First Division) as well as with the Ministry of Interior in Berlin. The Prussians, as we have seen, began with an attitude as negative to the Jews as that of the city, but this quickly changed. From demanding the expulsion of all Jews who immigrated in violation of Article 16 or were unpatented, and specifically of several Jews the Council had particularly condemned, First Division began championing Jews granted exemption from Article 16 and demanding hard evidence that the allegedly bad Jews were really bad.[78]

The Prussians adopted an ostensibly literalist interpretation of the 1808 law, complaining that the city had blatantly disregarded some provisions of the legislation and fabricated others (which, of course, it had), while the provincial government was merely upholding the law. It was not so simple. Prussian authorities also took many liberties with the decree. First Division overturned negative judgments by the City Council and granted patents to Jews who had never received the Council's recommendation, which was a stated prerequisite for the patent. It demanded evidentiary proof of Jewish wrongdoing when the Council withheld its endorsement, a degree of specificity the decree had never mandated.

We will explore the reasons for the Prussian change of attitude below. Suffice it here to say that where the city did not believe in the possibility of "good" Jews, the Prussians were much more open-minded. The method they employed to protect "good" Jews was the "philistine fussiness" about procedure that state bureaucracies elsewhere in Germany used when confronted with local resistance to their authority.[79]

Some of this was strategic posturing. Yet First Division was genuinely horrified at what, in its view, was the city's completely arbitrary manner of handling *Judenpatent* recommendations. The 1808 law, it repeatedly told the Council, specified only usury or illicit trade as grounds for denial of a patent endorsement, and such charges were to be substantiated. Yet the city had created whole new categories for denying endorsements, as well as denying them without justifying its grounds.

First Division rejected the Council's denials of patent recommendations to Jews who had not previously held patents and, when the Council based its denial on a charge of usury or illicit trade, demanded that it "set out in minute and scrupulous detail the particular facts" of the case.[80] First Division rejected, for example, the Council's denial of a recommendation to one Jew accused of dealing in stolen goods because the Council had submitted no evidence that a court had ever found the man guilty, while the Jew had marshaled considerable evidence of his innocence.[81] While later willing to accept something less than a court judgment against a Jew as grounds for denying patent endorsement, First Division continued to insist on specific, substantiated charges.

First Division meticulously reviewed minutes of City Council sessions on *Judenpatente*, noting changes in the status of a Jew from one Council deliberation to the next, as well as inconsistencies in the Council's treatment of Jews with ostensibly similar records.[82] It demanded explanations, insisting on clarity and, above all, on conformity to the rules as it saw them — treating the Council, in short, as the mere bureaucratic tool it judged the Council to be.

The Prussians even found fault with the Council's technical procedures. The Council voted on patent recommendations at meetings that lacked a quorum. The recommendations were not issued on properly stamped paper. Rather than issue each successful applicant a document signed by its members, the Council just drew up a list of successful applicants and signed that.[83] Particularly galling was the lackadaisical pace at which the city dealt with Jewish affairs. The Council took excessive amounts of time to process applications for patent recommendations and was especially slow in responding to First Division's increasingly frequent calls for clarifications, revisions, or, when an entire Council deliberation on *Judenpatente* was rejected, for special sessions.[84] In 1820, possibly in response to problems in the city, the office of the royal government in Cologne set strict deadlines for each phase of the *Judenpatent* process for the entire government district of Cologne.[85] Several bureaucracies were involved in the patenting process, and the City Council's role was pivotal. It was essential that Council deliberations be timely for any of the deadlines to be met.

Yet Cologne's Council was perennially late. What began with polite calls for speed ("Would you please advise me about this matter as soon as possible," Police President Struensee wrote the Mayor's Office in April 1820) soon turned nasty. "We summon you," First Division wrote the mayor's office some months later, "to return to us the revised, completed, City Council deliberations on the issuance of trading patents for the Jews of this city within three days, without fail."[86] Demands for speedy handling of Jewish affairs became a staple of the government's correspondence with the city, testifying, of course, to their ineffectiveness.[87] The ever-punctual Struensee, who needed the Council's full deliberations and final decisions on *Judenpatente* in order to make his own recommendations to the government, was driven to distraction by the city's behavior, imploring it to act with dispatch so that he could meet his own deadlines.[88] By the winter of 1821–22, First Division was excoriating the Council for its so "indecently delayed deliberations on Jewish patents."[89] Several months later it accused the city of deliberately obstructing the due process of law through chronic lateness.[90]

But the charge of passive aggression was only partly true, since the city also defied the Prussians openly and brazenly. One is inclined to take the city at its word when it explained delays and sessions held in the absence of a quorum. Members were out of town, particularly in the summer. Others were ill or attending to urgent business.[91] The mayor's office needed time to investigate the backgrounds of Jews applying for patents for the first time, yet the Chamber of Commerce, to whom it referred such cases, was itself not always prompt in responding.[92]

The Jews, moreover, were not the Council's most urgent problem, as it plainly told the Prussians on several occasions.[93] Cologne was in the midst of a serious recession exacerbated, in the Council's view, by Prussian policies. The city was fighting a desperate battle with provincial authorities against Prussian-imposed reforms of the city's revenue structure. Were it not preoccupied with problems of Prussian making, it implied, it would have time to deal properly with the Jewish question. But, as it pointedly told both Struensee and First Division in 1822, *Judenpatente* would simply have to wait until urgent work on property and trade taxes, forced on the Council by Prussian policies, was completed.[94] The city was already doing its job with regard to the Jews in a manner it deemed fitting. It simply lacked the time and energy (and, obviously, the sympathy) for the kind of meticulous documentation the Prussians were demanding. Nor was the Chamber of Commerce, on whom the Council attempted to foist the drudgery of processing endorsement requests, willing to follow Prussian directives.[95]

Above all, the Council pointedly noted, revealing its still smoldering rage about the loss of municipal police functions, if it was not being asked for its considered *judgment* about the Jews, but merely for a report on their criminal activities, then the entire matter ought to be referred to the police—into whose hands, it reminded Police President Struensee, Jewish affairs in Cologne had been delivered, in contrast to policy elsewhere.[96]

The Denouement

Matters began to come to a head in the winter of 1821–22 when, after four years of inconclusive sparring, First Division decided to get tough. It is worth following developments from this point closely, because it was in these years, during the tenure of the deputies, that the Council's audacity in defying the Prussians reached its height.

In December 1821, First Division nullified a very belated Council deliberation on Jewish patents that were to have been issued for that year. Charging that none of the required conventions had been observed, it returned the Council's minutes and ordered a new session held in scrupulous accord with the royal government's oft-repeated stipulations.[97] Several months passed before the Council responded, only to reject the Prussian demands.[98] The royal government, it said, was making the patenting procedure inordinately laborious by demanding individualized patent recommendations, each signed by the entire Council; that would amount to over 800 signatures.[99] The Council's practice of just listing recipients and rejectees had been established under the French (who, the Council implied, had been far more rational on the subject). The royal government, moreover, was misconstruing the Council's quorum requirements. A quorum *had* been present at the session in question.

Most important, the Council held fast to its position that it would grant patent recommendations only to those Jews whose "public reputation" was favorable and deny all others, whether or not there were specific, proven offenses.[100] The Council was clearly tired of hearing itself accused of arbitrariness and of having its professionalism impugned, asserting, "One must trust the integrity of the Council not to deny a patent without reason." Since there was nothing wrong, in its opinion, with its *Judenpatente* deliberations for 1821, the Council declared them valid — and blithely proceeded to forward to First Division its patent recommendations for 1822.

Given the gravity of the Council's provocation, First Division was remarkably restrained, limiting itself to some insults, a vague threat of "unpleasant proceedings" if the city remained refractory, and a point-by-point rebuttal of the Council's position.[101] Reiterating its nullification of the Council's proceedings, First Division again ordered deliberation of the patent requests for 1821 (this in the spring of 1822) as well as a new and "lawful" deliberation on the requests for the current year. It again rejected denials of patent endorsements that were not substantiated or that were based on grounds other than usury. The government, it insisted, would not accept judgments based on mere *"rumor* or on general *opinion"* (emphasis in the original).

But the City Council would not relent and began challenging the authority of First Division to oversee testimonial issuance. If ordered by "higher authorities," the Council said, it would prepare individual recommendations for each Jew, though this remained very objectionable. But it would not acquiesce to First Division's demand for hard evidence to substantiate denials.[102] The 1808 decree had never placed such a burden on the municipalities. On the contrary, the French law assumed all Jews guilty of usury until proven otherwise. It was for the municipality to attest the applicant's *innocence*, not his guilt, and this is what Cologne's Council had been doing.[103] First Division's stance was dangerous as well as mistaken, moreover, because it would never be possible to prove a case against each Jew denied a patent endorsement. If First Division's ruling were implemented, every Jew who applied for a patent would be granted one by default — and the Council, aided by the Chamber of Commerce, cited cases of patented Jews allegedly practicing usury and fraud to show the danger of such an outcome.[104] The city, accordingly, would stand by its earlier resolutions on this subject. It also reaffirmed several testimonial denials that First Division had specifically and repeatedly rejected.

In response, First Division again rejected the Council's deliberations, repeating its demand for prompt new proceedings on the 1821 and 1822 patents, to be conducted according to all the bureau's rules — which, it insisted, did come from "higher authorities."[105] The city fell silent for several months. When prodded angrily for a response, it answered that it had been unable to gather the full quorum on which First Division kept insisting. Should this number continue to be unattainable, might not First Division consider issuing patents according to the Council's previously forwarded recommendations?[106]

Temperatures rose on both sides; smoldering fury flared. First Division heatedly reiterated its demands, setting new "inviolable" deadlines, charging the mayor's office with a "special duty" to obey orders.[107] These, however, the Council once again rejected on the grounds that *its* proceedings, not those First Division had mandated, were more faithful to the injunctions of the 1808 law. As for First Division's concern that "rumors" might determine a Jew's fate, these were for Police President Struensee, not the Council, to investigate, since — the familiar barb — the Council lacked police power. As far as the city was concerned, it was enough that rumors existed.[108]

It was now early 1823 and an exasperated First Division decided to sidestep the Council. It issued *Judenpatente* for 1821, 1822, and 1823 according to its own judgment of the Jews' patentworthiness, overruling many of the Council's denials and issuing patents to other Jews on whom the Council had never pronounced judgment.[109] The Council, now headed by Mayor Steinberger, was incensed. It rejected First Division's instructions to deliberate patent testimonials for 1824 and announced its intention to seek "higher judgment" about the entire matter.[110] First Division fumed back that it was not the Council's business to question orders but to execute them, dutifully. How dare it presume to challenge First Division's instructions, which, the Council had already been told, issued from the Ministry of Interior?[111]

No one in the Council doubted the correctness of its stance on *Judenpatente*. Indeed, only extreme self-righteousness could have blinded the Council to the legendary professional loyalty of the Prussian bureaucracy, allowing it even to dream that the Ministry of Interior might overrule one of its own bureaus in the Council's favor.[112] Doubts did arise about the wisdom of refusing to deliberate patent testimonials for 1825 and, by this time, for 1826 as well, while the appeal was processed. The Council was split eleven to ten between extremists who considered further dealings with First Division an "utter waste of time" (*bloser Zeit verlusst*) and moderates, including Mayor Steinberger (who here insisted on his right to vote), who argued that it was the Council's legal obligation to deliberate testimonial issuance — according to its own lights, to be sure — while awaiting the verdict from Berlin.[113] The extremists won, setting the stage for the final grand act (though not the last skirmish) of the long dispute.

First Division received news of the Council's vote with cold fury. The time had come to break the errant Council. It informed Steinberger:

We have learned to our great displeasure from your report of December 31 and its appendix that the majority of the members of the . . . City Council have refused to deliberate the legally mandated endorsements for the Jews of this city for the purpose of drawing up the trading patents these latter have sought for 1825 and 1826.

We order you immediately to gather the entire Council at another time; to inform this latter once again of our instructions . . . and to enjoin the latter at the same time that since the City Council is legally bound to [hold] the deliberation in question, further refusal will constitute the crime of insubordination and will necessitate [the appropriate] investigation.

Should this communication and warning go unheeded . . . the refractory [Council members] at such a vote will be specified by name at the trial. You are charged, moreover, with seeing to it that the entire Council is present at this deliberation and that no member lacking legal grounds to be excused shall be missing from it.[114]

Several weeks later the eagerly awaited response from the Ministry of Interior arrived — upholding First Division. Any procedures that office had ordered, it said, originated in Berlin, and completely accorded with the "spirit" of the 1808 decree. The Ministry would countenance no appeals. The City Council was to execute patent proceedings exactly as directed.[115]

Amazingly enough, even this was not the end of it. The Council met in full strength and did deliberate *Judenpatent* endorsements for 1824 and 1825.[116] But it once again rejected the demand for specifics, much less proof of wrongdoing, in cases of endorsement denial. The 1808 legislation was *discriminatory*, it insisted. The Prussians were trying to make it fair. If proof were required of a Jewish trader's wrongdoing, how, it asked in bewilderment, would treatment accorded a Jew differ from that accorded a non-Jew? It was for the business community — i.e., "public opinion" — to decide a Jew's worthiness for membership, for this community to lift the suspicion of general Jewish guilt from his shoulders, or not. The Council would follow this verdict. The Council could not in good conscience fulfill its role in the patenting process in the manner the government was demanding.[117]

Indeed, when in subsequent years the Council withheld patent recommendations, it was because "public opinion" was negative and the Council was "not convinced that [the Jew] had never been guilty of any usury."[118] Undoubtedly because of Prussian pressure the Council did go to some lengths to obtain intelligence about applicants — its records after the 1825 "showdown" are replete with detailed police reports about individual Jews. These were almost always highly favorable and, together with vigilant Prussian prodding, resulted in the reversal of most of the Council's denials. The notably diminished role of the Chamber of Commerce in the Council's patent deliberations of 1822, the result, in all likelihood, of extreme tension between the two bodies, may also have been a factor in the reversals.[119]

But the Council never conceded its right truly to judge Jewish worthiness for patents rather than merely rubber-stamp the verdict of the Prussian-administered police and courts. Several years after the showdown between the Council and First Division, reverberations of this fundamentally opposing view of the city's competence continued. In May 1828 the Council denied its endorsement to a Jew who had the Ministry of Interior's permission to settle in Cologne as a merchant. It even urged the man's deportation because he had recently sold his belongings at auction to pay his debts and the city feared he was about to become a public charge.[120] First Division, in one of its most explicit pronouncements on the subject, bluntly informed Mayor Steinberger that "it is not for the City Council to decide questions of citizenship in general," nor had the 1808 decree given it such jurisdiction over immigrating Jews: Article 16 was the domain of the state. The only pronouncement the city was entitled to make about a Jew was with regard to usury, to which question exclusively it was to direct its attention in the case at hand.[121]

Jewish Responses

From the beginning, Jews denied the Council's patent endorsements appealed the decisions, to the Council itself, to the local police, or to Prussian authorities — Police President Struensee or First Division. While Jews who were denied endorsements figure prominently among the "transients" of the Jewish population who disappear from the records, most remained in the city, reapplied each year for patenting, and vigorously appealed their rejections.

There is no evidence that either the Consistory in Bonn or the synagogue in Cologne ever protested the Council's behavior to the Prussians or appealed denials in individual cases. The Consistory played its legally mandated role issuing the character references required for patents. As far as we can tell, it did so in virtually every case, and its endorsement sometimes played a role in reversing a negative Council decision.[122] But there was no institutional Jewish response to the Council's enforcement of the 1808 law or, after 1818, to the basic inequality of the law itself.

The behavior of Jews denied patents — their tenacity in pursuing vindication, the language they used when doing so — is the more noteworthy for being individual and undirected. Their petitions, preserved among the records of the City Council, are virtually the only materials in which Cologne's Jews speak in their own voices. Those voices are remarkably forthright, even adamant. They were also not without effect. Though it sometimes took years, the most persistent Jewish plaintiffs eventually won patents. Moreover, the abuses they reported heightened Prussian awareness of the potential economic costs of the city's *Judenpatent* policy and, arguably, even sensitized the Prussians to the human predicament of Jews living under the 1808 law.

Jews who were denied patents because of a negative City Council recommendation protested their verdicts from the outset. While unpatented Jews continued to live and work in the city, their business agreements and loans lacked legal standing; a Prussian ordinance forbade them to trade on pain of arrest.[123] With a patent, on the other hand, not only did a Jew's business enjoy legal protection, but the Jew had gained membership in the business community, which in Cologne meant honorable society as a whole.[124]

Given the stakes and the loose manner in which the Council withheld its recommendations, it is not surprising that Jews denied patents appealed the decisions. We can imagine the horror, for instance, of one Alexander Oppenheim at the predicament in which he found himself. In 1817, about to be married, Oppenheim was in the process of leaving a job as an employee in a Jewish firm to go into business for himself when he was denied a patent solely because he had had the bad judgment to declare his profession as "old clothes dealer." Oppenheim spent years trying to get himself reclassified in a more respectable occupational category so that he might gain the Council's endorsement, but every time he tried the Council came up with a new reason to deny him, including the fact that he had not previously been patented. Only after the showdown between the Council and First Division, when many Jews who had long been refused patents finally obtained them, did Oppenheim succeed — ten years after he first applied.[125]

Jews treated in such a fashion were indignant and expressed their emotions in their appeals. In the months before he was finally granted a patent in 1826, Alexander Oppenheim wrote to Mayor Steinberger:

I hear that the *Judenpatente* for 1826 have been distributed without my being sent one. I ask therefore, most respectfully, that this mistake be rectified and that a testimonial of my morality for the years 1824 and 1825 as well as for the current year 1826 be sent to the Honorable Royal Government [First Division] most graciously, and *in great haste* [emphasis in the original], since I have come into the position of needing a [*Judenpatent*] most urgently.[126]

It should be noted that when Oppenheim appealed his first *Judenpatent* rejection, First Division, then quite hostile to Jews, told him to drop the matter, since "your request is hereby denied once and for all."[127]

The Jewish merchant's need of a special patent, which could be withheld on the flimsiest of hearsay, was exploited by non-Jewish competitors seeking the Jew's ruin. The ever-present possibility of such abuse was one of the law's chief liabilities.[128] One Jew thus victimized wrote Mayor von Mylius:

It pains me deeply and most earnestly that while my other coreligionists have received the *Judenpatente* they sought, such a patent was *refused* [emphasis in the original] to me . . . because the present City Council has seen fit to deny me the legally mandated endorsement, alleging that I enjoy no good reputation.

I have lived here in Cologne for more than ten years, appear on the population list, pay all the taxes of a *Bürger* and have a second-class [general business] patent.[129] I am among those who had a *Judenpatent* already in French times and I find it absolutely impossible, therefore, to remain silent about the Council's proceedings. I therefore request Your Honor, most humbly, to have the complaints on the basis of which the Council saw fit to deny me a testimonial most graciously forwarded to me, so that I can vindicate myself as is right and proper.

Convinced of Your Honor's love of justice, I look forward hopefully to the granting of my request, and sign most humbly, Your Honor's most humble and obedient servant,

Salomon de Jonge Jacobs[130]

Jacobs did succeed in clearing himself. The following year he was granted the Council's testimonial, although only for a "second-class" *Judenpatent*, which, as we recall, was given to previously patented Jews who had given no cause to be denied patents yet who had somehow fallen short of the Council's full endorsement.

Perhaps the most striking example of the inequities and frustrations of the *Judenpatent* system was the case of one Lob Moises Pollack, a Posen-born resident of Cologne since 1807 and by far the Jew city authorities most loved to hate. Pollack was either a notorious one-time thief or, more likely, the victim of a case of mistaken identity. A Jew with this name had been a member of a robber band of mixed (Jewish and non-Jewish) composition that operated in Cologne's vicinity in the late 1790's.[131] Although there was some damning circumstantial evidence implicating the "Lob Moises Pollack" of the *Judenpatente* records in this earlier criminal activity, it does not seem likely that the two were the same person.[132] Lob Moises Pollack had settled in Cologne just ten years after the thief Pollack participated in a spectacular raid on Cologne's customs house. According to Prussian records, Lob Moises Pollack had also been granted a *Judenpatent* by the French in 1813, just a few years after the French had succeeded in curbing the depredations of the robber band.

The only uncontested blot on Lob Moises's record was that he had been arrested shortly after the allied takeover on charges of theft. He had also, by everyone's account, been acquitted for lack of evidence.[133] Pollack was nonetheless denied a *Judenpatent* by Cologne's City Council because of "his known association with thieves," a charge that, if true, constituted letter-perfect grounds for patent denial.

Pollack, a peddler, appealed the decision to Police President Struensee (again, unlikely behavior for a thief), bringing evidence of his court acquittal and other attestations of his good character. Struensee found it all rather compelling; the Council did not.[134] Pollack, whose ability to earn a living was being imperiled for lack of a patent, turned to First Division:

> If you please, most humbly, to grant me a temporary *Concession*, since I have lived here for twelve years and make my living outside the city through the sale of goods [*Waarenverkauf*]. I need this *Concession* in order to ply my trade, which has been forbidden me because of information sent to the local police by the Royal Procurator in Bonn concerning receiving stolen silver, which office, however, has written again to the local police to declare my innocence.
>
> Sustained by your understanding and knowledge that I am an oppressed, upright citizen, I hope that Your Most Honorable Government will allow yourself to feel my situation in your human heart, [to feel] how necessary it is for me to be granted such a *Concession* as soon as possible so that I can discharge my duty as supporter to my wife and children, so that I can be allowed to go on my travels as quickly as possible, something forbidden me for a year already.[135]

First Division ordered the Council to justify why it should not grant Pollack a favorable endorsement in light of the evidence. Von Mylius and the Council responded testily that their judgment was not "based only" on the now-overturned original police report (although they did not state on what grounds it *was* based) and that they saw no reason to change their minds.[136] They didn't — for over ten years. But in December 1827, at a point when the Council, most probably at Prussian behest, was thoroughly investigating Jews to whom it wished to deny patents, Pollack's case — he had been applying for a patent annually since 1817 — was reopened.[137] In the margin of a communication to First Division regarding patents for the following year, Steinberger noted, "Pollack has been denied a *Judenpatent* till now because he was under suspicion of association with thieves. One wonders how he has behaved since then, and whether he has earned a *Judenpatent* through upright and irreproachable behavior."[138] The mayor asked for a police report on Pollack. It read, "Moises Pollack has thus far conducted himself right well, given not the slightest complaint, and through honorable, irreproachable conduct has earned claim to a *Judenpatent*."[139]

Pollack was issued a Council recommendation on February 8, 1828, and a *Judenpatent* several weeks later. In the cover letter to First Division sent with the minutes of the Council's deliberations, Steinberger wrote blandly of the enclosure that it "concerned patents still to be granted to various local Jews." After a decade of being typed a dire threat to the welfare of the community — in 1817 First Division had excoriated the Council for even suffering his presence in the city — Pollack's tenacity had finally paid off. He was just another Jew.

Assessing the Conflict:
"Who Shall Say Who Belongs?"[140]

In his study of German home towns, Mack Walker has written that "community . . . implied outsiders."[141] Jews were not the only social outsiders on the German scene, but until full emancipation was granted and, arguably, even afterwards they were outsiders par excellence. If ancient patterns of exclusion made it possible to consider Jews alien to "the community" in localities where their presence was centuries old, we can only imagine how Jews must have appeared to the keepers of the communal gate in Cologne.

Disputes between state governments and localities over the right of controlling *Bürgeraufnahme* — accepting outsiders into the privileges of local citizenship — were rife in nineteenth-century Germany. State governments, seeking to extend the reach of their jurisdiction, tried to breach the exclusivity of ancient communities by liberalizing *Bürgeraufnahme* policies; localities resisted the intrusion into their ruling privileges and identities.[142] The "outsiders" in question were not primarily foreigners in the usual sense of the term, but anyone deemed outside the social fabric, to whom the right to permanent residence, to vote, hold office, marry, practice a trade, share in community property, or partake of poor relief might be denied.[143] The question of Jewish rights was clearly related to this broader struggle, as astute contemporaries realized.[144] In the politically fractured conditions of preunification Germany, more fundamental than the question of which rights Jews would enjoy was the question of who would decide: the state or localities?

Given Cologne's traditional control over this issue, it is easy to see how a struggle might have ensued once the city was free of the temporary, aberrant French precedent of state control of Jewish status and had returned to German rule. Still, we must ask if the struggle in Cologne was only this or whether other circumstances — a heightened sense of vulnerability, a perceived threat from other "outsiders" — sharpened resistance to Jews. Was there a broader context to Cologne's stance, and to Prussia's?

As we know, Cologne experienced heavy immigration after the Prussian takeover, and we might wonder whether the reaction to Jews was part of a broader xenophobic backlash. Interestingly, there is no known official reaction to the influx, which would seem to indicate that the immigration was not seen as a problem and was not resisted.[145] This only makes the phobic hysteria over the proportionately minuscule Jewish immigration — the dire warnings of the Chamber of Commerce about proliferating weeds — the more striking.

It would be tempting to ascribe the positions of the city government and

Chamber of Commerce on the Jews to a survival of "proud old *Reichsstadt*" traditions. Such an explanation could certainly apply to the City Council, whose members had long ties to the governmental order in Cologne and in some cases were actual holdovers from the previous era.[146] But it is not possible to write off the behavior of the Chamber of Commerce as a mere throwback, the extended death rattle of the Old Order. The Chamber was a quintessentially modern institution, created by the French on the ruins of the medieval guilds they abolished. While some of its members derived from Cologne's old elite and also served on the City Council, some of its most prominent figures were "new men": Protestants, immigrants, Catholics who had joined the Freemasons during the French era.[147] The Protestants themselves only gained full civic rights in Cologne under the French.[148] They certainly did not want to turn back to some mythical and, for them, dark period of ancient history.

Peter Heinrich Merkens, for instance, one of the avowed leaders of the "liberal" faction in the Rhenish provincial diets from the 1820's on, was the Protestant son of a baker from Mülheim.[149] Having achieved remarkable business success in Cologne — he started as an apprentice in a Protestant firm — and election to the Chamber of Commerce in 1810, Merkens utterly dominated the institution during the period in question.[150] Yet he signed many of the Chamber's most viciously anti-Jewish pronouncements.[151]

The label "liberal" is exceedingly problematic in this early period. It has been applied to Merkens because he adamantly opposed Prussian proposals to make distinctions in civil status between city and rural dwellers, because he worked doggedly to win the merchant class a voice in government, and because he championed such innovative enterprises as steamshipping.[152] Given his background, he was, of course, "completely unburdened by remembrances of the *Reichsstadt*," for whose old families he had a pronounced distaste.[153] Whenever secondary sources mention him in connection with Jews, it is with reference to his call in 1843 for their civic equality.[154] But the *Judenpatent* records attest that in the teens and twenties Merkens was an implacable foe of Jews settling in Cologne, much less having equal rights there.

Merkens's stance and that of the Chamber of Commerce cannot simply be lumped together with that of the City Council and ascribed to shared atavism. Moreover, the two institutions were at bitter loggerheads in these years. Jewish policy was one of few areas in which the Chamber and the Council agreed with each other, much less cooperated. What explains the common stance of Cologne's warring camps on the Jewish question?

If they do not fully account for it, a number of factors in Cologne's economic circumstances help contextualize this collaboration. Economic conditions on the Rhine as a whole and in Cologne ranged from depressed to unstable into the 1830's. The teens and early twenties, when the Chamber and Council first articulated their anti-Jewish positions, were particularly dismal years. Of special significance was a regional monetary crisis, in particular, a shortage of coin.[155] Interest rates rose and "wild rumors were thrown up everywhere about usurers."[156] Given popular stereotype and the fact that 20 percent of Cologne's Jews did practice some form of money lending, Jews could easily have loomed as a monstrous threat.

The Chamber of Commerce and the Council did accuse several Jews of exploiting conditions "particularly in this period when a general shortage of money has set in," especially of victimizing "poor people," "the lower classes and the petty seamen" through ruinous loan deals. One Jew was said to have "already ruined many" poor families (15 to 20 complaints had been lodged against him). Having brought these people "to the abyss, [the Jew] then behaved with the greatest mercilessness, often grabbing their beds from under their bellies, his house being a regular depot of such and similar items."[157] Another Jew was accused of circulating counterfeit foreign coins.[158]

Yet the source for these accusations is hardly objective; the Council made them while arguing that judiciary evidence of Jewish wrongdoing was both impossible and unnecessary to obtain. This information, then, attests but does not explain the city's position.[159]

Careful reading of the Council's deliberations, and of the Chamber of Commerce recommendations that deeply informed them, establishes that, self-righteous invective notwithstanding, it was not the Jewish usurer but the Jewish petty dealer who was the real target of the authorities. And it is here that specifically anti-Jewish animus and broader outlooks meet.

For all their rivalry, the members of the City Council and the Chamber of Commerce shared two basic traits: wealth and, in the near-absence of an industrial base in Cologne, domination of the city's trading sector.[160] The Council was the tool of the merchant elite — 74 percent of its members in 1817 were large-scale merchants. Even after Prussia began installing professional bureaucrats in the mayor's office (Cologne's mayor had traditionally been a wealthy businessman), "the influence of the business community" in Cologne "was so great, and the identity of interests between business and government so strong, that the office of mayor still served the interests of the urban economy."[161] The differences between the municipal government and the Chamber of Commerce were power struggles. Their economic character and interests were the same.

Both the City Council and Chamber of Commerce were also inbred and highly exclusive clubs — only 43 men served on the Chamber between 1815 and 1833, with the average term lasting over nine years — and both were determined to maintain that exclusivity.[162] The Prussians whittled away much of the Council's autonomy but did not challenge its internal composition. Prussian policies, however, twice challenged the nature of the Chamber's membership, and its response in both instances bears directly on our case.

In 1820 Prussia, having promulgated a new business tax, attempted to increase the number of businessmen eligible for it. This would have had the effect of broadening the category of "first-class" merchants, whose "merchants' rights" included the right to vote in Chamber of Commerce elections.[163] The Chamber, led by Peter Heinrich Merkens, fiercely opposed the changes and refused to implement them, appealing all the way to Berlin until Chancellor Hardenberg and Trade Minister Bülow themselves ordered compliance.[164] Twelve years later Berlin, after sanctioning the creation in several right-bank cities of new Chambers of Commerce with franchise requirements considerably lower than those in Cologne, ordered the eased franchise regulations applied in left-bank Chambers as well. Again, Cologne's Chamber balked. Members elected under the new rules refused to take office, while Merkens, his own humble origins notwithstanding, led the charge against the reforms.[165]

In 1820 and 1832 Merkens's argument was the same: the Chamber of Commerce was the proper preserve of a truly "first class" of businessmen, composed, that is, of representatives of old, established, and prosperous firms. The line between notables and "nonentities" — minor merchants — should not be effaced. What the government was proposing was not only unjust, since those paying higher taxes rightfully should have more say in fashioning public policy, it was perverse. If the government had its way, Merkens warned, "petty restauranteurs, artisans, fruit peddlers, dealers in second-hand goods, harpists, organists," would sit alongside bankers, great merchants, and manufacturers in representing the concerns of business before government.[166] Merkens resigned for a time from the Chamber, so insistent was he on preservation of the exclusivity of the business elite.[167]

This was Cologne's version of a *Bürgeraufnahme* conflict with the state and it is in this context that the city's struggle against Jews must ultimately be placed. The generally restrictionist mentality of Cologne's business elite, as well as the more inclusive outlook of Prussian authorities, carried over with regard to the Jews. Recall the fabrication by the Chamber of Commerce of a "second-class" *Judenpatent* category for Jewish petty traders (an innovation the City Council readily adopted), the denial of recommendations to Jews whose only misdeed was old clothes dealing — indeed, the city's entire policy of concocting pretexts for barring Jews from obtaining *Judenpatente* as well as the Prussians' policy of granting them.[168]

Cologne's business elite was tiny. A mere 171 men in the entire city possessed "first-class merchants' rights" in 1821.[169] It was, then, exceedingly vulnerable to dilution of its political influence through expansion of its ranks. Precisely such dilution was the goal of Prussian policy, according to Jeffry Diefendorf, which explains why Merkens, himself an arriviste, fought so hard against newcomers.[170]

The Jewish policy of Cologne's merchant elite, then, was in accord with its broader policies and strategies. It is certainly unsurprising that a general defense of privilege by "insiders" against "outsiders" was coupled with an extreme anti-Jewish posture. If, moreover, the Chamber believed its own propaganda about hordes of Jews poised to overrun Cologne, and I believe it did, the Prussian policy of granting *Judenpatente* liberally — elevating the Jewish hordes to the rank and privileges of the *Kaufmannschaft* — must have been terrifying.[171]

One noteworthy event bolsters the thesis that official resistance to Jews was tied to the business elite's revulsion at the prospect of sharing power with "nonentities." In 1822, in the midst of virulent anti-Jewish lobbying, the Chamber of Commerce elected the Jewish banker, Salomon Oppenheim, Jr., a member.[172] Although the histories of Cologne, the Chamber of Commerce, Cologne's Jews, and the Oppenheim house note the election, some hailing it as proof of the city's progress toward tolerance, its circumstances remain vague, and we can only hypothesize the obvious: Oppenheim's money compensated for his religion.[173]

The Oppenheim house had moved into the ranks of Cologne's largest banks within ten years of Salomon Oppenheim's immigration to the city. It was involved in the full range of financial activities alongside the most respected and politically powerful Catholic and Protestant houses of Cologne. In fact, Oppenheim's election to the Chamber of Commerce only capped his acceptance into Cologne's financial elite. Since 1819, together with Cologne's other major bankers, he had been deeply involved in the business and politics of replacing the French franc with the Prussian taler as the Rhineland's currency; his election seems to have been related to ongoing wrangling over this issue.[174] Given the influence Oppenheim already wielded, it would have been striking had he not gained entry into the body representing the city's business elite. In accepting the Jewish magnate into its ranks while resisting business licenses for petty Jewish traders, the Chamber was being truer to the spirit and letter of the 1808 decree than were the Prussians with their generalized economic liberality.

Was, then, the anti-Jewish stance of the City Council and Chamber of Commerce simply synonymous with plutocratic defense of power, and Prussian liberalism merely the extension of a larger policy of attacking and undermining that same power bastion? Were both "antisemitism" and "philosemitism," then, but the expression of something else?

Analysis of the behavior of the City Council and the Chamber of Commerce shows that a distinctly Jewish policy did exist, because the positions of both bodies on the Jewish issue differed significantly from those they took in the dispute over membership in the merchant elite. Whereas the mayor's office, under both the deputies and Steinberger, cooperated with the Prussian government against the Chamber of Commerce in the membership conflict, the City Council and the Chamber collaborated closely on Jewish policy against the Prussians.[175] If, we reason, the City Council shared the Prussian desire to see the power of the Chamber of Commerce diluted through expansion of its ranks, its antipathy to Jews was such that it would not consent to using them as tools even in this noble cause. Wealth, moreover, while generally helping the case of Jews applying for Council recommendations, did not guarantee favorable treatment; witness the Council's stubborn denial of a testimonial to a well-established, previously patented Jewish merchant from Münster, first on grounds that he was not a member of the local synagogue, then because he was a foreigner.[176]

If economic considerations alone had governed the Council's Jewish policy, we should expect it to have done what the Prussians did in this and other cases where Jews were economically attractive: recommended exemption from the clause in the 1808 decree barring immigration of merchants and facilitated *Judenpatent* issuance.[177] On the contrary, however, the Council not only shared the Chamber's loathing for Jewish petty trade, it apparently harbored an opposing fear: the fear of Jewish success and competition. Mayor von Mylius expressed it best in 1819 when, citing to First Division some scurrilous tracts purporting to tell the history of the Jew in Germany, he wrote, "As soon as a German city blossomed in the Middle Ages, it restricted or eliminated the Jews, who had gradually drawn all commercial transactions to themselves."[178] Jews, in short, would either subvert trade or monopolize it. Their economic activities, petty or grand, above- or belowboard, were a menace to non-Jewish society simply because Jews practiced them. No wonder Oppenheim was never held up, Mendelssohn-like, as an example of what Jews in Cologne could become. The exception, Cologne's government hoped, would not become the rule.

As we know, the city was willing to tolerate a small Jewish community, especially one of its own choosing. After the French left it did not press for a return to the status quo ante — total exclusion of Jews from the city and its economic life — but was content with the discriminatory 1808 decree, as long as execution was in city hands. This shows that the Council, for all its fear of Jews, did see some economic usefulness in a small, restricted Jewish presence. Paradoxically, though, the fact that the city did not deny a much greater percentage of endorsement requests also illustrates the genuineness of the anti-Jewish prejudice. Jews were not simply being used to thwart Prussian intervention. Faced with the Jews who actually applied for patents in Cologne, with reports by the police and Chamber of Commerce of upstanding, *bürgerlich* behavior in almost all cases, the Council granted the majority of endorsement requests (in one instance, the Chamber of Commerce, recommending a Jew for the Council's testimonial, lamented that the man's blameless conduct had left it no other choice).[179] But all the evidence did not allay its fundamental Judeophobia, the suspicion that good behavior by Jews was exceptional, worse, a ruse.

Consistency is not a hallmark of prejudiced thinking. The disparity between rhetoric and record in city *Judenpatent* policy is evidence not of disingenuousness in the service of strategy but of a deeply conflicted mentality in which Jews were both a lethal threat and, if controlled in numbers and behavior, economically useful. The crucial point was control.

The attitude of Prussian authorities to Jews was utilitarian, based on economic considerations. In the first three decades of the nineteenth century, John Gillis writes, Prussian officials, "trained in laissez-faire economics," were staunch advocates of "economic emancipation," and this was true of provincial officials on the Rhine as well.[180] First Division, which started out with an extremely anti-Jewish stance, quickly changed its attitude because of financial considerations.

First Division never spelled out the reason for its shift, but we can surmise it from a strange exchange of letters between First Division and Mayor von Mylius in 1819.

When the French abolished the Holy Roman Empire, and with it the electoral state of Cologne, the *Judenschaft* (corporate Jewry) of the territory owed the electoral treasury a considerable amount of money. Prussia, determined to collect that debt, set up a commission to apportion it among the Jewish communities of the former electorate.[181] Since there had been no Jewish community in the city of Cologne until French times, the Prussians tried to find a way to include the newly established community in the assessment.

First Division was assigned the task, and in April 1819 wrote to von Mylius with a seemingly bizarre set of questions.[182] By what right had Jews ever been excluded from the city, it asked, when, according to electoral archives, jurisdiction over Jews had been a prerogative of the electors? When, and under precisely which legal rubric, had Jewish settlement in the city resumed? When had Jews begun to pay city taxes? Now that Jews were back in the city, could not the old Jewry prerogative of the electors (*Judenregal*) be considered in force once again (this to staunch city patriot von Mylius)?

The letter betrayed striking ignorance of the city's history and equally yawning innocence of its more recent experience. When, it asked, had the left bank been seized, when annexed, by France? When, precisely, had the

Napoleonic code been introduced? The point of these questions is clear. First Division was trying to build a case for counting the new Jewish community of Cologne a constituent of the ancient electoral *Judenschaft*.[183]

Von Mylius answered the stiff, rudely worded letter with lengthy judiciousness, recalling the history of Jews in Germany from Roman times to the present, carefully demonstrating Cologne's legal right to have expelled the Jews in 1424.[184] Most important, he produced the requisite dates and facts to deny the Prussians what they wanted: an early date for the readmission of Jews to the city, a date preceding the introduction of French law and institutions. Autonomous Cologne, von Mylius stressed, had excluded the Jews for as long as it had the power to do so. The French had admitted them. No medieval Jewry privilege, therefore, included them and they could not be considered members of the old *Judenschaft*.

Facts notwithstanding, the Prussians counted the Jews of Cologne as members of the electoral *Judenschaft* and assessed them a special tax for the retirement of its debt. To financially pressed provincial authorities, no revenue source could be overlooked. With such an outlook the activities and potential contributions even of petty Jewish entrepreneurs were welcome, and, as we have seen, the Prussians by no means championed the cases only of wealthy Jews.[185] First Division's Jewish policy was in full accord with that of the Interior Ministry, which generally championed the needs of "lesser but rising businessmen" against Merkens's exclusivity.[186] Financial need was religion-blind, and broader economic philosophy was extended to Jews.

This policy violated the sensibilities and interests of the city's commercial elite, which did not trouble the Prussians but was not their primary intent. Had the Prussians used Jews merely as tools to undermine the city's political pretensions, they would have approved Jewish immigration and patent applications indiscriminately. Yet careful reading of the entire record shows that Prussian liberality on the Jewish question was not absolute; even First Division occasionally deemed Jews ineligible for patents.[187]

Financial need and economic pragmatism made the Prussians the best friends of the largely lower-middle-class Jews of Cologne and even engendered it seems, some appreciation of the humiliation and injury that Jews denied patents experienced. Thus, First Division in 1822 wrote to the mayor's office of its concern that "harshness and injustice" were too likely to influence *Judenpatent* proceedings if mere rumors were admitted as evidence against a Jew.[188] In another case, the Prussians ordered the Council to judge patentworthiness strictly according to the stipulations of Article 7 of the decree and urged speedy action so that the Jew who was recently arrived (and, albeit, had "extremely good attestations of his means") might "no longer be left in uncertainty" regarding his fate.[189]

The struggle over *Bürgeraufnahme* of Jews in Cologne touched on vital concerns for all the principals. For the Jews of this period, as for their forebears in the medieval era, the best hope lay with higher authorities, a reality they grasped quickly and exploited to good effect. If perhaps the long political history of the Jews of Europe helped those of Cologne assess their situation, it was just the opposite for city authorities. Centuries of zealously guarded independence ill prepared the city for modern realities. The French absorption was clearly taken as aberration, not portent. Better was expected when the city returned to a German realm. But unlike newly absorbed localities in Bavaria, Baden, and Württemberg, which were able to wrest a measure of autonomy from weak state governments in the early post-Napoleonic years,[190] Cologne experienced only a progressive tightening of the leash. Prussia was not Bavaria; Frederick William did not need to appease Cologne with even a partial restoration of home rule in order to keep a political hold on it. Prussia did not yield to Cologne on any issue of policy, including the "Jewish question." Of course, Cologne's municipal government had no way of knowing the Prussians would prove so intractable, but its *idée fixe* about restoring old glories did not speed the dawning of wisdom.

The resources of the protagonists were far from equal, and with hindsight the outcome appears inevitable. Yet in the end even Prussian authority was unable to bring an extraordinarily determined City Council entirely to heel. Although the city lost the war for control of Jewish affairs, its unrelenting recalcitrance managed to wear down the Prussians about a point central to the dispute from the beginning: the kind and degree of substantiation necessary to deny patent endorsements. Even after the 1825 showdown, the city continued to deny its recommendation on the basis of a Jew's allegedly "bad reputation" and on grounds other than usury.[191] All the Prussians could do after more than eight years of wrangling with the Council was to force police investigations of the individuals in question and revision of the Council's decisions.[192] First Division never succeeded in compelling the Council to accept its position on evidence. The Prussians won in fact, and what the Council had predicted did come to pass after 1826: virtually all Jews who applied for patents received them without further ado. But if the Council was vanquished, it was not utterly defeated. It never conceded in principle.

Cologne's ultimate failure to win control of its affairs, whether tariff, tax, and trade policy or Jewish status, should not obscure the significance of its attempt. Cologne's assertiveness in defense of its economic agenda was without parallel on the Rhine.[193] Its battle with state authorities over the Jewish question was also singular: no other city in the Rhine province mounted the kind of challenge for control of Jewish affairs that Cologne did. Moreover, while Cologne's economic offensive was pressed by the

Chamber of Commerce, its political offensive—the fight for control of Jewish affairs—was pressed by the city government, including the mayor, who was a Prussian civil servant. Such was the potency of Jews as a symbol of sovereignty.

The Limits of Acceptance

If Prussia's free-trade policies opened the door to Jews the city would have excluded from the *Kaufmannschaft*, not even the wealth of Croesus sufficed to gain Jewish admission into the anterooms of Cologne's *haute société*. Although Salomon Oppenheim was able to retain his membership in the local Freemasons, which he had acquired during the French years, he was not included when his business peers founded the exclusive Casino social club in the early 1820's.[194] As Pierre Ayçoberry notes, "The absence of Jews [in the club] is not surprising. It was acceptable to do business with Oppenheim, far less so to socialize with him."[195]

This, despite the fact that the Prussian government ("probably," according to Oppenheim historian Wilhelm Treue, "at the instigation of [Chancellor] Hardenburg") named him a "Royal Upper Court Agent" in 1822, an honorific title laden with status;[196] or that he became a member of the Chamber of Commerce in the same year; or that he owned a palatial residence near the cathedral, in one of the most prestigious parts of town. Oppenheim had acquired some of the furnishings of the previous owner, a former mayor, and a large collection of Dutch old masters, which he proudly displayed to important visitors; in 1828, Johanna Schopenhauer ranked it the third largest collection in the city. He dressed the part of the burgher patrician, with fashionably coiffed short hair and distinguished clothing, portliness proclaiming his worldly substance. As befitted his station, he dispensed civic largesse: aid to war-stricken civilians; corn during famine; funds to help build a safe harbor for use when the Rhine froze.[197] For all his wealth, indeed, because of it, he declared his belief in the *Bürger* ethos of frugality and self-restraint: "Just no ostentatious [literally, gluttonous] furniture!" He refused to own horses to pull his wagons, insisting on renting them when needed.[198]

If all this was meant to proclaim his status and serve as "an entry ticket to the circle of distinguished citizens," it was only partially successful.[199] Although two of Cologne's most prominent businessmen, Friedrich Peter Herstatt and Johann Philipp Heimann, served as witnesses at the legal proceedings when, in 1813, Oppenheim married off a fifteen-year-old daughter, by proxy, to a French Jewish banker, Oppenheim did not use one of the most powerful tools by which Cologne's business elite consolidated its ties:

intragroup marriage.[200] Although fully acculturated, Oppenheim did not break this most basic traditional Jewish norm: none of his children married non-Jews in his lifetime. Oppenheim, like his Catholic and Protestant counterparts in Cologne, arranged glittering matches for his children with wealthy business and banking families, but the Oppenheim matches, unlike the others, were anything but local. Spouses came from Jewish banking families in Amsterdam, Hamburg, Günzburg, Frankfurt am Main, Karlsruhe, Strasbourg, Paris. As we shall see, the firm's business connections were significantly enhanced by these ties. They did nothing, however, to secure Oppenheim's entry into Cologne's "society." That step was several years off, when conversion and marriage to non-Jews began to bring a kind of acceptance business success alone never could.[201]

In light of the city's overall Jewish policy and the limits to the social acceptance even (or perhaps, especially) Oppenheim could attain, the man's elevation to the Chamber of Commerce does not reflect significant progress toward the ideals of emancipation in Cologne.[202] Given the impressive "silent" record of de facto Jewish integration in the city, it is not in the behavior of the city's power elite that real signs of progress toward emancipation are to be found, but in that of average citizens, Jews and non-Jews.

The Business of Equality: Rhenish Liberals, Jewish Bankers, and Jewish Rights in Cologne, 1835–50

> We believe that, as long as we recognize religion as the foundation of our civic institutions [*bürgerlichen Einrichtungen*], it is impossible for us to grant [the] Jews equal rights with Christians without falling into contradiction with ourselves, the negative consequences of which we should feel soon enough. In our opinion, therefore, any legislation regulating Jewish status in a Christian state can deal only with greater or lesser restrictions on Jews but never with the complete suspension of restrictions.
>
> *Kölnische Zeitung*, July 6, 1842

> The strained relationship between Christians and Jews can be resolved only through full, unconditional equalization of [Jewish] status. Religion is a matter for each single church, denomination or sect, to which the state as such . . . ought not to tie any granting or withholding of civil rights. Everything which has thus far been done to improve the position of the Jews in Germany appears to us as mere patchwork.
>
> *Kölnische Zeitung*, August 4, 1844

With this stunning reversal, the most important organ of public opinion in Cologne and one of the most influential papers in Germany signaled the emergence of a new era in the debate over Jewish rights.[1] In Cologne and all over Germany, the "Jewish question" was being framed in new language in the 1840's. The very term *emancipation*, evoking sudden and total release from bondage, had only recently made its way to the Continent from England, where it had originated in connection with the Catholic struggle for civil equality. Now, to the chagrin of Judeophobes, the term was applied to the battle for Jewish rights, replacing the less dramatic and more ambiguous *civic betterment* in use since Christian Wilhelm Dohm's pivotal essay of 1781.[2]

Since the inception of public debate on the "Jewish question" in Europe, since the awareness that a Jewish "problem" existed, reform of Jewish status had always been conceived as part of a broad program of societal change.[3] The impetus for actual change emerged in France, Austria, and Prussia in the eighteenth century under absolutist regimes determined to boost the economic usefulness of their subjects: discriminatory measures based on religious differences were deemed a waste of civic resources. Reform of Jewish civic status was repudiated in Austria and Prussia after taking on revolutionary character in France, but, following several decades of reaction, a new generation of reformers in Germany, in and out of government, began to call once more for a new social order in which Jews would have at least enhanced, if not fully equal, rights and obligations.

The reformers were not necessarily motivated by philosemitism. The relationship between German liberalism and the movement for Jewish rights was complicated, many German liberals harboring personal as well as ideological antipathy toward Jews, refusing to back Jewish rights, and even justifying discrimination. Yet the Jewish and liberal causes were inextricably linked. As both the friends and foes of the Jews knew, Jewish emancipation was impossible in a society itself unemancipated from divisions by Estate and religion, and a society thus emancipated could not justify exceptional civil status for Jews. For all the ambivalence of German liberalism on the Jewish question, the record of the struggle for Jewish rights shows unmistakably that progress was tied to the political fortunes of German liberalism. And in the 1840's the star of German liberalism was rising.[4]

Endorsement of civil equality for Jews is not a position we would have expected from a newspaper based in Cologne, much less one that spoke for its business class, as the *Kölnische Zeitung* did. But the elite that dominated the city's economic life in the 1840's was not the same group that had doggedly resisted Jewish rights in the past. Nor was the city itself any longer a somnolent colossus on the Rhine, its face fixed toward the past. By the 1840's the structure of Cologne's economy had been fundamentally altered. The city was an integral part, in some areas, in the forefront, of developments now recognized as the beginnings of Germany's modern economic "takeoff." *Spedition und Kommission*, its once dominant forwarding and commission business, received a death blow in 1831 when Prussia and Holland concluded an agreement establishing unimpeded navigation on the Rhine. The city lost its staple right, for which it had fought tenaciously throughout the 1820's, making Cologne but one of eight free ports on the river rather than a necessary stopping point. Its port declined precipitously, with trade in colonial and luxury goods all but disappearing.[5]

Yet three years later Cologne became part of the Prussian-led *Zollverein* (customs union), which opened to its merchants a free-trade zone encompassing eighteen German states, with a total population of 23.5 million. Cologne's reorientation away from international trade brokering took place surprisingly quickly; even before the advent of railroads enormously facilitated overland traffic, Cologne had become a pole of local and regional commerce. In the 1840's, when it was served by a railway network, Cologne began a rise to preeminence as Germany's internal grain market. Because of the railroad, Cologne was also able to maintain its traditionally strong position as a trading center for iron and coal from the Ruhr district, just as these commodities and the Ruhr were becoming crucial to Germany's emerging industrial economy. The railroad made possible new international trading links via Belgium at a time when Antwerp was Europe's leading port of entry; as a result, Cologne became an important market for South American hides. By 1845, Cologne's custom office was second in Prussia only to that of Berlin.[6]

Yet, as Pierre Ayçoberry observes, it was not the volume of goods passing through the city that accounted for Cologne's dynamism and optimism at midcentury, since with the decline of *Spedition*, its overall trade volume had not increased from 1830. Rather, it was the willingness of Cologne's businessmen to use new modes of transport and trade. Cologne's business elite finally gave up the attempt to perpetuate the past.

The *Zollverein* and the railroad were the most dramatic and influential developments of the period, but other signs also signaled a changed mentality in Cologne, an outlook Ayçoberry has aptly termed "the end of localism."[7] As early as 1825, Cologne's Chamber of Commerce initiated proceedings to found a joint stock steamship company, which succeeded in obtaining a government concession the following year. The Rhine having recently become "romantic," a new cruise industry was unfolding which the Dutch threatened to dominate. Faced with this specter (Dutch tariffs on goods passing through Amsterdam were already causing Cologne's merchants grief), the business elite embraced the latest in technology as well as a relatively new financial expedient, joint stock companies then being rare on the Continent. The gamble paid off. Between 1827 and 1841 ridership of the line increased more than 25-fold and freight carried about 5-fold.[8]

This venture also meant a more forthcoming attitude to the outside world. Rhine cruises were a means of promoting regional tourism, and Cologne soon became a favorite stopping point. It was extremely significant for a city as inward looking and xenophobic as Cologne had been that a tourist industry began to develop in these years: there were 72 inns in Cologne in 1835 and more than double that fourteen years later. Other developments in transportation betokened a new attitude of engagement with the outside world. In the mid-1830's, a steam-powered wagon began carrying passengers between Cologne and Bonn. In 1838, the city's first commercial taxi company opened; a few years later, an omnibus began running from the city center to beyond its walls, where the newly opened Rhenish railway had its station.[9] Cologne remained girded by its ancient walls until 1870, contact with the outside limited to seven gates closed by night. Still, by the 1840's, the city's long-entrenched stance of self-isolation was much diminished.

By this time, Cologne had been part of a major European state — France or Prussia — for decades. A generation had come to maturity under the new conditions. Moreover, a completely new class had come into existence, a group that both symbolized and spurred the changed realities: a new immigrant middle class, largely Protestant, wholly enterprising and innovative. The immigration of this group began in the mid-1820's and became substantial after 1830. It was part of a larger migration that would help increase Cologne's population by 40 percent from 1834 to 1849, from 67,000 to 94,000.[10]

Except for the crisis years of 1846–48, the immigrants, in contrast to those of earlier years, were "more attracted by urban dynamism than propelled by rural misery."[11] This was especially true of immigrants from the more economically stable regions of the Rhineland and industrially advanced Berg, where mercantilist policies in the eighteenth century had generated a class of enterprising business people. The roster of the new elite, popularly called in Cologne the "Junkers of Berg," reads like a who's who of nineteenth-century Rhenish business and industry. It included the sugar refining magnates Langen, Joest, and vom Rath and the trade, banking, and manufacturing families of Carstanjen, Bredt, von Recklinghausen, Hölterhoff, Jagenberg, Brügelmann, Rautenstrauch, and Deichmann. It also included two Catholics whose activities and importance eventually extended beyond Cologne and the Rhineland: the future government ministers Ludolf Camphausen and Gustav Mevissen.[12] With tax payments well above the norm (August and Ludolf Camphausen and C. Joest were three of the wealthiest men in Cologne in 1848), the group quickly earned a prominent place among Cologne's business elite, which had counted a disproportionate number of Protestants even under the French. The perceived significance of this group was enormous; of twelve statues erected at century's end to honor Cologne's great men of affairs, only two honored native sons.[13]

The association of Protestantism and worldly success did not escape popular notice in Cologne, where wits asked, "Are you well off, or Catholic?" Yet to borrow from H. R. Trevor-Roper on the purported connection of Protestantism and modern capitalism, it was less the immigrants' religion that bred their success than the initiative and daring that drove them to migrate from perfectly adequate places of origin to Cologne, where the potential for gain, particularly after 1834, was far greater.[14]

Of course, this is what we have said about Jewish immigrants to Cologne from the beginning of French rule. While most Jews did not attain the wealth and economic power of the city's new immigrant elite, the existence of that elite is a sign that the possibilities for Jews were also much enhanced. Cologne's old social and economic structure had been breached, overwhelmed. Newness, once a mark of Cain in Cologne, which Jews had borne doubly as Jews and as immigrants, had lost its stigma.[15]

All of this is necessary background to understanding not only why Cologne became a bastion of political liberalism in the 1840's but why its most prominent liberals — Camphausen and Mevissen — backed Jewish equality, in contrast to many other German liberals. It is necessary background, yet not sufficient. Cologne had experienced significant immigration since the French occupation, immigration at all social levels, including the highest. Wealthy Protestants had been able to penetrate the municipal power elite from the beginning, first because the French applied civic equality with a vengeance, then because under Prussian rule Protestants shared the religion of state, passing out of minority status to that of privileged in-group. This penetration did not make the old power structure, or even the Protestants, liberal on the Jewish question until the 1840's.

Peter Heinrich Merkens was a Protestant immigrant from the French period who dominated the Chamber of Commerce into the 1830's and who, as we know, vigorously opposed Jewish rights in the 1820's. Yet Merkens spoke up forcefully on behalf of Jewish emancipation as one of Cologne's representatives in the Rhenish provincial Diets of the 1840's. Mayor Steinberger, a Catholic and an *Altkölner* who in the 1820's had joined the City Council in opposing Berlin's more forthcoming position on Jewish rights, also became an advocate of emancipation in the 1840's. Ultimately, Cologne's extraordinary evolution on the Jewish question can be ascribed neither to a Protestant connection — Camphausen and Mevissen were Catholics — nor to the iconoclasm of "new men," since "new men" had been quite capable of adopting a traditional, regressive position on Jewish rights in the 1820's, while "old men" (chronologically as well as metaphorically — Merkens was 67 in 1845) as well as young did the opposite two decades later.

The cause for the fundamental shift of Cologne's business and governing elite on the Jewish question must be sought not so much in the new names on its roster as in a new mentality, shared by initiates and veterans alike.

That new mentality was the result of profoundly changed economic conditions, unprecedented material opportunity, political frustration, and, I submit, a tight alliance with economically powerful Jews. To understand it, we must look more closely at the development of Cologne's business community in this period, at its political positions and its conflicts with Berlin. Not least, we must examine its tangled, often troubled, but vitally important connections to the Jewish banking house of Oppenheim, connections which, though mentioned in all the entrepreneurial histories, have never been examined systematically.

The Business Elite and the Oppenheims

Economic historians debate whether Prussian policies helped or hindered the development of industrial capitalism in Prussia and contributed to the improvement in economic conditions in the Rhineland beginning in the late 1830's.[16] Whatever the truth of the case, Cologne's organized business community did not view Prussian policies as helpful. Its tradition of opposition to Berlin intensified during this period, the Chamber of Commerce perfecting the role it had developed earlier. Dissatisfaction was no longer with the state's failure to protect the city's old economic patterns but its failure to foster new ones. The city's railroad initiatives in particular were accomplished despite Prussian policy.

While businessmen in Cologne and elsewhere in the Rhineland and Westphalia were among the first to anticipate the economic and military potential of railroads, Berlin was unconvinced of the need for them and extremely wary of their financial and political cost. It was an attitude best expressed in Frederick William III's remark that it was not worth sacrificing *Ruhe und Gemütlichkeit* (calm and easygoing comfort) merely in order to arrive in Berlin or Potsdam a few hours earlier.[17] The king's "calm and comfort" were also of a political nature, since an 1820 law barred the crown from incurring public debt without the consent of the Estates, which Frederick William was loath to convoke.[18]

Interest in a railroad had been sparked in Cologne in the late 1820's, when it was viewed as a potential panacea for a host of problems. A railroad could realize a historic dream of Cologne's merchants by opening direct access to the sea and, better yet, do so via an overland route that would outflank nettlesome Dutch control of the mouth of the Rhine. Thus, the railroad loomed as a means for Cologne to regain its primacy as an entrepôt just as it was losing its forwarding monopoly and taxing privileges on the river. Under the circumstances, Belgian independence from Holland in 1830 seemed downright providential, especially because the new Belgian government was eager to establish a railroad accord with Prussia. The obvious connecting points were the great sea and inland ports of Antwerp and Cologne, and by 1835 the first Belgian stretch was completed. It was the first railroad on the European continent.[19]

The next move was clearly Prussia's, but the state refused to play. Here, too, political as well as budgetary concerns were at work. Enhanced ties between the recently revolutionary Belgium and the Rhineland, whose loyalties to Prussia were always suspect, were not seen as a blessing. But Cologne's railroad enthusiasts would not be stilled. In 1833, eight of the city's leading businessmen formed a committee to promote construction of the German stretch of rail. The group included Mayor Steinberger as chairman, Ludolf Camphausen, then a corn merchant and member of the Chamber of Commerce, and Peter Heinrich Merkens, the Chamber's president. Mayor Steinberger lobbied the government for financial support for the Cologne-Antwerp line. Camphausen composed what is now regarded as one of the most important tracts in the annals of railroad promotion to argue for government funding of railroads in general and this one in particular. The committee's minimum goal was a government concession so that building of the railroad line could commence with private backing, if necessary. It got the concession. The state's financial support was limited to waiving tariffs on passengers and freight the future railroad might carry.

Undaunted, the committee proceeded to request and receive government permission to establish a joint stock company to finance the project. Construction was delayed when an equally zealous group of businessmen from Aachen, led by the wool manufacturer and insurance pioneer David Hansemann, formed its own railroad company and insisted that the proposed line include Aachen. Much to the irritation of the Cologne group, this was the plan Berlin ultimately approved. But the project was barely launched when its future was jeopardized by tremendous cost overruns. Yet even with the Rhenish Railway Company facing demise, Berlin still refused to intervene. The day was saved for the Rhineland's railway only by the Belgian government, which in 1839 bought several thousand of the company's depressed shares, infusing one million taler into the project. It was, in Eberhard Gothein's words, "the darkest page in the history of Prussia's railways."[20] Hansemann, who played a leading role in negotiations with Prussian and Belgian authorities to save the railroad, said of his experience, "I conducted the negotiations in Brussels in shame and sadness for my government, which in this regard is so very inferior to the Belgian."[21]

"Shameful" though this episode may have been, it yielded an important lesson for the Rhineland's would-be entrepreneurs: Prussian opposition to railroads was not absolute. While the government had refused to back a railroad venture, it had not exercised its ability to crush the initiative. Concessions as well as permission to form joint stock companies were government-held privileges, and Berlin, albeit ponderously, had granted the Rhenish enterprise both.[22] In fact, the Prussian policy of nonencouragement would prove sufficiently benign to allow railroad development in the Rhineland to continue, although at a retarded pace.

It was clear, however, that entrepreneurs would have to be persistent, inventive, and financially self-sufficient. This, in turn, necessitated creation of close, efficient networks including, given the vast sums railroads demanded, not just big banks but ones with strong connections to still larger financial institutions. Such networks developed in several Rhenish and Westphalian cities but nowhere more than in Cologne, and there, among the several banks of regional importance, none was more important in the history of railroad development than the house of Salomon Oppenheim, Jr., and Company.

As we know, the Oppenheim bank had become a leading force on Cologne's financial scene during the French period. But it was under Abraham Oppenheim, Salomon's son and principal business heir, that the bank catapulted itself into a position of central importance in local, regional, and, ultimately, national and international affairs, primarily through railroad investment. The bank got in early and decisively. Abraham Oppenheim was among the founders in 1837 of the Rhenish Railway Company, as well as its biggest shareholder. The 1,002 shares the bank purchased were more than double the number bought by the next largest investor, the Schaafhausen bank of Cologne.[23] But the Oppenheim involvement was not only financial. Abraham Oppenheim had been instrumental in negotiating with the Prussian government to get the company a concession in the first place, and his brother Simon played a crucial role in securing the Belgian funding to keep it going during the crisis of 1839. For over 40 years, first as a leading member of its managing board, then as vice president, Abraham took a decisive role in running the railroad.[24]

He played a similarly crucial role in launching and maintaining the Cologne-Minden railroad company.[25] It is testimony to the primacy that Cologne had achieved in regional banking by the 1840's that this line, which was the brainchild of Westphalian railroad advocate Friedrich Harkort and the organizational handiwork of David Hansemann of Aachen, got its financial life in Cologne. Of the three city banks that participated in its founding in 1843, the Oppenheim share again was the largest by far: at the unprecedented value of 8.5 million talers, the Oppenheims' was more than double the next largest investment. Here, too, the Oppenheim tie was long-standing and deep. No company stock or bond transaction took place without the bank's participation. Abraham served on the company's administrative council; another Oppenheim brother, Dagobert, sat on its managing board.[26]

The vast sums the Oppenheim bank invested in these and other enterprises were mostly the reserves of others. As Abraham Oppenheim observed, "The aim and art of banking consists not in using one's own capital but . . . the capital of others," and the Oppenheims had a legendary ability to mobilize other people's capital.[27] This derived in part from a shrewd marriage strategy begun during Salomon Oppenheim's lifetime, which linked some of the many Oppenheim offspring (eleven in all) to important Jewish banking families all over Germany and Europe: the Beyfus house of Frankfurt; the von Haber of Karlsruhe; the Obermayer of Augsburg; the Hertz and Heine of Hamburg; the Benoit and Fould of Paris; the Bischoffsheim of Brussels.[28]

These ties brought others, most notably to several branches of the Rothschild empire, to the Pereire brothers of Paris, to the Mendelssohn Company of Berlin, and to the S. Bleichröder Company of Berlin.[29] The links to the Rothschild house were the most glittering: one can imagine the impact on the public mind of the sight of "Rothschild ships" from Frankfurt docking at Cologne and unloading sacks of money that were then dragged through the streets into the cellars of various banks, a spectacle recounted by one of the city's larger bankers and presumably more jaded residents.[30] (The Rothschild-Oppenheim link led Simon Oppenheim to joke about the signatures the respective bank heads left on hotel register manifests when they traveled: "R. de Frankfurt," "O. de Cologne."[31])

Familial connections enabled the Oppenheim bank to achieve a standing it would not otherwise have attained, as one example will illustrate.[32] For reasons that will be explored below, the Oppenheims were not invited to the first meetings called to organize the Rhenish Railway Company—until it became clear that the necessary start-up capital would not be forthcoming without the services of foreign markets. Given the geopolitics of this particular railroad, the Oppenheims' connections in Brussels and Paris were especially appealing, but Oppenheim involvement was also found indispensable in subsequent Rhenish railroad and industrial ventures having no ties to foreign countries.

The amount of capital required for such projects simply could not be raised locally, if only because the Rhineland had no established, central capital market. Stock exchanges existed in Cologne, Essen, and Düsseldorf but were of marginal significance at this time. Promotional and issue business was handled through bankers, mostly on major outside stock markets—Berlin, Frankfurt, Paris, Brussels. But there were fewer than a dozen bankers in the Rhineland with the connections to place issues in the millions of talers. Four or five of them lived in Cologne, which accounts for much of the city's standing as a financial center. One of these was Abraham Oppenheim.

By the time Oppenheim received his invitation in the summer of 1836 to join some 170 other would-be founders of the Rhenish Railway Company, he already had a "Comparenten Liste" of 27 friendly (to him) firms, including the Rothschilds of Frankfurt, Paris, and Naples, Mendelssohn of Berlin, and Heine of Hamburg, whose support for the project he had painstakingly cultivated in anticipation of the summons to partake in it.[33] When sale of the shares occurred, the Oppenheim bank represented the three Rothschild branches as well as members of the Beyfus, Haber, and Obermayer families and their banks and numerous others, placing more shares than any other financial representative. The total backing the Oppenheims brought the venture, counting the bank's resources and others they had marshaled, was 25 percent of its total start-up capital.[34] Most of the railway company's capital in its first decade of existence continued to be raised on outside markets, and the Oppenheim role remained pivotal.[35]

The Oppenheims' involvement was equally crucial in mining ventures related to steam railroads. In 1839, for example, the bank claimed to control, on its own or through proxies, more than three-quarters of the capital of the United Mining Company, one of two important coal producers on the left bank.[36] The Oppenheim "connections" were critical, finally, in a third major area of activity, insurance. Like railroads, insurance was a new enterprise in the Rhineland. What existed was either limited in scope — the most important was David Hansemann's Aachen-Munich Fire Insurance Company, founded in 1825 — or foreign-held. In 1837, however, the Prussian government, concerned about the outflow of Prussian capital through premium payments to foreign companies, barred further concessions and forbade new contacts to foreign companies, opening the door for the creation of domestic ones.[37]

The Oppenheim bank had long been interested in insurance. Salomon Oppenheim had been among the founders of a shipping insurance company initiated by Peter Heinrich Merkens and another Cologne businessman in 1818.[38] By the late 1830's, the bank was in a position to do more than participate in the initiatives of others. In early 1837, Abraham Oppenheim learned, via his Fould and Fould-Oppenheim contacts in Paris, that both of the largest French insurance companies doing business in the Rhineland were on the verge of failure. When he also learned that Hansemann's Aachen outfit was secretly buying up the companies' policies, he hurriedly invited the Schaafhausen, Stein, and Herstatt banks, as well as P. H. Merkens, who was known to support the idea of a fire insurance company, to join him in creating the Cologne Fire Insurance Company, called Colonia. With three million taler in founding shares to place, this enterprise, too, required the services of outside banks, but this proved no problem. Oppenheim arranged for the Paris and Frankfurt Rothschilds to cofound the company, an association which also gave it an inestimable advantage for future expansion.[39] As Fritz Stern has written in another context, "In the private banking world of those days, personal ties were of greatest importance. Common ventures depended on mutual trust, and that trust had to be established by direct personal knowledge."[40] This the Oppenheims had in abundance.[41]

In all this the Oppenheims were more exceptional than unique. They did pioneer certain trends, specializing in banking earlier than the other merchant-banks of Cologne, "cultivating . . . industrial finance earlier and more intensively than all the other Cologne private banks."[42] But their methods were widely in force. All the major Rhenish private banks operated through familial and personal contacts with major outside markets, especially Frankfurt and Berlin. Unlike their English and American counterparts, they were all directly involved in short- as well as long-term funding operations of the enterprises they backed. They were also all deeply involved in managerial control of the companies they financed, undoubtedly because of the substantial returns of close control.[43] Simon Oppenheim, for example, was for years in charge of the buying and selling operation of the Phönix Metallurgical Company, whose government concession the Oppenheims had been instrumental in obtaining and which, not coincidentally, also sold much of its output to other Oppenheim-related enterprises, such as the Cologne-Minden Railway. But the Oppenheim example at Phönix could be matched by others from different banking houses and companies.[44]

Ultimately, it was Prussia's restrictive monetary policy that encouraged private banks to flourish in the Rhineland and elsewhere. As Richard Tilly observes, the "Prussian [Royal] Bank was designed not to compete with, but to strengthen the position of local bankers [including those] in the Rhineland."[45] The same market and political factors shaped all the banks' options, if not their inventiveness and luck in exploiting them. The Oppenheims were particularly aggressive, phenomenally successful, and conspicuous, but they did what a class of bankers did. They did not monopolize new types of financial ventures or the aggressive political brokering essential to business success. Influence-peddling and kickbacks to helpful government bureaucrats, activities in which the Oppenheims clearly engaged ("the tactics of corruption," as Tilly puts it), were common throughout Prussia.[46]

What is significant for our purposes is the fact that by the 1840's a Jewish house, which, as we shall see, wore its Jewish identity boldly, had become a leading force in entrepreneurial developments in the Rhineland: by 1846, Abraham and Simon sat on the boards of 25 to 30 enterprises.[47] They were a financial reality neither would-be entrepreneurs nor other banks could ignore, bypass, or undermine, as much as they occasionally tried.

For the Oppenheims were merely unavoidable, they were not necessarily liked. We have noted Ludolf Camphausen's initial attempt to do without their participation in the Rhenish Railway Company, a position the existing literature does not explain but which fits a long-standing pattern of Camphausen-Oppenheim antagonism. Yet, according to Mathieu Schwann, a Camphausen biographer, there was a broader pattern by Cologne's business elite of attempted and actual exclusion of the Oppenheims from major undertakings: from the steamship company spearheaded by Merkens and other Chamber of Commerce magnates in the 1820's; from the shipping insurance company backed by the same group — in which, as we have seen, Salomon Oppenheim ultimately participated but was overshadowed; from loans to the Cologne municipality for restoration of port buildings.[48] To Camphausen, for whom the railroad was as much a project for the welfare of state and society as a financial venture, the Oppenheims were the worst, if not the only, representatives of sheer avarice.[49]

Camphausen's dislike of the Oppenheims cannot have been tempered by the way in which his entry into public life in Cologne — his election to the Chamber of Commerce in December 1833 — came about. The Chamber was then in a state of turmoil, the Prussians having recently promulgated liberal election rules meant to dilute its powers and make it subservient.[50] The old guard, led by Merkens, refused to accept the new regulations and resigned en masse; a full complement of replacements could not even be found. It was under these highly irregular conditions that Simon Oppenheim served, briefly, as the Chamber's president. He was in office just long enough to preside over a counterattack by the old business elite, which succeeded in regaining control of the institution. Camphausen's election occurred as part of this counterattack and for this reason was contested, along with those of four others, by the "rump" Chamber under Oppenheim. The attempt to stop Camphausen failed. Oppenheim was soon replaced as president by Merkens; Camphausen's election to the Chamber was confirmed and he was immediately given a high post. But the indignity inflicted by an Oppenheim-led Chamber stuck.[51]

The animosity grew more bitter over the next few years as Camphausen struggled to realize his vision of a Rhenish railway. In a letter to his friend W. L. Deichmann, who ran the Schaafhausen bank (clearly, Camphausen's dislike of the Oppenheim bankers was not generic), he accused Abraham Oppenheim of turning spoiler after being denied his "vivid wish" to become a member of the railroad's board of directors — to partake in actually running the railroad company, not just in financing it. Oppenheim, he said, worked systematically and deviously to undermine public and official confidence in the project, then joined forces with the hated Hansemann of Aachen, whose competing railroad plan, it will be recalled, ultimately did win the government concession, supplanting Camphausen's.[52]

Hansemann, however, whose "purely private economic egoism" (in Schwann's paraphrase) Camphausen reviled no less than that of the Oppenheims, soon learned to his chagrin what an Oppenheim partnership meant: a bid—successful, as we have seen—for an effective measure of control. (In Camphausen's word, Hansemann directed his railroad company from 1837 only until 1844, when he was "bitten off the road by his protégé, Oppenheim."[53]) In fact, Hansemann tried to find alternatives to the services of the private (Jewish) bankers of Cologne and Berlin—Oppenheim and Mendelssohn, respectively—and found one to an increasing degree after 1840 in the new government of Frederick William IV. But even this association was insufficient to permit dispensing with the Oppenheims.

Was there a specifically anti-Jewish element to this power play? Undoubtedly, although, as we have seen, there was no love lost between Camphausen and Hansemann or between Camphausen and Mevissen, either. The animosity to the Oppenheims, which fairly drips from the published sources, was a mixture of personal aversion, high-stakes business competitiveness, and Judeophobia. Camphausen was probably involved in a newspaper campaign to smear the Belgian placement of Rhenish Railway shares and the "Cologne Jews" who backed it.[54] In the same letter to Deichmann cited above, he pointedly noted how the banker A. Schaafhausen, disturbed by Oppenheim's machinations in the Rhenish Railway, put his concerns before his (presumably more ethical) "Christian" colleagues in Cologne. Hansemann described how he turned to a "clever and frightful Jewish intermediary" in Berlin when he was looking for funding sources.[55]

The Oppenheims' success should be seen for what it was. The enterprise-finance partnerships they entered were marriages of convenience, sometimes of the shotgun variety. Even Abraham Oppenheim's relationship with Gustav Mevissen, which would blossom in the mid-1840's and beyond into an extraordinary collaboration and friendship, had a rocky start.[56] Mevissen immigrated to Cologne in 1840 from Dulken, where his father operated a prosperous spinning mill. A young man (he was born in 1815) of wide reading and travel who firmly believed in the social role of business and businessmen, Mevissen judged Cologne the place to make both his economic and political mark. He began to do so almost immediately, which made contact with the Oppenheims a necessity.

Mevissen met the Oppenheim presence in both his areas of passion: politics and business. In 1842 he joined the editorial board of the short-lived *Rheinische Zeitung*, an eclectic organ of social, economic, and political criticism, some of whose other contributors and sponsors were such radicals as Moses Hess, Karl Marx, Bruno and Eduard Bauer, Friedrich Engels, and, such was the inchoate nature of pre-1848 liberalism, another Oppenheim brother, the lawyer and entrepreneur Dagobert.[57] In the same year, he also joined the upper reaches of the business elite at a moment of financial distress: claims arising from a catastrophic fire in Hamburg severely hit the Colonia Fire Insurance Company, founded, we recall, by Abraham Oppenheim in consortium with several other magnates. The need for a reinsurance company, a pioneering idea, suddenly became apparent. Colonia's management appointed a committee to shape the project and invited Mevissen, an insurance zealot, to join. Oppenheim wanted Colonia put on secure financial footing; to Mevissen, providing protection from disaster and encouraging planning for the future were as much social as business imperatives. The partnership was struck.

Mevissen soon trod on the other main Oppenheim preoccupation: railroads. By 1843, organized resistance to Abraham Oppenheim's influence in the Rhenish Railway Company had crystallized within its board of directors to a point where a force-out was attempted. (The ostensible reason was conflict of interest between Oppenheim's many commitments.) When Oppenheim refused to go, the entire board resigned, leaving him reigning over a vacuum and the company in a tailspin, with investor confidence and the price of shares deeply depressed. Hansemann, who had nursed the railroad from its infancy, quit the company. It was at this critical juncture that Mevissen, a strong railroad enthusiast, was brought onto a reconstituted board of directors — for whose presidency Oppenheim, with the Belgian government's backing, then bid. He lost — to Mevissen, who was the unanimous choice of everyone else on the board. Mevissen held this office for the next 36 years, until the company was nationalized. Oppenheim had to content himself with the vice presidency.[58]

Pragmatism was a virtue Abraham Oppenheim knew how to practice as well as to exploit, however, and the two men not only made their peace but continued an avid business association. One project was the reinsurance company both badly wanted. Here, too, the Prussian government played unwitting marriage-broker by making the funding process so protracted and laborious that it necessitated long, intense collaboration by entrepreneurs and bankers. The plan, first introduced to the Cologne Chamber of Commerce in 1842, did not receive a government concession until 1846, by which time the money market was so unstable that actual funding had to be delayed for another six years. The company finally got off the ground only because the Oppenheim and several other Cologne banks raised one-third of its founding capital. The rest, two million taler, was raised, through Oppenheim's mediation, from the Paris Rothschilds.

In 1845 the Oppenheims and Mevissen realized a hefty 30 percent profit on a joint placement of a large quantity of Rhenish Railway shares. A year earlier, they had come up with a novel proposal for "priority shares" to stimulate investor interest in the railroad. Toward the end of the decade, they collaborated on formation of a life insurance company to be based in Cologne; it would come into being in the 1850's as the Concordia Life Insurance and Annuity Company. Oppenheim also lent his considerable reputation to another Mevissen insurance project, conversion of the Rhenish Shipping Insurance Company into one that insured ground and sea, as well as river, transport.

This cooperation, it should be noted, was extended during and after the clash of the two men for control of the Rhenish Railway Company.[59] Nothing could express more clearly the exigency of the business-banking partnership in Cologne and the Rhineland in the 1840's, a partnership which to a significant degree depended on Jewish financial power.

Cologne's Liberals and Jewish Emancipation in the Rhineland

While Abraham Oppenheim's activities on behalf of Jewish communal institutions and civil rights are noted in every history of Jewish Cologne and in all the writing on emancipation in the Rhineland, their nature and importance have never truly been assessed. One writer goes so far as to attribute the relatively favorable Prussian Jewry law of July 1847 to Abraham Oppenheim's personal efforts in Berlin, without substantiating this claim or recognizing that Rhenish liberals worked prodigiously to amend the government's earlier, more regressive draft of the law.[60] Another writer downplays the role of economic considerations in the debates and decisions of Rhenish liberals on the Jewish question, while acknowledging the importance of Abraham Oppenheim's lobbying efforts — the success of which, however, he attributes solely to Oppenheim's "academic training, spirit and mental acuteness."[61] Eleonore Sterling, who in a few paragraphs comes closest to a theory about support for emancipation in the Rhineland, posits a causal link between the interests of industrial capitalism and entrepreneurial advocacy of Jewish rights, yet does not mention the vital railroad interests of such advocates of emancipation as Hermann Beckerath, Ludolf Camphausen, and Gustav Mevissen, or their connections to the Oppenheims.[62]

The Oppenheim role in furthering Jewish rights was neither as central and determinative nor as peripheral as these treatments would suggest. Abraham's two-month sojourn in Berlin in 1847, when the government's proposed Jewry law was put before the First United Prussian Diet, capped nearly a decade of private and public activity — not just by him, but by

Simon and Dagobert Oppenheim as well — on behalf of Jewish emancipation. In 1841, Abraham and Simon sent the newly crowned Frederick
William IV a lengthy appeal for Jewish rights (see Chapter 6). The Oppenheims circulated this petition among their politically powerful business
associates; one of the Rhineland's most eloquent liberals, Hermann Beckerath, would borrow from it in a major address on behalf of emancipation
at the United Diet of 1847. Abraham and Dagobert personally lobbied for
the Jewish cause at the Rhenish Provincial Diets of the 1840's and the First
United Diet in Berlin in 1847. As we shall see, in at least one instance,
Oppenheim efforts led to the adoption of a pro-Jewish plank when this
would not otherwise have occurred.

Given the Oppenheims' importance to business ventures in which Cologne's entrepreneurs were either directly involved or on which the health
of the local and regional economies depended, it was surely the better part
of wisdom for these men to take the "correct" position on Jewish rights in
their public capacities: Merkens and Camphausen as Cologne's representatives to the Rhenish Provincial Diet; Camphausen, too, as a member of the
City Council, President of its Chamber of Commerce from 1839 to 1848, a
delegate to the First United Diet, and a major force behind the *Kölnische
Zeitung*; Mevissen, as a member of the Chamber of Commerce and delegate
to the Rhenish Provincial and First United Diets; Steinberger as mayor.
The same may have been true for David Hansemann, the region's most
prominent liberal, who did not live in Cologne but who had extensive
business dealings there and deep ties to the Oppenheim bank.[63] Given the
often tense relations between Abraham Oppenheim and these men, we can
also say that to the extent pro-Jewish positions were taken because of the
Oppenheim connection, it was surely not for love of the Oppenheim house.

But this does not mean that it was sheer expediency, either. Support of
Jewish rights was in far greater consonance with the broader visions of these
men than it was for their counterparts in south and southwest Germany.
Sterling and, to a greater extent, Reinhard Rürup, have shown how it was
possible for liberal parliamentarians in Baden, Württemberg, and Bavaria,
including some of the greatest theoreticians of German liberalism, to withhold support for Jewish emancipation and even rationalize antisemitism. In
part this flowed from deep personal prejudice. But the opposition was also
political: these liberals represented a town-dwelling, economically distressed artisan class that perceived Jews, most of whom practiced petty trade
and money lending, as competitors and predators. Given popular antisemitism — one liberal clergyman-parliamentarian in Baden said he "would
sooner bring the cholera back to his congregation than Jewish emancipation" — opposing Jewish rights could even be defended in the lofty name of
democratic principle.[64]

Post–World War II historiography, especially the works of Rürup, Uriel Tal, and Jacob Katz, has shattered any notion of an automatic alliance between liberals and Jews, thoroughly revising rosier assessments of the legacy of German and European liberalism on the Jewish question.[65] This work has been a necessary correction but itself has led to a distortion. Liberalism has been broadly tarred; pre-1848 German liberals are uniformly depicted as "unable to come forward with a consistent program in favour of Jewish emancipation," their positions being indistinguishable from "that of the Governments."[66]

Yet Rhenish liberalism of the 1840's resolutely backed Jewish civic equality. The region's major newspapers — the *Kölnische Zeitung*, *Aachener Zeitung*, the *Trierische Zeitung*, the *Düsseldorfer Zeitung*, the *Rheinische Zeitung*, all of which were liberal organs — took strong positions on behalf of emancipation in the 1840's. Liberals in the Rhenish Provincial Diets of 1843 and 1845 actively supported Jewish rights. Because of their efforts, these diets became the first representative assemblies on German soil to call for Jewish emancipation. Rhenish liberals also spearheaded an effort on behalf of Jewish equality at the First United Prussian Diet in 1847.

Recent historians have stressed that nineteenth-century German liberalism was a highly variegated movement with deep ideological, religious, class, and regional differences.[67] We would only expect such factors to create diversity on the Jewish question, as they did on other great social issues. The Rhineland in the 1840's was very different economically, socially, and politically from Baden, Württemberg, and Bavaria in the 1820's and 1830's, the decades from which Rürup draws many of his examples of liberal antisemitism. The Rhineland's economy was far more urbanized and its important cities, Cologne, Aachen, much larger and less provincial than Karlsruhe, Stuttgart, or Munich. Artisan guilds had been eclipsed in the north; in the south, there was clamor for their restoration. By the 1840's, most Rhenish liberals were leaders of business, industry, and finance whose political vision encompassed a unified Germany with overseas colonies (in the words of one detractor, theirs was "moneybags liberalism").[68] Their constituency was an educated, articulate upper bourgeoisie stymied by the Prussian censor and bureaucracy and disgusted with economic policies that favored estate agriculture over business and mechanized enterprise.

In contrast to the situation in the south, this liberal constituency backed Jewish rights, with great merchants, factory owners, bankers, and insurance entrepreneurs signing numerous petitions on behalf of the cause to the Rhenish Diets of the 1840's. While anti-Jewish outbreaks occurred in rural districts of the Rhineland in the 1830's, Rhenish cities, the cradles of Rhenish liberalism, were by the 1840's quite friendly to Jews.[69] By 1846, Jews served in the municipal councils of Bonn, Cleves, Deutz, Düsseldorf,

Goch, Calcar, Wesel, Essen, Neuss, Siegburg, Koblenz, Simmern — and even Cologne.[70]

According to Eleonore Sterling, pure economics explains the Rhenish liberal record on the Jewish question. Rhenish liberals and their constituents wanted a dynamic market economy and a government supportive of enterprise, committed to increasing wealth; to them, she argues, Jewish emancipation was part of a broader program of reform that would make government and society more rational and productive. Indeed, as we know, the same Prussian bureaucracy that made obtaining a railroad concession a nightmare (Mevissen once called this bureaucracy the national "cancer") kept Jewish rights frozen in the distorted pose of semiemancipation. A contemporary observer remarked that Jewish emancipation was the "touchstone of German liberalism because it is the only [issue] which will be fought for without material advantage for the liberals."[71] Yet according to Sterling, neither abstract principle nor love of the Jews, and certainly not altruism, but simple self-interest cemented the liberal-Jewish alliance in the Rhineland.[72]

While compelling, Sterling's economic theory does not account for everything. As we shall see, there was large variation in motivation and degree of commitment to Jewish equality within the Rhenish liberal camp despite its uniformly proemancipation stance in public. The alliance of a Rhenish urban elite with the Jewish cause is also far from self-evident. It is a striking departure from the "firmly anchored anti-Semitism [of] the urban culture of late medieval Germany,"[73] a stance that persisted well into the nineteenth century. In the fifteenth and sixteenth centuries, urban elites expelled the Jews from "most of the Imperial cities in the Rhineland . . . Bavaria, Swabia and Franconia," including, to give but a partial list of Imperial and other cities, Cologne, Mainz, Linz, Augsburg, Regensburg, Halle, Magdeburg, Salzburg, Nuremberg, Freiburg, Ulm, Colmar, Mulhouse, and Obernai.[74] Municipal elites ghettoized the Jewish populations of cities where Jewish residence was tolerated, like Frankfurt am Main, Worms, or Bonn, and restricted Jewish access to the urban economy through a maze of discriminatory regulations. All this persisted until the French revolutionary occupation and, in some cases, beyond it: in Frankfurt, city authorities revoked emancipation once the defeated French departed. In Lübeck, Jews were reexpelled. In Bremen and Nuremberg, Jews received permission to settle only in 1848 and 1850, respectively. We have seen the official hostility to Jews that persisted in Cologne into the late 1820's.

Urban hostility to the Jews had a clear genesis and, on the Rhine, a clear end point in the 1840's. It emerged when the urban economies of central Europe had developed sufficiently for there to be a Christian middle class capable of delivering the market and financial services for which Jews traditionally had been tolerated. As a sixteenth-century saying put it, "We don't need Jews anymore, there are other moneylenders."[75] Unlike Jews, the non-Jewish urban elites exercised an inherent rather than a negotiated claim on community and polity. They could portray Jews as interlopers on the privileges of Christian "natives" and, with growing political power, something Jews could never have, restrict or eliminate Jewish access to the urban economy. Doing so became politically imperative when Jews, who often held charters of toleration from feudal overlords, were used (as in Cologne) to assert the lord's sovereignty and quash emerging municipal autonomy, a common dynamic in central Europe. Finally, the animosity of municipal elites converged with escalating popular Judeophobia fomented by Franciscan and Dominican preachers, a hysteria manifested in increasingly frequent accusations of ritual murder in the thirteenth through sixteenth centuries.[76] It is in this context that hostility supplanted the benign policies that had welcomed Jews to cities since Carolingian times. By the turn of the seventeenth century, the hysterical element in Jew-hatred subsided.[77] Economic and political factors persisted.

Competition is often cited as a main factor in antisemitism, ancient and modern. However, even limiting the discussion to economic factors in Jew-hatred, "competition" would be inadequate to explain urban hostility to Jews, for were this truly its cause we would expect the Rhenish bourgeoisie of the 1840's to have been particularly anti-Jewish. It would seem that a crucial operative factor in "competitive" antisemitism was the perception that wealth, resources, economic activity itself, were finite, static. This being the case, it was essential to protect the privileges of rightful "insiders" against the incursions of "outsiders." A constricted view of the material world sustained in the urban elites an implacable economic hostility to Jews, as well as to other perceived "outsiders," like Protestants in Cologne.

This view persisted until industrial capitalism substituted a vision of dynamic, virtually limitless economic potential beckoning the most aggressive and inventive, of whatever religion, to create and enjoy wealth. Like the religion-neutral ground created by the Enlightenment for Jews and non-Jews who shared rationalist, humanist ideals, industrial capitalism created "neutral ground" inhabitable by the likes of Mevissen and Oppenheim but also, significantly, by a broader class of Jews and non-Jews riding the economic wave: witness the reports of non-Jews cheering Jews in pubs on hearing of the seventh Diet's historic decision on Jewish rights or the report of one newspaper that "it is not unusual to see Christian citizens [*Bürger*] joyfully shaking the hands of Jews."[78]

The potential of large-scale capitalist undertakings to level the importance of confessional difference had already been proved in Cologne when French policies made possible the remarkable rise of Protestants into the upper reaches of Cologne's economy. Peter Heinrich Merkens, one of these Protestants, would later take the young Ludolf Camphausen, a Catholic, as his business and political protégé, as fine an example as possible of Protestant-Catholic coexistence on the neutral terrain of modern capitalist endeavor.[79] It would take several decades for this dynamic to apply to Jews, decades of continued capitalist development and, crucially, of sufficient upward mobility among Jews for there to be a Jewish middle and upper class assimilable by a new capitalist elite that cared more about class similarity than religious difference.

It was only with the emergence of the industrial-capitalist view of the material world that a recast, benign evaluation of the Jews and their economic activity became possible.[80] It was only when this fundamental change in mentality occurred that cities and Jews, the dual bane of late-nineteenth-century antisemites, developed an extraordinary symbiosis. By the 1840's, the economic changes necessary to the new mentality had made sufficient inroads in the Rhineland to allow a sea change in attitudes about Jews by at least that segment of the population that spearheaded the emerging industrial economy. We have already seen the main features of the economic transformation in Cologne, which provided much of the leadership for the battle for Jewish emancipation in the Rhine Province.

Clearly, the traditional importance of religious difference had waned among Rhenish liberals and their constituency. Much of the Catholic population of the Rhineland and Westphalia in the 1840's, according to Jonathan Sperber, was influenced by enlightened ideas and was "religiously indifferent," or was without intellectual hostility to religion, yet "neglectful of its religious obligation." The inhabitants of Cologne and Düsseldorf, in particular, were noted for lack of religious fervor.[81] Jacques Droz has noted that all the leaders of the liberal movement in the predominantly Catholic Rhine Province were either Protestants or men with "minds absolutely detached from any positive faith."[82] While not necessarily hostile to religion in general or to some form of Christianity in particular, all supported separation of church and state and adamantly opposed notions of a "Christian state" then gaining currency in conservative circles, especially at court. Even a Catholic cleric serving in the Rhenish *Landtag*, the Canon Gisbert Lensing, spoke of the equality of all men before God and the law and against the "Christian state," whose form in Prussia would inevitably be Protestant and under which there would be "no security for the rights of the Catholic citizen."[83] Lensing also spoke strongly on behalf of Jewish emancipation.

Thus, not only a material weltanschauung but unique realities of religion itself promoted tolerance in the Rhine Province. The territory had a sizable Protestant minority (861,019 in 1840, compared to 1,929,660 Catholics), which, significantly, was itself religiously diverse.[84] Protestants were scarred by the experience of Catholic discrimination, some of it quite recent: in 1839, Catholic opposition caused Hansemann, a Protestant from Catholic Aachen, to lose his bid to represent the city in the Provincial Diet, despite the fact that the city's fortunes had benefited enormously from his. Along with Catholics, however, Rhenish Protestants also feared a militantly Evangelical Prussia in which the political rights of unrecognized Protestant sects were threatened. All this made advocacy of secular citizenship by Rhenish politicians an urgent priority.[85] In the Rhineland, the argument for civic equality regardless of religion was extended not just to minority Christian denominations but to non-Christians. Whether it was fear for their own freedom of conscience or the "simple religious conformity, approaching dogmatic indifference" of the urban upper middle classes, religion had ceased to play its traditionally negative role in determining Jewish civic status.[86]

Still, it is impossible to overstate the importance for the Jewish cause of the belief of the Rhenish entrepreneurs in material abundance and in the value of capitalist economic development. The emancipation debate in Germany had begun in 1781 with C. W. Dohm's essay, "Concerning the Civic Improvement of the Jews," which argued for the abolition of most anti-Jewish discrimination yet which was permeated with physiocratic abhorrence for the commerce most Jews practiced. Indeed, Dohm argued against anti-Jewish discrimination because discrimination had driven Jews into economic practices he viewed as morally corrupting. Of commerce he wrote:

The merchant is busy all the time keeping up profits . . . [his mind] continuously in anxious activity and tense alertness. . . . The continuous habit of looking at everything from the viewpoint of yield and profit necessarily causes a limitation of his outlook. Opportunities to increase his profit by little infringements on strict legality are too enticing not to cause him to succumb, at least sometimes. . . . Most merchants become somewhat uncertain and flexible in their principles. . . . They become narrow-minded, isolated, less inclined to be generous than other men of otherwise similar enlightenment and moral education. . . . Gambling is a natural vice in [the merchant] because commerce itself is a kind of gambling.[87]

Dohm wanted the state to end religious discrimination in order to open other occupational options to Jews, and he expected Jews to forsake the money economy to become artisans and farmers. The "civic betterment" Dohm had in mind was as much for Jews' moral state as their legal status, the former debased not by their religion (as opponents of emancipation argued, as we have seen) but by what Jews did for a living. So important was this occupational change that Dohm even justified state coercion and discrimination to bring it about.[88]

How different the declaration of Hansemann's mouthpiece, the *Aachener Zeitung*, only 50 years later that "agriculture . . . prevents a nation not only from being rich but also strong morally. By limiting needs, it turns the people back on itself; by suppressing all intellectual creativity, it paralyzes initiative." Commerce, on the other hand, "vitalizes the state, and without industry, commerce remains an idle fancy."[89]

While many of the Rhineland's most prominent liberals had reservations about the social consequences of industrialization and unrestrained economic growth, all viewed the economy as expansive and dynamic. The railroad was not only a private business obsession for these men but a powerful agent of economic and social betterment, a means to decrease unemployment, facilitate the flow of goods, lessen misery in bad years, and "equalize social contrasts."[90] Money, its accumulation and investment, was a good, at least in a state that (as Mevissen, for example, intended) would direct resources to the public welfare.[91] Ludolf Camphausen could argue not only the necessity but the human blessings of an abundant, rational money supply in an essay entitled simply, boldly, "About Money."[92] Camphausen had already argued the irrelevance of religion in a society ordered on such an economy, writing in his famous railroad essay of 1833, "Neither religion nor political ideals will stand in the forefront of this new age and if one were to dare to speculate what [idea] might be designated to take over this empty place, it would be the striving of all peoples after material well-being."[93]

Unlike Dohm and those who followed him in demanding that Jews transform their occupational profile, Rhenish advocates of emancipation wanted more of what Jews traditionally did, viewing the Jews' seemingly innate capacity for commerce with envy. "The finesse of the Jew and the speed of the eagle," wrote Hansemann, "were the qualities of the successful merchant."[94] Arguing for Jewish rights in 1847, Camphausen turned the tables on traditional prejudice by reminding his fellow delegates to the First United Prussian Diet that "the Jews are distinguished by certain talents, which are found more abundantly among them than among the Christian population. Not to mention what Jews have produced in poetry, literature and music, it is plain that they possess financial talent."[95] Precisely the qualities that had most stigmatized Jews were now positive attributes shared by the "best" elements of non-Jewish society and held up as ideals to the rest. As one remarkable petition to the Rhenish Diet put it, Jews did not practice "usury" (*Wucher*), they took "interest" (*Zins*).[96]

To the large urban constituency of Rhenish liberalism, increasingly middle-class Jewish city dwellers were not hostile competitors, much less fearsome aliens. They were *Verwandte*, kindred. The emancipation coalition in the Rhineland was built on foundations more reliable than self-sacrifice and more complex than simple self-interest. It was built on identification with Jews (albeit of the middle-class variety), a startling *novum* in Rhenish, and German, history.

The Emergence of a Political Movement for Jewish Rights

> In the matter of the Jews . . . we must not stay idle . . . for only through persistence will the . . . objective . . . be reached.
>
> Abraham Oppenheim to Joseph Wergifosse
> (delegate to the Rhenish Diet), August 2, 1844[97]

> The press . . . is to public opinion what the hand is to the clock.
>
> Karl Theodor Nauwerck,
> in the *Rheinische Zeitung* 226, August 14, 1842

The year 1840 is generally seen as a turning point in Prussian political history. It was a turning point in Rhenish liberalism as well, a divide between early and later phases.

The early movement, which began with the Prussian takeover, was made up of a bewildering diversity of adherents whose sole rallying point was opposition to Prussia. Devout Catholics — including clerics — jurists, wealthy merchants and industrialists, all joined in defense of "Rhenish law" (French criminal and commercial codes) and against Prussia's attempts to impose its General Code and system of local government.[98]

The strands of Rhenish liberalism began to untangle after 1840. The "Cologne troubles" of 1837, when the archbishop was arrested for refusing to sanction mixed marriages without a pledge to raise children as Catholics, radicalized the Catholic faction. Although liberal businessmen — Camphausen, Mevissen, even Hansemann, a Protestant — joined Catholic clerics in denouncing state interference in religious affairs, the Catholic faction became increasingly uncomfortable with the religious "indifference" of the rest of the movement and veered progressively toward ultramontanism.[99] Intellectuals and men of affairs soon parted company as well, their last great collaboration being the *Rheinische Zeitung*. The newspaper, launched in early 1842 under temporarily relaxed censorship rules, was quashed for its radicalism fifteen months later. Its short life proved sufficient to demonstrate the incompatibility of reformers and revolutionaries (on learning that such respected banking houses as Stein and Oppenheim backed the paper financially, the Prussian Minister of Interior could only sputter in amazement, "But why do they give their money to such an enterprise?").[100] After the demise of the *Rheinische Zeitung*, the two camps parted company.[101]

Businessmen, industrialists, and financiers, formerly a bloc in the larger liberal constellation, now dominated Rhenish liberalism, giving it a distinctly pragmatic, nonideological character, in contrast to the liberal movement in south and southwest Germany.[102] Aside from Hansemann, Camphausen, and Mevissen, its leaders were the banker-industrialist Hermann Beckerath of Krefeld and the merchant-banker August van der Heydt of Elberfeld. The group had internal divisions over tactics and substance; Camphausen clashed sharply with Mevissen and Hansemann over trade and tariff policies, for instance. But it was far more homogeneous than the old liberal consortium and far more capable of coalescing into an effective political lobby.

It was also staunchly pro-Prussian, the final distinction generally drawn between early and later Rhenish liberalism. The state was to be thoroughly refashioned, but the leaders of Rhenish liberalism were pragmatists and it was clear that the key to realizing their goals was a strong Prussia.[103]

Neither the literature on Rhenish liberalism nor that on Jewish emancipation has noted that support of Jewish rights was a further major distinction between the earlier and later liberal movements. We have seen how, in 1818, the same forces that fought to retain the French judicial system in the Rhineland—because its open, oral proceedings and juries better protected general civil rights, also advocated retaining the 1808 decree for Jews. Throughout the 1820's and 1830's, as the Rhenish liberal movement fought for civil equality for non-Jews—vehemently resisting, for instance, Prussian attempts to distinguish between the civic status of city and country dwellers—it manifested no similar commitment to civil equality for Jews.

Although Prussia lacked a single, statewide parliament until 1847, it had provincial assemblies that met from 1824 on in which the Jewish question was several times raised.[104] There was also considerable press and public debate on the subject. All the Prussian Provincial Diets, including the Rhenish, took negative positions on Jewish emancipation in the 1820's and 1830's.[105] The first Rhenish Diet of 1826 not only recommended retaining the 1808 decree on the left bank, but extending it to the right. It is true that this assembly, like the others, was heavily weighted in favor of landed nobility and that the anti-Jewish initiative probably came from this camp. But the Diet's anti-emancipation recommendations (it had consultative competence only) were passed by a large majority from which there is no reason to think the representatives of the cities, generally in the forefront of the fight for liberal "Rhenish law," departed.

One of Cologne's two representatives at that first assembly was P. H. Merkens.[106] We know what Merkens's record was on the Jewish question in Cologne during this period, and there is no reason to think it differed on the provincial level. Merkens, in fact, is a fine exemplar of the capacity of liberals in this early period — not just in southern Germany but in the economically advanced northwest, not just in towns but in big cities — to exempt Jews from the implications of their own highest principles. Merkens, a fiery orator, led the fight in the Diets of 1826 and 1831 for the civil equality of urban and rural dwellers and against introduction of Prussian-style privileges for the Rhenish nobility.[107] His efforts in this area have led one writer to characterize him as "that fighter [against] all social inequality."[108] But the full record, that is, the one that includes the Jewish case, says otherwise.

Indeed, with regard to the Jewish question, the early Rhenish liberal movement seems to have had more in common with its counterparts in the south and southwest than with its own successor: the Provincial Diets of 1833 and 1837 also opposed Jewish rights, with only the slightest indication at the latter of dissent by representatives of cities or those otherwise considered "liberal."[109] Rhenish liberalism only became liberal on the Jewish question after the region's economy had turned toward an industrial capitalist base; after its leaders were an elite not of education and wealth but of capitalist enterprise; and after the Oppenheim connection had been made. The turnaround that occurred at the Provincial Diets of 1843 and 1845 is inconceivable outside of this context.

Yet that turnaround was no spontaneous affair. In contrast to the impression liberal leaders wished to convey, support for the Jews did not simply well up and overtake the Diets. It was carefully crafted at the local level and orchestrated by the liberal leadership, which was the most politically astute, organized, and dynamic bloc at the Diets. There was also significant behind-the-scenes input from several Oppenheims. The outlines of this story have been sketched previously but the full story never told. That awaits a comprehensive history of Jewish emancipation in the Rhineland and is beyond the scope of the present work. Here we focus on the political metamorphosis that occurred in Cologne on the Jewish question and on the role its political leaders, and the Oppenheims, played in the movement for Jewish rights in the Rhine Province and in Prussia in the 1840's.

The Jewish question of that decade was framed in Berlin shortly after Frederick William IV came to the throne in 1840. The new king wanted to harmonize the multiplicity of legal systems regulating Jewish status in the kingdom, a problem exacerbated by Prussia's territorial acquisitions in the post–Napoleonic peace treaties. The bureaucracy and, at the king's behest, the Provincial Diets had wrestled with this issue several times since 1815 but never resolved it.[110]

In December 1841, Frederick William proposed a solution in keeping with his belief that religion determined nationality and that Jews, therefore, were unassimilable into the German Christian state.[111] Since he considered equality based on individual rights to be an artificial and destructive concept, he proposed grouping Jews into a legally recognized religious corporation, from which body alone they would draw their necessarily inferior civic status. Thus they would no longer be eligible to vote as individuals in municipal elections, a right the Prussian Municipal Law of 1808 had granted, but would have their interests represented by their "corporation." Neither could they vote, hold office, nor be elevated to military rank or to any other station involving the exercise of authority over non-Jews.[112]

The king's views regarding Jewish economic rights were less clear, so he mobilized the bureaucracy to study the question. Two ministries were ordered to institute what one writer has termed a "grand enquête," which resulted in "statistical and nonstatistical [material providing] an uncomparable [sic] record of Jewish life in Prussia of a kind never again compiled until, possibly, the . . . Nazi period."[113] Provincial governments were ordered to prepare detailed reports on local conditions so that the government might decide the limits of freedom of movement and occupational choice for Jews. This included assessment of the practical effects of discriminatory legislation already on the books. In the Rhine Province, this meant the 1808 decree.[114]

Provincial governors turned to local authorities for their "expert opinions," and thus it fell to Mayor Steinberger to be the first public figure from Cologne to voice an official position on Jewish rights.[115] In an extraordinary report, Steinberger forcefully backed emancipation, at least for the Jews of the Rhine Province, reversing his stand of some two decades before and opposing the king's current legislative plan. While supporting the right of Jews, like any other religious group, to enjoy such corporate rights as were necessary to secure their spiritual, educational, and welfare institutions, Steinberger denied that Jews needed or wanted corporate status of a more comprehensive nature. Any such grouping, he asserted, "regardless of whether this is meant to benefit or harm those placed in the exceptional category," "would go against the grain of our [provincial] laws," which, except for the 1808 decree, he alleged treated Jews equally. It would also violate the "Volksgeist," the spirit of the people.

Steinberger was pragmatic in his arguments; he had no love for Jews as such. It was simply that exceptional legislation to protect Christians from alleged Jewish wrongdoing had been tried and never found effective. Humiliating or injuring Jews by restricting or withholding their civic rights would never lead "Jews to cease being Jews, that is, Jews in the sense that has been complained about from time immemorial, everywhere. Were this the route to this result, we would not be discussing the question once again. . . . In any case, there can be no question of erecting such [Jewish] corporative societies in the Rhine Province, which would result in putting the Jews in an isolated position" to the detriment, apparently, of Christians as well as Jews.

Several of the points on the government questionnaire circulated to local officials reflected concerns of eastern provinces with large, unacculturated Jewish populations and had little bearing for a big-city Rhenish mayor: the advisability of granting Jews freedom of movement throughout the monarchy, forbidding their settlement in the countryside, or allowing them to run rural inns. Steinberger addressed these issues anyway, always stressing the same point: discriminatory legislation was either ineffective or counterproductive. It was also superfluous, because any crimes Jews committed were already covered under the general criminal code.

All the questions being raised about Jews, in fact, touched on general concerns that required broader policy formulation. Population movement, whether from outside Prussia or within, and the strains placed on cities, especially by the influx of poor migrants, were larger, societal problems. Economic discrimination meant to influence the course of Jewish migration, prohibition of their settlement in the countryside "was . . . not the way to lead [Jews] to better, more generally agreeable culture and breeding [*Bildung und Gesittung*] . . . or the way to make their talents and capacities more readily available." It would only encourage their concentration in certain areas, especially cities, precisely the "evil" targeted by the lawmakers for eradication. Shutting them out of legitimate pursuits like innkeeping would likewise drive them into the very activities perennially denounced. The only rational course was "general equality," instituted gradually, if necessary, but furthered by the state by all possible means.

As for the 1808 decree, one law Steinberger could judge from long personal experience, "the formula for its so-called *Judenpatente* [affirming a Jew's innocence from usury and other illicit business] . . . has to a large extent lost its practical effectiveness in this city." The prescribed granting of the "detested [patent] testimonials by the City Council is largely a formality. . . . Time exercises its inexorable right in this as in so many other matters," the mayor mused. Only once in many years had Cologne's Council denied its endorsement, and that action was later overturned.[116] "Certainly little . . . success for a piece of exceptional legislation which every year inflicts anew great humiliation on a large population group," he noted.

The law was also self-defeating. "To burden a priori a single group of citizens [*Staatsbürger*], much less an entire religion, with the stain [of criminality] can only lead to the same behavior [here] as [in general]. . . . He who is once judged a rascal and is watched everywhere with guarded mistrust all too easily succumbs to the temptation of being that which is feared and anticipated he already is."

Steinberger agreed that usury was a scourge in both the cities and countryside but asserted that there were no data to indicate Jews were particularly guilty of it — and even if they were, this would only prove the futility of exceptional legislation. What was needed was tough laws against "any and all" usurers, because many Christians were also accused of this crime. Stein-berger concluded by pleading that in the event discriminatory legislation were introduced elsewhere in Prussia "it would appear only just and reason-able that the Jews of this place" [the Rhine Province], "whose civil, social and moral" standing warranted equality, "not be made to suffer by it. They ought to be able to expect that any general [Jewry] legislation for the entire monarchy not deprive them of the rights and benefits of existing laws, that . . . the good intended by [having] a single [nationwide] law not be for them a step backward."

Frederick William's proposed Jewish law sent shock waves through Jew-ish communities across Prussia because it denied the fundamental premise on which the struggle for emancipation was based: that Jews were not a nation in the political sense but only members of a faith community.[117] It also did violence to the liberals' view of the state, which, as Hansemann once put it, "must be entirely indifferent about whether someone reveres religious relics or worships them, or does neither. . . . The Prussian state must be absolutely secular."[118] In advocating the Christian state, the new king, whose reign had initially been greeted with special enthusiasm in the Rhineland and Cologne, inadvertently did much to galvanize the emerging liberal movement.

In Cologne, the proposal set off a running polemic between the *Rhein-ische Zeitung*, then the city's liberal organ and the most important journal of the opposition in pre-1848 Germany, and the *Kölnische Zeitung*, edited by K. H. Hermes, a supporter of the Christian state and a friend of the regime in Berlin.[119] The *Rheinische Zeitung* sharply attacked the Jewry ordinance and the broader political philosophy that underlay it. The very notion of special legislation for Jews, whatever its content, was outdated and without popular mandate, it argued, while the idea of a Jewish "corporation" was absurd. The proposal to subject politics to religion in the Christian state was as untenable as it was dangerous, an idea the nineteenth century was simply too "mature" to tolerate. If the state truly wanted to follow Christian principles, it would be guided by the injunction to love one's enemies and would protect all religions with equal political rights.[120]

Hermes in the *Kölnische Zeitung* defended religion as the necessary cor-nerstone of the state, denouncing "Vernunftrechtler" (advocates of natural law) like Bruno Bauer and the other Young Hegelians at the *Rheinische Zeitung* for advocating "the destruction of Christianity and all religious sentiment," which philosophy alone made possible the promotion of civil equality for Jews.[121]

The *Rheinische Zeitung* was quickly silenced by the Prussian censor, but, happily for the Jewish cause, Hermes soon lost his job at the *Kölnische* over charges of accepting Prussian bribes. His successor, Karl Andree, held markedly different views, and the paper was thoroughly reshaped into the liberal mouthpiece in Cologne. The shift in editorial policy away from support for the Christian state and, in the words of its owner, toward support of "progress, of national development, of the German middle class" (*des deutschen Bürgertums*), also signaled a more favorable stance on the Jewish question.[122] Karl Andree served from November 1843 until the summer of 1845, the crucial period when the seventh and eighth Diets took their votes on emancipation. He unequivocally supported the movement for Jewish rights, which the paper placed squarely in the larger struggle against feudal oppression. As its Easter edition of 1845 declared, "The full legal equality of our Jewish fellow citizens is a matter which will no longer be eclipsed . . . because the contemporary consciousness [*Zeitbewusstsein*] will simply no longer be content with the position Jews have thus far been alotted [in society]. Fairness, a sense of justice, humanity, ordinary reasonableness, urgently demand this equality; public opinion presses for it as it does for the abolition of serfdom and bondage."[123]

The *Kölnische Zeitung* made its turn to liberalism just as newspapers in general were becoming potent tools through which local Rhenish leaders, lacking true parliamentary power, attempted to influence state policy. From 1842 to 1848, as he battled the Prussian bureaucracy for adoption of protectionist tariffs crucial to his textile interests, David Hansemann, for instance, made the *Aachener Zeitung* his mouthpiece. After the Diet of 1845, the first in which he served as a delegate, Hansemann also used the paper as a platform from which to press for constitutional government and civil liberties, making it one of the important organs of the Rhenish liberal movement.[124] Gustav Mevissen had moved to Cologne in part because the city seemed a good possible base for a major newspaper in which he could promote his business and political ideas. He participated actively in the *Rheinische Zeitung* and, during Karl Andree's tenure, in the *Kölnische*. After 1845, the *Kölnische Zeitung* became Camphausen's organ; a new editor, Karl Heinrich Brüggemann, was his choice as much because of Brüggemann's support for Camphausen's views on free trade as for his liberal political credentials.

Camphausen and Hansemann used their newspapers to square off on the tariff issue. What is significant for our purposes is that both journals, the two most influential in the Rhine Province (the *Kölnische Zeitung* had over 8,000 subscribers in the mid-1840's), strongly backed emancipation at the seventh and eighth Rhenish Diets and at the First United Diet in 1847, helping to create and direct the surge of popular, but hardly spontaneous, pro-Jewish support that emerged in those years.[125]

The *Bürger* petitions for Jewish rights, for example, were given careful attention and encouragement by the *Kölnische Zeitung*. In 1843, the paper reported approvingly that the petition on emancipation presented to the seventh Diet was signed by "a considerable number of the most distinguished local citizens" (including the paper's publisher), as well as their counterparts in Bonn. In 1845 it went further, telling readers the locations where they might go to sign a similar petition themselves.[126]

Attached to the 1843 petition was a supplementary appeal for Jewish equality, which came from Cologne and was signed by a long list of its most illustrious citizens, including several members of the City Council and Chamber of Commerce. Citing the anachronism, injustice, and self-defeating character of current and proposed discrimination against the Jews, it asked, "Who among us does not sufficiently know honorable followers of that confession with whom he would gladly share concern for the good of the Fatherland and at whose side [he] would sit in deliberations thereon?"[127] The appeal, which called for full civic equality for "our Jewish brothers and fellow citizens," was presented to the Diet by none other than P. H. Merkens.

The 1845 petition to the Rhenish Diet on behalf of emancipation originated in Cologne and was circulated by its liberals to those of other provincial cities before being presented to the Diet. Thanks to some personal letters by Ludolf Camphausen, we can get a glimpse of how this support for Jewish rights was forged in the backroom politics surrounding the Diets. The information does not revolutionize our view of liberal support for the Jewish cause, but it does round it out, removing it from the realm of the near-heroic to the more recognizable one of everyday power broking. It also affords some valuable insight into the ways the Oppenheims used their position to further the Jewish cause.

To place these letters in context, we should note that the petitions on Jewish rights submitted to the Diets in 1843 and 1845 had their genesis in a broader petition campaign orchestrated by urban liberals and Diet deputies. Since the Diets had only consultative status, engineering manifestations of "popular" will was the best way to exercise indirect power.[128] Cologne's liberal elite was particularly articulate and active and had an excellent sense for the drama necessary to successful parliamentary politics. In June 1843, for example, over a thousand Cologne *Bürger* had sailed conspicuously to Düsseldorf, where the seventh Diet met, to present a torchlit recessional in honor of the liberal deputies who had fought the government's proposed penal code.[129] A petition backed by this group would have impact.

Ongoing defense of "Rhenish law" against the Prussian legal code and the debate over tariffs were the main concerns of Cologne's representatives at the seventh Diet; at the eighth, it was press freedom, open Diet sessions, and the demand for some form of national assembly. It is clear from several letters that Camphausen wrote to his brother Otto that he, at least, did not view Jewish emancipation as an essential concern and that it entered the agenda only through the dogged efforts of the Oppenheims. As Ludolf told Otto shortly after his election to the *Landtag* in 1843,

There are a variety of unreasonable demands [*Zumutungen*] for the *Landtag*. Abraham Oppenheim handed over to me an earlier petition [he had] presented to the King and delivered himself of a long, clever discourse in which he recommended that I raise myself up for the emancipation of the Jews.[130] A delegation of pharmacists hoped I would support their opposition to the cheap sale of their dispensaries. The shoemaker Schutzenbach, in the name of six hundred craftsmen, wanted to challenge a new trade ordinance through my intermediacy. David Hansemann asked for an interest guarantee for the share capital of the Rhenish Railway.[131]

There is no hostility to Jewish rights here, nothing approaching the rationalized Judeophobia of Karl Rotteck, a leading liberal in Baden, just a lack of zeal. It was a vacuum another Oppenheim rushed to fill. Once again, in Camphausen's words to Otto, this time describing the politicking preceding the eighth Diet,

After one consultation . . . there was another . . . whose prudence, determination, and unanimity not only satisfied but delighted even your friend [Dr. H.] Claessen [a prominent Cologne liberal]. The city of Cologne petitioned for calling the Estates of the Realm, for press freedom, the greatest possible openness at the proceedings of the impending Provincial Diet and (to please Oppenheim), for Jewish emancipation. All the notables, with few exceptions, will probably sign. The other cities will undoubtedly follow, as far as the Catholic church [*der Katholizismus*] does not prevent it.[132]

In fact, as Joseph Hansen tells us, it was not the "city" of Cologne that drafted these two petitions, but a group of its most important *Bürger*, gathered in Koblenz, where the eighth Diet was to meet. At the behest of Claessen and Gustav Mevissen, the group assembled three times in the second week of January 1845 to hammer out its platform. This is where the impetus for the plank on Jewish rights originated. That the Oppenheim the Cologne group sought to "please" was Dagobert, not Abraham, emerges from another reference.[133]

Realizing this is an important corrective to an almost heroic picture of Rhenish liberalism on the Jewish question, but it does not revise the picture fundamentally. The impassioned language of the petition on Jewish rights speaks for itself (see Appendix A). Nor is there any indication that anyone in the group from Cologne or on the floor of the Diet objected to the plea for Jewish rights. Cologne's *Bürger* may have seen this as the Oppenheims' "issue," but once raised it was accepted as compatible with other, ostensibly larger concerns considered the core of the liberal agenda.

Moreover, once the petition was made part of the Cologne program it received equal backing when Mevissen peddled it to representatives of the other Rhenish cities to which Camphausen had alluded. Jewish rights alone of all the petition's points encountered resistance in Mülheim—but only because, in the words of a local business associate to whom Mevissen had sent it for shepherding, "It is to be hoped the time is near when we may offer our humiliated fellow humans more [than this]; it is not worth playing the grand benefactors for so puny a thing [as a petition for equality]."[134]

Cologne's two petitions, which in Mevissen's estimation "were powerfully effective," were introduced onto the floor of the Diet by Ludolf Camphausen.[135] On March 12, 1845, a resolution calling for full Jewish emancipation passed the Diet by a margin of 56 to 16.[136]

Would Jewish rights have been endorsed by the Rhenish Diets without the Oppenheims' intervention? Conceivably. There was a substantial base of support for it, as we shall see, and at least one non-Jew, Mevissen, was a zealot for the cause. The Oppenheims were a persistent and efficacious prod but not the cause for liberal support of Jewish rights.

Cologne's prominence in that support, however, is attributable to the Oppenheims. Camphausen, we have seen, was no crusader for Jewish equality. Neither was Cologne's other Diet delegate, Merkens, nor for that matter was Mayor Steinberger, all of whose support for the cause was pragmatic. Of course, it is extremely significant that by the 1840's pragmatism recommended a stance in favor of emancipation, but it is important to realize that not all who backed Jewish rights were zealots.

One does wonder how Merkens's transformation on the Jewish question came about, but the rest of his long political career shows that he was capable of equally radical policy switches. The very longevity of his tenure in the Rhenish liberal movement indicates a capacity to adapt, since, as we have seen, the movement itself underwent fundamental change. Merkens made a complete turnaround on one of the core issues splitting the factions of the early liberal coalition: the attitude toward Prussian rule. Into the 1830's, he was a stubborn advocate of virtual autonomy for the Rhine Province, arguing that it be granted "its own legislature, administration and provincial representation."[137] In 1845, however, during the Rhenish Diet's debate over popular representation in a proposed national assembly, Merkens declared, "Above all, we want to be more Prussian than we are [now]."[138] We have also seen that Merkens's relations to the Oppenheims changed radically, from attempted shunning, first of Salomon and then of Abraham, in various business ventures to eventual partnership with Abraham in an insurance company by 1840.

As we know, Merkens's opposition to Jewish rights in the 1820's was partly visceral aversion to Jews, partly general elitism, and partly fear that the Chamber of Commerce would lose power through state-instigated dilution of its exclusivity. Far from losing power, however, the Chamber's influence grew in the 1830's and 1840's, becoming one of the most important organs of opposition to Prussian policy in the Rhine Province. Cologne's economy was expanding in unimagined directions and scale, a development in which the Oppenheims were instrumental. By the 1840's, the problem was not newcomers encroaching on the business community's privileges and status but the possibility that Berlin's economic policies would stymie further development. Cologne's Jews, by midcentury a predominantly middle-class group, were unobjectionable. So was the rest of the Rhineland's urban Jewish middle class. Discrimination was senseless, as Steinberger had argued, and Oppenheim, ever vigilant. Jewish equality was good business, good politics.[139]

But not all of Cologne's liberals, or those of the Rhineland, were as apathetic about emancipation as Camphausen, Merkens, and Steinberger. For all the unanimity of their public positions on emancipation, there was a wide range in the kind and depth of commitment they brought to the cause. Aside from the "pragmatists," there were two other "types" of liberals on the Jewish question: "rationalists," men of ideas whose broader philosophy necessitated support for Jewish rights but who lacked sympathy for real Jews, and "true believers," who felt the Jewish cause deeply and who needed no prodding or reward to support it.

Bruno Bauer and the other "Young Hegelians" at the *Rheinische Zeitung* were in the former category; so was Karl Heinrich Brüggemann, editor of the *Kölnische Zeitung* from October 1845 to 1855.[140] Brüggemann came to the paper with a proven liberal record. He had been a member of a politically radical *Burschenschaft* (student organization) in Heidelberg and a leading participant in the Hamburger *Fest* of 1832, which had called for a German constitutional republic. Prosecuted for "demagoguery," he was imprisoned, sentenced to death, and freed only by the amnesty Frederick William IV declared in 1840. Born a Catholic, Brüggemann had joined the liberal Protestant *Lichtfreunde* (Friends of Light) in Berlin and was an outspoken opponent of ultramontanism and of any clerical influence in politics. Barred by his political past from the academic career he would have preferred, Brüggemann was an anomaly in the business-dominated Rhenish liberal movement, which unlike its south German counterpart was relatively untheoretical and undogmatic. But Brüggemann was a man of ideas, author of several tracts on political and economic questions, and a former contributor to the *Rheinische Zeitung*. His appointment to the *Kölnische Zeitung* signaled that paper's decisive break with the Catholic party in the city and the province and its adoption of an oppositional stance to the government.[141]

Although not opposed to religion per se, Brüggemann wanted to see citizenship secularized and confession made irrelevant to civil status. Staunchly opposed to the "Christian state," he backed Jewish emancipation. But he did not like Jews very much, nor did he respect their religion and culture. As he confessed, Fichte-like, in a private letter in 1847, when the Jewish question was raised at the First United Diet,

As for the Jews, if all of them had but one head which lay right under the guillotine and I came along just then, I really don't know whether I wouldn't slice the rope and let the axe fall. Although I know valiant men among the Jews, the multitude of them is still less than agreeable to me. However, since they are already among us, I want to see them fully emancipated because the ongoing injustice corrupts their souls and ours. A brave attack which passes over like a lightning flash harms nothing, but a lingering rot and a stupid injustice darken [the] spirit's image of justice itself and brutalize it. The long injustice against the Jews has already so confused the Christians that most of them do not feel at all anymore the injustice which they inflict on the Jews through their laws.[142]

When Brüggemann attempted to turn the tables on the charge that he, and the *Kölnische Zeitung*, were "indifferent" to religion, and for this reason could support Jewish emancipation, he published the following in the paper:

The promotion of freedom of religion, or better, freedom of belief [*Konfessionsfreiheit*], is for us not the outcome of [religious] indifference but rather of religious confidence. We fight for the emancipation of the Jews precisely because their non-emancipation is Jewish [weil ihre Nichtemanzipation jüdisch ist], precisely because their emancipation is a consequence of the Christian state of our time and the realization [of that state's] deep trust in the omnipotence of the Christian spirit.[143]

Brüggemann did not so much champion the Jewish cause as oppose the government's policy. Jew-hatred might be understandable, but it made poor social policy.

Rhenish Liberals and the Jewish Question at the First United Diet, Berlin, 1847

If practical considerations brought businessmen to the Jewish cause and principle brought the theoreticians, it was something of both and more that brought the "true believers" — Mevissen of Cologne and Hermann Beckerath of Krefeld. There is a completely different tone to Mevissen's private and public utterances on the subject and to Beckerath's many speeches on behalf of Jewish rights at the Rhenish Diets and the First United Diet in 1847, than to those of Merkens, Camphausen, or Brüggemann.

By that year, the most onerous provisions of the infamous decree of 1808 had passed quietly out of existence through enactment of the General Trade Ordinance of 1845. The law abolished all trade restrictions, including the special business licenses required of Jews (with the exception of peddlers, of any religion, who would still require special permits).[144] But Jewish freedom of movement remained restricted under Article 16 of the 1808 decree, while many other disabilities under Prussian law or administrative ruling remained. Further, there was the threat of the king's proposed Jewry corporations and the reiteration of Jewish exclusion from high academic posts and public office, central features of draft legislation on the Jewish question that the government had submitted to the United Diet.

Frederick William was forced to call the United Diet because of a crisis in state finances, but the government also intended to use it to enact measures that would mold an officially Christian and unconstitutional Prussia. Liberals, Rhenish and otherwise, had a different agenda, including institutionalizing the Diet, expanding its competency, and pressuring the king to agree to a constitution assuring civil rights and responsibilities. To both throne and liberals, then, the status of religion and the churches was a vital concern, and this made the proposed Jewry law a central concern as well. A state in which enjoyment of full civil and political rights depended on membership in the church — and the right one, at that — was anathema to Rhenish liberals and a threat to their own freedom of conscience. Hansemann, Camphausen, Merkens, Mevissen, Lensing, and Beckerath led Rhine Province delegates to a resounding 44-to-14-vote endorsement of a Beckerath cosponsored proposal granting full emancipation — which the United *Landtag* rejected by a vote of 220 to 186.

Jewish rights and self-interest were intertwined for all the members of this group, but self-interest can be understood and expressed in different ways. Hansemann, for instance, who like Camphausen felt considerable ambivalence about Jews, argued pragmatically that discriminatory legislation would drive them out of Prussia to more liberal states, much as persecution had once driven Huguenots and old Lutherans to more tolerant environments.[145] "In the interest of the state, in the interest of the welfare of the country, I implore you," he asked the delegates, "accept [Beckerath's] proposal."[146]

Beckerath's reasoning was of a different order. Beckerath was a Mennonite. Any suggestion of religious tests for political rights (the government had proposed making active and passive voting rights to the Diets contingent on membership in "tolerated Christian communities") was a chilling reminder of past discrimination and a threat to his own group's civic status.

A deeply religious man, he argued passionately against religious coercion or favoritism in public life and against the Court's projected Christian state:

> Gentlemen: religious convictions, the relation of a man to his creator, lie entirely outside the sphere of the state. It is a sacred prerogative of the individual. . . . Political rights are the noblest of man's possessions. His best powers remain undeveloped if he is deprived of active participation in the state, and it cannot surprise [us] if bitter feelings seize those whom the Fatherland rejects unloved. . . . Christianity is a religion of love, justice, of the noblest humanity. How then, can it lead to cruelty, to unjust and inhuman acts?
>
> The Christian character of the state rests not on confession . . . [but] on the spirit of Christianity. . . . I beg you, let us remember the dictum: what you would not wish on yourselves, do not do unto others. Let us not exclude anyone upon whom God has imprinted the everlasting seal of his likeness from the circle of human rights. Let us not deprive any of our brothers of a right because he holds fast to that which is highest to each of us, namely, that he serves God according to his own persuasion.[147]

Rising again to speak for the full civil equality of Jews — till now he had been arguing on behalf of members of Christian sects not yet recognized by the state — Beckerath made similar points, appealing to the delegates' moral self-interest: "We are not only talking about justice for the Jews but [about] preserving our own state interest, [about] whether the principle of Christian morality, of right and freedom in the state, is to be realized or renounced. The injustice which we perpetrate on the Jews has negative repercussions on us. So long as the Jews are not free, we ourselves are not free."[148]

It was similar with Mevissen, who was outraged by the government's proposed Jewry law. His remarks on the subject have not been studied by Jewish or German historians. I quote them here because of Mevissen's immense importance in nineteenth-century Germany history but especially because of the central place that Jewish civic equality held in Mevissen's social vision and in his German nationalism.

The 1847 law, Mevissen said, "threatens to hurl this question [of Jewish civic status] backward several centuries."[149] It represented a betrayal of the religious tolerance and freedom of thought that Germany had learned with such pain after its religious wars. The fact that freedom of the spirit had first emerged through the struggles of German history was one of Germany's greatest national glories and one of the "greatest events of world history." The government's plans would have matters "revert to the religious notions of previous centuries, which were vanquished in bloody battle. . . . [But] I do not believe that we, after having overcome [intolerance], would consider it progress to return to harshness and obstinacy, as is now happening. I believe, rather, that this phenomenon is the most unwelcome and deplorable, the most malignant to national development."

The government had proposed a clause in the law that would bar non-Christians from academic positions in law, philosophy, or history on the grounds that such subjects needed to be infused with "Christian spirit." Mevissen responded:

Sirs, I ask you. Let us ponder the consequences of this clause, because it pertains to the deepest, most powerful, and most dangerous [of proposals] we have examined. . . . If it can be granted, even for an instant, that a certain spirit can be made statutory by the state . . . then this is the end of freedom of inquiry [*freien Wissenschaft*]. Could we even recognize freedom of knowledge . . . of research and teaching, where a government imposes on the representatives of knowledge the requirement of arriving at a fixed result, at a government-set conception of the Christian spirit? . . . Freedom of knowledge exists only by . . . throwing off all bonds, all assumptions . . . by acknowledging as correct and true only that which it has discovered on the road of free inquiry.

If you wish to postulate the Christian state . . . it is the end of further development of our people, indeed of all Christian humanity. I would hold such a moment as the saddest . . . of my life. . . .

Therefore, I ask you, I beg you, gentlemen! Let us keep all religious divisions far from us, let us honor the free spirit of German knowledge, let us recognize that our people has ascended too high in its culture [*Bildung*] to give room to any religious intolerance, [to] any unjustified coercion of mind.[150]

In another address to the Diet on emancipation, Mevissen argued, Dohm-like, that whatever clannishness Jews demonstrated was the result of Christian persecution, not Mosaic law, as the government maintained: "After centuries of having been forced to live despised, degraded, isolated, and dispersed among Christians, it would be a wonder if a spirit of hatred, separation, and enmity against Christians had not developed among these Jews." Yet despite oppression, the small Jewish minority had contributed mightily to European intellectual life. "Could we imagine German philosophy without Baruch Spinoza [or] the efforts in the sphere of humanity at the end of the last century without Moses Mendelssohn? And has not the Jewish spirit grown in a thousand directions with all the [spiritual] endeavors of the present?" Jews, admittedly, tended to journalism, to the literature of "despair and *Weltschmerz*," a genre they were chiefly responsible for introducing to Germany. But "who could maintain today that he had remained untouched by this . . . outpouring, that he had absorbed nothing from this spirit of derision and perplexity?" If Germany wanted less of this kind of creativity, it must stop the oppression, "that accursed state of affairs," that produced it, a reform that would redound even more to the general benefit than to that of the Jewish minority.

By contrast, the government's proposed Jewry law, he said, would perpetuate the very ills it decried:

We all have the greatest interest in [seeing] national unity in our Fatherland come about, in [seeing] all division and isolation vanish. This division . . . can only disappear, however, when equal rights and equal duties are granted to all citizens, when consciousness of freedom and equality establish and sustain in all the love of the Fatherland. We demand, as we must demand of Jewry, that it become Prussian, that it become German; we cannot allow that the Jew shut himself out from the Fatherland, that he consider himself not as our equal co-citizen but as a scorned, rightless alien. In our own interest, we cannot, we must not [allow] it. [But] in order for the Jew living among us to become Prussian . . . to belong to our state with heart and soul, we must grant the rights which the human in the Jew [der Mensch in dem Juden] claims, the rights which he demands as the inalienable possession of his human nature.

Mevissen closed with an appeal for a vote in favor of full emancipation, less for the sake of the Jews than the non-Jews, that the Christian spirit might demonstrate itself free of the fetters of prejudice, "that we Christians might become free of the guilt which the past has transmitted to us, of the sin with which we ourselves burden the present through ongoing injustice."[151]

Even more telling than Mevissen's passionate public utterances on the Jewish question are several personal letters he wrote after the United Diet had convened but before the question had come up for formal debate. They show dramatically that the Jewish cause was not only one of Mevissen's highest political priorities but a personal crusade central to his identity.

"Yesterday and today," he reported in May 1847, "one of the greatest questions of the day, the separation of church and state, came up for discussion. The Chamber is not yet ripe for this question, however, and rejected this great principle by 308 to 159. A bad omen for the Jewish question," he concluded.[152] Several days later, in a letter to his wife, Elise, Mevissen wrote:

There are still very few men indeed who have the courage to lift their gaze beyond their own narrow interests to the free and beautiful ideal of humanity, few who dare to be completely sincere. As [is the case] everywhere, so here in Berlin, too, the truth is not always a welcome guest. But this observation, renewed [by what I see here], cannot distract me either in my faith or my hope. What does not happen today can happen tomorrow, and if not tomorrow — then the day after. The question for the individual is only how much perseverance, how much vigor he possesses. He who for years anticipates the future waits calmly at the lookout; youth will gradually follow. What today is heresy and madness will be truth and wisdom ten years from now. For the most part, it is difficult for each person to remain true to himself . . . [not] to violate his own conviction. The Jews have lost the battle for now. The Chamber rejected political rights for all without regard to religion . . . by 312–159. Thus, two-thirds of [the men in] the Chamber are, for now, religious minors—and the German people wants to complain that the princes take it for political minors!

As long as the German people is not able to recognize the purely human in everyone and the rights founded on this reality, so long as people with privilege fight only for their privileges [and] not for everyone, not for an infinite and universal idea, the German people is not worthy of freedom. I cannot relinquish this idealism which dwells deep within me. It is the center of gravity of my entire personality, the Archimedean screw, by means of which I have remained myself, through each metamorphosis of life till now.

This idealism, this zeal and unshaken belief in all which ever was, is, and will be great and holy . . . I place with trust in your lap, . . . I give it to you as a pledge . . . with thanks for everything beautiful that you have given me. . . . Forward without looking right or left! Only the valiant will triumph, and if he falls in battle, he falls with honor.[153]

Such sentiments clearly surpassed material or political self-interest. If "obsessed" is perhaps too strong a characterization for Mevissen's commitment to Jewish equality, he was certainly preoccupied with it. In a letter to the editorial staff of the *Kölnische Zeitung* reporting on the United Diet's early business, the government's proposed Jewry law was the first of five items he mentioned; Jewish rights were hardly the afterthought for Mevissen that they had been in a similar letter Camphausen, we recall, wrote during the seventh Rhenish Diet.[154] Having written to alert Abraham Oppenheim about the law so "the Jews might energetically protest it," Mevissen confessed himself "pleased [to learn] that . . . Oppenheim is coming here [to Berlin]. This Jewry law is hideous [*scheusslich*] in its present form and nevertheless will be defended by the government with the utmost determination, perhaps the most fiercely of all laws. This law infuriates me to the depths of my soul, and that could certainly be the point where I could lose my remaining restraint toward the government."[155]

Although the United Diet ultimately rejected emancipation by 215 to 185, Mevissen had the satisfaction of seeing the government's proposal amended substantially for the better, subject, of course, to the king's desires. ("What the final upshot of the deliberation will be, I don't know at this moment," he wrote on June 19. "A good one, I hope!"[156]) As the Chamber's debate on Jewish rights came to an end, Mevissen reflected contentedly on his own role in it:

My best wishes accompany this question of humanity [elsewhere he called it "this highly significant matter"]. Today in the Chamber I delivered a very short speech [which,] however, if I do not deceive myself, [was] an effective address for the freedom of German thought and German belief, a speech which powerfully affected all hearers with its true inner enthusiasm. I think this speech will constitute the culmination [*Schlusspunkt*] of my current endeavors, were it not that the great question of press freedom requires me to take the stand . . . yet again. I am pleased with my work here, and in any case I take a clear conscience home [knowing that] I fought in the front ranks with my best powers and best determination for the development of the Fatherland in the greatest historical moment of the century. All future United Diets will be placed in the shadow of this first one, because the foundation of a great national structure can be laid but once.[157]

History would soon prove this last assessment false. More important than Mevissen's prognostication, however, was his conviction that the Jewish and broader German struggles for constitutionally guaranteed freedom of conscience were indivisible and that the Jewish question, far from being peripheral, was the very heart of the matter.

As we have seen, not all of Cologne's liberals who backed Jewish emancipation saw the centrality of it. Some who did understood its importance intellectually but did not feel it emotionally, as Mevissen did. Given the diversity of attitude behind a common outward stance, no one factor can be said to have caused the groundswell for Jewish rights among the middle class, business elite, and intellectuals of Cologne and, I would venture, of the Rhineland. Oppenheim influence appears to have been decisive with Cologne's City Council and Chamber of Commerce; it was superfluous with Mevissen and would probably have been counterproductive with Brüggemann. Of course, given Cologne's economic and political primacy in the Rhine Province, the support of its official and semiofficial organs was a great asset to the Jewish cause. The leading role that Cologne's representatives played in the Provincial Diets was a tremendous accomplishment for the movement for Jewish emancipation in the Rhineland and Prussia and a reflection of Oppenheim clout. It is the more impressive given the City's reactionary stance only two or three decades (not to mention centuries) before.

Cologne underwent extraordinary transformation in these years. One sign of the radically altered circumstances was the election of Abraham Oppenheim to the City Council shortly after the enactment of Prussia's Communal Statute of 1845.[158] Oppenheim served briefly, but in heady times. He was in office in 1847, while the First United Diet was in session, and he undoubtedly used his influence to have the following paragraph included in a lengthy petition the Council addressed to Cologne's representatives at the Diet, Camphausen and Merkens:

Full equality of civil and political rights for Jews: It is futile to seek justification for the hitherto existing restriction of the Jews in their moral and national circumstances. In its origin and duration, [Jewish] oppression is based on an intolerable encroachment into a sphere from which the influence of political power should be removed. According to the experience of foreign states [France], no danger but rather a beneficial effect is to be anticipated from Jewish equality. This measure promises justice to Christian citizens [*Staatsgenossen*], especially the reward . . . that they will contribute powerfully toward establishing . . . religious tolerance in followers of Christian denominations.

The other points on the petition were the central issues of the Rhenish liberal agenda: open sessions of all Diets, abolition of censorship; and securing of personal freedom.[159] Fifty years after emerging from physical and social segregation, the Jews of Cologne had emerged from the political ghetto as well.

CHAPTER SIX

Profile of the Jewish Group in the Era of Liberal Ascendancy, 1835–48

Vormärz, the years between the Restoration and the Revolution of 1848, was a time not only of political and economic transformation, but of tremendous demographic change in the Rhine Province and Cologne. Between 1816 and 1844, the population of the province grew from 1.8 to 2.8 million.[1] Although the pace of industrialization and urbanization intensified, particularly after 1850, significant migration to cities, especially to the old commercial and manufacturing centers, began earlier. The populations of Cologne, Aachen, Elberfeld, Barmen, and Krefeld grew tremendously (from 49,000 to 88,000, 32,000 to 50,000, 21,000 to 35,000, 19,000 to 35,000, and 13,000 to 35,000, respectively). The average rate of urban increase was 84 percent for the period, most of this the result of immigration.[2] Cologne remained the most populous city in the province.

Jewish Migration and Urbanization

Provincial officials in the 1830's were very concerned about Jewish immigration, viewing it as virtually out of control. The Jewish population did increase substantially, largely because of immigration, although at a less spectacular rate than that of the general population: from 1823 to 1843 it rose by 33 percent, from 20,762 to 27,570.[3] But there was also considerable Jewish movement within the province, contributing, perhaps, to the exaggerated official impression of immigration.[4] While not all the internal migration was to cities — Rhenish Jews, like other German Jews, did not necessarily move only to cities in these years — there was a clear Jewish trend to urbanization on the Rhine well before midcentury.[5] As Table 10 shows, the populations of all but one of eight Rhenish cities with relatively large Jewish settlements in 1823 increased substantially during the next twenty years, with an 85 percent increase overall. While Rhenish Jewry remained over-

TABLE 10
Jewish Population Growth in Rhenish Cities, 1823–42

| City | Population size | | Increase (%) |
	1823	1842	
Bonn	474	1107	133
Cologne	354	784	121
Düsseldorf	315	553[a]	76
Krefeld	248[a]	592	139
Koblenz	256	349	36
Trier	232	369	59
Mülheim	220	123	−44
Aachen	114	223	96
TOTAL	2,213	4,100	85

SOURCES: Kober, *Cologne*, pp. 328-29; Sterling, "Der Kampf", p. 307, n. 2; *Statistik und Hand-Adressbuch;* Keyser, ed., *Städtebuch Rheinland;* id., *Rheinisches Städtebuch;* Ayçoberry, "Histoire Sociale," 1: 4–5, 2, "Population de la ville de Cologne."
[a]Approximate number.

TABLE 11
Increase in the Total and Jewish Populations of Cologne,
1837–49

Year	Total population	Jewish population	Jewish %
1837	65,296	454	0.7
1840	70,999	615	0.8
1843	78,513	784	1
1845	85,195	824	1
1846	85,446	974	1.1
1848	86,671	981	1.1
1849	88,356	1,286	1.4

SOURCES: Ayçoberry, "Histoire Sociale," 2: 4–5, 105–6, 97, Table 13a. Figures for the Jewish population in the years for which Ayçoberry provides no data are taken from Kober, *Cologne*, pp. 328–29.
NOTE: Kober's figures for the total and, at times, the Jewish populations often vary with Ayçoberry's.

whelmingly (61 percent) rural, the segment living in larger cities had risen to 26 percent in 1843, more than double the percentage (11 percent) of the total population living in middle-sized and large cities combined.[6]

Cologne was clearly one of the more popular choices of urbanizing Jews. Its Jewish population increased from 454 to 1,286 in the twelve years between 1837 and 1849 alone (see Table 11), with immigration responsible for much of that growth. According to my reconstruction, 668 Jews came to the city between 1835 and 1846 alone (the only years for which data are available for a yearly calculation of immigration; see Table 12). Immigra-

TABLE 12
Jewish and General Immigration to Cologne, 1835–46

	No. of general immigrants (including Jews)		No. of Jewish immigrants	
	Yearly average	Total	Yearly average	Total
1835–37	357	1,071	40	120
1838–40	1,190	3,570	45	136
1841–43	1,778	5,334	56	168
1844–46	1,331	3,933	81	244
TOTAL		13,908[a]		668[c]
		13,240[b]		

SOURCES: Ayçoberry, "Histoire Sociale," 2: 8–9, App. 3, 3A. *HASK,* Oberbürgermeisteramt, 403, Abteilung 11, Caps 23, Band III; 400, II-4-B-1; *Judenpatente;* 400, II-4-D-1, Jewish population lists of Jan. 19, 30, 1844, Sept. 1844 (3758/3, no. 2756), Sept. 1, 1845, Sept. 2, 1846 (1ten Bezirk), Sept. 2, 1846 (2ten Bezirk), Sept. 4, 1846 (4ten Bezirk), and Sept. 4, 1846 (5ten Bezirk). See also Kober, *Cologne;* Brisch; and Weyden.
    NOTE: For the methodology used in this table, see Appendix B.
[a]Including Jews.
[b]Excluding Jews.
[c]Represents 5 percent of the total immigrant pool.

tion seems to have remained high even during the crisis years preceding the 1848 revolution, since the Jewish population increased by some 350 between 1846 and midcentury.[7] There was a 23 percent increase in the number of names (from 175 to 215) appearing on the synagogue tax lists between 1845 and 1848, a rise surely due largely to immigration.[8] The Jewish pattern of continuing immigration even in these years contrasts with that of the non-Jewish population, whose immigration to the city dropped sharply between 1845 and 1848.[9]

As noted above, Cologne's total population increased enormously from the Prussian takeover to the mid-1840's, half of this growth coming from immigration.[10] Between 1835 and 1846 some 1,000 immigrants a year, excluding Jews, came to Cologne, a yearly immigration rate of 8 percent (see Table 12). Yet, even in this context, the rate of Jewish immigration was remarkable; Jews, who never constituted more than 1.1 percent of the total population during this decade, made up 5 percent of the immigrants (see Table 12). The Jewish rate of natural increase, moreover, was higher than that of the general population.[11]

As before, Jewish immigrants to Cologne came overwhelmingly from the Rhine Province and neighboring Westphalia, nearly half from towns and cities of no more than 10,000 inhabitants, 58 percent from Jewish communities numbering 100 or fewer Jews. The move to Cologne meant a radical change from small settlements and Jewish communities to a huge metropolis and a relatively large Jewish community.

Why did these Jews come, and how did city and state authorities respond to the influx?

Historians of German Jewry have shown that migration, whether local or long distance, internal or to foreign destinations, was a major means of betterment for Jews, the vast majority of whom were poor at the beginning of the nineteenth century.[12] Because provincial officials required immigrants to apply for settlement permission and state their reasons for moving, we have rich information about the motives of Cologne's Jewish immigrants and can see how consciously they tied migration to betterment.

Jews gave three sometimes overlapping reasons for immigrating: to follow family members or acquaintances who had settled in Cologne; to seek superior educational facilities; and, the overwhelming majority, to seek greater economic opportunity and betterment.

Ties of family and friendship served as a lure for Jews of all economic classes to join relatives and friends in Cologne. A poor Jewish widow from Deutz hoped to join her sons living in Cologne and there nurse her failing health; an elderly butcher from Mülheim explained that while he was no longer capable of running his business independently, he could operate it jointly with a son living in Cologne.[13] Two members of the Oppenheim family also joined their relatives in Cologne, one to pursue banking, the other living off his means, all within close proximity of each other in a wealthy part of town.[14] Dates on the immigration records of other Jews indicate that relatives and friends from the same town often immigrated together or within a short time of one another, a common pattern among immigrants of all nationalities, reflecting a conscious attempt to mitigate the disruptive emotional effects of migration as well as to facilitate upward mobility.[15]

The superior educational facilities of cities are known to have drawn upwardly mobile Jews and was the stated reason of several Jewish immigrants to Cologne.[16] One Jew from a small town near Cologne wanted to enroll his handicapped child in an institution for the deaf and dumb in the city (he also said he wanted to expand his business as a butcher, livestock dealer, and cloth manufacturer).[17] Hermann Hersch, an author and poet from Juchen, held clerical positions in Jewish businesses in Düsseldorf but moved to Cologne to pursue the higher education he needed in order to enter university. Hersch was able to gain the support of the editor of the *Kölnische Zeitung*, as well as that of another local man of letters, and did eventually matriculate at the University of Bonn.[18]

The most common reason for wishing to move to Cologne was the hope of economic improvement. Two brothers from Ehrenbreitstein, a small town of some 2,000 inhabitants near Koblenz, wished to relocate their business in manufactured goods to Cologne "because they expect to be able to pursue [it] with greater profit here." A Jew from Düsseldorf wanted to immigrate in order to become a master in a cigar factory and "improve his circumstances." A businessman from Elberfeld, one of the Rhenish cities experiencing significant population growth in these years, nevertheless wished to move to Cologne "because the expansion of his business makes it necessary to found an establishment in this city," by far the largest in the province. A butcher from Deutz wished to move "because he [already] has many customers here" and because he expected "to be able to provide a better living for his [seven] children, of whom one is a doctor and two attended the higher *Bürgerschule*" of Cologne. Even a Torah scribe foresaw better opportunities in Cologne, stating that "the local Israelite community is more numerous and therefore the possibility better for making a living."[19]

Municipal attitudes toward Jewish immigration were a mix of broader concerns about immigration, poverty and poor relief in the city, and a specific posture toward Jews. Despite some local sentiment to the contrary, from the French years on, Cologne was open to immigration, without a "means test" or other municipal controls on internal migrants. Even when city poor-relief services were severely strained in 1846 by the immigration of desperate migrants from the countryside, the City Council, led by liberal members, refused to limit immigration to those able to pay an admission tax.[20] Jewish immigrants, however, were subject to Article 16 of the 1808 decree, which, from the mid-1820's on, had been used largely as a means test to keep poor Jews out. Thus, while there was plenty of middle-class anxiety about immigration of the poor, the only immigrants to Cologne the city actually controlled for wealth were Jews.[21]

In contrast to earlier years, documents from City Council sessions in which Jewish petitions for settlement permission were considered show that while occupational background and occupational intent mattered, wealth ultimately decided a prospective immigrant's case. The same documents show that Prussian provincial authorities, who had the final say in immigration questions, showed particular solicitude for the applications of wealthy Jews.

Thus, Mayor Steinberger strongly recommended approval of the settlement petition of a Jew from Hamm who had no trade but who "lives off his not inconsiderable means [and who] is known personally by the Governor [of the Rhine Province] to be . . . wealthy." The Mayor pointedly noted that the Ministry of Interior desired a positive outcome to the man's settlement petition. The Ministry was not disappointed.[22]

Another Jew, originally from Hannover, more recently from Elberfeld, not only had positive character endorsements, the City Council reported but nearly 7,000 taler that he had placed at the disposal of a local (non-

Jewish) entrepreneur. He soon had official settlement permission as well.[23] The application of another Jew, who in 1849 would appear on a list of the city's most endowed citizens, received the special consideration of provincial authorities, who also took the extraordinary step of referring to the man as "Bürger Horn" (this, in contrast to two less well-endowed applicants, called in official correspondence "the Jew-brothers Goldschmidt").[24] The City Council, equally uncharacteristically, expressed its approval for Horn's request directly, rather than taking refuge in the double negatives it usually used in cases involving Jewish settlement: "The City Council spoke for the approval of this request," it said, instead of its formulaic, "The City Council has nothing against this request."[25]

Poor Jews, on the other hand, Jews without fixed and secure livelihoods, and Jews with a history of past financial difficulties, were quickly denied settlement permission. The widow from Deutz mentioned above failed to win provincial or municipal approval for her settlement request. "She barely has any means," the City Council noted, "and lives off the earnings of her children" (both of whom were artisans and none too secure themselves). The Royal Government rejected her settlement request "because she is without means and incapable of work [while] her children's earnings are very uncertain" and denied subsequent appeals.

In only one instance was Article 16 of the 1808 decree cited in support of a denial of a settlement request, but the objection that the applicant (here, too, a woman) had no intention of becoming a farmer was an absurd pretext, because this was true of all the Jews who received settlement permission. The Council's real concern was the bankruptcy the woman's husband had suffered some years before and the fact that she herself was a petty dealer of manufactured goods. "This community is overburdened with petty dealers of this sort and it is, therefore, to be feared that she would not be able to find a livelihood here," Mayor Steinberger wrote. "Not a welcome addition," noted the deputy mayor, who first suggested Article 16 as a means to keep the woman out.[26]

We should note that official settlement permission was required for receipt of a *Judenpatent*, without which the immigrant could not conduct legally recognized business. In a commercial center of Cologne's size, full control over Jewish immigration was impossible and the documents amply illustrate that many Jews lived and worked in the city for years without one or both papers. The authorities, therefore, could not simply "[pick] the Jews who might settle in Cologne," unerringly filtering out the poor, as Adolf Kober implies. Poor Jews did immigrate to Cologne, as Kober himself notes.[27] The mayor himself testified that such Jews often turned not to city poor relief, to which they were legally entitled, but to the Jewish com-

munity, "[becoming] a burden to their coreligionists residing here, in ill-
ness and other misfortunes [making] claims [on them] rather than on
public welfare."[28]

Age Structure, Household Size, and Composition

Economic vigor is directly related to age. While the records show that Jews
in Cologne remained economically active into their 80's, significant change
in type or scale of occupation was more likely to occur among the young.
Analysis of several house-to-house surveys of the Jewish population in 1845
and 1846 shows that Cologne's adult Jewish population was relatively
youthful: 91 out of 154 economically independent men and married women
were between the ages of 22 and 41. Some 60 percent of 190 Jewish households in 1844 consisted of married couples, and most of these had children
living at home.[29] This, too, would make for an economically active population, especially since 30 percent of Jewish couples had five or more children
present in the home in 1844 (see Table 13). These demographic data depict
a Jewish group brimming, as Pierre Ayçoberry says of Cologne as a whole,
"with the traits of an optimistic and vigorous society" transformed from
what it had been just a decade or two before.[30]

Occupational Structure and Mobility

In the history of Jewish emancipation in the Rhine Province, 1845 was
arguably as great a watershed as 1848. It was the year of a new *Gewer-
beordnung* (trade regulation) that, among other reforms, abolished the
economic discrimination of the 1808 decree.[31] Discrimination did not
cease, as the framers of the "infamous decree" had intended, because Jews
had abandoned commerce for crafts and farming but because of a broader
Prussian policy favoring minimum government regulation of the economy,
a continuation of the laissez-faire economics that underlay Prussian support
for Jewish settlement and trade in Cologne in the 1820's.

The 1808 decree was not so much abolished as retired, succumbing to
the anachronism with which it had been afflicted since birth. Yet, while the
Jews of Cologne did not change their occupational profile in the ways the
decree had demanded, like other segments of German Jewry in this period,
they did undergo some important occupational change.[32]

The following analysis examines Jewish economic function and mobility
separately. The aim first is simply to map out what Jews did for a living
during this period compared to the earlier one and to assess how their

TABLE 13
Jewish Family Size, 1844

	Number of Children											
	0	1	2	3	4	5	6	7	8	9	10	13
Families with that number	5	19	21	22	19	6	10	8	2	6	1	1

SOURCE: Population survey of Jan. 19, 1844, *HASK,* Oberbürgermeisteramt, 400, II-4-D-1.

NOTE: Out of a total of 190 families, 115 had children. The total number of children was 442; the average per family was 3.8. Although the source does not specify if the number of children listed was the total born to the family or only those then living at home, it is likely that the number reflects a count only of resident children.

activities fit into the broader economic scene in Cologne. Only then can we grasp the range of opportunities for occupational mobility open to Jews, measure change in the type and scale of occupation Jews practiced, and evaluate the success Jews were able to achieve in years when precisely those sectors of the economy in which they were concentrated improved.[33] The questions are, To what extent did Jews enjoy the fruits of a rebounding economy even while their legal status languished in a state of "half citizenship"?[34] What difference did inequality make to the material advancement of Cologne's Jews?

Table 14 compares Jewish occupational stratification in 1835 and 1844 and shows three major areas of change. Most striking is the sharp decline in Jewish banking activities at all levels, from 20 percent of occupations to 6 percent. Lottery collecting, which blossomed in the 1820's and 1830's as a form of petty banking, especially as a side occupation of economically marginal Jews, shrank from one-half to one-third of all Jewish credit activities, and from 10 to 2 percent of Jewish occupations overall. Money changing, common in the French and early Prussian years, virtually disappeared. The decline in these branches is attributable to a more stable and homogeneous currency supply and to a more developed banking system, including a city-chartered savings and loan that served Cologne's poorer classes (an institution, albeit, run by Jews until midcentury).[35]

The second important change is in the increase (from 8 to 13 percent) in the proportion of Jews engaged in crafts, striking because Cologne's artisanal class grew increasingly stressed in these years.[36] Yet, as we shall see, Cologne's Jewish artisans, and their non-Jewish counterparts, were a varied lot and not by any means all poor. We know from evidence elsewhere that crafts were often an avenue of upward mobility for poor Jews, who used them to secure a minimal livelihood, to learn a trade that could later be practiced independently, and, often, to enjoy the benefit of board that came with apprenticeship, all without capital investment.[37] Indeed, evidence

TABLE 14
Jewish Occupational Structure, 1835, 1844

	1835		1844	
Occupation	No.	% of total	No.	% of total
Commerce				
Trade	26		64	
Business ownership	1		5	
Butchering	13		21	
Commission sales; commodity brokering	5		5	
Peddling	2		1	
TOTAL	47	54	96	51
Money and Credit				
Banking	5		3	
Director of savings and loan			1	
Currency changing	3		4	
Lottery collecting	9		4	
TOTAL	17	20	12	6
Manufacturing				
Writing materials	1			
Oilcloth and wallpaper	0		1	
Distilled spirits	0		1	
TOTAL	1	1	2	1
Crafts				
Watchmaking	0		4	
Gold- and silversmithing	2		5	
Bookbinding	0		3	
Tanning	0		3	
Oil, oil and gypsum or rock milling	2		2	
Master tailoring	0		1	
Master shoemaking	0		1	
Hatmaking	1		2	
Stocking weaving	0		1	
Metal and stone engraving	1		1	
Typefounding	0		1	
Saddler	1			
TOTAL	7	8	24	13
Salaried employment				
Business assistant	2		3	
Cashier's assistant	0		1	
Railroad management's cashier	0		1	
TOTAL	2	2	5	3
Services				
Commodities forwarding	0		1	
Innkeeping	3		3	
Rental of horses, books	3		0	
TOTAL	6	7	3	2
Professions				
Teacher				
Hebrew	2		0	
Other languages	1		2	
Music	1		0	
Unspecified			1	

TABLE 14
(continued)

	1835		1844	
Occupation	No.	% of total	No.	% of total
Headmaster of trade school	0		1	
Doctor	2		5	
Optician	0		2	
Lithographer	0		1	
TOTAL	6	7	12	6
Synagogue functionary				
Cantor	0		1	
TOTAL	0	0	1	0.5
Pensioners	1		6	
TOTAL	1	1	6	3
Without a trade	1		26	
TOTAL	1	1	26	14
TOTAL for all occupations	88		187	
TOTAL individuals	81		187	

SOURCE: See Table 12.

NOTE: This table shows the number of times a given occupation was practiced by Jews. Because some individuals practiced more than one occupation, the number of occupations is higher than the number of individuals.

from Cologne shows that immigration for betterment and the practice of a craft could be linked, as in the case of a Jew from Düsseldorf who asked for settlement permission in Cologne in order to work as a master in a cigar factory run by non-Jews, through which appointment he intended "to better [his] position."[38] The upswing in Jewish crafts in Cologne was part of a broader if short-lived phenomenon in German Jewry in the first half of the century, linked to a corresponding decline in such occupations of poverty as peddling, menial work, and domestic service, which had earlier typified German Jews.[39] The growth of a Jewish artisanal class, therefore, should not necessarily be taken as a sign of economic distress, but may in fact signal a route for betterment by some of the community's poorest members. Both trends in Cologne — the shift out of money trades and the growth of Jewish crafts — accord with Avraham Barkai's observations about the occupational structure of German Jewry during the period of early industrialization.

The third major change was a marked increase in the proportion of Jews designated as *ohne Gewerbe*, without a trade. The reasons for this are not clear, nor is the real meaning of being "without a trade," which does not necessarily signify unemployment and poverty. Occupational titles were very inexact in this period. Wealthy Jews could have been listed with this title although they were not unemployed but economically inactive by choice, as was the case of one *Rentner*, a very wealthy pensioner, listed on the 1844 population survey as "without a trade."[40] Thus, we cannot know what the increase in this group really meant and can only say the designation covered a heterogeneous group.

How does the occupational structure of Cologne's Jews compare with that of the rest of Prussian Jewry in these years? Heinrich Silbergleit and Jacob Toury provide comparative data for 1834 and 1848, respectively.[41] Silbergleit's figures exclude the heavily rural province of Posen; Toury's include it. In both cases, we find Cologne's Jews more concentrated in trade of all kinds, including money trades (56 percent of Jews in Cologne in 1844 compared to 49 percent in Prussia in 1834 and 45 percent in 1848), with fewer salaried employees and day laborers (3 percent in Cologne compared to 10 and 14 percent in Prussia in 1834 and 1848); and, in 1848, with a higher percentage of professionals (8 percent in Cologne compared to 3 percent in Prussia). In 1834, around 10 percent of Jews in Cologne and in all of Prussia, excluding Posen, practiced a craft. With statistics from Posen included, the middle-class character of Cologne's community emerges more sharply: 20 percent of Prussian Jews, compared to 12 percent of those in Cologne, practiced a craft; 10 percent of Prussian Jewry (excluding Posen, where there was much Jewish poverty) were peddlers in 1834, compared to the virtual nonexistence of peddling among Cologne Jews in 1844.

Most comparisons of Jewish and non-Jewish occupational stratification in nineteenth-century Germany survey state or national populations. So constructed, they pit a predominantly mercantile and relatively urbanized Jewish population against a predominantly agrarian and rural non-Jewish one and draw the classic conclusions about Jews and precocious embourgeoisement.[42] It is particularly telling to make the occupational comparison *within* a large urban context—and still find a distinct Jewish economic character.

As comparison of Tables 14 and 15 shows, there were glaring distinctions between the Jewish and non-Jewish economic profiles in Cologne at mid-century. Half of the working Jewish population practiced some form of trade while half of the non-Jewish population practiced some level of crafts. A much higher percentage of the Jewish group was professional, while no Jews were in government employ ("functionaries") — a significant occupational category in a city with a major military and administrative presence, and one closed by law to Jews. Absent, too, are Jews earning their livelihood from cultivation of the land, as some 2,000 non-Jews did as late as 1860,[43] eloquent testimony, were any needed, of the inefficacy of efforts to steer Jews into farming.

Other distinctions in the economic function of Jews and non-Jews not visible in Tables 14 and 15 are important to note. Manufacturing was an equally weak sector in both groups, a legacy of Cologne's anti-industrial

TABLE 15
*Occupational Structure of the Non-Jewish Population
in Cologne, 1846*

Occupation		Number	Percentage
Agriculture		478	3
Commerce (all categories)		3,349	19
Manufacturing		424	2
Factory workers		2,290	13
Master artisans		4,544	25
Journeymen		4,043	22
Transportation		1,054	6
Professions		174	0.9
Pensioners		613	3
Artists		150	0.8
Functionaries		889	5
TOTAL	N=	18,008	100

SOURCE: Ayçoberry, "Histoire Sociale," 2: 70, App. 11.
    NOTE: Together, the categories of master artisans and journeymen
constitute 47 percent of all those with occupations.

past. Yet by this time there was a small but economically powerful group of
Protestant immigrant sugar refiners who were among the richest of Co-
logne's new elite. Although new economic sectors lacking traditions of anti-
Jewish exclusion often offered Jews opportunities for success, and though
Jews in other German cities entered industry, we know of no Jews among
the industrial elite in Cologne.[44]

Another booming subsector of the economy not visible in these tables
was land speculation and development. Cologne was a very small city physically, growing increasingly cramped because of the population growth. As
the price of land shot up, a powerful if short-lived speculation and building
boom ensued (it burst with devastating impact in 1846). Yet Jews, including the Oppenheims, were not represented in this phenomenon.[45] Finally,
there was an important new sector within trade from which Jews were also
absent: the wholesale business in raw hides, which was dominated by a
small, economically powerful group of merchants who, like Jews, were
heavily immigrant.[46]

Still, the overall picture in these years as in earlier ones is one of Jewish
economic integration within the sectors they inhabited. Thus we find Jews
involved in the increasingly important metal trade, as well as a Jewish lithographer of some note, one of a group of around 30 in the city serving the
souvenir trade spun off by Cologne's burgeoning tourist industry.[47] The
ability of Jews to integrate so widely speaks powerfully for the openness of
opportunity in Cologne, despite the Jews' lack of legal equality. The level of
official hostility toward Jews was also markedly diminished from previous

decades. Wealth was now the City Council's overriding concern regarding Jewish immigration. It was the same with regard to *Judenpatente*, quite a shift from the days when even respectable Jewish businessmen were denied patent recommendations.

Two decades after the city-state showdown on Jewish policy, a new approach to enforcement of the 1808 decree had emerged, a revised version of the original Prussian stance, shared now by city and state. Economic considerations determined enforcement, but no longer did the Prussians value petty economic contributions. In an era of middle-class consciousness and power, class, rather than religion or newness to the community, was the city's basis for anti-Jewish discrimination. A City Council in which newcomer Ludolf Camphausen served and that represented the interests of a business elite dominated by innovative Protestants and immigrants did not speak in the voice of its staid, inbred *Altköln* predecessor. That was good news for Jews — or at least for minimally established Jews who conformed to the remaining tenets of the emerging *Bürger* ethos: industriousness, solidity, and stability.

City Judenpatent *Policy*

In 1838, the mayor of Cologne wrote to the mayor of Strasbourg, France, for information about a Jew who had lived in Strasbourg for several years and now wished a *Judenpatent* in order to do business in Cologne. With no apparent sense of irony, the German mayor patiently explained that this license was required by the French "law of 17 March 1808, which is still in existence here," though it had long passed from the books in France.[48]

The City Council took Article 7 of the law, which mandated the yearly licenses, very seriously, meeting frequently to deliberate applications and conducting thorough investigations into the business reputations and financial standing of applicants.[49] Resident Jews were as subject to these controls as immigrants. The application of one Levi Schnoog for renewal of his *Judenpatent* was easily granted because this horse and cattle dealer had proof "that he has conducted his trade in a steady and orderly, indeed, in an exemplary fashion," while that of another Jew, a former teacher in the Jewish school who now ran a lending library and did lottery collecting, was summarily dismissed because he had suffered a bankruptcy.[50]

More serious was the case of Maximilian Hirschbach, a petty Jewish dealer whose application was rejected on grounds of suspected usurious loans to minors — unlike bankruptcy, this was stated grounds for patent denial under the decree. Unspecified information furnished by the police as well "by several [unnamed] members of the City Council" was cited as justification, although the police report admitted the absence of court-admissible evidence. For this reason, apparently, the given reason for denial was Hirschbach's failure to procure the requisite character reference from the Jewish Consistory of Bonn — a pretext Hirschbach challenged, appealing to the Council, which, he said, represented "70,000 inhabitants without regard to religion, . . . not to prolong the misery of my family . . . over a one-sided insinuation." He failed.[51]

For all that this case appears to have been manipulated — Hirschbach claimed that the Consistory had refused him a character testimonial because it had been informed of the Council's opposition to his patent application — there were other cases where Jews of dubious backgrounds were allowed to marshal evidence and reverse negative Council opinion or where the Council itself inquired after patented Jews whose names failed to appear in yearly renewal lists.[52] The Council, then, did not obstruct Jewish petitions per se. With evidence in the case of immigrants that proper settlement permission had been obtained (which, of course, would already have weeded out economically marginal cases), and in all cases that applicants had reported to the tax authorities and been assessed the appropriate level of *Gewerbesteuer* (trade tax), patenting proceeded without incident, money literally buying admission into the respectable business world.

As was true in even the worst years of Council resistance, the overwhelming majority of Jews who applied for *Judenpatent* endorsement got it (see Table 16). As in the previous era, this says a great deal about the economic character of the applicants, but in this period it also speaks for a Council for which Jewish policy had lost its explosive political significance. *Judenpatente* were now merely a means of "quality control" for Jews at the portals of economic society. The whole institution of *Judenpatente* remained, of course, discriminatory. For city authorities, however, the 1808 law was a given. The question is how the city government used its license to discriminate, and it is clear that the values that informed city administration of Jewry law were not targeted solely at Jews. The electoral ordinance of 1845, backed enthusiastically by the liberal business elite, disenfranchised the vast majority of Cologne's adult male population. It was not an egalitarian world into which Jews were being integrated; half the Christian population — women — remained unenfranchised on the basis of gender. Nevertheless, the emerging middle-class economic order did accept middle-class Jewish men well before the revolution of 1848.

Wealth, Class, and Mobility

Immigration policy favored the financially stable and established. *Judenpatent* policy did the same. Economic conditions in this period were vastly improved over previous decades, and all signs point to de facto economic

TABLE 16
City Council Judenpatent *Recommendations
Requested and Granted, 1838–45*

Year	Requested	Granted
1838	72	70
1839	72	71
1840	80	78
1841	85	85
1842	103	103
1843	111	109
1844	137	132
1845	139	138

SOURCE: HASK, *Judenpatente*, Oberbürgermeisteramt, 400-II-4-C-1.

NOTE: This count includes all Jews applying for patent endorsements in the course of the year (applications were often received and processed after the annual *Judenpatent* request lists were compiled). It also includes the final results of applications held for further investigation; cf. Müller, p. 66, Table 2. A City Council endorsement always resulted in Prussian approval of the *Judenpatent* in these years.

This count is of patent applications made and granted, not the number of individuals asking for or receiving patent endorsements (partners running a business applied for a single *Judenpatent*). Thus it reflects the number of Jewish businesses, not the number of Jews, licensed. Only independently employed Jews needed *Judenpatente*; professionals, pensioners, those working for a salary, or a husband or father, did not. Not all Jews who by law should have applied for these patents did. *Judenpatente* lists, therefore, are not an accurate source for the group's economic profile or occupational distribution.

integration in years when powerful spokesmen of the business and political elite publicly called for the civil equality of Jews. Not since the early years of the French presence were conditions as auspicious for a Jewish "takeoff." Given all this, were Jews in these years able to better themselves and their children to an extent not possible earlier?

Occupation is the single most important element in determining mobility and class.[53] It is far from a perfect index, especially for a population heavily concentrated in commerce, since the most typical occupational title, *Kaufmann* (merchant), covers a broad range of activities and was applied to small and middling as well as wealthy businessmen.[54]

Analysis of the occupational distribution of Cologne's wealthiest Jews (who were listed on a citywide compendium of Cologne's most endowed citizens in 1849) shows the difficulty of constructing a meaningful occupational ranking with which to measure Jewish mobility. As Table 17 shows, the preponderance of all Jews on this list, which had three wealth rankings, practiced trade: 40 percent of Jews in the uppermost class, 68 percent of those in the middle one, 62 percent of those in the third class. The only occupations that truly distinguished the wealthiest were banking (with the title *Banquier* used) and living off a pension. The rest of the Jews on the list were in occupations we would expect to find among the wealthy — manufacturing, professions — as well as in occupations not normally associated with wealth — crafts, butchering, salaried employment.

A clearer and more direct index of wealth is level of tax assessment. Fortunately, this often rare source is abundant for Cologne's Jews in these years and provides a solid basis for study of the group's income and class structure. Table 18 shows a pyramid-shaped Jewish class structure in 1844, with a broad base composed of lower and marginal groups (combined, these constituted over half of the Jews), a sizable middle class (41 percent of Jews), and a tiny elite (4 percent). We can best appreciate the significance of this configuration in comparison with that of the Jewish group in a previous sample year and in comparison with that of non-Jewish society in Cologne at the same point in time.

The first comparison (Table 18) shows that dramatic change had occurred in Jewish class structure since 1835. The uppermost class declined in relative size, while the middle class proportionately more than doubled, to a point where it comprised almost half the Jewish population. While opportunities for the wealthiest had shrunk, those for a far larger segment of the Jewish group had increased significantly. Although the proportion of Jews in the lower classes remained stable at roughly half the population (merging the two lowest categories in 1844), the overall picture is one of real improvement from 1835, when Jewish society was sharply split between haves and have-nots (see Chapter 3).

Was the growth of a Jewish middle class in Cologne, however, largely the

TABLE 17

Occupations of Cologne's Wealthiest Jews as Classified in the Meistbeerbten *List, 1849*

	Class			
Occupation	I	II	III	Total
Trade (including butchering)	4	26	47	77
Money and credit	3	2	4	9
Manufacturing	0	0	3	3
Crafts	0	2	5	7
Salaried employment	0	1	0	1
Service	0	1	0	1
Professions	0	1	8	9
Synagogue functionary	0	1	0	1
Property owner	0	2	0	2
Pensioner	3	2	3	8
TOTAL	10	38	70	118

SOURCE: *Verzeichniss der Meistbeerbten der Stadt Köln,* 1849.
  NOTE: On the methods of analyzing this list, see Chapter 6, n. 72; and Appendix B.

TABLE 18
Jewish Income Stratification, 1835, 1844

Ranking	1835		1844		Combined %
	%	No.	%	No.	
Uppermost	23	13	4	8	
Upper middle			6	10	
					41
Middle	20	11	35	64	
Lower	57	32	16	30	
					55
Indigent	0	0	39	72	
TOTAL	100	56	100	184	

SOURCES: For 1835, *HASK*, Oberbürgermeisteramt, 400, II-4-D-1 (see Chapter 3, n. 37); for 1844, *Verzeichniss der Meistbeerbten der Stadt Köln*, 1849. See also Appendix B.
    NOTE: For the methodology used in this table, see Appendix B. On bracketing for 1835, see Table 5. Fuller information and a larger population allowed more brackets for 1844. The wealth categories for 1844 are bracketed as follows:
    Uppermost: Class I of *Meistbeerbten* and/or *Gewerbesteuer* of 48–240 taler, or *Grundsteuer* of 42–65 taler.
    Upper middle: Class II of *Meistbeerbten* and/or *Gewerbesteuer* of 36–42 taler, or *Grundsteuer* of 24–30 taler.
    Middle: Class III of *Meistbeerbten* and/or *Gewerbesteuer* of 14–30 taler, or *Grundsteuer* of 9–23 taler.
    Lower: *Gewerbesteuer* of 8–12 taler or *Grundsteuer* of 6 pfennigs to 7 taler.
    Indigent: no tax assessments or other indicator of wealth.

TABLE 19
Tax Assessments of Resident and Immigrant Jews, 1844

Ranking	Resident		Immigrant		Overall	
	%	No.	%	No.	%	No.
Uppermost	6	5	6	5	6	10
Upper middle	8	6	3	3	5	9
Middle	34	27	42	37	38	64
Low	24	19	10	9	17	28
Indigent	28	22	39	34	34	56
TOTAL	100	79	100	88	100	167

SOURCE: *HASK,* Oberbürgermeisteramt, 400, II-4-D-1; *Verzeichniss der Meistbeerbten der Stadt Köln.*

result of an external factor — immigration — or an internal one — upward mobility of longtime-resident and native-born Jews? In a population that doubled in size between 1835 and 1844 largely because of immigration, this is an essential consideration.

We have seen that, in the economically troubled 1820's and early 1830's, long-settled and native-born Jews lost ground and that as a group they were far less well off than immigrants. Between 1835 and 1848, however, the fortunes of this group improved. I was able to trace the tax assessments of 34 longtime residents and natives from 1835 to 1844 and found that the number of these Jews assessed a middle level of tax rose from 6 (18 percent of the group) in 1835 to 16 (47 percent) in 1844, while the number assessed little or no taxes dropped from 22 (65 percent) to 14 (41 percent).

A comparison of the tax levels of residents and immigrants in 1844 (Table 19) confirms the economic rise of Cologne's Jews. While immigrants retained a slight edge of wealth, we find that the gap between them and long-term residents had narrowed to insignificance. Class structure in the two groups was virtually identical, powerful evidence of improved economic conditions and, crucially, of Jewish access to opportunity. For if immigrants arrived with the high level of wealth the statistics depict, resident Jews attained it in the city.

Furthering Mobility

Fortune smiled on Cologne's Jews during these years. But they also worked prodigiously for their success and laid the groundwork for that of the younger generation in a number of concrete ways.

Partnerships

The *Judenpatent* records show a continued pattern of professional and personal relationships that enhanced Jewish business resources. Proposed partnerships were commonly cited as a reason for immigration. This bolstered an immigrant's chances of obtaining settlement permission, since, if the partner in Cologne was financially established, the newcomer could assure the authorities of a definite, secure livelihood. Business ties were often combined with ties of kinship and marriage. They were a demonstrable means by which Jews lacking the ability to establish their own businesses were able to achieve self-employment and to better themselves.

One case of such mobility was that of Salomon Koppel. An immigrant and employee in a large Jewish textile firm, Koppel had been in Cologne some four years when he applied for formal settlement permission and a *Judenpatent* in order to enter a partnership with an even more recent immigrant. The latter, Jonas Moses Katz, owned a "considerable dry goods business" and was among "the most highly taxed merchants." Much of Katz's business remained in Paderborn, his home town, but he now wished to relocate it partially to Cologne, as well as to open another business. Koppel's requests were granted. Partnership had made an employee a *Kaufmann*.[55]

Women's Work

Although the sources on women's employment are sporadic, it is clear that Jewish women at all levels of wealth contributed actively to family income. We most often hear of widows assuming their husbands' *Judenpatente*, including Therese Oppenheim, Salomon Oppenheim's widow.[56] If widows were able to pick up their husbands' businesses, however, it was because as wives they had long been active in them. In fact, we have evidence of women, not only widowed but married and single, working to support themselves and others. This is not surprising, since a bourgeois doctrine of female domesticity was not yet current in German society, so had not yet been absorbed by acculturating Jews.[57]

Thus, we find mention of three daughters of a Jewish army veteran from Deutz, Collman Bielefeld, who had been wounded in service and was unable to continue work as a jeweler. His daughters had learned the millinery business and intended to support themselves, and him, thereby. On the strength of *their* business prospects, Bielefeld, certified as an "invalid . . . incapable of work," petitioned for permission to settle in Cologne—and got it.[58]

Another woman, who had been running a dry goods business since her husband's bankruptcy, sought settlement permission in Cologne on the strength of her own independent business reputation. The Royal Prussian Government, writing to the mayor's office about the case, referred to her as the "trader wife" of Simon Jakob Bier; the mayor of Barmen, her previous place of residence, confirmed that Amelia Bier had withdrawn her funds from her husband's business and was truly independent. Cologne's City Council and, at its prompting, Mayor Steinberger, withheld their endorsement after struggling to establish that, as a married woman, Amelia Bier could not separate her business reputation from that of her husband, although the fact of her independent economic function was incontrovertible.[59] Another woman, a widow from Deutz, sought settlement permission in Cologne for herself and her five sons in order to establish a jewelry business and tobacco factory. On the strength of a recommendation from the mayor of Deutz and, apparently, a solid business reputation, her request was granted.[60] The wife of the Jewish operator of the city-run savings and loan worked as his assistant, and his daughter ran the cashier office with him.[61]

Jewish women appear only occasionally in the *Judenpatente* records, but when they do, their work, contribution to, or responsibility for, family income is assumed. The very fact that their activities were unremarkable to contemporaries is what we must note. Women's work was clearly the norm and a factor in Jewish upward mobility.[62]

Education

Forming partnerships and using the productive labor of all family members meant that Cologne's Jews were rationally organizing and exploiting their group resources, a strategy that would increase their chances for success. Education would help secure success for the future generation, something the Jews of this era, as those before them, understood well as they continued making disproportionate use of the city's *Realgymnasium*. The percentage of Jewish boys in the school increased from between 4 to 6 percent in the 1830's (when Jews constituted 0.7 percent of the city's population) to 9 percent in 1850/51 (when Jews were 1.4 percent of the total city population).[63] Jewish use of the *Realgymnasium* reflects both a level of wealth that made it possible to dispense with the labor of teenage boys and a belief in the economic value of vocational education. Both characteristics distinguish the city's Jews from the most economically distressed non-Jews, who were heavily concentrated in the artisanal sector and who underutilized the city's schools because, in Ayçoberry's words, these "did not appear to be a means of upward mobility for children, even the most gifted."[64] As we have seen, Jewish boys from all income levels attended the *Realgymnasium*, the first Jewish graduates finishing their schooling in the 1830's and 1840's. They and others, who attended for a time without graduating, clearly saw a link between education and betterment, most often declaring their intended occupation to be commerce.

Occupational Mobility

In general, the younger generation of Jews in Cologne favored butchering, crafts, and the professions over banking and commerce. Significantly, none of the younger generation was synagogue functionaries. The cantor's son, Jacob (later Jacques) Offenbach, the famed composer, retained his father's involvement in music but not his association with the Jewish community; he eventually converted.[65] David Levy Elkan, son of the synagogue's first teacher (who himself had become a petty trader), became the lithographer we have noted above; although Elkan also produced works on Jewish themes and remained very active in community affairs, his professional identity and livelihood were not bound to the synagogue. The unpopularity of Jewish communal work among the younger generation of Cologne's Jews is an expression of the general stagnation of communal affairs in these years, as we shall see.

Immigrant Occupations

If there was no real difference in the income stratification of immigrants and longtime residents, there were some important distinctions in their occupational patterns.

TABLE 20
Occupational Comparison of Resident and Immigrant Jews, 1844/46

Occupation	Resident		Immigrant	
	%	No.	%	No.
Commerce				
Trade	28	23	51	49
Butchering	16	13	5	5
Subtotal	44	36	55	54
Money and credit				
Banking, currency changing, lottery collecting	15	12	0	0
Manufacturing	1	1	1	1
Crafts	9	7	16	16
Salaried employment	1	1	6	6
Service	3	2	3	3
Professions	7	6	7	7
Pensioner	4	3	5	5
Without a trade	16	13	6	6
TOTAL	100	81	100	98

SOURCE: See Table 12.

Compared to 15 percent of resident Jews who practiced some form of money or credit activity, no immigrants did so (see Table 20). The general decline in Jewish banking, then, was not occurring evenly among all Jews but was concentrated among younger Jews and new arrivals, groups which, given their relative numbers, would set the direction of future trends. Banking, that most traditional of pursuits among medieval and early modern Jewry, was clearly on the wane in this community, forged entirely in modernity.[66]

A far greater proportion of immigrants than resident Jews worked in crafts, also a trait they shared with the younger generation. Far more immigrants were in salaried employment, which, like crafts, was an easy entry occupation for less well-established newcomers. A much higher percentage of immigrants than residents practiced trade; a much lower proportion were butchers. The latter pattern seems the result of broader city policies; city tax authorities strictly controlled the importation of meat, making meat provisioning a difficult market for newcomers to penetrate. One immigrant butcher from Mülheim cited the decrease in the amount of nontaxed meat allowed into Cologne "in the last few years" as his reason for moving to the city; he would be better positioned to do business as a resident. The fact that he had a son in the business already living there made his move economically feasible, but also suggests the difficulties facing other prospective butchers not similarly connected.[67]

This difficulty might have been compounded by the fact that the meat trade had a surfeit of Jews — 21 percent of all Jews in commerce were in the meat business in 1844 (Table 14) — and by the fact that butchering had a high degree of professional heredity among Jews. The sons of butchers tended overwhelmingly to continue in this line, 17 percent of the younger generation, compared to 6 percent of fathers, making its living in this way. If butchering had become something of a family affair among Cologne's Jews, it would have been a less feasible option for outsiders.[68]

Comparative Wealth of Jews and Non-Jews

In a time of improved economic conditions but continued discrimination, how were Cologne's Jews doing compared to the population as a whole?

While we know the occupational structure of non-Jewish society, we do not know the relative wealth of its classes.[69] However, given the stark differences in occupational profile between Jews and non-Jews, a rough gauge of relative wealth can be made by comparing the overall health of the city's trading and artisanal sectors. Although both included subgroups of lesser and greater means, commerce was clearly a much more vigorous sector than crafts. There was more upward mobility within trade: the retailing elite (merchants "with open stores") increased by a third in the 1840's alone; the number of merchants paying higher amounts of trade tax increased more than the number paying lower amounts. By contrast, all indices show a continuous decline in the crafts in this period, in good years as well as bad.[70]

Even the crafts Jews did practice tended to be the less stressed — precious-metal smithing, watchmaking — while no Jews were found in the most acutely depressed trades — shoemaking, carpentry, building. Several Jewish craftsmen are known to have been masters, that is, members of the artisan elite, while seven craftsmen were wealthy enough to be included on a list of the city's most well-endowed citizens — 6 percent of all Jews listed. A number of these appear in city *Adressbücher* as "Firma."

Analysis of the list of the city's wealthiest citizens (*Meistbeerbten*) yields a number of striking contrasts. Compiled for purposes of designating electors under the Municipal Ordinance of 1845 and limiting the franchise to the wealthiest men, it is of special interest because it was based solely on the income, class, and property taxes, not the older and far more common *Gewerbesteuer* (trade tax).[71] These restrictions and the 400-taler minimum level of assessed wealth left fewer than 4,000 adult males, out of a total population of over 80,000, with voting rights.

TABLE 21
Proportion of Jews on the Meistbeerbten *List, 1849*

Ranking	Jews	Total	Jewish percentage
First Class	10	246	4
Second Class	37	879	4
Third Class	71	2,715	3
TOTAL	118	3,840	3

NOTE: Totals are based on my count of names on the published *Meistbeerbten* list of 1849; cf. Gothein, p. 513.

Despite all this, Jews constituted roughly 4 percent of each of the three wealth categories on the list, and 3 percent overall of the city's "wealthiest," although Jews then constituted only 1.4 percent of the city's population in 1849 (see Table 21). Calculating differently, we find that while 4 percent of the total population was represented on that list (assuming women and children as included in the households of husbands and/or fathers), 9 percent of the Jewish population was so represented, and this may well be an undercount.[72]

There certainly were poor Jews in Cologne — 39 percent of the group, according to our study of Jewish tax records (see Table 18). There is, however, no way of measuring this against the percentage of poor in the city as a whole or, in the absence of religion-specific poor-relief statistics, of comparing the criteria used to judge poverty. This is a crucial consideration, since inability to pay business or property tax and to put bread on the table represent very different levels of poverty. My reasonably substantiated impression is of a Jewish group relatively well-off compared to the general population, a group that could easily earn the solicitude of the bourgeois establishment.[73]

The general economic situation of Cologne's Jews also compared favorably with that of the rest of Prussian Jewry, only a third of which, according to Jacob Toury's reckoning, was in a combined upper and middle class, over a quarter of which he classed as "petty" and 40 percent of which as "marginal" in 1848.[74] The situation of Cologne's Jews compared favorably, too, with that of Jews of another major trading city, Hamburg, where in the late 1830's only a third of Jews enjoyed a "secure existence" while the rest were evenly divided between those living on "minimum" means and those in economically stressed or impoverished circumstances.[75] The general trend is clear. Cologne's Jews not only participated in the economic "miracle" remaking German Jewry in the age of emancipation. They were in its vanguard.

Backlash

> For three years I have run a dry goods business under the
> name of Stern and Company, and have . . . managed it
> with growing success.[76]
> Nathan Stern, Jewish businessman, 1841

Given all this, we must wonder about resentment of Jewish success and
resistance to it. Despite muted official discrimination and clear signs that
Jews were accepted at all levels of the economy, there was at least one
instance when competitors of the Jews attempted to use the 1808 decree to
thwart Jewish success. Because the case is unusually well documented in the
words of many of the principals, it also affords precious insight beyond the
quantitative data into the human realities of Jewish economic integration in
these years.[77]

Pierre Ayçoberry has noted the economic distress in many sectors of
Cologne's class of artisans and small retailers during these years.[78] It is here
more than among the city's new business elite that we would expect friction
over Jewish interlopers, and it is here, among one of the most threatened
groups, that it emerged.

In August 1841, a large group (in the characterization of city authorities) of cloth retailers complained to the municipal government about four
Jews who, they said, were auctioning goods below cost and undercutting
the complainants' businesses. The Jews were able to sell below cost, they
alleged, by obtaining goods dishonestly. The Jews were also audaciously
running "extremely long advertisements" to boost their sales.

The mayor's office asked the Chamber of Commerce to investigate. The
Chamber's report began by noting that some of the complainants had
themselves engaged in auctions and that it was normal for businessmen to
try to undersell one another. Still, it concluded, the complainants were
insisting that the Jews' "constant selling" did *not* (emphasis in the original)
take place in a "natural and legal" manner and that, in the Chamber's view,
"so large a number of respectable *Bürger* would not have signed the accusation . . . without mature consideration." The request for action against the
Jews deserved support, insofar as such action was consonant with state law
on freedom of trade.

The Chamber's report presumed the complainants were "honest Bürger," making no such presumption about the Jews. This may have been
simple prejudice, but it may also have been because the original complaint
(not extant) had alleged that two of the Jews had questionable business
histories, one of them having gone bankrupt twice before immigrating to

Cologne. According to a Council paraphrase of the document, the retailers cited Prussian law forbidding bankrupts from carrying on independent business until they had been rehabilitated and argued that "it would be strange" indeed "if a Jew, whom the lawgiver deemed needy of comprehensive, strict supervision [the 1808 law], would do better in this regard because he went bankrupt abroad." This Jew and two of the remaining accused, moreover, came from the right side of the Rhine and therefore were also liable to the immigration restrictions of the 1808 decree, which certainly ought to be applied.

The fourth Jew named in the complaint was Nathan Stern, son of Joseph Stern, the first Jew to settle in Cologne and, since 1834, director of the municipal savings and loan. Standing was obviously not an issue here and, since Stern had been born in Cologne in 1805, neither were immigration technicalities.[79] Stern's business history, however, was checkered. He had fled the city in 1833 under an arrest warrant and had returned to Cologne in 1838 under a cloud of suspicion about his business practices in Strasbourg, France, in the interim.

As his father explained the 1833 affair to the City Council, however, Nathan had been guilty of nothing more than youthful brashness. After a dispute between them regarding Nathan's share of his mother's inheritance, Nathan had fled with a large sum of money that one of Joseph's sons-in-law had deposited with Joseph, and left instructions for Joseph to deduct the amount from the disputed inheritance. The son-in-law summoned the authorities, but before they could find him, a remorseful Nathan returned the entire sum to his brother-in-law. Rather than return to Cologne and face a judicial inquiry, Nathan went to Strasbourg, where he found employment with a respectable businessman, whose daughter he eventually married. Unable to establish himself there, however (because, Joseph Stern explained, local authorities knew about the charges in Cologne), Nathan returned to his home town, only to be refused a *Judenpatent*.

But Nathan's early offense was not the only reason the City Council withheld its endorsement. Its inquiries to Strasbourg produced an accusation that Nathan had staged a fraudulent bankruptcy and fled France to avoid prosecution.

The case against Nathan Stern and the other Jews seemed damning. Yet Council investigations of its own records found that the first three Jews had good character references and had conducted their businesses without the slightest complaint until that point. They all had formal settlement permission and held valid *Judenpatente*. Under provisions of the 1808 decree as well as Prussian law on freedom of trade, the Council informed the complainants, the Jews could not be stopped from doing business in the current year. Their applications for *Judenpatent* renewal, however, would be scrutinized.

Nathan Stern, on the other hand, who had been conducting his business without a *Judenpatent*, would be shut down immediately by the police.

Stern, who had been pleading for a *Judenpatent* since 1838, responded in long, impassioned letters to the mayor and the City Council and the local office of the Royal Government, arguing that, while unlucky, he was upright. Yes, he had suffered several bankruptcies, yet he had still met his obligations punctually. He had always obtained his goods honestly and openly; in proof, he attached various bills and receipts, as well as a character reference from no less than the firm of Salomon Oppenheim, Jr., which had approved him for credit. He had been cleared by a Royal Cabinet decree of charges growing out of the original "youthful prank," and the Strasbourg charges were unsubstantiated. What had occurred there was simply the failure of an honest business run with his brother-in-law. Yes, he had fled France, but only to avoid ruination. His brother-in-law in Strasbourg had cleared the business of all charges; proof, again, attached.

Stern's troubles with the Cologne authorities, he charged, were the result of the malicious jealousy of business competitors. The fact that he was both a Jew and "not possessed of the license bound to this identity" ("dass ich Jude bin und das mit diesem Predikat verbundene Patent nicht besitze"), eased their task. But the 1808 decree was directed against usury and illegal trade and he had *never* (emphasis in the original) been guilty of these. He could sell cheaply not because he had obtained his wares dishonestly but because his behavior, personal and professional, had been temperate and frugal, because he bought wisely and worked hard, as a good number of the city's most respected businessmen (named) would attest. (Stern's repeated references to his connections to "the best merchants" and bankers was obviously meant not only to establish his respectability but to highlight the pettiness of his enemies' businesses before city officials, who were themselves prominent businessmen.)

His efforts succeeded. The Royal Government first granted him a two-month "exceptional" permit to conduct his business, during which time he was to procure the prerequisites for a *Judenpatent* or again be barred from business. Within a month, Stern had convinced the City Council of his worthiness and after more than three years of trying, secured its endorsement of his *Judenpatent* application, which the Prussians then approved. Ironically, his competitors' campaign resulted only in Stern's being cleared of the suspicions that had long blocked his obtaining a *Judenpatent*. Two of the other accused Jews were also cleared; the fourth drops from the records.

It is a commentary on changed times that the "target Jew" of these years was an ingenious if bumbling, successful, and well-connected businessman, while that of the previous period, Lob Moises Pollack, had been a hapless peddler. Even the "problem" Jews in these years were middle class.

There was another attempt by business competitors of the Jews to use the 1808 law to their advantage. In 1843, a group of textile retailers protested auctions of imported goods by Jews. The complainants wanted a return to medieval-type guilds and strict control of "a class whose complete civil rights the state itself has not recognized, because in the specifics of their moral, religious, civil, and economic life it sees elements contrary to its own essence and to its most lofty goals." The Chamber of Commerce turned a deaf ear to both appeals.[80]

The failure of petit-bourgeois attempts to win official support for anti-Jewish discrimination is very noteworthy. In the Stern case, not only did Prussian authorities reverse themselves once the facts were established, so did the City Council, whose early communications about Stern had been very hostile. This, too, is telling commentary on changed times, further evidence that economics and middle-class credentials mattered more than religion in determining Jewish status.

Yet these cases also show that Jewish economic integration was not entirely smooth and painless; that, in an age of bourgeois, liberal acceptance, lower-class antisemitism persisted — this is not the first time we have seen petty competitors of Jews attempt to use the 1808 decree to drive Jews out of business. The middle-class base of Jewish acceptance clearly had a flip side in lower-class antagonism.

These cases also suggest that, if the city's immigration and *Judenpatent* policy favored the formation of a relatively well-off community, innovative and aggressive Jewish behavior in the marketplace secured and furthered mobility. Finally, they are noteworthy in light of the role Jews are known to have played in pioneering the ready-made clothing industry and in department-store retailing in Germany.[81] The four accused of cheap, bulk sales of textiles (Stern readily admitted to "an abundant turnover") were clearly headed in that direction. Indeed, by the mid-1840's, just a few years after being threatened with ruin, Stern and another of the four appear in the city address books as proprietors of ready-made menswear shops. Nor were they alone. A single Jewish family in the same line of work, "Emanuel, Abraham und Gebrüder," had six such listings in the address book of 1846.[82]

"A Jew, Yet a Subject and a Human Being": Jewish Attitudes to Their Environment

The documents relating to Nathan Stern yield yet another kind of insight, into Jewish attitudes about their place in non-Jewish society. Both Nathan and his father Joseph wrote many letters, composed in the tone of aggrieved victims. Their writing tells us much about the expectations average Jews had of the Gentile world and about their self-perceptions in it.

The letters of both men assume that non-Jews in power and Jews in trouble share a common humanity and that the non-Jews are not only capable of understanding the predicament of Jews but are likely to do so if only they can be made to see the full picture. While Jews had been appealing to Gentile authorities for compassion for centuries, the concepts and terminology used in the Sterns' correspondence are modern, composed in the language of Enlightenment humanism — of emancipation.

Joseph Stern's letter to the City Council on behalf of his son is written in a familiar tone; because of his position in the municipal savings and loan, he reminded the members, he did know some of them personally. He freely shared with them his feelings as a father who, now advanced in years, wants nothing more than to see his children settled in life in secure employment. The right honored members could surely feel with him ("recht innig mit mir fühlen") the despair over a son's difficulties. Surely they could also understand how it is in families, fathers and sons at loggerheads over the disposition of family affairs, the misunderstandings and "unpleasantness," the rash behavior of "youthful folly." Surely they could grasp, too, the marital stress that an uncertain livelihood had placed on Nathan, whose wife, though "exemplary," reproached him at every turn.

Mayor Steinberger, it turns out, had tried to help Nathan when he first returned to the city and applied for a *Judenpatent*. In a letter to the mayor, Nathan recalled the "fatherly interest" Steinberger had shown him and the certainty this had produced in him that Steinberger's love of justice extended to each of his *Mitmenschen* (fellow humans), regardless of religion.

But Nathan also made a personal appeal to officials of the Royal Government to grasp the desperation of a "brokenhearted" "father of a family, threatened by the greatest misfortune, [who] although a Jew, [is] yet a subject and a human being" ("wenn auch Jude, doch Untertan und Mensch"). Nathan had three small children and a wife who had become crippled in her most recent birth. Every "feeling man and head of a family," he wrote, could realize that learning a handicraft at his age was not feasible and that if he were not allowed to pursue the only trade he knew, he and his entire household would be reduced to beggary (a prospect sure to evoke horror, if not empathy, in the good *Bürger* of the City Council).

Most striking are numerous references in the letters of father and son to Cologne as *Vaterstadt* (homeland) and to Christians as *Mitbürger* (fellow citizens). Joseph Stern referred to himself as "an old father and *Bürger*." Nathan wrote to Steinberger, "I support myself, as do each of my Christian brothers. . . . I have . . . earned the trust of my fellow men [*Mitmenschen*] through diligence and the strictest integrity." He begged justice as "a fellow citizen, albeit an Israelite" and believed he would get it "because indeed, we all believe in one God and are brothers." Then, too, he was not only an "homme d'honneur" (honorable man) but "a born *Kölner*" rightly returned to his *"Vaterland"*; "I certainly do not seek . . . a Fatherland in France," he added.

Of course, we would expect flattery and hyperbole in letters like these, but their language does not seem merely tactical. Because Stern's case and those of the other Jews were substantiated by evidence, we have no way of knowing whether the "justice, charity, and humanity" of Cologne's authorities were as strong as Nathan asserted them to be. That he and his father saw themselves as entitled to such sentiments, there is little doubt.

Acculturation and Continued Identity

There is evidence that broader segments of Cologne's Jews had imbibed cultural values from non-Jewish society.[83] Of fifteen families for which we have information in 1846, all had given most of their children — 51 of 62 — non-Jewish names, at least "officially." (That the 11 other children were given such names as Sarah, Rebecca, and Abraham gives credence to the many more called Sibilla, Bertha, Juliana, Moritz, Max, Adolf, and Gustav; Jews were not simply germanizing their children's names for the sake of the police survey, which is the source of our information.[84]) Although the 51 children may well have been given Jewish names as well, the German names are a clear sign of acculturation and hopes for integration.

Other factors — occupation and residential distribution — served to reinforce a separate Jewish identity. Although I would not argue that Jews deliberately chose certain occupations in order to foster continued distinctiveness, their choices nevertheless had this effect, as attested by the intragroup partnerships and marriages that resulted. Such associations both derived from and perpetuated particularity.

Jewish residential patterns worked similarly. More than they had in the past, Cologne's Jews lived near other Jews during these years; 57 percent of Jewish households were in two of the city's six sections, the third and, especially, the fifth (see Table 22 and Map 2).[85] The reasons for this are not clear. The synagogue (marked on the map, by me, with a star) was in the district most heavily populated by Jews, but this was also where the *Kreutzgasse* secondary school and such important avenues of trade as the Schildergasse and five of the city's "gate streets" (east-west roads through the city walls) were located.

As we have seen, occupation influenced the general residential pattern in Cologne and may have influenced the Jewish pattern as well.[86] The fact that

TABLE 22
Location of Jewish Households by City Section, 1844

City Section	Number of Households	Number of Individuals	Percentage
I	5	25	3
II	29	114	16
III	35	138	19
IV	23	82	11
V	81	278	38
VI	17	94	13
TOTAL	190	731	100

SOURCES: *HASK,* Oberbürgermeisteramt, II-4-D-1, Jewish population lists of Jan. 19, 30, 1844, Sept. 1844 (3758/3, no. 2756), Sept. 1, 1845, Sept. 2, 1846 (1ten Bezirk), Sept. 2, 1846 (2ten Bezirk), Sept. 4, 1846 (4ten Bezirk), and Sept. 4, 1846 (5ten Bizirk).

NOTE: The average size of Jewish households was four persons, but this figure is distorted downward by the number of single men (57) and women (2).

so much of the Jewish community was in the middle-income range itself may have led to geographic concentration in the fifth section of the city, in which neither the wealthiest nor poorest *Kölner* tended to live; relatively few Jews lived in the northern and southernmost sections, which had significant pockets of poverty. The Jewish pattern was probably caused by a confluence of factors. Whatever the causes, geographic concentration could only have fostered group cohesion at a time when other social and economic forces worked powerfully toward integration.[87]

Converts, Critics, and Radicals

Not all of Cologne's Jews identified with the community. Although a minority, those whose ties were attenuated or severed in these years tended to be the more conspicuous, culturally, economically, and politically. They, too, are part of the story.

Alienated Jews ranged from the merely indifferent, such as the previously mentioned poet and dramatist Hermann Hersch, who "was little moved by the question of his Jewish identity," to converts to Christianity, of whom we know of some twenty between 1830 and 1850.[88] For a population of between 450 and 1,300 during these years (see Table 11) the number of converts is insignificant, in contrast to trends in some other German cities, particularly Berlin, whose yearly conversion rate one scholar has put at 11 percent (2,000 converts) for the years 1816 through 1854.[89] Students of German Jewish apostasy have stressed that conversions came in "waves" or "movements" linked to political developments.[90] The period under study

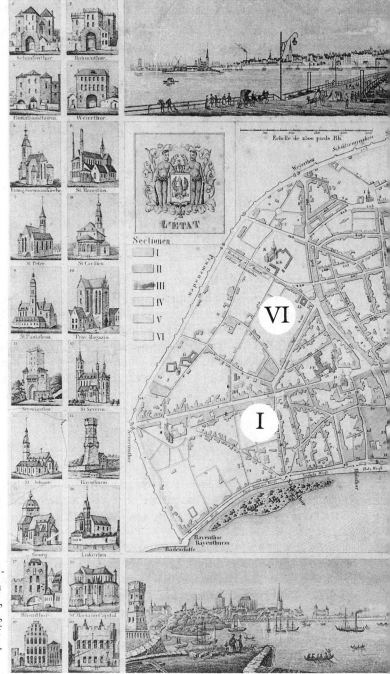

Map 2. Jewish residential distribution in Cologne, 1844, by city section, with the location of the synagogue.

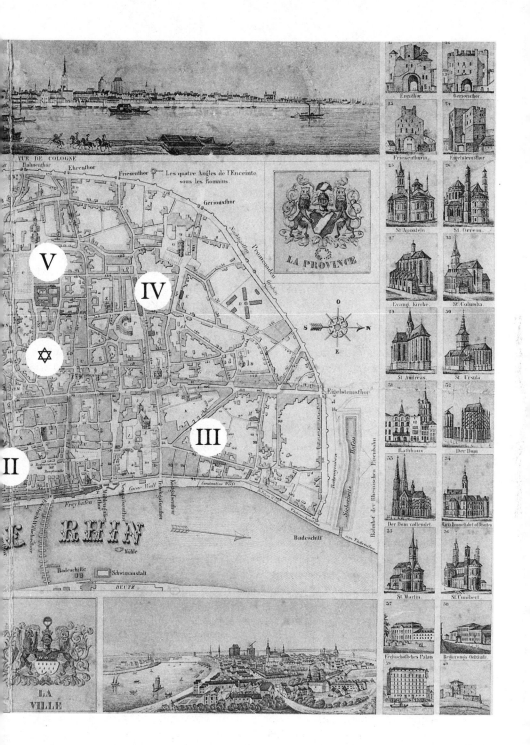

VUE DE COLOGNE

Halmenthor Ehrenthor Friesenthor Les quatre Angles de l'Enceinte
sous les Romains.

Geriousthor

LA PROVINCE

LA VILLE

RHIN

Mühle

Freyhafen

Gruer-Wall

Constantins Werft

Badeschiffe Scheimanstalt

DEUTZ

Badeschiff

Eigelstemsthor

Bahnhof der Rheinischen Eisenbahn

Ehrenthor

Geriousthor

Friesenthurm

Eigelstemsthor

St Aposteln

St Gereon

Evang. Kirche

St Columba

St Andreas

St Ursula

Rathhaus

Der Dom

Der Dom vollendet

Caro Bromantstadt of Dondes

St Martin

St Cunibert

Erzbischöfliches Palais

Regierungs-Gebäude

here, when rights extended by the French were restricted or revoked, was a time of increased conversions as Jews who had tasted equality sought relief in conversion, "an attempt at . . . personal emancipation," in the words of one scholar.[91]

Rhenish Jewry had drunk as deeply of equality as any of Germany's Jews, yet conversion rates in the Rhineland between 1822 and 1846 were among the lowest in Prussia.[92] We can only speculate about one possible reason: perhaps political activism in this hotbed of Prussian provinces gave (male) Jews an alternate vehicle for expressing discontent and a group, rather than individual, approach to fighting inequality and attaining emancipation.

If the number of Jewish conversions in Cologne was small compared to conversions in some other major cities, the Jewish apostasy rate was far higher than that of Catholics in Cologne, only thirteen of whom converted to Protestantism between 1827 and 1847 out of a total Catholic population of between 55,300 and 85,000. The relative pressures on Jews to adopt either Christian faith, and Jewish susceptibility to them, were obviously far greater than the pressures on and susceptibilities of Catholics to adopt the religion of state. This is not surprising, since Catholics were the vast majority of the population in Cologne (Protestants numbered only 3,500 to 10,000 in these years), while Jews were a tiny minority. The differential is eloquent testimony, however, to the magnitude of the pressure on Jews to convert or at least to minimize cultural difference.[93]

The small number of conversions in Cologne makes the ones that occurred the more interesting, particularly because fifteen of twenty were to the Evangelical church, and these were evenly divided between (seven) women and (eight) men.[94] More than three-quarters of all Jews who converted to Christianity in Germany in the nineteenth century became Protestants, so the breakdown in Cologne is in line with the general one, except that the overall statistics represent the conversions in predominantly Protestant as well as Catholic states, while Cologne was overwhelmingly Catholic.[95] The choice of Protestantism in Cologne indicates that the conversions were motivated primarily by desire to escape inferior legal status and for social betterment, since conversion to the religion of state would do far more for the convert than conversion to Catholicism.

Deborah Hertz and others have shown that gender was a very significant factor in German Jewish conversions to Christianity.[96] Men, stymied in their careers by occupational discrimination, tended to convert opportunistically; among the better known are Heinrich Heine, Ludwig Börne, and Eduard Gans. Women, barred by gender discrimination in the larger society from even dreaming of occupational opportunities closed to Jews, tended to convert either out of religious conviction or in order to marry non-Jews, civil marriage not being an option in Prussia until 1874. These marriages could be socially advantageous or motivated by affection, or both; the most famous examples are of the Jewish women of the Berlin salons at the turn of the nineteenth century, who wed members of the nobility and the intellectual elite. These marriages could also bring material benefits, such as the right to reside in Berlin, which had anti-Jewish settlement restrictions until 1812. As Hertz notes, "Both poor and rich women . . . achieved a kind of emancipation when they converted or married out. . . . [For] women, intermarriage, rather than educational or professional opportunity [from which women were barred by gender discrimination], was likely to be the way a converted woman made actual the higher status made possible by conversion."[97]

Social considerations may well have factored in the conversion of Eve Oppenheim, Salomon Oppenheim's daughter, who joined the Evangelical church sometime before her marriage in 1831 to Carl Friedrich Ferdinand Kusserow, originally of Berlin. Oppenheim was 22, Kusserow, 38, when they married; one suspects that the conversion and marriage were tied and, given the age difference, that social and material considerations, respectively, were at work. Kusserow's father, a government official, had died when the boy was a few years old; the boy was bright and ambitious but poor. The coupling seems to conform to a pattern in which upwardly aspiring but impoverished Prussian males of good family ("status rich" but "cash poor," in Hertz's words) acquired Jewish wealth by marrying converted Jewish women.[98] If desires for social and financial betterment figured in the match, they were certainly realized: Kusserow had a brilliant military career, attaining the rank of general, then elevation to the nobility. The families may have repeated the pattern in the next generation, when a son of the Oppenheim-Kusserow marriage wed the converted niece of Abraham Oppenheim's wife. The girl, orphaned shortly after her birth in 1846, was adopted by her childless aunt and uncle; she later converted to the Evangelical church, explicitly in order to marry *Legationsrat* Heinrich von Kusserow. The Oppenheim-Kusserows thus participated in another pattern established in the era of emancipation: a tendency for families with converted Jews to marry members of other such families.[99]

We know of at least one case where conversion was genuinely religious. Andreas Gottschalk, a former employee of the Oppenheim firm, was by the 1840's a physician to Cologne's poor and their passionate advocate. He converted in 1841 after sincere study, according to church records whose testimony historian Arno Herzig accepts: career obstacles could not have pressured Gottschalk since medicine, unlike law, was open to Jewish men.[100] Gottschalk, who became a founder of the German workers' movement and was one of Cologne's leading radicals during the revolution of 1848, said that his conversion stemmed from a conviction that Christianity, not Judaism, was a true basis for "ethical socialism."[101]

The conversions of the other Jewish men appear to have been opportunistic. For all the improvement in the local climate, Cologne's Jews were also Prussian Jews and as such labored under severe disabilities aside from those imposed by the 1808 decree. Prussian law or administrative rulings barred Jews from holding "public" or state office, whether political, military, or civilian. Thus Jews could not sit in local (*Kreise*) or provincial assemblies. They could serve only as "general soldiers" but could not be promoted to the officer corps. Jews could not hold teaching positions in state-sponsored institutions and thus were barred from university careers. After these were defined as "public" offices, Jews were barred from serving as land surveyors, master builders, auctioneers, executioners, even night watchmen. Jews were ineligible for state certification as lawyers, so could not pursue careers in justice administration. Jews were even barred from serving on juries. While not a career impediment, the latter was an insult to civil dignity and to the judicial principle that underlay the ideal of "juries of one's peers," a proud centerpiece of "Rhenish law." At the same time, Jews were required to use the special "Jewish oath" in judicial proceedings, a particularly degrading holdover from the medieval era.[102]

Under such circumstances, men whose secular educations and university socialization attenuated their ties to Judaism often converted.[103] Such considerations are known to have caused the conversions of David Oppenheim, brother of Abraham and Simon (and Eve), who joined the Protestant church in 1839 in order to be admitted to the licensing exam for assistant judges. Dagobert, as he was renamed, studied in the philosophy faculty at the University of Bonn and the law faculty of Heidelberg, finished his training in Berlin, and joined the Prussian justice administration — "a normal career," in the words of Oppenheim historian Wilhelm Treue, except that it was open to him only because he had converted.[104] The immediate benefits of conversion are apparent even in one reference in the *Judenpatent* records, in which the police director, investigating the reputations of Jews who had applied for Council patent recommendations, informed the mayor that because one (particularly wealthy) merchant, Ezechiel Ritter, had converted to the Evangelical faith, he no longer needed a *Judenpatent* and could be stricken from the records.[105] We have no testimony from those who converted opportunistically; it appears that Dagobert Oppenheim, at least, like his contemporaries Heinrich Heine and Ludwig Börne, resented the circumstances of his conversion (see below). Like them, he did not seek to hide his Jewish origins, which was not a real option anyway. As we have seen, Dagobert worked vigorously for Jewish emancipation well after his conversion.

Some Jews alienated from Judaism adopted socialism with quasi-religious fervor, without formally renouncing Judaism. Moses Hess, born in 1812 to an orthodox family, abandoned Jewish traditionalism along with his father's sugar refining business. Hess is of interest here not for his signal contributions to German socialism or, after 1862, to Jewish nationalism, but because he represents a type of Jewish intellectual and social activist and because his memoirs furnish precious insight about a class of alienated young Jewish men in Cologne in the late 1820's.[106]

In his nationalist phase, Hess would recall his pious grandfather adoringly: "My . . . grandfather was one of those revered scholars who, though not using the Torah as a means of subsistence, yet possessed the title and knowledge of a rabbi. . . . Tears fell upon [his] snow-white beard . . . as he read [the] stories . . . concerning the exile of the Jews from Jerusalem."[107] Yet, as an adolescent, Hess had little patience for Talmudic studies. It was the same for a group of young Cologne Jews from middle-class homes who, according to a Shlomo Avineri, restlessly sought but failed to achieve acceptance in larger society.[108]

Left in a cultural and social void, they frequented saloons, theaters, and art galleries and read cheap novels. Hess was saved from this aimlessness by his relative Leopold Zunz, one of the founders of *Wissenschaft des Judentums* (the Science of Judaism). Zunz sent him more refined books and awakened him to the European Enlightenment; Hess devoured it all.[109] Slowly and painfully he lost his belief in Judaism and then was left with "nothing, nothing. I was the most miserable person in the world. I became an atheist. The world became a burden and a curse. . . . " But "I [could not] remain a skeptic for the rest of my life," and Hess soon discovered that lost belief in a personal God could be replaced by faith in a "moral world order," a realization nourished particularly by Spinoza and Heine.[110] It was the beginning of his socialist odyssey. We do not know how his young friends resolved their conflicts.

Hess's story also affords insight into the attitudes of traditional Rhenish Jews to Cologne and into the generational conflicts exacerbated there in particular. Hess's family came from Bonn, where Moses was born. In 1816 or 1817 the father, a merchant, moved to Cologne, apparently for economic reasons. He ran a grocery store, then went into sugar refining with a Christian partner. Yet he left the five-year-old Moses behind in Bonn to be educated by the grandfather described above, since Jewish educational facilities in Cologne were poor and the father wanted the boy to become a Talmud scholar. Thus we see that while traditional Jews responded to the economic lure of the big city, those concerned with transmitting a high level of Jewish learning to their sons may have left families behind rather than bring them to a Jewish "wasteland."[111]

As a result of these circumstances, Hess grew up in Bonn's Yiddish-speaking Jewish quarter. Receiving only private lessons in German and French, he never attained the fluency and style of those with a *Gymnasium* education. When he moved to Cologne following his mother's death in 1824, the size of the city and its lack of a Jewish quarter overwhelmed him. Suddenly he felt his linguistic inadequacy and set out to learn proper German and manners. As he wrote to the German Jewish writer Berthold Auerbach in 1840, "Dass Du die English language lernst, I have heard by my brother, and I do it also. Auch reinige ich täglich die Zähne und bringe mein Haar in Ordnung [I also clean my teeth daily and arrange my hair]."[112] Hess's behavior in the big city fulfilled his father's every fear. The two quarreled about religious observance and Moses's (alleged) aimlessness, since he was not going into business. The rift never healed. It was one of many conflicted relationships between parents and children during the cultural upheaval that transformed Jewish society during the era of emancipation.

The Rhineland's contrasting history of liberation and repression in the early nineteenth century may have produced a particularly high incidence of this kind of conflict and of radical solutions to it.[113] The region certainly was home to a large number of Jewish-born social critics and activists. Heinrich Heine, Moses Hess, Andreas Gottschalk, Ludwig Börne, and Karl Marx are only the best known of a list of such men, not all of whom converted.[114] In addition to Gottschalk, Marx, and Dagobert Oppenheim, a disproportionately large number of men affiliated with the Jewish community were involved in founding and running the *Rheinische Zeitung*: Abraham Oppenheim, Samuel Benjamin Cohen, Jacob de Jonge, Hartwig Lazarus Hellwitz, Moritz Morel, and Abraham Ochse-Stern (a son-in-law of Joseph Stern).[115] As we know, the paper was founded in 1841 as a liberal-radical counterweight to the *Kölnische Zeitung*, then the conservative mouthpiece. Small wonder that its editorial staff was disparaged by Cardinal Giessel as consisting of "Protestants, young Jews [*Jungjuden*], in confederation with unchurched Catholic [*dekatholisierten*] Hegelians."[116]

Little wonder either, that the paper resolutely backed Jewish emancipation. Even Marx, whose antipathy for Jews and Judaism was well developed by this time, considered the political equality of the Jews a necessary development in the unfolding and ultimate demise of bourgeois society.[117] Accordingly, in the summer of 1842, Marx, then in Trier, wrote to Dagobert Oppenheim for copies of anti-emancipation articles appearing in the *Kölnische Zeitung* so that he might write a refutation and, if not lay the "Jewish question" to rest, utterly redirect its analysis.[118] The promised article never appeared in the paper, probably, as Edmund Silberner notes, because by the fall of 1842, when Marx became its editor, the *Rheinische Zeitung* was struggling to survive pressures from the Prussian censor. Marx's intention to pronounce on Jewish rights finally found expression in his "On the Jewish Question," a more jaundiced theoretical exposition than a piece of advocacy.[119]

Yet in that same year, at the height of the lobbying effort surrounding the seventh Rhenish Provincial Diet, Marx declared his readiness to assist in practical efforts for emancipation—for the right reasons, of course. As he wrote to fellow radical Arnold Ruge (who detested Jews), "The leader of the local [Cologne] Israelites has just come to ask me to write a petition for the Jews to the *Diet*, and I am going to do it. Repugnant as the Israelite faith is to me . . . as many holes as possible should be driven into the Christian State in order to smuggle in . . . the rational [point of view]. At any rate, one must try to do it," for even if reforming efforts failed, precisely this would radicalize the malcontent and serve the ultimate cause, for "embitterment grows with every petition that is turned down with protest."[120]

At this stage in his life, Hess's pronouncements on Judaism were only slightly less vitriolic than those of Marx. We do not know if the Jewish backers of the *Rheinische Zeitung* were aware of how hostile the paper's chief ideologues were to Judaism. Their motivations, however, might have seemed a fine point in the early 1840's, with Jewish rights under intense public and official debate and the city's most important newspaper, the *Kölnische Zeitung*, backing the Christian state.

Jacob Toury has described the predominantly conservative, loyalist stance of German Jewry in these years. It was an attitude born of the religious traditionalism that still typified the majority of Jews and a combination of middle-class and specifically Jewish anxiety about "law and order," since "the authorities" were the Jews' only hope against anti-Jewish mob violence.[121] Liberalism, however, was the Jews' only hope for improved legal status. For the growing numbers of acculturated and acculturating Jews, it was also the only hope for a deeper rapprochement with German society, for acceptance and belonging beyond material success. This awareness, sharpened as details of Frederick William IV's intended re-segregation of Jews became known, fed Jewish willingness to participate actively in the political and physical battles of 1848.[122]

We have no way of knowing whether Toury's breakdown of the political orientation of German Jewry during the 1848 revolution— 50 to 55 percent loyalist, 30 to 35 percent moderate liberal, 14 percent radical democratic, 1 percent socialist—holds for the Jews of Cologne.[123] We do know that two Cologne Jews were in Gottschalk's radical camp (one was Moses Hess's brother Samuel), and that two served in the civil guard—the aforementioned etcher-illustrator David Levy Elkan and former *Rheinische Zeitung* supporter and city loan office manager Abraham Ochse-Stern.[124]

Yet labels can be very misleading in describing the allegiances of Jews during these years. In 1846, the *Allgemeine Zeitung des Judentums*, German Jewry's most important newspaper, reported the election to Cologne's City Assembly (as the City Council was renamed after 1845) of Abraham Oppenheim, describing him as a "candidate of the conservatives," although, according to city historian Gothein, there were no "true conservatives" in Cologne.[125] Several scholars have noted this newspaper entry and commented on the significance of Oppenheim's party adherence.[126] Jacob Toury, who explains why a Jewish-conservative alliance could never develop in Germany, reports that Oppenheim's conservative connections were indeed short-lived and that he "transferred his political adherence from the conservative to the liberal camp immediately upon the outbreak of the Revolution."

As we know, however, Abraham Oppenheim was no conservative in the sense usually used in Prussian politics, in the sense Toury himself uses the term: a defender of the privileges of the Protestant, aristocratic, estate-owning power establishment, a backer of a Christian state and of minimum government stimulation of the industrial economy. Abraham backed the radical *Rheinische Zeitung* financially and, as Wilhelm Treue notes, Dagobert Oppenheim's managerial post at the paper hardly put him in disgrace with his brothers.[127] Not only did Abraham and Simon address a forthright petition for Jewish rights to Frederick William IV in 1841 (see below), Abraham, we recall, joined the liberal opposition at the First United Diet in Berlin in 1847 to lobby against the King's proposed Jewry law.

Nor were Abraham's oppositional politics limited to Jewish affairs. On April 16, 1847, Dagobert Oppenheim wrote from Cologne to Mevissen, then at the United Diet in Berlin, about a "small gathering" that he and Claessen, a prominent member of the Cologne liberal clique, had organized the previous night to find "a legal?" means to publicize news of the Diet's deliberations, which censorship was keeping out of the newspapers. Dr. Feist, a member of the Jewish community, was at the gathering; so was Abraham Oppenheim.[128]

More than Oppenheim's political label, it is the election of so conspicuous a Jew to Cologne's municipal government that is the true commentary on the times, further evidence that in the bourgeois age, class took precedence over religion. Oppenheim's election was the result of the new electoral system introduced by the Municipal Ordinance of 1845, a creation of Rhenish liberals, which established a three-class, wealth-biased, male-suffrage system and secured the hegemony of the wealthy.[129] It is also noteworthy that this election occurred in the middle of the economic crisis of 1846, when the lower classes were becoming radicalized and middle-class anxiety was escalating.[130] Abraham Oppenheim was no democrat. He had as much at stake in the preservation of law and order as those who elected him, but it was the *new* social order to which Oppenheim belonged. It was precisely because *Cologne's* erstwhile conservatives — its old Catholic, merchant families — had been eclipsed by a new elite that an Oppenheim could sit on its municipal council.

For all this, Treue tells us, Oppenheim did so with remarkable lack of interest, resigning his post in May 1848 because, as he wrote the mayor, other responsibilities left him no time to discharge a public office.[131] Yet, just a year earlier, City Councilman Abraham Oppenheim had found the time for a two-month stay in Berlin to lobby for Jewish rights — against the king.

Social Integration

In the absence of memoirs it is not possible to judge the kind and quality of social relations between Jews and non-Jews in these years. Evidence from elsewhere in Germany, though for the years after midcentury, suggests that Jewish economic success was not accompanied by social acceptance and that the acceptance that did occur was more in public than private spheres, that economic relationships did not extend from marketplace to home. Even Jewish and Christian children maintained social distance in the schools they increasingly frequented together.[132]

Jacob Toury has noted that social relations were influenced by class and locale, with relationships between Jews and non-Jews more likely to develop in big cities and among the well-to-do, than in towns and villages and among Jewish and Christian *Kleinbürger* (lower classes).[133] Attitudes to Jews in Cologne seem to follow these class lines. We have seen evidence of *Kleinbürger* resistance to Jews. While there were no popular outbreaks against Jews in Cologne such as occurred elsewhere in Germany and Europe in 1848, the strain of the lower-class antisemitism that had developed by the early 1840's reached political expression in radical circles during the Revolution.[134]

Ironically, much of this was directed against Andreas Gottschalk. Despite his conversion, opponents in the workers' association he helped found labeled his proposals *jüdische Hinterlist* (Jewish fraud) and accused Jews in Vienna, Prague, Pest, and Paris of manipulating *das Volk* (the people) for selfish ends, that is, emancipation. Several years later, Cologne's radical worker's journal would label Ferdinand Lasalle, Germany's foremost socialist, a "Jew" and an "egoist," interchangeable epithets.

Internal wrangling within the leadership of the Cologne workers' association was surely a factor in this vituperation against Jews. The language bears the unmistakable imprimatur of Karl Marx, who in 1848–49 was waging a winning battle against Gottschalk for control of the organization.[135] How deeply anti-Jewish sentiment permeated the rank and file of the organization we do not know, and generalizations from the behavior of the leadership may not be warranted. The 3,000 to 4,000 workers who attended Gottschalk's funeral in 1849 (he died of cholera after treating the poor during an outbreak) obviously did not believe that he was a selfish manipulator of their cause.

If competition divided upwardly mobile Jews and distressed petty Christian *Bürger*, ideology created common ground for some Jews and non-Jews of *Besitz- und Bildung* (property and education). The "Young Germany" group that created the *Rheinische Zeitung* and the paper itself were "neutral ground," to use Jacob Katz's term, if ever such existed: a terrain of common interests and commitments in which religious background was irrelevant.[136]

Dagobert Oppenheim's Jewish origins, his efforts on behalf of Jewish emancipation well after his conversion, and the conspicuous Jewish associations of his brothers Abraham and Simon, did not impede his acceptance into Cologne's liberal clique. His place in its politics is amply documented in the correspondence of movement activists.[137] A casual reference in a letter Mevissen wrote to his brother-in-law in 1845 shows that Oppenheim was considered a comrade as well as a colleague. Describing government efforts to quash the Cologne group following its successful petition campaign to the eighth Provincial Diet, Mevissen wrote, "For the time being, Claessen, Oppenheim, and Haan are involved in an inquiry concerning evasion of censorship in the dissemination of the Cologne petition, and are threatened with a fine of 10 taler. The public hearing this week, at which Wittgenstein [a high-ranking city official], the mayor, the entire City Council, and I hope to be summoned as witnesses, will be exquisite fun."[138] (This because Cologne's entire municipal apparatus was in the liberal camp and none of its members was likely to provide testimony helpful to the government.)

Because of the Oppenheims' prominence, virtually all our information about Jewish social integration concerns them, and we cannot, of course, generalize from their exceptional case. Even then, we know more about Oppenheim efforts at integration than any success they may have achieved, especially in local Cologne society. Thus we know, for example, that the Oppenheims, like other wealthy families of Cologne, bought land outside the city: a rural property southwest of it; a "summer residence," consisting of houses "in antique style," gardens, and a court, in the northern outskirts.[139] Pierre Ayçoberry evaluates such behavior as less financially motivated than a "reflex behavior of parvenus" mimicking the nobility.[140] The fact that the Oppenheims were but one family in a class of such parvenus may not have eased their way. As we have seen, even the socially advantageous intermarriage of Eve Oppenheim was not to a local son and insider but to a Berliner.

Still, the Oppenheims took care to be model citizens of a type befitting their station, joining 40 of Cologne's most respected *Bürger* on the executive committee for the completion of the Cologne cathedral. The *Dom* was of enormous symbolic importance in Cologne and beyond. While still crown prince, Frederick William had visited the structure, expressing his admiration for it and his desire to see the building, begun in the Middle Ages, completed. Thereupon it became a symbol of hoped-for German unity. At the festivities celebrating the laying of the foundation-stone in September 1842, Frederick William called the centuries-long work on the cathedral an effort "of fraternity [*Brudersinn*] of all Germans of all confessions." Oppenheim support ensured that Jews, too, were included in that company. Simon Oppenheim, the most culturally interested of the brothers, pledged a substantial donation to the project, earning a lifelong honorary membership on the executive committee — and a home visit by the royal couple, the prince, and a host of Prussian nobility.[141] Triumphs of this sort did not necessarily bring social acceptance, though they certainly signal the hope for it.[142]

The Gemeinde *and Its Affairs*

> "A reform faction does not prevail here, therefore no
> splits exist."

This cryptic remark, buried in an otherwise prosaic report by the synagogue executive board to the mayor in 1843, stands out as much for its perception of the communal impact of Reform Judaism in the 1840's as for its commentary on the state of Judaism in Cologne.[143] Written before the Reform rabbinical conferences of the 1840's but after the eruption of bitter disputes in several of German Jewry's most important communities around issues of prayer language, synagogue decorum, and rabbinic authority, it showed acute awareness of the divisive potential of organized religious change and relief at its absence from the local scene.[144]

Nevertheless, the board also made clear that there were serious deficiencies in the structure of religious life in Cologne's community. Here as in the business world, French law still held sway over Jewish affairs. The Napoleonic decree that established the centralized consistorial system in France continued to govern Jewish religious life in the Rhineland. Cologne's Jewish community, by this time among the largest in Prussia, had no rabbi of its own. Instead, it continued to be served by the *Ober-Consistorial Rabbiner* of Bonn — an anamolous office, given the nonexistence in Prussia of the consistorial hierarchy headed by a chief rabbi. The rabbis of this period — Abraham Auerbach, originally from Alsace, and his son, Aaron — were but an occasional presence in Cologne, visiting periodically to speak in the synagogue or examine school children. Yet under the consistorial system they exercised total control over administrative and religious life in Cologne's community.[145]

Crippling, too, was the community's inability to enforce dues payments by synagogue members, a "highly desirable" right vouchsafed by the law, community leaders wrote, but which "the government, for now, does not yet permit."[146] Dues to the consistorial synagogue in Bonn were inescapable (130 to 140 taler a year were collected from Cologne under government supervision), while the local synagogue had to depend on voluntary contributions. As a result, the community's debt stood at a considerable 1,350 taler, the report stated.

Cologne's communal leadership chafed at its enforced subservience to Bonn. The compilers of the May 1843 report (written in response to a state-initiated survey of Jewish affairs) soon turned to provincial authorities with a petition to end Cologne's communal tutelage. The appeal did not propose abolishing the consistorial system but redistricting its loci of power: Cologne would be removed from the Bonn Consistory and made part of the Consistory of Krefeld—whose district consistorial seat would then be transferred to Cologne. The appeal failed.[147]

Had it been granted, Cologne, of course, would have had to select its own rabbi, and we can only speculate about the choice that would have been made. For all the purported absence of a reform group in Cologne—one version of the 1843 report states the absence of a reform party; the one actually delivered to the mayor's office states only that such a party was not dominant—it is clear that the communal leadership wished at least a "modern" if not a "Reform" type of Judaism. The 1843 report noted that "the service is held in Hebrew, but for the last six months or so, a rabbinical student has been provisionally engaged for occasional sermons in German on Biblical texts; he will be paid through voluntary contributions." The preacher's subject matter—the Bible, rather than rabbinic law—as well as his language of instruction—German, rather than Hebrew or Yiddish—mark him as a "modern."[148]

The fact that the preacher's salary was not drawn from communal funds but was privately financed would indicate the existence of an interest group of modernized Jews. Their ability to have such a man preach in the synagogue (the same innovation was the subject of bitter conflict in Breslau) indicates that these Jews were powerful in the community, or that there was little opposition to the new practice, or both. The authors of the 1843 report, Isaac Cohen and David Hess, were undoubtedly in the modernizing camp, since their petition for communal autonomy a few months later complained about the community's inability to hire a man who, in Adolf Kober's paraphrase, would "educate the young,"[149] 1840's code language for a modern-type rabbi able literally to speak the language of the younger generation and draw it into the synagogue.

Yet the latter complaint is puzzling because the situation in Cologne was very different from that in Breslau, for example, where reformers tried to introduce a new type of rabbi, Reform leader Abraham Geiger, into communal office because the "old" type of rabbi was an intransigent antimodernist. Rabbi Aron Auerbach of Bonn, though Orthodox, was university educated, even the holder of a doctorate.[150] Cologne's move to separate from Bonn, therefore, is attributable less to reformist strivings, though these clearly existed, than to a desire for local control and greater rabbinic presence.[151] Indeed, a number of references in the 1843 synagogue board report expresses disapproval for certain religious innovations — confirmation for children, clerical dress — which had "an exclusively Christian character or mimic Christian practice."[152]

Jewish education, never a strong point in Cologne, sputtered along under persistent prodding from the city school commission about its curriculum and physical plant. A school for boys and one for girls operated out of run-down, community-held property. Both were considered private institutions, although the girls' teacher was licensed and both teachers were recognized as private instructors. Costs were defrayed through tuition and community subvention.[153] Fewer than 60 elementary-age children — 22 boys and 33 girls — were enrolled in the two schools in the 1830's. While Jewish school enrollments in ten other major German Jewish communities rose between 1841 and 1861 (declining in six others), in Cologne, even with the enormous increase in the Jewish population by 1848, enrollment was up only to 108, fewer "by far" than the number of children eligible, according to a city education official.[154]

The gender disparity in enrollment may have been caused by the respective curricula: boys' studies were heavily traditional, girls', strikingly modern. Of 39 hours of weekly study for boys, 20 were devoted to Hebrew and religious subjects, only 11 (later 13) to German.[155] Girls, by contrast, received fifteen hours of German weekly and only five of religion — as many as were allotted each for math, handiwork, and French.[156] With an increasing number of Jewish families expecting boys to succeed in the world of business and pass, at least, in German society — recall the enrollment statistics for the *Realgymnasium* — it is little wonder that parents saw the Jewish school as poor preparation, even for the *Gymnasium*.

The modernity of the girls' curriculum is less surprising than might appear. Formal education for Jewish girls had never been a traditional priority because girls were not expected to become scholars or leaders in the community, and rabbinic law did not obligate females, as it did males, to

Torah study in its own right. Traditionally, girls were taught at home the basics of Hebrew and Yiddish literacy necessary for prayer and reading of popular, pietistic works, and the essentials of Jewish law and ritual for the spheres under women's control: the kitchen and the marital bed. The fact that the curriculum in Cologne gave girls more secular study than boys does not indicate conscious modernizing of girls. Rather, it was an outgrowth of traditional values according more importance to the study of Jewish texts than to secular subjects (since girls were not taught the first, they could learn the second) and of the precapitalist expectation that girls would contribute to family income, thus, their need to learn German and math (middle-class Jewish families had long considered it a status symbol for girls to know some French).[157] Jewish education in Cologne was in a dismal state, as community leaders, complaining about the lack of a resident rabbi to oversee the school, clearly knew.

On the Eve of Revolution

The most elaborate Jewish protest from the Rhineland against the lack of emancipation came from Abraham and Simon Oppenheim in 1841. Addressed as a "most humble" appeal to the newly crowned Frederick William IV, it was anything but circumspect. At 45 printed pages, its very length bespoke the authors' sense of its importance.[158]

The tract shows solid familiarity with Prussian and Rhenish history and law and with the king's beliefs about the centrality of religion in public life. While joining him in denouncing religious indifference and rejecting notions of a secular state, however, the Oppenheims argued that religious affiliation should be irrelevant to all public positions except those with "true, inner, living" connection to religious concerns. These they do not define, but they explicitly exclude the legal, teaching, and military professions, drug dispensing and jury service — precisely the areas in which Jews suffered discrimination. Passionately, bitterly, the Oppenheims decry the hypocrisy and opportunism engendered by laws purporting to protect and elevate religious principle, and they implore the king to lift the oppression that forces "the best among" his Jewish subjects to "buy" advantage "through confession" — opportunistic conversion.

Particularly desperate, they say, is the generation that grew up in the second decade of the century, after the proclamation of Prussia's 1812 Edict of Emancipation and before administrative rulings in the 1820's closed public service to Jews. A generation educated and trained toward a certain life path found itself betrayed and adrift, understandably choosing "to regain what was lost through a change of faiths." The appeal describes the predicament of Jews ready to give the best of themselves to society, to whom the state responded, "If you have a sense of honor, let it rot. If you have talents, let them lie fallow, I cannot use them. If you have gained knowledge for yourself, bury it, I can apply it to no useful sphere of activity. . . . Eat your bread with shame; disgrace and humiliation shall be your inheritance." The prominence and bitterness of the plea against state-pressured conversions leaves no doubt that the appeal, composed just two years after Dagobert Oppenheim's conversion, had personal wellsprings. Indeed, Dieter Kastner is probably right in suggesting that it was Dagobert himself, a jurist, we recall, who authored the petition, his more prominent and influential brothers signing and presenting it to the king.[159]

Deftly maneuvering around France's reputation as the first European state to emancipate its Jews, the Oppenheim essay recalls the excesses of the French Revolution along with the ignominy of the 1808 decree, implying that a king who reviled the first must also reject the second. Prussia, moreover, did not need a foreign model to guide its Jewish policy. Its own Edict of 1812, loosed from the administrative fetters that had bound and betrayed its spirit and extended finally to all Prussia's provinces, was a solution with both justice and national integrity.

This, of course, was not the solution Frederick William and his advisers had in mind, and the king's terse reply to the Oppenheims two and a half months later spoke volumes: "I have read your petition and the accompanying text concerning the situation of the Jews in the Prussian state and have familiarized myself with their contents. Since the subject in question has already been taken up by the Council of State, I refrain for now from any judgment on it and await the proposals of the Council of State."[160]

It is a measure of the glory Cologne's Jewish community enjoyed, by virtue of the city's importance, that Rhenish Jewry's response to the king's 1847 law emerged in Cologne, initiated and led by a special committee of the synagogue executive board.[161] On April 26, 1847, this committee, which included Simon Oppenheim, formally asked Abraham Oppenheim to represent Rhine Province Jewry in its opposition to the law at the United Diet in Berlin. Oppenheim departed for the capital six days later. In fact, Mevissen's correspondence shows that Oppenheim had already resolved to go to Berlin before the Jewish committee ever met and that Mevissen, not Rhenish Jewry (as community historian Carl Brisch would have it), prompted the trip.[162] The Oppenheims undoubtedly learned from Mevissen about the Jewry law long before notice of it appeared in the *Kölnische Zeitung*, the ostensible catalyst for Jewish communal response (as we know, the paper received its intelligence about the Diets from liberal delegates), and it was undoubtedly the Oppenheims who alerted the Jewish community and called forth *its* response.

Be that as it may, it was a remarkable prominence that the Jewish community of Cologne had attained only 50 years after resettlement: one of its own huddled with some of German Jewry's greatest spokesmen — Gabriel Riesser, Moritz Veit, Johann Jacoby, Sigismund Stern — to work for the future of Prussian Jewry.[163] The 1847 law had little time to effect change in Jewish civic status. The revolution of 1848 declared, and the 1850 Constitution affirmed, the separation of civil and political status from religious affiliation. The principle of secular citizenship and civil equality in Prussia would subsequently be compromised grievously through "restrictive administrative practices" developed "into a fine art."[164] In 1850, however, to the Jews of Cologne, some of whom had experienced Jewish readmission to the city, the times must have appeared momentous, indeed.

The Free Imperial City of Cologne, viewed from Deutz. This is the only view most Jews would have had of Cologne until the French annexation and Jewish resettlement.

Cologne's City Hall, site of decades of debate on the city's "Jewish question."

Adolf Steinberger, mayor of Cologne, 1823–48. A Prussian appointee, in 1824 Steinberger took part in a daring challenge by the City Council of Prussia's relatively liberal enforcement of Jewry legislation in Cologne. In the 1840's, he argued for emancipation, also in opposition to Prussia.

Peter Heinrich Merkens (1778–1854). A leading Cologne businessman, longtime head of the city's Chamber of Commerce and one of its representatives at the Rhenish Provincial Diets. Originally a fierce opponent of Jewish rights, Merkens later supported Jewish equality.

Salomon Oppenheim, Jr., (1772–1828). A court Jew in electoral Cologne, merchant, entrepreneur, and founder of the Oppenheim banking house, Oppenheim was often called on to represent Jewish interests. He served in this capacity, albeit reluctantly, at Napoleon's Assembly of Notables in 1806. He was made a Prussian senior royal court agent and member of Cologne's Chamber of Commerce in 1822, at a time when the chamber opposed Jewish rights.

Abraham Oppenheim (1804–78). A banker and railroad, mining, steam shipping, and insurance maverick, Oppenheim campaigned tirelessly for Jewish rights, lobbying politically prominent business associates who were dependent on his bank for loans, as well as Prussia's Frederick William IV, on behalf of Jewish emancipation.

Gustav Mevissen (1815–99). Railroad, insurance, and newspaper entrepreneur, and leading Rhenish liberal. A long-standing friend and business associate of the Oppenheims, he argued passionately for Jewish emancipation at the First United Prussian Diet in 1847.

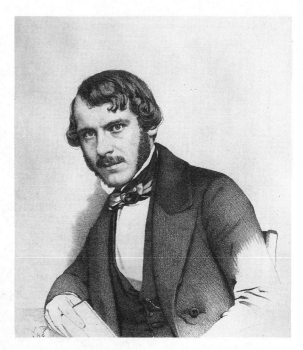

Ludolf Camphausen (1803–90). Like Mevissen, an entrepreneur and prominent Rhenish liberal. Bearing both a personal and a professional animosity against the Oppenheims, Camphausen nevertheless went along with support for Jewish rights.

Nouvelle synagogue de Cologne, fondée sous le patronage de M. Abraham Oppenheim, et construite sur les plans de M. E. Zwirner, architecte de la cathédrale.

The original caption of this reproduction reads, "The new synagogue of Cologne, founded under the patronage of Mr. Abraham Oppenheim and built according to the plans of the cathedral architect, M. E. Zwirner." The synagogue was inaugurated in 1861.

Glockengasse synagogue, street scene. A member of Cologne's Municipal Assembly called the structure a "credit to the city."

ZUR
EINWEIHUNG
DER NEUEN
SYNAGOGE
ZU
COELN

Interior, Glockengasse synagogue.

Facing page:
Invitation to Cologne municipal assemblyman, Dr. Nückel, to attend the dedication of the synagogue.

Rabbi Dr. Israel Schwarz (1828–75). The first rabbi to serve in Cologne, Schwartz was Orthodox yet willing to use such innovations as a catechism to reach acculturated Jewish youth. A vigorous advocate of Jewish education, Schwarz won permission to give religious instruction to Jewish students in public schools, just as priests and ministers were permitted to do for Catholic and Protestant students.

Regierungsbezirk von Köln.

Patent
für das Jahr 1827.

Auf den Grund des Dekrets von 17. März 1808, und der Königlichen Kabinets-Ordre vom 3 März 1818, imgleichen auf das Zeugniß des Gemeinderaths der Stadt *Coeln* wird dem *Marcus Schilo Schubach*

hiermit die Befugniß ertheilt, das Gewerbe als

im Regierungsbezirk Köln während des Jahrs 1827 zu betreiben

Gegeben Köln, den 1827.

Königliche Regierung. Abtheilung des Innern.

Judenpatent for the Jewish hides dealer Marcus Schilo Schubach, issued on March 20, 1827.

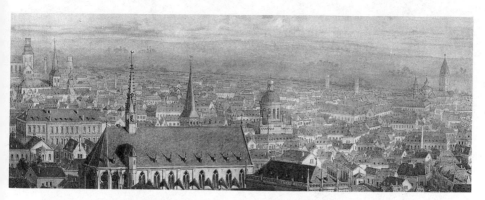

City vista, late nineteenth century, with spires of some of Cologne's ancient churches and the dome of the synagogue.

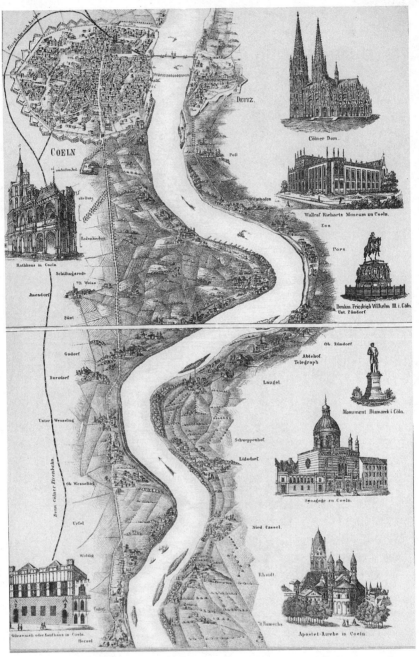

Souvenir map of Cologne, late nineteenth century. The synagogue (right, second from bottom) is pictured among the city's most notable sites, including its ancient churches, Cologne Cathedral, City Hall, and statues of Bismarck and King Frederick William.

CHAPTER SEVEN

"A Large Gemeinde Like Cologne": A Community Comes into Its Own, 1850–71

The Roots of Jewish Revival

In 1852, the leaders of Cologne's Jewish community wrote a forthright letter to the highest-ranking Prussian official in the Rhine Province about the need for fundamental reorganization of the structures of community life. Any such change required government ratification, and community leaders had to convince the *Oberpräsident* that the need for change was pressing and that Cologne's Jews merited his attention. Accordingly, the letter stressed the growth of Jewish settlement in the city, ending with the plea that only a firm new institutional base would allow "a large community like Cologne" to realize its rich potential.[1]

There was no disputing the facts of the petition. By midcentury, 52 years after resettlement, the Jewish community of Cologne was the fifth largest in Germany, and the third largest in Prussia, after Berlin and Breslau (see Table 23). Though far smaller than those in Hamburg, Berlin, Breslau, and Frankfurt, it was sizable enough to have made a mark on the communal landscape of a still predominantly small-town and rural German Jewry.[2] Within the Rhine Province, Cologne's community of nearly 1,300 Jews far outnumbered that of Aachen (223 in 1840) or Koblenz, the provincial capital (349 in 1843).[3] Between 1851 and 1866 Cologne's Jewish community more than doubled, from 1,275 to 2,720. By 1871, the Jewish popula-

TABLE 23

Jewish Population Growth in the Seven Largest Jewish Communities in Germany, 1850, 1871

Community	1850	1871	Absolute Increase	Percentage of Increase
Hamburg	10,000	13,796	3,796	38
Berlin	9,595	36,015	26,420	275
Breslau	7,384	13,000	5,616	76
Frankfurt/Main	5,200	7,620	2,420	47
Cologne	1,286	3,172	1,886	147
Munich	1,252	2,903	1,651	132
Leipzig	320	2,551	2,231	697

SOURCES: Wilhelm, p. 59; Richarz, ed., *Jüdisches Leben*, p. 31.
NOTE: Berlin, Breslau, and Cologne were located in Prussia.

tion was 3,172, constituting 2.4 percent of the city's total population, up from 1.4 percent just twenty years before (see Table 24).

More than size established the community's significance. Its communal leadership, a highly self-conscious group, as we shall see, also basked in the borrowed glory of Cologne's importance as a regional economic pole. The liberal movement, which had catapulted the city to political prominence in the 1840's, was not nearly as active and conspicuous in the 1850's but Cologne's place in commerce and, especially, finance only grew more important after midcentury, assuring its Jewish community some status by association.[4]

With a growing sense of self-importance came increased communal assertiveness. Evidence of this came as early as 1843 in the effort by members of the communal leadership to make Cologne the seat of the consistorial synagogue and to gain the right of compulsory taxation of members (see Chapter 6).

Grander efforts came in the wake of the Jewry law of July 23, 1847. The original draft of this law, we recall, was the bane of Rhenish liberals and organized Prussian Jewry because of its fundamental compromise of Jewish civic equality. But the law that was actually enacted, though it barred Jews from a broad range of state positions, actually held rich potential for reorganizing and strengthening Jewish community life. This was because the "Jewry corporations" that Frederick William IV had sought were transformed from humiliating institutions effecting "the collective exclusion of the Jews from modern society" to "synagogue-communities," membership in which was compulsory.[5]

The full impact of the 1847 law on the organizational life of Prussian Jewry has not been studied, but it stands to reason that its effects would have been beneficial: state recognition of the community and compulsory membership were powerful conserving forces in a time of unprecedented integration.[6] The boon of the legislation is dramatically evident in Cologne where communal affairs, sunk in a dismal morass before midcentury, began to show dynamism and creativity thereafter. The communal leadership made major initiatives in three areas: reorganization of internal affairs, relations with the rest of Rhenish and Prussian Jewry, and relations with municipal authorities. These initiatives have been chronicled, but their significance has not been explored or appreciated. On the contrary, the impression left by Adolf Kober is one of communal drift and decline in the postrevolution years.[7]

Kober's portrait accords with Jacob Toury's assessment of organized German Jewish life in this period. Toury, borrowing the judgment of Ludwig Philippson's *Allgemeine Zeitung des Judentums*, has written that there was a noticeable "slackness" in German Jewish communal life after the revolutions of 1848, an "unsteadiness," a "lack of public spirit, of esprit de corps." This "weakening of communal cohesion," as Toury puts it, resulted, he says, from attrition of the Jewish best and brightest away from Jewish concerns toward those of a larger society now receptive to their "political and scientific" contributions.[8]

Aside from the fact that such receptivity was very short-lived—Toury himself illustrates how dismal was the record of German states on Jewish rights (especially political rights) in the "years of Reaction"—there is strong evidence of a surge of Jewish communal creativity and vitality in the

TABLE 24
Growth of the Catholic, Protestant, and Jewish Populations of Cologne, 1851–71

Year	Total Population	Catholic	Protestant	Jewish	Other	Jewish Percentage of Total
1851	90,085	80,235	8,566	1,275	9	1.4
1854	99,703	88,147	9,942	1,605	4	1.6
1855	100,470	88,258	10,385	1,823	3	1.8
1862	115,889	100,699	12,794	2,392	4	2.1
1863	119,596	103,535	13,605	2,452	4	2.1
1865	116,995	101,493	12,872	2,610	9	2.2
1866	121,072	105,056	13,217	2,720	9	2.2
1871	129,594	108,656	17,327	3,172	439	2.4

SOURCES: "Die Civil Bevölkerung der Stadt Köln betrug nach der letzten Aufnahme in Jahre 1851," *Verhandlungen des Gemeinderaths der Stadt Köln* (1851); "Jahres Bericht über den Civilstand der Stadt Köln," ibid. (1855); "Jahres Bericht," ibid. (1856); "Anlage zu den Verhandlungen der Stadtverordneten Versammlung vom 7 Juli 1864," "Bericht pro 1863 über den Civilstand der Stadt Köln," ibid. (1863); "Anlage zum Sitzungsprotocoll vom 1. Februar 1866," ibid. (1865); "Sitzung vom 7. November 1867," ibid. (1867); Ayçoberry, "Histoire Sociale," 2: 106, App. 15.

NOTE: In 1851, Jews were 2.24 percent of the population of Berlin; 5.29 percent of Hamburg; 6.16 percent of Breslau; 0.73 percent of Munich; 0.65 percent of Dresden; 0.79 percent of Leipzig; 8 percent of Frankfurt am Main; 2.05 percent of Bremen; 0.19 percent of Nürnberg, and 1.44 percent of Stettin. Barkai, "German Jews," p. 125, Table 1.

post-revolutionary era.[9] While acknowledging the financial and religious crises that beset Jewish communities all over Europe in this period, Salo Baron argues that "the Jewish bodies were intrinsically so strong and tenacious that they ultimately emerged from the trial with renewed vitality. In fact, the very preoccupation of writers [like Philippson, we might add] with the shortcomings of the existing [communal] order not only testified to their intense interest in the preservation of their community, but often stimulated new thinking and gave rise to a variety of proposals which pointed the way to . . . healthy reforms."[10]

This was certainly true in Cologne's organized community. The dynamism of its leadership deserves study not only because this revises an incomplete, even inaccurate picture of one community, but because the whole image of German Jewry floating rudderless in this period may need reassessment.

It seems odd to attribute any beneficial effects to Prussian Jewish policy, and we must stress that this result was completely unintentional. The active hostility of the Prussian state to Judaism's continued, viable existence is amply documented.[11] Prussia's ultimate goal for the Jews was collective disappearance, whether through progressive assimilation or conversion. Such statesmen and civil servants as Wilhelm von Humboldt or Christian Wilhelm Dohm foresaw assimilation as a natural consequence of emancipation and were content to let the process take its own course, but the government actively fostered the Society for the Promotion of Christianity Among the Jews, with which it had a close, if unofficial, relationship.[12] Ismar Schorsch has shown that Prussian state policy intended to withhold respectability from the Prussian rabbinate and undermine it in order to weaken Judaism; writing in 1899, Leopold Auerbach, a Jewish legal historian, characterized Prussian Jewish policy since 1812 as geared toward ignoring, fragmenting, and dissolving German Jewry.[13] Frederick William IV and his ministers, who considered adherence to the Jewish faith and full German citizenship mutually exclusive, certainly did not wish to promote the survival of Judaism.

If the government fostered the persistence of organized Jewish communities, it was for other reasons. One writer argues that "the governments of Western Europe [including that of Prussia] did not seek the demise of the organized Jewish community" because of the continuing usefulness of those communities, especially at the local level; Jewish educational and social welfare needs continued to be met by Jews, although as taxpaying citizens they were entitled to drink from the larger civil cup.[14]

It seems, however, that organized Jewish communities had another kind of usefulness to the Prussian state. The communities maintained religious distinctions and prevented Jews from simply melting into the growing and, in the state's view, insidious mass of the religiously indifferent. At the same time, because being Jewish entailed considerable civil disabilities, compulsory membership in the Jewish community paradoxically made Jews feel the price of affiliation, indirectly encouraging defection to Christianity.

Official recognition of the community was intended to be pernicious in other ways. Recognition brought suffocating government regulation of the community's governing structure. Far from being free organizations, able to set and execute their own priorities, *Gemeinden* like Cologne's were unable even to draft their own constitutions without government approval. Even the religious school's curriculum and the appointment of community officers came under state control.

Prussia, unlike Napoleonic France, or Bavaria until 1838, did not use its regulatory power to force modernization of Judaism. On the contrary, the state opposed Jewish religious reform; in the 1840's, and after 1848 in particular, it feared any challenge to traditional authority. Moreover, as Schorsch notes, "By preserving religious forms which no longer accorded with the tastes and needs of Jews integrating into German society, the government hoped to accelerate and finalise the process of alienation" from Judaism.[15] Prussia also blocked all attempts of individual Jewish communities to form regional or statewide associations. The intent was to isolate each community, making each dependent on its own limited resources, and to undermine any larger sense of Jewish solidarity.[16]

Undercutting the rabbinate, enforcing membership in communities with severely limited competency, and maintaining civil disabilities on Jews was Prussia's way of "orchestrat[ing] the assimilation of its Jewish population."[17] Yet the net effect, at least of compulsory membership in the community, was to affirm the collective existence of the Jews. Unwittingly, this policy did much to further Jewish group survival.[18]

In Cologne, the 1847 law and several subsequent legal enactments strongly encouraged a *preexisting* desire by the communal leadership to invigorate the *Gemeinde*. Thus I would not argue that Prussian legislation caused a communal revival in Cologne. External forces could not work a communal renaissance. Moreover, since the law was hardly salutary in intent or design, only determined, creative adaptation by Jews could have brought about an invigorating result.

In this chapter we shall examine three initiatives undertaken by Cologne's communal leadership in the 1850's and 1860's. One effort, to reorganize and invigorate the local community, was partially successful. Another, to organize regional and statewide Jewish communal structures, failed completely. The third initiative, to win from the municipality treatment for the

Jewish communal school equal with that accorded Catholic and Protestant schools, was a great triumph. That is a very respectable record for a period when the pressures against organized Judaism were substantial. But in all these cases, the effort, as well as the outcome, is significant for what it tells us about Jewish attitudes to communal survival and to the non-Jewish world.

A note about sources: the *Judenpatent* system lapsed in 1845, so we lack for the years under consideration here the meticulous records available for previous decades. There is, however, a relative abundance of other sources, rare for the preceding period, on Jewish communal life. Preserved in the archives of governmental bodies charged with regulating community affairs, the records' very existence bespeaks the preserving role of official policy after 1847.

Initiatives for Communal Reorganization: Regional and Statewide

In the early years of the post-revolutionary Reaction, there was much uncertainty about the legal basis of organized Jewish life in Prussia. The 1847 law had not been implemented before the outbreak of the revolution of 1848, which, having declared Jewish equality, nullified the law. After the revolution, it was unclear how much of the status quo ante would be restored. In the Rhine Province, for instance, what was the status of the consistorial system, which the 1847 law was to have replaced and which the revolution had also abolished?[19]

Even the short-lived, unconditional emancipation the revolution decreed, although welcome, raised the anxiety of communally minded Jews. The absence of any state framework for synagogal life threatened German Jewry with atomization and individual communities with dissolution. It was in this context that Ludwig Philippson, among others, sounded the alarm. Editor of the *Allgemeine Zeitung des Judentums*, activist for emancipation, and a rabbi, he wrote after promulgation of the 1848 Prussian constitution:

Complete suspension of all state influence on our communal affairs, unconditional independence not just of communities but individuals . . . can be a dangerous gift . . . if it will be used to destroy all communal bonds, to unravel all synagogue life. The elements of such decomposition, splintering, are among us. . . . Do we want this dissolution? . . . Is the hour of freedom also to be the hour of death?[20]

The solution was to weave individual communities into a voluntary union. Prussian Jewry would send delegates to a Congress to be held in

Berlin to decide questions of religious and educational reform and reorganization. Philippson's suggestion, the continuation of his long-standing advocacy of national synods of German Jewry, yielded no results, but he was not alone in supporting such an idea.[21] In March 1850, the new, vigorous leadership of the Berlin community invited the Jewish communities of Prussia to form a federated, central organization to address their common problems. The seat of the organization would be Berlin, but meetings would rotate among four other major communal centers: Königsberg, Posen, Breslau, and Cologne.[22]

Cologne's *Gemeinde*, too, devised several ambitious schemes for communal reorganization. With the promulgation of the 1847 law, the community leadership called for formation of a regional organization of Rhenish and Westphalian communities.[23] The proposal seemed even more urgent after the revolution. In late October 1850 the synagogue board called on all the communities of the Rhine Province and Westphalia to send delegates to a conference to found a "unified corporate organism." The body would address common problems of internal management, ritual (*Kultus*), and education.[24] "We want order at last," as a correspondent to the *Allgemeine Zeitung* put it.[25]

The "Congress of Cities," representing fourteen of the larger Rhenish communities, met in Cologne on January 29 and 30, 1851.[26] The delegates agreed that the most urgent need of the communities was corporate rights, without which such basic activities as buying or selling property and collecting or borrowing funds were impossible. With no secure financial or even physical base, communities could not provide religious and educational services. The 1847 law had granted synagogue communities the rights of a juridical person with regard to property, but the law applied only to communities that were part of Prussia before 1847, and even then excluded Posen. The Revised Prussian Constitution of January 31, 1850, had declared that religious and spiritual associations (*Religionsgesellschaften, geistlichen Gesellschaften*) lacking corporate rights could attain them, but only through special legislation.[27]

What was needed, the congress resolved, was a general law on Jewish life granting all Jewish communities corporate rights. Accordingly, it appealed to the Prussian Ministry of State to call Jewish delegates "from all points of the monarchy to Berlin" to draft the law (under government supervision) and to work on structures to regulate Jewish communal and educational affairs (emphatically not, it assured Berlin, on "questions of a religious nature," in which the government, of course, had no interest). The congress urged the remaining communities of the Rhineland and Westphalia to join the appeal. It also sent word of the gathering and its resolutions to the main communities of the rest of Prussia and urged them to take similar steps.[28]

Several months later, the Ministers of Religious Affairs and the Interior denied the request of the communities. Corporate rights would be granted to individual communities only, on a case-by-case basis.[29]

The proposal of the Congress of Cities had sought to prevent atomization of Prussian Jewry, but this was precisely what Prussian policy sought to achieve. No attempt to found a Jewish umbrella organization would ever receive the slightest countenance from the government. It was the end of the Cologne initiative.

Regardless of the outcome, however, the congress's effort was very significant. A new community had taken the lead in confronting a fundamental challenge of German Jewish modernity: creating structures for the continued group existence. Without such structures, no religious invigoration would have soil in which to root. No wonder Cologne's initiative won Philippson's enthusiastic endorsement, receiving prominent and frequent play in the *Allgemeine Zeitung*.[30] "Bravo!" was how he opened the paper's first report, the lead article, on Cologne's call for a community congress.[31]

In these early years of the Reaction, while the promise of the new Jewry legislation, but not yet the antipathy of the bureaucracy to collective Jewish survival, was apparent, ideas could be grand, even grandiose. Not apathy, but extraordinary dynamism characterized Cologne's communal leadership in these years.

Local Communal Reorganization

The concern of the leadership of Cologne's community for the coherence of Prussian Jewry was an extension of its concern for the local community. In fact, the community executive board issued its call for the Congress of Cities just four days after completing ambitious work on Cologne's internal communal structure.

Community leaders knew only too well the dire need of Jewish communities for corporate rights. As they and the police director of Cologne noted in official letters in 1850, the two original buildings purchased by the community in the beginning of the century were small and decrepit, completely inadequate to house religious services, a school, and apartments for the teacher and sexton. Yet, because the community lacked the legal rights of a corporate body, it could not repair them or purchase a different property: since the community was legally incompetent to conclude contracts, its board could not enter into business transactions.[32]

The problem was more serious than crowding or aesthetics. It threatened the community with financial paralysis and schism. Because the synagogue buildings were far too small to accommodate the 1,235 Jews living in the city in 1850 (numbers had swelled "particularly in the last years through immigration," the police director noted), only longtime residents, some 140 to 190 families, were members of the community and had any financial stake in it. The rest, some 90 to 125 families, stood outside the organized community. Newcomers were also put off by the uncertainty of the *Gemeinde*'s legal status, reluctant to join a synagogue whose organization might soon be overhauled from the still-extant consistorial system to something based on the 1847 law.

The divisions in the Jewish community, the police director stressed, were not doctrinal; the parties in Cologne did not correspond to the "Orthodox, liberal and those standing midway between both," which had crystallized in other large German cities. Division, therefore, could be remedied relatively simply. Left untreated, it would only worsen as the Jewish population continued to grow. The solution was to sell the old properties which, because of their prime location, would bring a high price, and buy or build larger facilities at a less central, inexpensive site. With new members charged admission fees as well as regular membership dues, the financial investment of longtime residents and immigrants would be equalized and the Jews could constitute a single "encompassing communal alliance [*Gemeinschaft*]."[33]

The communal leadership also deemed internal reform crucial, as we shall see, but resolution of this issue was fundamental, and the new Prussian Jewry legislation promised a way out. Indeed, the board was not even sure it had to apply formally for corporate rights in respect to property, since these the 1847 law had granted.[34] Still, the community applied for them. Without them, the executive declared in language almost identical to that of the Congress of Cities in its appeal to Berlin, the community could "have no secure existence, and [such] a secure existence the state, too, must surely desire."

In fact, the Ministry of Interior responded positively, although it did order that the constitutionally mandated prerequisite be met: passage of special legislation, a draft of which, it said, would be undertaken immediately. This, however, required drawing up a *Statut* (community regulation), which would need ratification by the membership, as well as state approval.[35]

Based on its own reading of the 1847 law, the executive had anticipated the need for a *Statut* and had begun drafting one before it petitioned Berlin for corporate rights.[36] It moved swiftly now; a general assembly met to work on the draft immediately upon receiving the Minister's ruling.[37] This body met fourteen times in less than three months, between early August and late October 1850, and produced its document. With 101 articles it covered nineteen printed pages: hardly the behavior of a lethargic laity.

Although the 1850 draft proceeded under the close direction of the

police director of Cologne, who was a state official, higher Prussian authorities required revisions to bring the statute into strict accord with the 1847
law (one demand was that the democratic-sounding "General Assembly"
be replaced by a more restrained "Representational System").[38] The community again proceeded quickly. In just eight months, between April and
December 1851, the *Statut* was amended according to government specifications, set before the board for approval, and circulated to the membership. Elections of a new board and a representative assembly were held
according to regulations set down in the 1847 law. The new administration
forwarded the revised *Statut* to the police director who, on instructions
from higher authorities, returned it for signature by the general membership — 228 of whom, out of a total of 260, signed "within a few days" at a
gathering called "immediately, for the purpose of speedier return [of the
document] to the government." (The 32 members who did not sign, the
synagogue executive stressed, were ill or absent at the time of the meeting;
"many" had since added their names.) The document was then forwarded
back to the police director for higher processing. In order to expedite matters in the future, the *Statut* empowered the synagogue executive to ratify
any future revisions the government might require.

Sadly for the obviously eager members of the synagogue administration,
the wheels of the higher Prussian bureaucracy turned slowly on the matter.
Worse, the Ministry of the Interior rejected the *Statut* in February 1853 on a
number of technicalities. Several months later the government ruled that, in
the interim, a new board and representatives would administer the synagogue community of Cologne (which was now also to encompass the Jews
of three nearby towns) in strict accord with the 1847 law. The police director would conduct the new election; another statute was to be drafted.[39]

Matters would drag on for years, and it was not until 1861 that the
Cologne community finally obtained corporate rights. In the meantime
(and actually, well before this), all was far from quiet within the community. The dissension seems to be the key to the unnatural haste with which
the *Statut* deliberations proceeded. Why, indeed, the rush to have the document framed and ratified and the eagerness to show its overwhelming support in the community? Why, too, the simultaneous push for communal
rights to be granted *all* Jewish communities of the monarchy — for the Cologne initiative and the Congress of Cities took place in the same months?
Why this hedging of bets, applying individually for Cologne's rights while
at the same time seeking a comprehensive approach?

Communal dissension was a growing feature of Jewish life across Germany after 1848. Tension between lay leadership and rabbis was especially
pronounced, in large part because the organizational structures that states
imposed on the communities overwhelmingly favored lay over rabbinic

control. This was certainly true of Prussian Jewry legislation.[40] As synagogue executives began to exercise enhanced power, they evoked the resistance of rabbis seeking to protect their traditional authority and status.

A conflict of this nature erupted in Cologne between segments of the lay leadership and Rabbi Aron Auerbach, the consistorial rabbi based in Bonn whose jurisdiction included Cologne. Cologne's lay leadership detested the consistorial system, which, it contended, had lost all legal validity with French evacuation of the Rhineland. The Consistory's continued "factual" existence had proven "completely impractical and inhibiting to the thriving development of religious life" in individual communities. Until 1847 there had been no choice but to work within the limits of the system, and efforts to invigorate Jewish life in Cologne had to be confined to the attempt, made in 1843, to have the consistorial rabbinical seat moved there. The 1847 law, however, in the words of the synagogue administration, opened up "a new era" for communal affairs in Cologne. A particular boon of the new legislation was the community's ability "at last" to conduct its affairs, "such as election of its religious officials," independently.[41]

As it had been in the 1843 complaint against his father and predecessor, Abraham, the stated problem was not the ideology but the personality of Rabbi Aron Auerbach. Community leaders alleged that he lacked dynamism or even basic commitment to Cologne's community. Under the truncated consistorial system in effect in the Rhineland, communities lacking guidance from a higher central organization, to which rabbis were accountable, were left to the "good intention, the energy and the competence of individual . . . rabbis, a nuisance which has proved very regrettable in this community, in particular." Auerbach, community leaders alleged, had been elected by synagogue notables fully cognizant of the deficiencies of communal life in Cologne who wished to relieve themselves of its burdens, and even then "purely out of consideration for and at the urgent request of his deceased father." "During his entire term in office," they charged, Aron Auerbach had been passive. "The fact that all the efforts of our community have not prospered and that it . . . remains behind most of the smaller communities of Prussia . . . we can only attribute to this apathy."

Communal independence was essential to any invigoration of Jewish life. The challenge was getting new structures instituted before the rabbi could counterattack, which he quickly did. Hence, I submit, the rush to complete a *Statut*—a legally correct one, as the synagogue leaders kept insisting it was—because time-consuming revisions would only give Auerbach an opening. Similarly, demonstrating the overwhelming popularity of the reforms was meant as a counterweight to the rabbi's opposition.[42]

While Prussian authorities deliberated the new *Statut*, synagogue officials who had been elected under its rules proceeded with an ambitious development program. In less than two years, they reorganized the elementary school (always a weak point, we recall) and moved it to new, more suitable quarters. They appointed four teachers (three male, one female); hired a "musically and scientifically trained cantor" (*Kantor*) to replace the deceased, traditional *hazzan* (*Vorsänger*), and advertised the position of preacher, since the man who had earlier occupied the post had left to become chief rabbi of Rotterdam. The preacher had been enormously successful, they said, and "we recognize in this important office one of the chief conditions for advancing the religiosity and harmony of a community." Finally, they had collected a substantial 1,510 taler in building funds from new members, a duty imposed by the new *Statut*.

Although the lay leadership spoke of the need to "elevate worship," "to place the community on a level suitable to the demands of the times," and "especially to have such education imparted to the youth as is indispensable to the training of good citizens, in the interest of the common welfare," they did not institute any serious reform of traditional ritual. There were none of the changes that marked reform services elsewhere in Germany: no tampering with liturgy or with Sabbath or festival observance, no suggestion even of enhanced decorum, let alone the infamous organ. Everything done was well within the bounds of change historians of German Jewish religious reform deem "moderate." As was true in the 1840's, the lay leadership of Cologne sought a modernized, not a radically reformed, Judaism. This is confirmed by the nature of Auerbach's objections, which were political, not doctrinal.[43]

The point of open conflict with the rabbi came in 1851 when the synagogue administration "of course" authorized the new cantor to administer "oath(s) according to Jewish ritual" (probably a reference to the special oath *more judaico*, which Jews involved in civil court proceedings were required to take, usually in the synagogue). The administration sought from Auerbach the rabbinic approval customarily bestowed in such instances, since "until the position of preacher [*Prediger*] is filled" it continued to recognize Auerbach as rabbi and "wished to hold open to him the sphere of purely ecclesiastical matters" (*rein geistlichen Handlungen*).[44]

Auerbach clearly perceived the attempt to supersede him. Having opposed the community's efforts, in the words of the leadership, "from the outset," he now declared the new synagogue constitution void (before Berlin did so) by reopening the positions of the synagogue executive. (He also refused his approval to the cantor.) Auerbach apparently based his actions on the fact that Frederick William's government had never formally abolished the 1808 law that established the consistorial system.

Synagogue officials, in turn, dismissed the validity of the rabbi's actions, but the "singularly dark wording" of his letter to them had signaled that he was bent on disturbing "tranquility and unity in our peace-loving community." Therefore, in June 1852, they appealed to the *Oberpräsident* of the Rhine Province, von Kleist-Retzow, to order Rabbi Auerbach (the consistorial rabbi, as they always referred to him) to cease all interference in community affairs, pleading with Kleist-Retzow to recommend approval of the new *Statut*, "the keystone" of communal existence, to his superiors in Berlin.

But Auerbach had supporters in the community. Even as the Bonn Consistory refused to approve Cologne's 1852 budget, with its appropriation of a salary for a new rabbi or preacher (some 30 candidates had already applied), and Auerbach considered moving to Cologne, a group of 28 members opposed to the executive's 1850 *Statut* emerged (we know nothing about their motives).[45] Hamstrung, the synagogue administration resigned in late 1852. It was replaced first by consistorial appointees, then, at Berlin's order, by a new administration, which continued work on yet another *Statut*. Ongoing internal dissension as well as snags in Berlin delayed promulgation of the document, which finally occurred in 1861, only shortly before the *Gemeinde* dedicated a new synagogue building—built, in the end, not with communal funds but through Oppenheim largesse.[46]

The ultimate failure of the attempt to win communal independence should not obscure some notable successes the *Gemeinde* administration was able to attain, even in the contention-ridden 1850's. The single most important goal of the earlier synagogue administration—a rabbi of Cologne's own, and one of the right sort—was realized in 1857 with the appointment of Israel Schwarz.

Schwarz was the embodiment of the modern yet orthodox German rabbi. The experienced scion of a rabbinical family from Bavaria, he was also university trained, having studied philosophy and philology at Heidelberg and received a doctorate at Jena. Jewish education, a major item on the "reform" board's agenda, was his special concern. Soon after assuming his post, Schwarz petitioned city school authorities for the right to give religious instruction to the "not inconsiderable number" of Jewish boys studying in the *Realgymnasium*, as priests and ministers did for Catholic and Protestant students during scheduled "religion hours." The *Realgymnasium*'s Jewish student numbers were sure to increase, he said, because "Jewish youth above all seek commercial training," and it was "urgent" that they also receive some knowledge of their religion. The authorities granted his request.[47] Education was an area in which Schwarz was willing to innovate, instituting confirmation for boys and girls, writing a catechism. He also innovated in the synagogue, preaching in German, introducing a (male) choir and German prayers for the Fatherland on special occasions. In 1862 he joined the synagogue administration in abolishing *piyyutim* (liturgical poetry) from the holiday service in order to shorten it and enhance its appeal. Though unenthusiastic, he agreed to abolish the *Kol Nidre* prayer on Yom Kippur (this formula renouncing regretted vows was a particular target of opponents of Jewish emancipation, who used it to impugn Jewish trustworthiness; even the neo-Orthodox leader S. R. Hirsch countenanced its abolition for a time). Yet Schwarz refused to consider introducing an organ, archsymbol of Christian worship, into the synagogue. He also declined to participate in a synod of Jewish religious reformers called in Leipzig in 1869.[48]

Religious change in Cologne thus continued to be moderate; by the 1860's there was certainly nothing shocking about removing *piyyutim* from the liturgy. But, as several synagogue administrations, whatever their other differences, had clearly wished, religion in Cologne was modernized and, finally, placed in the hands of an able, energetic rabbi.

Rabbi Auerbach was never formally deposed, and the new constitution finally approved in 1861 provided for his continued financial support, as well as for payments from Cologne's community toward the administrative costs of the Consistory.[49] The consistorial system established by Napoleonic law in 1808 was abolished on the left bank of the Rhine only in 1863.[50]

"Equal Duties, Equal Rights": Relations with Municipal Authorities

Although there was in these years nothing like the struggle for Jewish emancipation waged in the 1840's, there was a significant and ultimately successful campaign for Jewish rights in the city. Unlike the earlier one, this campaign was conducted with little fanfare, waged not by great figures in the world of business and politics but by the synagogue leadership. It focused not on abstract questions but on the community's elementary school. Yet this seemingly mundane issue triggered fundamental questions about the place of religion and the nature of society in Cologne. Was the city Christian, divided among Catholics and Protestants and merely suffering Jews, or religiously plural, officially recognizing religious diversity? Would all citizens, regardless of religion, enjoy equal civil status?

In order to appreciate the significance of the local struggle we need to bear in mind the state of Jewish civil status in Prussia in these years. The 1847 law distinguished between Jewish "inhabitants" and Christian "citizens." While abolishing much other economic discrimination, it confirmed Jewish ineligibility for the civil service, which covered a broad range of positions from teaching in state institutions to jobs in the post. The law also restricted Jewish political rights. The Prussian Constitution of December 5, 1848, which declared unconditional civil equality, was as short-lived as the Revolution that had created it. Articles 4 and 12 of the Revised Constitution of January 31, 1850, declared the equality of all Prussians before the law and the secular nature of civil rights, but Article 14 of the same document stated that, "notwithstanding the freedom of religion guaranteed in Article 12, the Christian religion shall form the basis of all institutions of state concerned with religious practice."[51] In subsequent years, Article 14 governed enforcement of the law.

Judaism did not enjoy equal status with Christianity in Prussia. Rabbis were severely disadvantaged vis-à-vis the lay synagogue leadership in Prussian Jewry legislation; the 1847 law did not even give rabbis a seat on the community's governing bodies. By contrast, Lutheran and Catholic clerics were recognized as civil servants and given such privileges as exemption from municipal taxes and the right to help supervise public schools. When Rabbi Schwarz asked to be paid for his religious instruction in the *Realgymnasium*, he was refused, told by the Ministry for Religious Affairs in Berlin that Judaism could not have the same status as Christian denominations.[52] Churches were subsidized; synagogues were entirely self-supporting. This is why compulsory membership was crucial to the communities.[53]

The 1847 law (paragraph 62) did require synagogue communities to maintain facilities for religious instruction but did not oblige Jewish children to attend them. Unsubsidized, lacking recognition as *öffentliche Schulen* (public schools), such schools were bound to remain inadequate and unattractive — which, of course, was the point. Christian and private schools were open to Jews; they made use of them. We have observed the weakness of the Jewish school in Cologne since its inception and the marked preference of Jewish parents for non-Jewish educational institutions for their children (see Table 25), behavior reflecting both the pressures of Prussian law and Jewish aspirations for betterment.

In light of all this, what took place in Cologne between 1851 and 1870 was quite remarkable: the Jewish school went from being a purely private, languishing institution to one wholly subsidized by the city, operating under the same supervision given Catholic and Protestant schools.[54] The transformation was possible because community leaders perceived opportunity in the 1847 law and relentlessly pursued its fullest realization, even beyond the letter of the law.

The basic presumption of the law was that Jewish children would attend "public" (tax-supported) institutions or take private instruction. But the law also allowed for establishment of "special Jewish public institution(s)" in places where the population count warranted it.[55] If approved by local Prussian authorities, such schools could apply for support from municipal

TABLE 25
School Enrollment of Jewish Children, 1846–69

Year	Elementary schools				Secondary schools (non-Jewish)
	Jewish	Catholic	Protestant	Private	
1865/6	189	31	53	100	101
1867	189	23	55	102	98
1868/9	231	64[a]	64[a]	163	133

SOURCES: "Auszug aus dem Beleitungs-Berichte des Städtischen Schulinspektor vom 19. Dezember 1846," *Verhandlungen des Gemeinderaths der Stadt Köln* (1846–48); "Bericht des Gemeinde Vorstandes über die Verwaltung und den Stand der Gemeinde Angelegenheiten zu Ende des Jahres 1851," ibid. (1852); "Bericht des Gemeinde Vorstandes," ibid. (1854); "Verwaltungs Bericht für 1858," ibid. (1858); "Anlage zum Sitzungs Protokoll vom 5. Januar 1865," ibid. (1864); "Anlage zum Sitzungsprotokoll vom 24. Januar 1864," ibid. (1866); "Sitzung vom 7. November 1867," ibid., (1867); "Anlage zum Sitzungs-Protocoll vom 2. Dezember 1869," ibid. (1869); Kober, *Cologne*, p. 263; Brisch, 2: 161; this volume, Tables 23–24, Chapter 6, notes 11, 29.

NOTE: Statistics on the enrollment of Jewish children in non-Jewish schools and in private instruction are not available for the years 1846–64, but the numbers must have been substantial, given the low levels of enrollment in the Jewish school in years when the total Jewish population, heavily composed of young families with children, ranged from roughly 1,300 to 2,600. Available figures for enrollment in the Jewish school in these years are 107 in 1846, 103 in 1851, 142 in 1852/3, 155 in 1857/8, 180 in 1859, and 210 in 1864.

In the years 1865–69, for which full statistics are available, the same number of children were enrolled in the Jewish school as in all the non-Jewish alternatives combined; in other words, 50 percent of Jewish children enrolled in the Jewish school in those years, when the municipal subsidy to the school increased tremendously (see Table 26).

The Jewish school only covered elementary education; at the secondary level, all Jewish children attending school went to non-Jewish schools or had private instruction.

There is a typographical error in Kober, *Cologne*, p. 339, App. C. The number of Jewish children in lower public schools and private schools in 1867 should read 467, which is Kober's actual total.

[a] A total of 64 students were enrolled in both the Catholic and Protestant elementary schools in 1868/9.

funds if education in the locality was generally so supported. The amount of the subsidy would be set by the amount of taxes Jews paid toward support of public education and the benefit derived by the larger school system from the existence of a Jewish school.

The public school system in predominantly Catholic Cologne was under Catholic auspices, but provisions had long been in effect for municipal support of Protestant institutions according to the ratio of the two groups in the population. The Jewish community, therefore, had legal grounds to claim municipal support for its school, and by 1851 (or, according to another source, as early as 1848) the community executive had successfully petitioned the Municipal Assembly (successor to the City Council under the municipal law of 1845) for a subsidy.[56]

The very fact of the grant, not its size (a minuscule 100 taler), was significant. As School Inspector Brandenberg observed many years later, it was the first step toward equal recognition of the Jewish school alongside those of Christian confessions, something the synagogue board, which had long been requesting assistance, fully realized.[57] Increasingly self-confident and aggressive, the board made ever greater requests: for larger subsidies,

for a city-donated school building, for a complete city takeover of the
school—which was nevertheless to retain its Jewish character. The record is
one of consistent and stunning Jewish victory.[58] (See Table 26.)

Whence this remarkable political clout? For we should not forget that
although the 1847 law gave the Jews a case for municipal support of Jewish
education, it nowhere established the principle of equal treatment of Jewish
and Christian schools. Indeed, such a notion, which would have accorded
to Judaism the same status as Christianity, was antithetical to Prussian
policy. Yet it was precisely this, *Parität*, which the synagogue executive
claimed and eventually won from the Municipal Assembly of Cologne.

Two factors, in addition to remarkable persistence, account for the Jewish success: the disproportionate share of taxes that Cologne's Jews paid
(the law having linked any subsidy a Jewish school might receive to the
level of Jewish tax payments) and, despite some pronounced and at times
crude opposition, a Municipal Assembly whose larger political concerns
made it basically sympathetic to Jews. We take the second point first, since
this as much or more than the legal strength of any Jewish claim would
determine the hearing Jews received.

Although Cologne's local politics underwent a "reaction" in the 1850's—
Mevissen had graduated to state politics, Brüggemann was ousted from the
Kölnische Zeitung—things were not as extreme there as elsewhere.[59] There
were two mayors during this period, both politically middle-of-the-road,
both loyal Prussian civil servants—men not likely to resist a claim clearly
grounded in Prussian law, although also unlikely to go beyond strict legal
requirements. Three parties crystallized in the Municipal Assembly in these
years. On the left were the Progressives, successors to the democratic radicals of the 1840's; their leaders were Johann Classen, Bernhard Joseph

TABLE 26
Municipal Subsidies to the Jewish School, 1851–69

Year	Amount (taler)
1851	100
1855	150
1859	200
1862	334
1863	800
1865	1,200
1867	1,500
1869	1,679

SOURCES: "Budget der öffentlichen Elementarschulen zu
Köln," *Verhandlungen des Gemeinderaths der Stadt Köln*, 1853;
1856; 1858; 1859; 1860; 1861; 1862; 1864; 1865; 1866; 1867; 1868;
1869; Brandenberg, p. 6; Weyden, p. 290.

Klein, and Wilhelm Anton Hospelt. The liberals of the previous era now regrouped in the (dominant) Constitutional party, led by Dr. Benedict Nückel, the highest municipal medical officer, and Heinrich Claessen, an old Oppenheim friend and now general director of Concordia, a Mevissen-Oppenheim insurance company.

True to its past, this party represented industrial and banking interests, had a distinctly "capitalist stamp," and was mortified even by the "reasonable demands" of the "aspiring masses" represented by the Progressives and the third party, the Catholics. The latter group, increasingly an opposition party to left-wing interests, had two influential leaders in the assembly, Friedrich Baudri, whose brother was the suffragan bishop and who "everyone knew" spoke for the Cardinal Giessel, and the one cleric of the body, a canon who also happened to be city school inspector, Dr. Johann Jakob Broix.[60]

The three parties represented distinct and even antagonistic interests, yet they quickly reached consensus on the era's "Jewish question." One might especially have expected the Catholic and Progressive parties — for different reasons, of course — to oppose extension of privileges to the Jewish school or, at least, favor the most restrictive interpretation of the law. Yet both not only supported subsidies but argued for *Parität*, equal treatment of the Jewish school with that accorded Protestant institutions. The Constitutionals, erstwhile liberal allies of the Jews, while also backing subsidies, were generally far more circumspect. Outright opposition also existed. Yet convergence in favor of Jewish rights occurred. While some assembly members seemed sincere in their support of Jewish claims, it was less the Jews than what they represented, less Jewish rights than the broader societal implications of those rights, that were at issue and the reason convergence was possible. Each group saw some essential interest of its own furthered by a policy favorable to Jewish claims.

Thus Baudri, leader of the Catholic party, supported *Parität*. His position derived, I believe, from well-grounded Catholic anxiety. Although Catholics remained the overwhelming majority in Cologne — 89 percent in 1851, 86 percent in 1865 (see Table 24), they were a political minority in the Prussian state. The church-state conflicts of the 1830's (see Chapter 5) remained a bitter memory, while the Catholic Church had reason to feel insecure in the reign of Frederick William IV. Though the church, spearheading a militant revival in Cologne in these years, moved vigorously to prevent Jewish rights from going too far in the city, it may have welcomed the emergence of a "third force" to blunt Protestant power in an area where exclusive church control was already undermined, municipal funding of elementary school education.[61]

The church faced an equally serious threat from a different quarter: the

Progressives, who believed in separation of church and state. *Justizrat* Kyll, for example, of the Progressive camp and a man with long democratic credentials, came out for retention (though not increase) of the subsidy to the Jewish school in 1853 but simultaneously denounced the whole notion of "separate schools." Arguing that the municipality was obligated to build and maintain only "general school institutions with no regard to various confessions," he urged that any group establishing a confessional school be denied municipal support. In a telling remark obviously based on the emergence of a third denomination in the city, Kyll cited the situation in North America, where a city might have "several dozen" religious sects, and evoked the chaos that would ensue were each to have its own confessional school. Hospelt, Kyll's close party associate, seconded this position, albeit only in theory; confessional education, however regrettable, was the practice in Cologne, in which case, he said, the Jews ought to get equal treatment. Böcker, another party member, labeled separation of schools by religion *verwerflich* (thoroughly reprehensible).[62]

Catholic leader Baudri supported *Parität* for the Jewish school on pragmatic as well as philosophical grounds. Since it was in the general interest of society that Jewish children, too, receive a good education (something the synagogue board had been arguing for years), municipal support was in order. But he also pointedly pleaded the principle of confessional education, the abolition of which "would be an act of the greatest intolerance."[63] Public financing of Jewish education meant support for the principle of confessional education, a chief Catholic priority in Cologne and the Rhineland as a whole.[64]

Several hostile Progressives notwithstanding, the most outspoken and consistent support for the Jewish claim came from the leadership of the left-wing Progressives—Klein, Hospelt, and Classen—who pushed parity, by name, from the outset. Progressive principles, of course, were most compatible with a policy of absolute civil equality for members of the various religions. But there is no evidence here (as there was, for instance, in the earlier principled advocacy of Karl Brüggemann) that conviction and sentiment clashed. Assemblyman Klein once even argued that the Jewish school deserved municipal support because the Glockengasse synagogue was "a credit [*Zierde*] to the city."[65] Still, without impugning the sincerity of the Progressives, support of parity for the Jewish school was doubtless also meant as a blow to the Catholic Church in an area of traditional power, education. Having the city recognize the Jewish claim would further relativize the claims of the Catholic Church. It was the next best thing to abolishing confessional education altogether, as Hospelt had all but said.

The relative reticence of the Constitutionals, especially Heinrich Claessen, whose liberal credentials and history of friendship with the Oppenheims would lead us to have expected more, seems attributable both to fiscal and political conservatism: in the post-revolution years, there was now a left-wing to which the Constitutionals played center. But the reticence was that and nothing more. Claessen never opposed a municipal subsidy to the Jewish school in principle; he even argued for complete municipal subsidy of its rental costs (though not of its total educational outlay). Like Mayor Bachem, he did not back parity, following instead the "strict interpretationist," invariably restrictive, line of the city's School Commission, the views of which he officially represented on the Municipal Assembly. Like the commission, Claessen was more likely to argue limited municipal responsibility by citing the 1847 law or the synagogue's 1861 *Statut*, which in accord with that law obligated the community to run an elementary school. The letter of the law, plus substantiated, justified costs and elaborately prorated subsidy amounts: they were the arguments of an account executive.[66]

Although Johann Classen (the Progressive) believed absolutely in the principle of parity, in 1862 he introduced into the debate a consideration that accorded with reigning bourgeois political values and was likely to appeal even to those who did not share his broader egalitarian convictions: the "equality of the taxpayers."[67] The "argument from taxes," as we might call it, established in the 1847 law itself, ultimately proved a most powerful weapon in the Jewish arsenal: according to the income tax roll for 1867, Classen informed the *Gemeinderat*, the Jews of Cologne, 2.2 percent of the population, were assessed 7 percent of the tax burden (nearly 17,000 of 240,000 taler).[68] This and the fact that the Jews did not avail themselves of the municipal welfare services they supported to such a disproportionate degree made it imperative, Classen argued, that the city "finally behave equitably to the Jewish population." It was an argument fiscal conservatives and even hardened opponents of the Jews could not easily resist. Another member would later chide the assembly for making the Jews approach the city like beggars.[69] Ultimate success of the Jewish quest for city assumption of the school's costs, achieved by 1870, undoubtedly owed much to the emergence of the tax realities in 1867.

Stiff opposition did exist in the assembly. This is especially noteworthy, since there was unambiguous sanction under Prussian law for the Jewish school to receive public support. One assembly member attempted to use a clause of the 1847 law making creation of separate Jewish schools conditional on their being in the "general educational interest" to deny funding to Cologne's Jewish school. "The city," he said, "only has an interest in having such education imparted to its school children as is necessary for ordinary life [*gewöhnliches Leben*] and may not be obliged, therefore, to have Jewish children educated in the Israelite belief and other subjects which afford the Jews a particular interest."[70] The teachings of Catholicism and Protestantism, of course, were of general, not "particular," interest, in this view.

Another member was even more blunt, his remarks betraying a Hegelian-derived contempt for Judaism typical of the German left. *"Advocat* Böcker," the official minutes read, "declared Judaism — this state within a state — as something inferior to Christianity, something which is no longer in accord with the times. . . . He cannot favor municipal funds being sacrificed for its preservation." Böcker, a Progressive, raised a host of other objections — Cologne already had all the elementary schools it needed, municipal support was in contradiction to the synagogue's 1861 *Statut* — but clearly his opposition was fundamental.[71] It never wavered in the many years the Jewish school question was debated, whatever the proposal under discussion.

Yet it is significant that while several other assembly members also opposed the idea of a municipal subsidy for a Jewish school, opposition was almost always to particulars — how high a subsidy, how good a new site for the school building — rather than to the principle of a subsidy itself. At heart the issue was *Parität,* although this concept had no legal basis whatever. Except for the two members just mentioned, everyone on the assembly agreed that the city owed the Jewish community something. This relatively moderate climate made the dogged efforts of the synagogue executive efficacious in the end.

The very fact that the Jewish communal leadership made and then relentlessly pressed a claim on the civil government ensured that the question of civic rights and religious equality — the very nature of society in Cologne — was on the municipal agenda for decades. Both the behavior of the synagogue executive and the assembly, therefore, deserve close attention.

It was a major victory for the Jews that the debate became focused on *Parität.* The original subsidy had been granted, as the law stipulated, merely in recognition of the benefit to the non-Jewish school system resulting from the existence of a separate Jewish school — less crowding, reduced demand for staff. This approach, however, used city expenses as a reference and did not measure the actual costs of running the Jewish school — teachers' salaries, building maintenance, rent. Thus the immediate and ongoing Jewish efforts to have the amount of the subsidy increased.

By what measure, however, was the increase to be reckoned? What was a fair subsidy amount? What did *fair* mean when it came to Jewish claims? The assembly considered four possible ways of calculating the subsidy: according to the size of the Jewish population relative to that of the Catholic (as the Protestant subsidy was figured); according to the total number of Jewish school-age children in the city (some of whom, apparently, were educated elsewhere); by the number of Jewish children attending any elementary school in the city, including the Jewish one; or according to the number of children in the Jewish school. While the last method, the one actually followed, might seem most logical, it also produced the smallest subsidy, since only about half the community's children attended the school.[72] The school was particularly stressed under this system, because such fixed costs as teachers' salaries and rent were the same for the four-grade Jewish elementary school as for those with greater enrollment, while tuition receipts and municipal aid were lower.

No wonder the Jews and their friends on the assembly tried to shift the focus from enrollment figures to the fixed costs of a school building. The inadequacy of the school's physical plant was a festering problem, which, as we have seen, the synagogue executive had raised forcefully in other contexts. The executive had always maintained, and continued to assert before the Municipal Assembly, that this deficiency was partly responsible for Jewish underutilization of the school.[73] The school had moved quarters no fewer than six times by 1870, ever searching for appropriate accommodations.[74]

In May 1862, the synagogue executive asked the city to furnish the Jewish school an appropriate building from city property. This was one claim that could be argued only on the basis of parity: if Catholic and Protestant schools were given buildings by the city, so should the Jewish school. Unlike proportionate reckonings, which would work against a tiny minority of the population, this was an absolute, objective need.

Said the Jews. Some assembly members contested the claim of inadequate facilities, even visiting the Jewish school to see for themselves.[75] Still, by early 1868, after extensive debate, the assembly agreed in principle that the city ought to provide a building for the Jewish school, and by October of that year the city's School Commission recommended a site.[76]

Rather than proclaiming the substantial victory achieved, the leadership of the Jewish community unanimously rejected the site because its location was too far from the city center. Since Jews lived all over Cologne, it argued, the school had to be centrally located (on more expensive real estate, we would note) to be a viable option for Jewish children of elementary school age (five to nine years.)

In arguing this point, the synagogue executive drew an analogy to parish schools, which stood in the middle of their districts. The analogy effectively argued for full confessional equality of all the faiths. It also implied, surely unconsciously, that Cologne was a Jewish parish.

There followed some comical, if not ridiculous, discussion of the merits of long walks for the health of young children, Assemblyman Böcker (not a friend, we recall) arguing that distance could not "be considered a drawback since boys must accustom themselves to marches from the outset," and that "no greater benefit can be rendered children than to see to it that aside from mental nourishment, they are strengthened physically." Whereupon another member reminded the assembly that they were discussing not secondary school students, but "little, little children" who "could not walk four times a day through the whole city, to its very limits, to go to school."

In 1872, the city and the Jewish community finally settled on a desirable site in the Schildergasse. Then, however, the tug-of-war continued over the amount the Jewish community would contribute to building costs. The city asked 3,000 taler; the *Gemeinde* declared itself ready to put up 2,994 taler and 15 silbergroschen — and the parties called it a deal. When the building plans called for use of one classroom in the new Jewish school by a nearby *Ober Realschule* the community refused, and the city backed down, insisting, however, on the clear understanding that the Jewish school was to be considered — municipal. To which the community responded that while the *building* was municipal property, the *character* of the school was to remain unambiguously Jewish.[77] It was an extraordinary turnaround from the situation just two decades earlier, when the authorities insisted that the Jewish school was the purely private affair of the Jews. It is also telling evidence that the Jews saw themselves as both citizens and Jews, entitled to both identities, just as Catholics and Protestants were entitled to a religious identity and citizenship. It was a major statement in the era of emancipation.

During the extended debate over the Jewish school question, a number of theoretical positions were voiced in the assembly that are noteworthy for what they say about attitudes to the Jews and civil rights and about local perceptions of Prussia. The remarks show that on this issue as in earlier struggles over Jewish status, larger questions were bound to the particular.

Precisely because the Jews had no legal right to claim anything but subsidies, their advocates on the Municipal Assembly had to appeal to higher moral, as well as material, values in arguing for parity. One member summoned the Christian conscience of his fellows, urging them to give the Jewish community the treatment they would wish for themselves. "Natural legal sense," moreover, dictated that those who bore equal civic burdens be granted equal civic privileges. The Jews "partake in the weal and woe of the community," he said, "often in surpassing manner, and have bled for the Fatherland as well as Christians have. How painful it must now be for the Israelites of Cologne to hear how the Christians reach boldly into the municipal purse when the need arises to build permanent school houses for themselves, while the Jews must be satisfied with a lump sum and move to and fro with their children as renters."

Because the assembly, however, was not legally obligated to do what the synagogue executive was asking and could no more sacrifice the financial interests of city inhabitants than could a guardian those of his wards, this assembly member proposed a compromise: the Jewish community would purchase whatever property it deemed fit for the school, which the city would then recognized and fund on the basis of parity.[78]

Baudri found this reasoning unseemly and condemned as "deplorable" the ongoing recourse to the formal, legal merits of the Jewish claim or references to the Jewish share of taxes when the only relevant principle ought to be "equal duties, equal rights." The wrangling over the amount of the municipal subsidy to the Jewish school and its legal basis was missing the essential point: what the Jews were fighting for and ought to be granted was not a few taler more or less but a "point of honor" — recognition as full, equal citizens of the community. Classen agreed. Principle, not mathematics, he said, was at stake. As for the guardian-ward metaphor to express the Municipal Assembly's relationship to Cologne's inhabitants, Jews were as much its "wards" as were Christians. Jews, in short, were not civic outsiders who needed to indemnify society for satisfying their needs, but legitimate and equal claimants.[79]

Classen also introduced a note of local chauvinism into the debate when, after introducing the statistics on Jewish income taxes into the assembly records, he suggested that Cologne ought to maintain a higher moral and political standard than that followed by Prussia. The state, he sniped, does "not yet" recognize the religious equality vouschafed by its own constitution, discriminating against Jews in [state] appointments while subjecting them to equal tax and other civic burdens. "Such behavior on the part of the state cannot serve as a model for the city," he said, which would do far better to follow the more enlightened example of "other Rhenish cities," Mülheim an der Ruhr and Krefeld, which already recognized municipal Jewish schools.[80]

He again expressed his contempt for the high-handedness of the Prussian governing style when he opposed attempts by some assembly members to have municipal support limited on grounds that the Jewish community's 1861 *Statut*, which included a community obligation to operate a school, constituted a contract that voided Jewish claims on the city. We recall that the 1861 *Statut*, however, was more the work of the Prussian government than the Jews, and Classen snapped, "There can be no question of a contract here. The synagogue statute was imposed on them; there was no contract between equals, rather the might of the stronger struck judgment."[81]

Although recognition of the Jewish school as officially "public" did not come until 1881, municipal support for its budget was reckoned alongside that for Protestant schools — tacit recognition of the principle of parity — as early as 1868. Municipal assumption of its costs began in 1870. It is testimony to the tenacity of the synagogue executive, whose claims an assembly member once suggested granting if only to get the Jewish school question "finally off the daily agenda once and for all."[82]

The inventiveness of the executive, and municipal receptiveness to it, are particularly evident in the tax ploy used in 1867. Since government tax records were not religion-specific, it would appear that the executive itself gathered the data about Jewish tax payments from the synagogue member- ship and furnished this information to the Jews' friends on the Municipal Assembly. Nothing could better convey the ingenuity and self-confidence of the Jewish community's leadership — or the substantial grounds for it.

In assessing the behavior of the synagogue executive in the school affair, we should note that while parity was without doubt, as Baudri had per- ceived it, a point of honor, it was also a financial imperative. "The local Jews are rich, they say so themselves," as one member of the assembly put it bluntly.[83] Yet, approximately half of the children enrolled in the Jewish school (220 in 1867/68) paid partial or no tuition,[84] while the government in 1860 refused the synagogue executive's request to have taxes for support of the community school made legally enforceable, on the grounds that the school was a private institution.[85] "Going municipal" was the only means for survival, at least for vigorous competition with other, non-Jewish alter- natives, a fact borne out by the increasing enrollment statistics once the Jewish school gained public funding, supervision, and legitimacy, especially after 1881.[86]

The synagogue executive's efforts to have the Jewish school integrated into the city system was clearly not an instance of co-optation or willful assimilation, since the members kept insisting to government authorities that the school retain its Jewish character even when its nonreligious cur- riculum was harmonized with that of other municipal schools.[87] On the other hand, the board firmly rejected a proposal by Rabbi Schwarz in 1859 that the community found a Jewish *Realschule*. Schwarz had suggested this because, he said, very few of the Jewish children attending secondary in- stitutions (174 of 455 in 1865) were receiving any religious instruction (obviously, Schwarz made this proposal before receiving permission to offer religious instruction to Jewish students in the general school).[88] The board's opposition may have been for financial reasons, but perhaps, too, because the proposal smacked of excessive separatism. It was one thing to teach young children the fundamentals of Judaism in a Jewish elementary school and another to keep Jewish youths separate from their Christian counterparts during young adulthood and career training.[89] Neither assim- ilation nor segregation, but integration with continued identity, was the board's goal.

Maintaining a viable, much less a vigorous, Jewish identity, was the basic problem facing all modern Jewries in the age of emancipation. It was clearly the central issue of Jewish communal life in Cologne in these years. The statistics on Jewish school enrollment testify to the forces of assimilation and the dimensions of the challenge to Jewish continuity. But there is no doubt that the lay leadership of Cologne's community recognized that challenge and attempted to meet it creatively and forthrightly.

For the Jewish community of Cologne, 1861 was a banner year. Frederick William IV, would-be architect of Jewish civil segregation in Prussia, died on the second day of the year. Several months later, the central government finally granted Cologne's Jewish community the rights of a corporation and approved a synagogue constitution, ending the organizational limbo in which the *Gemeinde* had hung for more than a decade. Then, in August, the community celebrated perhaps the greatest symbolic event of its existence: the inauguration of a monumental new synagogue building on the Glockengasse.

The building had been designed by the city's foremost architect, Ernst Zwirner, who was also in charge of the completion of the Cologne Cathedral, then underway. Cologne was a center of architectural design, and the cathedral was a powerful symbol in the Rhineland and Prussia as a whole. To have no less than the cathedral architect design the synagogue was a powerful statement about the place of Jews and Judaism in the city.[90] But by 1861, both had achieved a remarkable degree of official acceptance. Representatives of the crown, the city, and all the religious denominations took part in the festive ceremonies to inaugurate the synagogue.[91]

As in earlier strides toward Jewish acceptance, the Oppenheim hand was heavily engaged in this triumph. Abraham Oppenheim had secured Zwirner's services — Abraham and his brother Simon sat on the board of the Cathedral Building Society, to which both contributed generously.[92] Oppenheim money also funded the synagogue, on which no expense was spared.[93]

Following a fashion that had become current among European Jews since the 1850's, the synagogue was built in Moorish style. Horizontal stripes girded its facade; with several gilded cupolas, minarets, and a great central cupola rising 120 feet into Cologne's landscape, it proclaimed the Jewish presence and typed it as distinct, even foreign.

It would seem an odd statement for the Jews of the city, let alone the Oppenheims, to make. Why so conspicuously announce Jewish otherness when the battle for equality and acceptance was not yet won?

Precisely because the notion of Jews as somehow alien was ineradicably etched in the popular image, for the Jews of Cologne and Europe as a whole, distinction was unavoidable. The only choice was that of stereotype.

Some chose to accentuate "Orientalism" because fascination with the exotic East was on the rise, Semitic culture and architectural images glorified in English gardens and novels and Paris salon painting.[94] In an age where "Mosaic" and "Israelite" were the polite terms for "Jew," minarets on the synagogue could enhance group image. Unlike unambiguously "Jewish," that is, rabbinic images, Eastern ones could even serve to remind Christians of the Biblical heritage Jews and Christians shared and perhaps recall the debt Western culture owed to the religious genius of Israel.[95]

The need to connect with and glorify ancient origins, already pronounced in an age of growing nationalism, could only have been heightened by the publicity and excitement surrounding the completion of Cologne's cathedral, being carried out according to newly discovered medieval plans. Jews must have been affected by so broad a current in popular culture, and this too, may have contributed to the sense that the eastern motif was appropriate. Jews certainly could not have appropriated for the synagogue the neo-Gothic style for which Cologne was renowned, because Gothic represented the national heritage of Christians, while Jews "were supposed to be [Eastern]."[96] Even if they had wanted to, it is unlikely that Zwirner would have gone along with a Jewish caricature of the great *Dom*, symbol of the "renaissance of the city, [and] the nation."[97] Gothic architecture, he felt, was "an expression of the Germanic spirit. Islamic architecture [was] most expressive of the spirit of Judaism."[98]

Thus the choice of Moorish style could placate non-Jewish expectations of Jews by expressing difference in a way non-Jews could tolerate, and even approve. Yet Moorish style could also express pride in Jewish identity. As Carol Herselle Krinsky observes, it was often used as a "celebration of uniqueness," an assertion that Jews could be "culturally separate but otherwise equal to their fellow citizens."[99]

As she also notes, such pride in Jewishness could only be flaunted in environments where Jews felt confident despite their difference. It was precisely those Jews "who felt secure and optimistic in their European towns [who] felt it good to develop a distinctive architectural style. As long as their position was improving . . . they found that looking different, even exotic, was a harmless way of appearing proud of their religious difference. . . . Jews who had a comfortable self-image found suitable an Eastern style that was not used in European church architecture."[100]

At the laying of the cornerstone of the Glockengasse synagogue, Rabbi Schwarz proclaimed the aims of the community as the "attainment of unity within and prestige without."[101] Clearly, the community had already made major strides toward both goals.

Conclusion

The substantial economic and political gains that Cologne's Jews achieved in the 73 years since readmission are telling evidence of Jewish striving for betterment but also of the transformation of a non-Jewish society in the age of emancipation. Cologne was one, in many ways singular, German city, and its history and that of its Jews cannot be considered paradigmatic. Still, its odyssey on the Jewish question and the rise of its Jewish community are important signs of mutual accommodation in an age when Germans and Jews were rewriting the rules of their relationship. We can learn much from studying the conditions and behaviors that fostered such accommodation in a specific locale. For all its particularity, society in Cologne wrestled with dynamics of resistance and integration and with the Jewish drive for betterment, acceptance, and continuity, and these were the essence of the emancipation experience in Germany.

Cologne's metamorphosis on the Jewish question was the product of a thorough economic, political, and religious remaking and of Jewish efforts, deliberate and directed. The city's immense but slumbering potential was awakened when French, then Prussian, policies swept away outdated economic patterns (the medieval transshipping and forwarding business, guilds), made it part of vast new markets (Napoleon's Continental System, Prussia's customs union), and abolished the religious discrimination that had made the city inhospitable to Protestants and exclusive of Jews, depriving it of both groups' economic contributions. Heavy immigration marked the years under study here, further undermining traditional social structures. A new social order arose that welcomed Jews and their middle-class pursuits. The new elite brought with it an optimistic, pragmatic, energetic civic mentality, replacing the xenophobic outlook that had gripped the city for centuries. It was also disgusted with the religious intolerance that Prussian policies would promote and which, in the peculiar conditions of the Rhineland, threatened Protestants and Catholics as well as Jews. This elite not only accepted but welcomed religious difference, seeing in officially tolerated religious pluralism the best protection for its own freedom of conscience.

Cologne's "old" elite was like that of such other major German cities as Lübeck, Bremen, Frankfurt am Main, and Nürnberg, whose historic enmity to Jews had led to expulsion, exclusion, or ghettoization of Jews from early modernity until well into the nineteenth century. But while these cities regained self-rule after the French interlude and could set their own Jewish policies, Cologne did not. Cologne's governing elite encountered modernity through humiliating loss of control over many fundamental issues, including Jewish civic status. The history of Jewish emancipation in Cologne is a study in the mentality and policies of an "old" urban elite toward the Jews, as well as those of an emerging "new" one that, like those of some other German cities, notably Berlin, were remarkably open to Jews.[1]

Many of the members of Cologne's new elite were immigrants, or Protestant, or both. These factors alone, however, do not account for their support of Jewish rights. Immigration, Protestant and otherwise, had been substantial since the French annexation, yet those who historians say were "liberal" in the first decades of the century became liberal on the Jewish question only in the 1840's. In some instances, "new" men who actively opposed Jewish rights in the first decades of Prussian rule — Peter Heinrich Merkens and, with less vitriol, Mayor Adolf Steinberger — reversed themselves and championed Jewish equality in the 1840's.

A number of factors made for the change. The men of Cologne's new elite, who constituted much of the leadership of the Rhenish liberal movement of the 1840's, were unabashed capitalists and zealots about economic innovation. Their view of the economy as expanding, with virtually infinite potential, rendered obsolete and self-defeating an older mentality obsessed with protecting the access of "insiders" to finite resources and excluding "outsiders" through religiously rationalized discrimination or arguments (such as Merkens's) for elitism. Rather than seeing enterprising Jews as hostile competitors, they welcomed them as kindred spirits, fellow workers in the vineyards of plenty.[2] Most significantly, they had a broad base of support in the Rhenish urban middle class that felt similarly.

Religion lost its divisive force in this worldview, serving instead, if at all, as a broad humanist base for coexistence and tolerance. Relentless Oppenheim pressure on men dependent on the bank's resources for realization of their business and political goals surely played a role. While it did not simply cause liberals to take a pro-Jewish position, pressure reinforced the sense that such a stance was rational and pragmatic — important considerations to men of business and politics, like Steinberger, Merkens, or Ludolf Camphausen. For others, like Gustav Mevissen and Hermann Beckerath of Krefeld, no inducement was needed; the Jewish cause was a passionate commitment, identified with the cause of a free, enlightened Germany, which was the core of their whole political vision. For yet another group, including Karl Marx and Karl Heinrich Brüggemann, editor of the influential *Kölnische Zeitung*, Jewish equality was the necessary, if unpalatable, concomitant of larger philosophical convictions.

The pro-emancipation motivations of Cologne's liberals were complex and varied, but their public record in the crucial 1840's was steadfast and unequivocal. The Rhenish story is an important chapter in the larger history of German liberalism and the Jewish question in the years before the 1848 revolution. It corrects the impression, given by a focus on south and southwest Germany, that German liberalism was incapable of applying its highest and presumably universal principles to Jews.

Wealth and class were pivotal factors in the acceptance Jews ultimately won. For all its avowed physiocratic motivation, the clear message of the 1808 decree had been that emancipation was for bourgeois Jews. The Jews of Cologne showed that they understood that message well, working prodigiously to better themselves. Following a pattern true of German (and French) Jewry in the nineteenth century, a significant minority of Jewish immigrants to Cologne, from the first settlers on, came to the city with some wealth. The Jewish group as a whole used a variety of means — business partnerships that pooled resources and skills, women's work, vocational education for sons — to create and perpetuate wealth. While acquisition of *Bildung* — education, culture — was undoubtedly the route of entry into German civil society for significant segments of German Jewry,[3] the Rhenish story suggests the importance of material factors and social reality in creating change toward Jewish equality and acceptance. As the tax records show, by the 1840's Cologne's Jews were solidly middle class. As school enrollment statistics and other records show, they were eager to acculturate — to use proper German, to give their children German names. The culture that Cologne's Jews acquired was decidedly middlebrow, but it was precisely this that made them fit into Cologne's bourgeois society, since the city, unlike Berlin, was not an intellectual center. By the 1840's, several Rhenish mayors, including Cologne's, realized that "their" Jews had become respectable, upstanding *Bürger*, making the kind of discrimination practiced in the 1808 decree or proposed by Prussia misplaced and counterproductive.

By becoming solidly bourgeois, then, Jews had not only bettered themselves economically. They had also influenced official perceptions of Jews, laying the groundwork for change in Jewish policy. The Rhenish bourgeoisie, itself transformed from what its early modern forebears had been, could identify with the new bourgeois, acculturated Jews, because these Jews had made such identification possible. Jews, then, were not simply "emancipated" by non-Jews, nor were they mere beneficiaries of high-level Oppenheim lobbying, lavish Jewish expressions of gratitude — a magnificent gold chalice presented by Rhenish Jewry to Abraham Oppenheim in 1847 — notwithstanding.[4] Jews were not passive recipients of changed attitudes. They participated actively in fashioning them. Emerging in the 1840's, the new perception of Jews is strongly evident in the debates in the Municipal Assembly in the 1850's and 1860's over funding for the Jewish school.

Commitment to tolerance and mutual accommodation in Cologne thus flowed less from abstract notions — Rhenish liberalism generally and that of Cologne in particular were largely nonideological — than from pragmatism and identification with bourgeois Jews. In an age of general economic improvement, this was stable bedrock for Jewish acceptance. In contrast to other situations where liberal Jewish policy was out of touch with public sentiment — Prussia in 1812, for instance — in Cologne, Jewish policy coincided with broader social reality.

Unlike the situation in Germany in the last third of the nineteenth century, when a backlash against modernity targeted Jews as prime symbols of modernity and all its ills, particularly industrial capitalism, in the Rhineland in the 1840's, 1850's and 1860's, the association of Jews and the new urban economy worked powerfully to Jewish benefit.[5] The evidence from Cologne and the Rhineland cautions us against reading back into the middle of the century the cultural and political pessimism that pervaded Germany after the crash of 1873 and that undergirded late nineteenth-century antisemitism.

Religious demographics also helped the cause of Jewish rights in Cologne and the Rhineland as a whole. Many though not all of the liberals were Protestant, bearing an abiding hatred of the religious intolerance that had plagued Protestants in Catholic areas of the Rhineland and that continued to threaten "dissident" Protestant denominations — Mennonites, Quakers — under Prussia. Yet under Prussia, Catholics, although the overwhelming numerical majority of the city's population, themselves became a political minority. This gave Catholics a vested interest in having the government barred from interfering in religious matters — a prime liberal tenet — and, by the 1850's and 1860's, an interest in promoting the right of unpopular religious groups (like Catholics) to self-perpetuation. Threatened, too, by the growing political power of secularists who challenged so basic a Catholic priority as publicly funded confessional education, Catholics in Cologne's Municipal Assembly backed Jewish claims for such funding for their religious school. Thus, for all their differences with one another, Protestants, Catholics, and the religiously indifferent, liberals and nonliberals (activists in an increasingly strident Catholic Church), all came to share a political vision favorable to Jewish rights and even to official recognition of Jewish religious claims.

Local hostility to Prussia worked against the Jews through the early 1830's. Much as they had been in the medieval period, Jews, detested in their own right, were also seen as agents of the overlord's efforts to crush city autonomy. While there was some truth to this suspicion, the Prussians had broad economic as well as political reasons for being relatively liberal on Jewish rights in the city. Yet the fixation of city authorities on the past triggered a replay of the medieval dynamic well into the nineteenth century.

From the 1840's on, local hostility to Prussia worked strongly in favor of the Jews, because the city's government and representatives in the Rhenish Provincial Diets saw regressive Jewry policies as part of a pattern of state policies that were harmful to the city. In having Jewish concerns defined as part of a larger agenda rather than as a set of inimical interests to be fought, Jews had won ultimate political integration, even in the absence of full civic equality.

The record of Jewish economic integration and upward mobility in Cologne bespeaks an environment open to Jewish activities well before mid-century. Aside from hostility in the city's business and government elite in the early Prussian decades, there was also popular resistance: some who felt themselves the losers in Cologne's capitalist transformation — former members of once-powerful guilds, now petty artisans — attempted to exploit Jewish disabilities under Napoleonic law to gain advantage over Jewish competitors. Their efforts failed because targeted Jews fought back strongly and because the authorities, state and eventually municipal, refused to support them. In the absence of effective resistance, Jews made solid gains even in decades when discriminatory legislation was in force. By utterly belying any contention that anti-Jewish discrimination was either natural or necessary, the very facts that Jews integrated into economic life, lived where their incomes and tastes dictated, and sent their children to regular schools laid the groundwork for public acceptance of Jewish legal equality. Thus, the "facts of life" in Cologne during the era of emancipation did not just exist in static tension with legal realities. Gradually, they undermined them and made legal equality, rather than discrimination, seem natural and necessary.

The *Judenpatent* system was a humiliating nuisance but not, for most, a serious hindrance to betterment. The 1808 "infamous" decree, intended to direct Jews out of commerce and into crafts and farming, was out of touch with powerful forces in the economy and society that kept Jews in commercial and financial pursuits. Overwhelmed by reality from its inception, the law served more as a cover for local opposition to the Jews — and to the Prussians — than as an agent of Jewish occupational restratification.

The Napoleonic consistorial system, on the other hand, stifled religious initiative and development for decades, making Cologne's growing community a neglected stepchild of Bonn. Studies of German and French Jewry have established that urban immigrants were often more "adventuresome" culturally, to use Paula Hyman's term, than those who remained behind in small towns and villages.[6] Given the immigrant base and increasing acculturation of Cologne's Jewish community, and the size and political vitality of the city, we might have expected to find some organized religious reform effort in Cologne, yet there was nothing even approximating the developments that occurred in Berlin, Breslau, Hamburg, or Frankfurt, centers of the German Jewish reform movement.

The structure of the organized community, as decreed by Napoleonic law, was a factor in this conservatism. Cologne's synagogue was dependent on Bonn, meaning that a reform initiative within the synagogue would have to overcome traditionalist opposition there as well as locally. A reform initiative outside the synagogue was unlikely, because membership in the consistorial synagogue was a prerequisite for receiving a *Judenpatent*. For this reason, the first efforts to invigorate Jewish communal life, begun in the early 1840's, concentrated on achieving independence from Bonn within the consistorial framework.

The Prussian Jewry law of 1847 opened the possibility of something far more ambitious, since it aimed at decentralizing supercommunal institutions like the consistory and creating individual Jewish "synagogue communities." Nothing but the most moderate religious reform emerged in Cologne anyway, for several reasons. The political climate after 1848 was not conducive; the reform movement stagnated in Germany in the years after the revolution. The predominantly Catholic character of the city probably impeded the emergence of Jewish reform, because Reform Judaism derived much of its theoretical apparatus from liberal Protestantism and flourished in Protestant milieus. Religion in Cologne, moreover, was conservative, the city becoming a center for Catholic resurgence after 1850. There was thus no model in the larger society for Jewish religious innovation; the little that began to emerge in the 1860's was easily quashed. Finally, Cologne was not an intellectual or cultural center. Its one claim to fame was its architectural school — and it is here, in architecture, that the Jewish community did make a major symbolic statement.

In intolerant settings, Jewish distinctiveness is imposed from without and, short of conversion, is unavoidable. In liberal settings, Jewish survival is possible when the will to adapt is accompanied by a will to maintain distinctiveness in viable, acceptable ways. Cologne in the period studied was neither wholly intolerant nor wholly liberal, and Jewish persistence derived both from outside pressure and an internal will to persevere.

The Napoleonic system made affiliation with the synagogue mandatory de facto; the Prussian law of 1847 made it so de jure. Both functioned, unintentionally, to preserve Jewish identity.[7] But from midcentury on, the Jewish communal leadership of Cologne also demonstrated a creative and tenacious commitment to Jewish cultural survival. It perceived opportunity in a law not meant to strengthen Jewish communal life and used the law to constructive ends. Unlike the first generations of communal leaders in Cologne, which were apathetic about the Jewish school, Cologne's later communal leadership realized the centrality of education to minority group survival and waged a persistent battle with the city government to secure the financial base and cultural independence of the Jewish elementary school. Farther than the first community leaders from the primacy that traditional Jews placed on Jewish education, the later leadership had a commitment generated entirely in conditions of unprecedented openness and acceptance. Theirs was a wholly modern commitment to Jewish continuity, born in, and because of, emancipation and the cultural pluralism they chose to see in Cologne's society. Yet by winning parity of treatment with the Protestant and Catholic schools, Cologne's Jewish communal leadership did much more than secure the existence of one Jewish school. They also won legitimacy for Judaism. That was a major accomplishment in Cologne, and Prussia.

While Jewish protest against injustice — abuse under the 1808 decree — was purely private and individual in the 1810's and 1820's, the fight for fair treatment in the 1850's and 1860's was led by the organized community, openly and aggressively. Far from co-opting or eviscerating the Jewish communal will, as such prominent critics as Asher Ginzberg, Gershom Scholem, or Hannah Arendt have alleged, the fight for emancipation emboldened the Jews of one major German city, Cologne, to press both for equality and acceptance, *and* for conditions favorable to Jewish cultural survival.[8] It was only in 1893 that a German Jewish organization was founded to fight antisemitism and (later still) to assert the right of German Jews to express their Jewish identity freely, even as they claimed to be fully German.[9] Well before this, the Jews of Cologne had begun to elaborate a clear, adamant sense of self as both Germans and Jews.

In 1714, the English deist John Toland, writing on the "Reasons for Naturalizing the Jews in Great Britain and Ireland," argued that toleration of

Jews carried demonstrable material benefits to societies enlightened enough to let them live and trade in peace. Intolerance, on the other hand, was benighted and harmed the intolerant as much as their targets. "What a paltry fishertown was Leghorn," he wrote, "before admission of the Jews. What a loser is Lisbon since they have been lost to it [through expulsion]." As further illustration he cited

several cities where they are infamously lock'd up every night in a quarter by themselves, under a peculiar guard, as in Prague; and in others, as at Colen, [where] they are not permitted to dwell within the City, but whenever they come over from Deuts, on t'other side of the Rhine, they must pay so much for every hour they continue in the town, which they must also leave before Sun-set: whereas, if the citizens of Colen understood their own interest, they shou'd rather give 'em immunities and privileges, with a Synagogue into the bargain, in order to inhabit among 'em.[10]

Cologne was a great success story in the history of German Jewish emancipation not because lofty proclamations on the meaning of civil equality issued from there but because its experiment with the reality of more equitable relations between Jews and non-Jews made such remarkable strides in 73 years. By the 1840's, there was a sea change of opinion in Cologne, which would transform the city from the archetype of intolerance it had been in Toland's day, a realization that went beyond the truth of Toland's words. Ultimately, Jews were accepted not just pragmatically, but because different and even antagonistic elements of Cologne's society had developed a broad perception of the civic self that included Jews. By 1871, when the German Reich was proclaimed and Jewish civic equality fixed in a new constitution, much of the essential groundwork in social custom, which historians of emancipation agree was ultimately more determinative of actual Jewish rights than formal legislation, had been laid in Cologne. Fifty years after city officials recoiled in phobic horror at the prospect of proliferating Jewish "weeds," a member of the Municipal Assembly called the synagogue an asset, and a souvenir mapmaker featured the synagogue along with Cologne's Cathedral, Romanesque churches, medieval City Hall building, and statues of Frederick William III and Bismarck as the city's proudest and most representative sites.

A liberal theoretician wrote in 1850:

The emancipation of the Jews . . . cannot be said to be truly established merely because it may be decreed in constitutions or in *Reich* and state legislation; indeed, it will come to pass only if and when the *non-Jewish* part of the population is persuaded by legal and political enlightenment to recognise emancipation in its consciousness as just and to confirm such recognition by action and in real life. In other words: if and when the non-Jewish part will stand by the relevant principles of the philosophy of law or of reason not only in theory but also in practice.[11]

There were few places in the Germany of 1850 where this observation could have been made on the basis of experience. By 1871, Cologne was a study in its essential truth.

During the era of emancipation, Jews, a minuscule percentage of Cologne's population as they were of Germany's, occupied a hugely disproportionate place on the public agenda because of all they symbolized. What they symbolized changed as the struggle over municipal autonomy receded, yet Jews continued to be invested with enormous symbolic importance. Jews were outsiders within; a group, as the Colonais and the Germans as a whole felt themselves to be, with an anomalous identity, struggling to secure their rightful place and define their modern identity. The fact that Germans made it so difficult for Jews to secure that place and define that identity meant, of course, the persistence of a civic ambiguity that mirrored the Germans' own. The ongoing, seemingly endless debate about the Jews, then, was really a debate about the Germans. Society in Cologne could ultimately make peace with and integrate the Jewish presence because it took major steps to resolve its own civic identity. That evolution, a sign of a certain civic maturity, was matched by a maturation in the Jewish community, expressed in its insistence on both civil rights and the right to perpetuate Jewish culture.

Cathedral, city hall, and synagogue: time had not stripped the Jews of Cologne of their symbolic significance, but, by 1871, they had come to represent the acceptance and integration of once-irreconcilable realities.

Reference Matter

Abbreviations

ANF	*France: Archives Nationales*
AZdJ	*Allgemeine Zeitung des Judentums*
CAHJP	Central Archives for the History of the Jewish People
HASK	*Historisches Archiv der Stadt Köln*
HO	*Hausarchiv Oppenheim*
HSTA-D	*Hauptstaatsarchiv Düsseldorf*
HSTA-D-K	*Hauptstaatsarchiv Düsseldorf, Zweigarchiv Schloss Kalkum*
JTSA	Archives of the Jewish Theological Seminary of America
LBINY	Archives of the Leo Baeck Institute, New York
SA	*Stadtarchiv Bonn*
SRH	Baron, Salo W. *Social and Religious History*

Complete authors' names, titles, and publication data are given in the Bibliography. All documents cited by date and/or signature only may be found in *HASK*, Oberbürgermeisteramt, 400, II-4-C-1, *Judenpatente*.

Petition on Behalf of Jewish Rights Presented by the City of Cologne to the Eighth Rhenish Provincial Diet, 1845

The proposal for the full political and civil equality of the Jews, which the Seventh Rhenish Provincial Diet laid before the steps of the throne, constitutes one of the finest pages in the history of this Diet.

Rejoicing resounded throughout Germany about a vote that, based on the natural, inalienable legal equality of all, rose above the barriers which for thousands of years has disgracefully oppressed the human dignity of those who profess another belief, asserting absolute freedom of conscience for Jews, as well as Christians, claiming the full right of universal development and expression for their spirit.

The Seventh Rhenish Diet was permeated with the conviction that the whole organism of state was diseased as long as one of its members was shut out of its rights and duties. It was convinced that the legal equality of all citizens must be the first step on the ladder toward freedom and humanity. Legal equality demands the Christian precept of love of one's fellow. Legal equality demands the political idea of our century. Legal equality is the urgent summons of progressive intelligence. Legal equality is the foundation as well as the only enduring guarantee for the right[s] and freedom of all. After the fine precedent of the Seventh Rhenish Diet, the request for civil and political equality for Jews under the law requires its more precise foundation at the Eighth Rhenish Diet.

His Majesty the King has also most graciously proposed considering the fulfillment of this request of the Seventh Diet in the prorogation [*Landtagsabschied*] laid before the Diet at its dismissal. But each moment lost is costly when it concerns the holiest interests of humanity, when it concerns the abolition of a burden which encumbers the conscience of the privileged

Christian and violates the divine teachings of Christianity. So that the moment of the secure, full legal equality of the Jews be hastened, so that the heavy guilt of today's society be nullified more quickly and the road to further progress be smoothed, we address the most obedient request to your sublime High Assembly of the Estates, that you once again raise your voice loudly for the holiest interests of humanity and freedom, which [are] yet oppressed in the Jews, and that you renew the proposal for full political and civil equality for the Jews before His Majesty the King, and implore its speedy, gracious fulfillment.

SOURCE: *HASK,* 1023/C21. A slightly different version is in Kastner, 2: 851–56; see also Jost, pp. 309–11.

Measuring Immigration and Assessing Jewish Wealth: Sources and Methodology for Tables 12 and 18

Measuring Immigration: Table 12

There is no source recording yearly Jewish immigration to Cologne. My calculation is based on dates of immigration cited in settlement petitions and the "date of first mention" method, in which I count the year a Jew first appears in any type of record as the year of immigration (see Chapter 2, note 3). In addition to its inexactitude, the latter method makes years of unusually copious record keeping — 1844, for example — appear as years of unusually heavy immigration. I address this problem by averaging three years' figures. I exclude from the immigration count children of resident Jews reaching adulthood and appearing on occupational and other records for the first time. The family identity of such people is sometimes explicit in the sources; otherwise, I reconstructed it from sources detailing Jewish household composition in Cologne in these and previous decades.

Because the sources focus largely on male immigrant householders and do not consistently report on family members accompanying them, I calculated immigration by counting the number of independently employed adult Jews who immigrated singly, considering each an immigrant household. (Thus, a family with six working members who immigrated together would be counted as one immigrant household, while two brothers who immigrated separately, applying individually for settlement and work permits, would be counted as two immigrant households.) The number of Jewish immigrating households was 30 in 1835–37, 34 in 1838–40, 42 in 1841–43, and 47 in 1843–45. Because average Jewish household size in Cologne during this period was four, I multiplied the immigrant household count by four to obtain total immigration figures by year. In order to establish symmetry with the three-year averages in Ayçoberry's Table 3A, I averaged these figures for three-year intervals, then multiplied by three to obtain the total number of Jewish immigrants for each three-year period in Table 12. I multiplied Ayçoberry's yearly averages for each three-year period by three in order to obtain the total number of immigrants to Cologne during 1835–46 (13,908).

All this does not account for population growth due to births. Using birth statistics in Kober, *Cologne*, p. 328, App. B, I estimate a total of 366 Jewish (presumably live) births for 1835–46. Subtracting this sum from Ayçoberry's Jewish population figure of 974 for 1846 (2: 106) yields a net Jewish increase of 608 due to immigration, a total close to my count. Cologne's population increased by 20,150 between 1837 and 1846 (see Table 11). If 13,908 of these were immigrants, 6,242 were births, a finding in accord with Ayçoberry (1: 276).

Jewish mortality figures, infant or otherwise, are lacking. There is also no record of Jewish emigration from the city, so the transience or permanence of long-settled or immigrant Jews is not measurable.

Assessing Jewish Wealth: Table 18

There were several population surveys of Cologne's Jews in January 1844. One (*HASK*, Oberbürgermeisteramt, 400, II-4-D-1, dated Jan. 30, 1844) recorded the Jews' occupations and amounts of assessed business and property tax (*Gewerbesteuer, Grundsteuer*). This is the chief source for analysis of Jewish wealth stratification in the 1840's.

An important auxiliary source is the published list of electors in the city of Cologne in 1849, the *Verzeichniss der Meistbeerbten der Stadt Köln,* compiled according to the specifications of electoral law favoring the wealthy. I also consulted the Cologne *Adressbücher*, which list occupation as well as address.

The Prussian *Gewerbesteuer* was introduced in 1820 and remained in effect without major modification until 1891. Although an apportioned tax, it was levied according to a predetermined average payment set by the fiscal authorities and probably overstated assessments. (On the *Gewerbesteuer*, see Ayçoberry, "Histoire Sociale," 2: 47–48, 57–58, App. 9, App. 10; and Müller, p. 198, n. 1.)

Nevertheless, the *Gewerbesteuer* is the most extensive source for gauging the level of Jewish economic activity in the city: of 184 Jews or Jewish-owned businesses that appear legibly on the Jan. 30, 1844, list, 82 (45 percent) paid the business tax (information about another six Jews on this list was unreadable). Eleven Jews not on this list were assessed the property tax, which serves as an indicator of their means. The economic standing of a further nineteen Jews with no assessed taxes, but who possessed considerable means, was gauged from their appearance and ranking on the list of the wealthiest citizens (*Meistbeerbten*). A total of 70 Jews were assessed neither levy and show no other evidence of means.

The business tax was levied on twelve occupational categories. Three of these were combined commercial and manufacturing categories, ranked by scale. We know the predetermined maximum, minimum, and average tax assessments of the upper two of these categories, "merchants with" and "without merchants' rights" (*Kaufleute mit/ohne Kaufmännische[n] Rechte[n]*). The maximum for the first group was 240 taler; the minimum, 12 taler; the average, 30 taler. In the second group, the maximum was 18 taler; the minimum, 2 taler; the average, 8 taler (Ayçoberry, "Histoire Sociale," 2: 47–48; cf. Müller, p. 198, n. 1).

These values give us a sense of the parameters for brackets into which to divide Jewish taxpayers, the full range of whose actual assessments I use to modify the bracketing amounts. (The lowest amount of recorded business tax assessed a Jew, 8 taler, was considerably above the minimum of 2 taler the law set for businessmen; I used that amount, rather than the legal minimum, to set the floor amount for the "lower" bracket.)

I used the values that delineate business tax brackets to evaluate and rank property tax assessments, which were an important auxiliary source for evaluating Jewish wealth. In cases where Jews were assessed no business tax but were assessed on their property, this was the wealth indicator. When Jews were assessed both types of tax but at discrepant levels, I gave evaluative preference to the more common business tax.

The *Meistbeerbten* list showed all citizens eligible to vote under the *Gemeindeordnung* (Community Statute) of 1845, which set up a three-class voting system. Electors in Cologne (amounts varied in different cities) were adult males assessed yearly incomes of 400 taler or more, ranked into three classes by level of wealth above the minimum. Jews were included on the list, which I used to augment and, for two categories, to correct, analysis of data contained on the 1844 population survey: members of the professions and pensioners were not liable for the business tax and so appeared on that survey as having been assessed no tax. In the absence of a property tax assessment, such people would be judged indigent, which for these two categories would be mistaken, because Jewish professionals and pensioners figure prominently on the *Meistbeerbten* list. All but one of the professionals were in the third class of *Meistbeerbten*, pensioners evenly divided among all three. On the basis of this information, I ranked professionals in the middle wealth class and pensioners in the upper middle.

Class level on the *Meistbeerbten* list generally coincided with the level of tax assessment with which it is coupled in my ranking system. When the two measurements varied — business tax assessment indicating a middle level of wealth while the *Meistbeerbten* classification indicated a higher level of wealth, for instance — I follow the business tax, if there is no property tax to corroborate in either direction. If there is only a property tax assessment and a *Meistbeerbten* classification at odds with it, I follow the latter, since it encompassed several variables in determining wealth (see the section in Chapter 6 entitled Comparative Wealth of Jews and Non-Jews). This method generally gives greater weight to indicators for lower wealth.

Religion is not indicated on the *Meistbeerbten* list. I identify Jews on the basis of the Jan. 30, 1844, population survey and accumulated evidence from *Judenpatente* records, supplemented by data in Brisch, Weyden, and Kober. There is an obvious problem in using a source dated 1849 (whose base data may have been compiled in 1848) to fill out information for 1844. Yet it is extremely unlikely that any Jews made their wealth between 1846 and 1848, years of severe economic crisis.

Five wealth categories emerged: the three highest using the *Meistbeerbten* classification in addition to direct tax information; the next lowest based on level of tax assessment; the lowest made up of Jews assessed neither form of tax who also did not appear on the *Meistbeerbten* list. In the absence of communal welfare records or any other means to gauge the extent of Jewish poverty in Cologne, I thought it important to distinguish economically marginal Jews (those assessed even a minimal amount of tax) from poor ones, rather than to collapse the groups into a general "low" category.

Notes

Introduction

1. Rürup, "Jewish Emancipation," p. 70. Salo Baron emphasizes this same point; see Baron, "Newer Approaches"; and id., "Civil versus Political Emancipation."

2. Rürup, "Jewish Emancipation," p. 68.

3. See J. Katz, "The Term 'Jewish Emancipation.'"

4. Some of the important works on the legal and political aspects of Jewish emancipation in Germany are Freund; S. Stern, *Die Preussische Staat*; Auerbach; Dubnow; and Horst Fischer.

5. I first conceived the idea of a local case study of German Jewish emancipation after reading Allen.

6. On the pace of German Jewish urbanization, see Lowenstein, "Pace of Modernisation"; Toury, *Soziale und Politische Geschichte*, pp. 27ff.; and Barkai, "German Jews," pp. 124–25. Statistics on Rhenish Jewry are drawn from Kober, "Aus der Geschichte," p. 79.

7. There are multitudes of German — and now English and Hebrew — histories of German Jewish communities, written by rabbis, community leaders, and local scholars. They are of varying quality: some apologetic, even hagiographical; others, scholarly. On Cologne, see n. 10 below.

8. See Toury, "Probleme Jüdischer Gleichberechtigung," pp. 267–86; and id., "Types of Jewish Municipal Rights," pp. 55–80.

9. Walker, p. 1.

10. There are two nineteenth-century histories of Cologne's Jews: Ernst Weyden's *Geschichte der Juden in Köln* and Carl Brisch's *Geschichte der Juden in Cöln*. Adolf Kober, a scholar of Rhenish Jewry and rabbi of Cologne's largest synagogue before the Second World War, wrote *Cologne*. All three works, particularly Kober's, are solid, careful, and useful. They are narrowly focused, however, and all are narrative, recounting rather than analyzing or contextualizing events.

Zvi Asaria's *Die Juden in Köln* is largely an update of earlier works, which Asaria does not always credit. Rolf Hahn's "Das 'schändliche Dekret,'" a doctoral dissertation in the Law Faculty of the University of Cologne, treats the purely legal aspects of emancipation in Cologne.

Alwin Müller's *Die Geschichte der Juden in Köln* is a methodologically sophisticated social history of the Jews in Cologne in the first half of the nineteenth century, but it is Jewish social history only, neither analyzing political developments (the city's stance toward the Jews) or Jewish communal behavior nor embedding Jewish occupational and economic patterns into those of the city.

Müller and I differ in some important areas of interpretation and, occasionally, fact, as stated in these notes.

11. I use Ayçoberry's two-volume thesis rather than his book, *Cologne entre Napoléon et Bismarck* (Paris, 1981), because the thesis includes his invaluable statistical data and graphics.

12. It is odd that the place of the battle over Jewish rights in German history should now have to be argued; contemporaries on either side of the issue understood this well. Writers as diverse as Heinrich Heine, Ludwig Börne, Bruno Bauer, Karl Marx, Moses Hess, and Ludwig Philippson, editor of the *Allgemeine Zeitung des Judentums,* all agreed that the issue of Jewish rights was part of a much larger German social question. Their understanding of the larger problem and their proposed solutions differed greatly. They did not share a common view of Judaism, nor did they all necessarily feel sympathy for Jews as a real group, as opposed to a symbolic abstraction — representatives par excellence of feudal victimization. But all recognized that to challenge the historically circumscribed place of the Jews in German society was to challenge the authority of the circumscribers — church, state, Estates — who had oppressed not only the Jews but society as a whole. As Bauer wrote in his famous essay "Die Judenfrage," "Not only Jews, but we, too, want to be emancipated." On the other side, Heine cautioned Jews against believing that their emancipation could be achieved while the rest of German society labored under the remnants of feudal tyranny. The fate of Jews and Christians was inextricably linked, he said, and Jews "ought not to claim as Jews what was due to them as Germans long ago." See citations and analysis in Herzig, *Judentum und Emanzipation,* pp. x–xi and 93ff.

13. This approach typifies the older works of Heinrich von Treitschke, who was no friend of Jewish historiography (see his *Deutsche Geschichte im neunzehnten Jahrhundert*), and Franz Schnabel (*Deutsche Geschichte im Neunzehnten Jahrhundert*). But it is also apparent in more recent studies. H. W. Koch's *History of Prussia* contains three references to the legal status of Jews, two in the context of antisemitism, the pervasiveness of which is assumed without being analyzed; see especially p. 180. Several other postwar works on specialized topics close to the concerns of this study ignore references to Jews and the Jewish question that abound in the primary sources they study. Elisabeth Fehrenbach, in "Rheinischer Liberalismus," pp. 272–94, makes no mention of the Jews although, as we shall see, the "Jewish question" was very prominent in the Rhenish liberal discussion of the German constitutional question. Helmut Asmus, in "Die 'Rheinische Zeitung,'" pp. 135–67, does not mention the pioneering vocal stand of this newspaper on behalf of Jewish rights. Beate-Carola Padtberg, in *Rheinischer Liberalismus in Köln,* does not mention the wrangling in Cologne's Municipal Assembly in the 1850's and 1860's over funding for the Jewish school, much less assess the significance of this debate for the place of liberalism in city politics.

By contrast, Thomas Nipperdey, in *Deutsche Geschichte,* pp. 248–55, includes a section on the Jewish minority in a chapter entitled "Leben, Arbeiten, Wirtschaften." Reinhard Rürup includes a section on Jewish emancipation in his *Deutschland im 19. Jahrhundert*, pp. 105–9. See also Rürup, *Emanzipation und Antisemitismus*; id., "Emanzipation der Juden in Baden," pp. 225–38; id., "Emanzipation und Krise," pp. 1–56; id., "Jewish Emancipation and Bourgeois Society"; id., "Emancipation and Crisis"; id., "German Liberalism"; id., "The Tortuous and Thorny Path"; id., "Emanzipation und Antisemitismus"; and id., "European Revolutions of 1848," pp. 1–62. Hajo Holborn's classic *History of Modern Germany, 1648–1840* and *History of Modern Germany, 1840–1945* also give serious contextual attention to Jewish legal and economic status.

I wrote these remarks before several similar critiques, which enlarge on important aspects of the historiographical problem, appeared. See Rürup, "Appraisal of German-Jewish Historiography"; Zimmerman; and Meyer, "Jews as Jews."

14. See, for example, G. L. Mosse, *Germans and Jews*; id., *Crisis of German Ideology*; F. Stern, *Gold and Iron*; Volkov, *Rise of Popular Antimodernism in Germany*. The literature on German antisemitism is vast; two important historiographical analyses are Schorsch, "German Antisemitism"; and Volkov, "Antisemitism as a Cultural Code."

15. By contrast, see W. E. Mosse, *Jews in the German Economy*; and Prinz, *Juden im Deutschen Wirtschaftsleben*.

16. Neither Theodore S. Hamerow, *Restoration, Revolution, Reaction*, nor Martin Kitchen, *Political Economy of Germany*, contains a single reference to Jews. One recent anthology on German social history introduces Jewish material only under the rubric of German genocide; see Ulrich. Some important recent social histories of the European and German middle classes by two scholars who consistently write integrative German Jewish history do include consideration of the German Jewish case. See Volkov, " 'Verbürgerlichung' of the Jews"; and G. L. Mosse, "Das Deutsch-jüdische Bildungsbürgertum."

17. The important developments in nineteenth-century German Judaism are not treated in the fourth volume of Franz Schnabel, *Deutsche Geschichte*, entitled *Die Religiösen Kräfte*. Nor are they covered in James J. Sheehan's more recent *German History*, though Sheehan notes Moses Mendelssohn. By contrast, Michael Meyer clearly grounds the ideology of German Jewish religious reform in its German context; see his "Reform Jewish Thinkers"; id., *Response to Modernity*.

18. Thus, despite its title, David Sorkin's *Transformation of German Jewry* is actually about the German Jewish intellectual elite.

19. Hamburger, "One Hundred Years of Emancipation," p. 11.

20. Kaplan, *Making of the Jewish Middle Class*.

21. See the work of Toury; Richarz; Hyman; Caron; Rozenblit; and Lowenstein.

22. See Barkai, "German Jews," p. 135.

23. Important exceptions are Toury, *Soziale und Politische Geschichte*; and Grab and Schoeps, eds. In her history of Würzburg Jewry in the era of emancipation, *Vom Schutzjuden zum Staatsbürger*, Ursula Gerhring-Münzel also notes the paucity of study of Würzburg in these years, p. 1.

24. See Kaschuba, p. 410; Kocka, ed., *Bürger und Bürgerlichkeit*; Conze and

Kocka, eds.; Lepsius; Zunkel, "Das Verhältnis des Unternehmertums"; Blackbourne and Eley; Engelhardt; and Blackbourne and Evans, eds.

25. See G. L. Mosse, *German Jews Beyond Judaism*; id., "Jewish Emancipation"; id., "Das Deutsch-jüdische Bildungsbürgertum"; Sorkin, *Transformation*; id., "Invisible Community"; and Volkov, "'Verbürgerlichung' of the Jews."

26. See Arendt; Scholem, *On Jews and Judaism*; id., *From Berlin to Jerusalem*; Schorsch, *Jewish Reactions to German Anti-Semitism*; and Lamberti, *Jewish Activism*. See also Toury, *Die politischen Orientierungen*; Tal; and G. L. Mosse, *German Jews Beyond Judaism*.

27. *HASK*, Oberbürgermeisteramt, 400, II-4-C-1. This collection, labeled *Judenpatente*, contains minutes of City Council sessions and correspondence with the Chamber of Commerce and various Prussian bureaucracies.

28. *HASK*, Oberbürgermeisteramt, 400, II-4-D-1.

Chapter One

1. For texts of the charters, their significance, and Jewish legal status in medieval Christian Europe, see Aronius; Parkes; Marcus; Chazan; Bachrach, pp. 66–105; Baron, *SRH*, 4: 43–53, 171–96; and Kisch, *Jews in Medieval Germany*.

2. See Baron, "'Plenitude of Apostolic Powers'"; and id., *SRH*, 9: 135ff.

3. On Cologne's economic importance in the Middle Ages, see Ennen, "Köln als politisches"; and Kellenbenz, "Der Aufstieg Kölns." On the Jews as private property and sources of income, see Parkes, pp. 93–154. On the economic activities of medieval Jews and their restriction to money trades and petty commerce, see Kellenbenz, "Die Juden in der Wirtschaftsgeschichte"; R. Straus, *Die Juden in Wirtschaft und Gesellschaft*; id., "The Jews in the Economic Evolution of Central Europe"; Elbogen and Sterling, pp. 32ff.; and Liebeschutz, "The Relevance of the Middle Ages." On the atomization of authority over the Jews, see Baron, *SRH*, 9: 193ff.

4. Kober, *Cologne*, pp. 12, 26–27, 38; and Bauer, pp. 17–18.

5. Strait, p. 144. See also Koebner; Lau; Diederich, pp. 41–58; and Herborn. On the conflict between city and archbishops, see Stehkämper. On medieval "nationalism" and its impact on the Jews, see Baron, *SRH*, 11: 193ff.; and id., "Medieval Nationalism and Jewish Serfdom."

6. On the Jewish quarter, see Kober, *Cologne*, pp. 68, 84 ff.; Strait, pp. 34, 81; and Asaria, 71ff.

7. Twice, in 1252 and 1258, the question of the Jews was raised in settlements terminating major hostilities between the archbishop and the city. Despite these explicit references, scholarship has virtually ignored the Jewish factor in the municipal-archepiscopal power struggle. An exception is Wenninger, *Man Bedarf Keiner Juden Mehr*, a study of Jewish expulsions from German imperial cities, including Cologne, in the fifteenth century. Wenninger, however, reduces the expulsions in general to manifestations of economic distress. Salo Baron's analysis of developments in Cologne is the most satisfying; see his *SRH*, 9: 170ff., 323–25, nn. 44–48. The histories of Weyden, Brisch, and Kober catalog but do not analyze this issue. Parkes, pp. 200–201, recounts the increasing authority of the city over the Jews without mentioning the municipal-archepiscopal power struggle. Bauer, pp. 30–31, details the legal

aspects of the conflicts and notes the importance of the city's Jewish policy, but studies only Jewish legal status and does not evaluate the Jewish aspect of the power struggle. Lau's *Entwicklung* is a constitutional history of the city, treating the Jews in a subsection. Stehkämper's article, "Über die rechtliche Absicherung," is presented as a full treatment of the municipal-archepiscopal conflict in the thirteenth century, but, despite emphasis on the importance of revenue sources in the dispute, it does not mention the Jews once, a baffling omission.

8. The archbishop faced challenges to his authority from within the church hierarchy as well as from secular authorities. The Cathedral Chapter several times objected to the liberal terms of the archbishop's Jewish privileges and tried, unsuccessfully, to quash them. See Brisch, 1: 108–9; Weyden, pp. 167–68; Baron, *SRH*, 9: 191; and Bauer, pp. 71ff. For its services in 1324, the City Council received a fee of 300 marks. See Kober, *Cologne*, pp. 63–64; and Lau, p. 181.

9. On anti-Jewish violence in the Rhineland, see Roth. For a broader context, see Ben-Sasson, ed., pp. 385–602. The massacres of Jews during the Black Death dwarf any that had occurred previously and had severe demographic, legal, and economic consequences for central European Jewry. See Baron, *SRH*, 4: 260–70; and Poliakov, pp. 107ff. On the events of 1348–49 in Cologne, see Weyden, pp. 188ff.; Brisch, 1: 129ff.; and Kober, *Cologne*, pp. 114ff.

10. Brisch, 1: 137ff.; Weyden, pp. 194ff.; and Kober, *Cologne*, pp. 116–17. Kober reports that both the cathedral and the City Hall were beautified with funds from confiscated Jewish assets.

11. See Diederich, pp. 45ff.; Lau, pp. 136ff.; and K. Hegel.

12. See Kober, *Cologne*, pp. 123ff.; cf. Brisch, 2: 2; and Weyden, pp. 200–201. According to von den Brincken, p. 313, it was the patriciate, newly victorious over the weavers, that sought the readmission of Jews to the city. The archbishop's actions were in line with his broader policy of encouraging Jewish settlement in the archbishopric. On the readmission of Jews to cities from which they were expelled during the Black Death massacres, see Littmann.

13. While the Jewish community in the thirteenth century and the first half of the fourteenth century had grown, between 1372 and 1424 it never numbered more than 150 to 200, with no more than 31 tax-paying households. See Weyden, p. 174; and Kober, *Cologne*, pp. 122, 361–62, n. 38.

14. Brisch, 2: 7ff.; Weyden, p. 206; Kellenbenz, "Die Juden in der Wirtschaftsgeschichte," pp. 223–24.

15. Kellenbenz, "Die Juden in der Wirtschaftsgeschichte," p. 221. See also R. Straus, "Jews in the Economic Evolution," pp. 15ff.

16. See Kober, *Cologne*, pp. 128–29; and Bauer, pp. 86ff. On the Fourth Lateran Council and the Jews, see Grayzel; Kisch, "Yellow Badge in History"; and Baron, *SRH*, 11: 96. On the lag in enforcing the council's decrees, see Elbogen and Sterling, pp. 51–52.

17. Weyden, p. 239. See also Bauer; and Kober, *Cologne*, pp. 362ff., n. 42.

18. Kober, *Cologne*, p. 126.

19. "Wir binnen unserer Stadt setzen und entsetzen mögen, was uns für unsere Stadt nützlich zu sein denkt." Cited in Brisch, 2: 50; and von den Brincken, p. 317, who analyzes the 1431 document and argues for more acceptance of the city's

alleged religious motivations for the expulsion. Rationalizations usually contain elements of truth and, to be effective, must be cast in an idiom of shared beliefs and values. While rationalizations may be sincerely believed, this does not obscure the distinction between motivation and justification. Von den Brincken is not convincing. Cf. Wenninger, pp. 94–101, who argues for purely economic motives.

20. Brisch, 2: 41. The number of Jewish tax-paying households declined steadily between the second of Dietrich's court summonses in 1417 and the expulsion. Kober, *Cologne*, p. 362, n. 36. The Jews had a year's notice of the impending expulsion to liquidate their assets. Not all were successful in doing so, in which case the city confiscated their property.

21. Between 1300 and 1500, the Jews were expelled about 150 times (more than once from the same place) in southern and central Germany. See R. Straus, "Jews in the Economic Evolution," p. 23; Bonn, p. 54; Israel, pp. 5–34; Hsia, pp. 65, 83, 86ff., 163ff.; Baron, *SRH*, 11: 275; Kellenbenz, "Die Juden in der Wirtschaftsgeschichte," pp. 225–26; Kober, "Jewish Communities in Germany"; and id., "Aus der Geschichte," pp. 41ff.

22. See Israel, pp. 8, 9, 23.

23. East Prussia, Mecklenburg, and Saxony had no Jewish populations before the eighteenth century. See Cahnman, p. 215. Modern Jewish resettlement in Germany began only in the late sixteenth century and even then was subject to great local variations. See J. Katz, *Out of the Ghetto*, pp. 12ff.; Kober, "Jewish Communities in Germany"; and Israel, p. 23.

24. Brisch, 2: 51–52; and Heimann, p. 109. See too, Kober, "Aus der Geschichte," pp. 63ff.

25. See Brisch, 2: 61; Ennen, "Die jüdische Gemeinde in Bonn"; and Schulte, *Bonner Juden*.

26. Kober, *Cologne*, pp. 142, 153, 154, 365, n. 44; Keyser, ed., *Rheinisches Städtebuch*, pp. 77–78, 85; and Schulte, *Dokumentation zur Geschichte*, p. 226.

27. The small size of Jewish communities in electoral Cologne was typical for the region. See Kober, "Aus der Geschichte," pp. 52ff. On Jewish supra-*Landgemeinden* in territories with small communities unable to provide all their own religious needs, see J. Katz, *Out of the Ghetto*, pp. 19ff., n. 32, 225–26.

28. See Pollack, pp. 1–14, 85–95, for a general description of Jewish housing patterns and dress; for a treatment of one location, see Kopp, pp. 358ff.

29. On the position of the Estates, see Kober, *Cologne*, pp. 142–43, 146; and Carsten.

30. See Kober, *Cologne*, pp. 142ff.; id., "Aus der Geschichte," pp. 46ff.; Brisch, 2: 106ff.; Weyden, pp. 257ff.; Kellenbenz, "Die Juden in der Wirtschaftsgeschichte," pp. 224ff.; and Ehrlich, pp. 246–63.

31. Each member of the community contributed toward the cost of the corporate license from which he (only males held membership) and family members derived legal status and protection. The state preferred the corporate tax, which had to be paid regardless of the size of the community; the Jewish community wanted as many tax-paying members as possible among whom to distribute the tax burden and so sought to limit the number of Jewish poor, who could not share the community's financial burden but would make demands on its social services. See Glanz; and G. Hoffmann, p. 34.

32. Hoffmann, pp. 22, 37–38.

33. On court Jews, see Stern, *The Court Jew*; Carsten; Arendt, "Privileged Jews," pp. 3–7; Weinryb, "Prolegomena"; Treue, "Das Verhältnis"; R. Straus, *Die Juden*, pp. 5ff.; and Priebatsch. On court Jews in northwest Germany, see G. Hoffmann; Heinrich Schnee, "Studien zur Institution"; and id., *Die Hoffinanz*. Schnee has been sharply criticized for unhistorical and antisemitic statements, although the breadth of his research is acknowledged. See Carsten; Weinryb, "Prolegomena."

34. See Hegel; Braubach, *Die Vier*; id., *Maria Theresias jüngster Sohn*.

35. See von Lojewski.   36. Schnee, *Die Hoffinanz*, p. 17.

37. See Brilling.   38. Schnee, *Die Hoffinanz*, pp. 36ff.

39. Kober, "Rheinische Judendoktoren"; and id., "Reichsstadt Köln." Jewish doctors were in particular demand in the second half of the seventeenth century during epidemics; see Klersch, pp. 3, 216. Conversions were relatively rare in the sixteenth and seventeenth centuries but increased in the eighteenth; Capuchin monks established a mission in Cologne and made the city something of a conversion center for Jews. The lists of converts in Klersch show a wide range of places of origin. Doubts were raised concerning the sincerity of some of these conversions; Jewish testimony from 1643 indicated that some Jews converted in Cologne went to Holland, where they reverted to Judaism; Klersch, pp. 211ff. See also Brisch, 2: 133ff.

40. Klersch, p. 211, reports the case of a Polish Jewish musician coming from Amsterdam who was arrested on Cologne's wharf while on his way to family in Bebber, where he was to celebrate the feast of Tabernacles and play at a wedding. The grounds for the arrest were that he lacked the proper certification for his "visit" in Cologne.

41. See Kober, "Reichsstadt Köln," for details and the text of a letter from Emperor Karl VI to the city of Cologne in 1714 on behalf of his court agent, Emanuel Oppenheimer, who was experiencing the usual problems there.

42. On these crypto-Jews, see Kellenbenz, "Die Juden in der Wirtschaftsgeschichte," pp. 229ff.; and id., *Sephardim*.

43. In this period the *Landrabbinat* of Cologne moved to Bonn. As control of Deutz was long disputed among the city of Cologne, the archbishop-electors of Cologne, and the Dukes of Berg, it often came under attack and sustained severe damage.

44. Brisch, 2: 115–16.

45. Kober, *Cologne*, pp. 156–57; Kober, "Reichsstadt Köln," p. 413. The Cologne City Council was also capable of sheer nastiness, as the Cologne Jewish community's *Memorbuch* records: "In the year 1699, Cologne's Council had a gallows erected in the Jewish cemetery at Severins Gate, in order to revolt the Jews through its use. Through the grace of the Elector, the Jews obtained a cemetery in Deutz. . . ." The slightly different Hebrew version reads as follows:

"בשנת תני'ט נחרב הבית הקברות בקוליניא על ידי עירוני העיר ויקימו שם עג
לתלות עליו את הרוצחים כדי לחרף ולגדף את המקום. בשנה ההיא נתן
הקורפירשט לקהל דייץ את קברות החדשה סמוך לרחיים על זנטקויל."

JTSA, History Mic. 8600, p. 19.

46. Kober, *Cologne*, p. 158; the original German is in id., "Reichsstadt Köln," p. 413.

47. On reforms in Jewish status under the old regime, see Mahler, pp. 18ff., 229ff.; Hertzberg; Israel, pp. 42–44, 64–65. On aborted reform of Protestant status in Cologne, see Diefendorf, pp. 40ff.

48. As Biro notes, 1: 305, by 1795 "municipalities or town councils were set up in Spires, Worms, Aix — in fact, in every city on the left bank but Cologne. The preservation of Cologne's Senate was due to its persistence, its eloquence, its logic, its pleading, and its reminding France that the latter still owed it 3,000,000 livres expended to assist France in 1756."

49. See Biro; a full but partisan account of events in Cologne is in Gothein, pp. 4ff.; cf. Klersch, pp. 219ff.

50. Biro, 2: 877; cf. 901.

51. Biro's paraphrase, 2: 853.

52. See Biro. On the Protestants in Cologne, see Gothein; and Becker-Jákli.

53. Cited in Schulte, *Bonner Juden*, p. 61; on this issue, see Kober, "French Revolution."

54. Weyden, p. 27.

55. From Brisch, 2: 146–47; Weyden, p. 275.

56. This incident is cited by Brisch, 2: 146.

Chapter Two

1. The memoir is in the Cologne community *Memorbuch*, JTSA, History Mic. 8600. According to a Prussian record of 1820 (*HASK*, Oberbürgermeisteramt, 400, II-13-C-10, "Nachweisung der in hiesiger Stadt wohnhaften Juden" of June 29, 1820), Stern and his family came to Cologne in 1794, but this is contradicted by the testimony in the *Memorbuch* and by what we know about conditions in the city before French annexation of the left bank. See, too, the handwritten "Chronik der Stadt Köln," by the city archivist in this period, Fuchs; *HASK*, "Chroniken und Darstellungen," no. 229.

2. Posener, pp. 281, 290.

3. My count, based on analysis of various population records. There were two house-to-house surveys of the Jewish population. The first, conducted in 1806, listed 124 Jewish adults and children (*HASK*, Französische Verwaltung, 2470); the second, conducted in 1808, listed a total population of 132 (ibid., 4884, list dated September 16, 1808, and "Registre des Juifs" dated August 15, 1808). Thereafter, the French recorded only adult male Jews granted the *patentes* required by the 1808 decree, obviously only a small part of the total Jewish population. I believe that even the population statistics of 1806 and 1808 are an undercount, however, since quite a few Jews whose names do not appear on such counts appear incidentally in other records, such as communications to or from the mayor or police chief. My method of calculation was to count any Jew mentioned in any source as living in Cologne, then deduct as transients any whose names drop from the records during the French period or fail to appear in Prussian records. I took the earliest date a person's name appeared in the records as the date of immigration.

I also used some Prussian records to calculate population during the French period when these cited an immigration date falling in the French period. One is the previously cited "Nachweisung" of 1820 (n. 1); the other, in the same collection, is the "Nachweisung Sämmtlicher in Stadtkreise Köln wohnenden Jüdischen Glaubensgenossen," of April 19, 1817. This was a particularly rich source because it also listed the number of children. When the number of children per family recorded exceeded the number listed in Kober, *Namensregister*, I estimated the number of children likely to have been born between 1808 and January 1814, the end of French rule, and included them in the population count. Information about Jewish births in 1811 is given in *HASK*, Französische Verwaltung, 2479. This is how I arrived at the count of 211 Jews in the city at the end of French rule.

4. Keyser, ed., *Rheinisches Städtebuch*, pp. 34, 41; Kober, "Aus der Geschichte," pp. 96, 97.

5. On Cologne's economy, see Gothein, pp. 57ff.; Pohl; and Diefendorf, pp. 24ff.

6. See Schwering; and Becker-Jákli, pp. 2ff.

7. Protestants showed a similar eagerness to immigrate to Cologne, and as a group they flourished, particularly in industry and banking. See Pohl, pp. 23ff., 150ff.; and Becker-Jákli, pp. 93ff.

8. Analysis of data available for 54 immigrants shows 12 to have been born in electoral Cologne; 19 elsewhere in the northern Rhineland; 9 in the Rhineland-Pfalz and Saar regions and in Hesse; 7 in Bavaria; 4 in Holland; 2 in Lithuania; and 1 in Lübeck.

9. There were 53 children aged fifteen or younger in twenty Jewish households out of thirty officially recorded in 1806; calculated from *HASK*, Französische Verwaltung, 2470.

10. Calculated from ibid., 2477. Seventeen infants' or children's deaths were recorded in the same years, when I estimate between 65 and 70 fertile Jewish couples living in the city. In 1806, 20 of 39 women were in their twenties; ibid., 2470.

11. Related in Weyden, pp. 275–76, who records it as a piece of oral history from one of Stern's daughters.

12. Sources for information about the immigrants' intermediate migrations are *HASK*, Oberbürgermeisteramt, 400, II-4-C-1, "Nachweisung" of April 19, 1817, and "Namentliches Verzeichnis" of September 25, 1817; and Schulte, *Bonner Juden*, p. 248. Statistics on population size are in Keyser, ed., *Rheinisches Städtebuch*; id., *Hessisches Städtebuch*; id., *Bayerisches Städtebuch*; Petri; and Petri and Droege, eds.

13. Jews constituted 85.3 percent of Grodno's population in 1816, 20 percent of Amsterdam's, and 20 percent of Fürth's. Statistics cited or calculated from figures cited in "Grodno," "Netherlands," *Encyclopaedia Judaica*; and Keyser, ed., *Bayerisches Städtebuch*, 1: 208, 210.

14. See Toury, *Soziale und Politische Geschichte*, p. 19; and Winter.

15. Salomon Oppenheim paid 23 Reichstaler; the other contributors paid between 9 and 3.30 Reichstaler. Calculated from Kober, *Cologne*, p. 319; and "Gemeindeordnung," LBINY-K, Box 7, 2–3.

16. An English translation of the document is in Kober, *Cologne*, pp. 317–27. Kober's German transcription of the original is in LBINY-K, Box 7.

17. *HASK*, Französische Verwaltung, 2474, 2470, "Nachweisung," 1817, "Nachweisung," 1820; and Weyden, p. 275. Identification of the "Joseph Levy" listed on the "Négotians" list as "Joseph Stern" was made using Kober, *Namensregister*. The

"Nachweisung" of 1820 says Salomon Oppenheim had been in Cologne since 1797, but this is not possible. Schnee says Oppenheim arrived in 1798 or 1799; in any case, he was among the first Jewish immigrants. See Schnee, "175 Jahre Bankhaus," p. 71.

18. Oppenheim's first child had been born in Bonn in July 1798; Stern's first child had been born in Mülheim in 1797; Cohen married in 1798 and his first child was born in Cologne in August 1799. See *HASK*, Französische Verwaltung, 2470, "Nachweisung"; and Kober, *Namensregister*, pp. 88ff.

19. Levels of wealth have been deduced from notations in French or reliable secondary sources, occupational titles, city addresses, amounts of membership dues paid to the Jewish community in 1802, and amounts paid by synagogue seats. See *HASK*, Französische Verwaltung, 2470, 2474, 4888; Weyden, pp. 274–78; Brisch, 2: 146–51; Kober, *Cologne*, p. 319; and *HSTA-D-K*, Königliche Regierung, 3691.

20. Kober, *Cologne*, p. 183, characterizes the community as "generally engaged in petty trade." Gothein, p. 313, states that the earliest Jewish settlers were "poor beggars, peddlers and petty pawn brokers," who came from "the little Jew city [*Judenstädtchen*] Deutz."

21. *HASK*, Französische Verwaltung, 2470, 4884.

22. On "servants" and women as apprentices, see Shorter, pp. 32–37; and Tilly and Scott, pp. 13ff., 83, 95, 108–9, 116ff., 153–54, 181–82. Wealthier Jewish families tended to have more children (at least, children present in the household) than did nonwealthy families. This agrees with Shorter's findings, pp. 32, 46.

23. On agriculture in the city during this period, see van Eyll, "Wirtschaftsgeschichte," pp. 178ff.; and Diefendorf, p. 29.

24. On the occupations of Roer department Jewry, see *HSTA-D*, Französische Abteilung, II Div., 1 Bureau, nos. 1791, 1798. On meat shortages in the city under the *Reichsstadt*, see Pohl, p. 54.

25. See *HASK*, Französische Verwaltung, 2468, document 2, letter of the police commissioner dated 20 Brumaire, An 8.

26. *Memoirs of Glückel of Hameln*, pp. 32–33.

27. The complaint (eventually dropped) was about swindling. One of the guillotined Jews was punished for theft; the crimes of the others are unknown. See *HASK*, Französische Verwaltung, 2468, documents dealing with Michel Mayer, Jacques André, and Moyses Abraham; ibid., 2466, document 4, letter of the *souspréfet* of 29 Frimaire, An 11; and Kober, *Cologne*, p. 185.

28. The lengthy and colorful correspondence regarding Levi Samson, alias Joseph Modemann, is in *HASK*, Französische Verwaltung, 2468. Samson claimed to have lived in Cologne for eight years when he was ordered imprisoned and deported in 1808. The authorities agreed only that he had been present in the city at the address he claimed, not that he had acquired legal residence rights. Samson/Modemann drops from the records after early 1809. Mention of the unmarried woman with "illegitimate" children is in Kober, *Namensregister*, p. 14.

29. *HASK*, Französische Verwaltung, 2473, letter of the mayor to the prefect of April 25, 1808.

30. See Krohn, *Die Juden in Hamburg, 1800–1850*; and id., *Die Juden in Hamburg, 1848–1918*.

31. There are two extant documents written by Jews, that is, not transcribed by scribes or translators, that testify to the Jewish vernacular. One is the record of the sale of synagogue seats in 1802; *HSTA-D-K*, Königliche Regierung, 3691. There are fourteen lines of text, plus the record of the proceeds of the sale. The language is a mixture of Hebrew and German, written in Hebrew characters, except for the French date, which is written in French in Latin characters. The preponderance of the words is German, as is the syntax. Hebrew is used for reference to such synagogue customs as the preferred seat on the eastern wall; German, to describe rules and procedures of the sale. Obviously, the Jews who composed the document (the rabbi and two community leaders) and those meant to understand it (synagogue members) understood at least business German, which is to be expected.

The second document is a wholly German letter written by the cantor and school teacher of the community in 1805 in response to a government inquiry about Jewish males eligible for that year's draft. See *HASK*, Französische Verwaltung, 2468, document 1; see also the directive issued to mayors of Roer department cities by the prefect in 1803, *Recueil des Actes* (1803), pp. 53–54.

Since the handwriting of the text, which uses both Latin and Gothic script, and the signature are the same, I take this as a specimen of Jewish language. In it, Seligman Ochs attests that, according to the circumcision records in his possession ("gemös der von unss[e]ren Glaubensgenossen in meine hände sich befundeten Ceremonien zeichen"), there were no Jewish males in Cologne born between September 1784 and September 1785. The German and the handwriting are very rough, but it is German, with no Hebrew admixtures; this Jew, at least, was literate in German. That all Jews, including women, were literate in Hebrew, and many in German as well, is attested to by their signatures on the record of their adoption of fixed, Europeanized names in 1808; see *HASK*, Französische Verwaltung, 2481.

Not surprisingly, Cologne Jews had far less facility with French than German; their communications with French authorities are all either written in German or translated into French. This limitation must have been true for much of the population.

32. The source on the Mendelssohn subscription is Kober, *Cologne*, p. 184; the population count is according to my reconstruction of the records.

33. Mendelssohn's translation was also meant to combat christologically motivated translations by Christians and shoddy translations by Jews insufficiently versed in Hebrew. See Altmann, pp. 242–45, 274–75, 286, 344, 355, 368–72, 374–77, 500–502; and Sorkin, *Transformation*, p. 71.

34. Altmann, pp. 344, 355.

35. J. Katz, *Tradition and Crisis*, pp. 245ff.; id., *Out of the Ghetto*, pp. 28ff.

36. Weyden, pp. 286–87. One of these families was that of Salomon Oppenheim; the Cohen family Weyden mentions is that of Samuel Benjamin Cohen, son of Rabbi Bunem Cohen of Bonn.

37. According to the 1806 police survey, 19 of 30 Jewish households were located in the second and third sections, where some 60 percent of the general population also lived. See *HASK*, Französische Verwaltung, 2470; *Recueil des Actes* (1809), p. 249.

38. Eighteen male householders signed the founding constitution. Jewish law

defines a male of thirteen years or older as an adult, so the possible number of *minyan* participants was somewhat higher than this but still very limited. The small size of the community also created a problem for its only *kohen* (priest), for whom tradition preserved certain honors, such as being called up (*aliyah*) to make the first blessing at Torah readings. Since it was customary for honorees to make a donation to the synagogue on this occasion, Samuel Benjamin Cohen received constitutional protection against overpayment of fees, given that this honor would accrue to him at least three times a week, more frequently on holidays.

39. See Endelman, pp. 3ff., 118ff. Unfortunately, we have no data on the daily behavior of Jews in Cologne, especially their social habits, although their indifference to Jewish schooling (see below) indicates apathy in one crucial area of traditional behavior.

40. Wolf Cassel, the "friend and intimate" of Rabbi Bunem Cohen of Cologne, was named chairman of the community executive committee by Rabbi Cohen. Joseph Stern from Mülheim and Samuel Benjamin Cohen, Rabbi Cohen's son, were named as its other members. Cohen, Salomon Oppenheim, and one other member of the community (Cassel Stern) paid nearly half the total membership dues of the community in 1802 (50 of 111 Reichstaler, 48 Stiver) and bid a similar share of the total sum pledged at the synagogue seat auction (148 of 281.50 Reichstaler). These figures were calculated from fees listed in Kober, *Cologne*, p. 319, and on the seat sale document, *HSTA-D-K*; Königliche Regierung, 3691.

41. On Cohen, see *HASK*, Französische Verwaltung, 2469, documents 1–4. On the costs and inconveniences entailed by the Assembly of Notables, including those borne by Roer-department Jews, see Anchel, pp. 139–56.

Oppenheim's request for exemption is preserved in *HSTA-D*, Französische Abteilung, II Div., 1 Bureau, no. 1799 I. By 1814 Oppenheim's French was fluent, as attested by a letter in his hand written to Paris on consistorial matters; JTSA, History Mic. 8600, Consistorial Correspondence, Box II, 1814.

Oppenheim is routinely depicted as a member of the communal leadership of Cologne, but this was so only unofficially; the constitution does not name him as an officeholder. Of course, Oppenheim's stature mandated the greatest honor and deference in the community — he signed the constitution first, Kober tells us, and his was also the first bid recorded at the seat auction — but he was certainly not involved in running its day-to-day affairs. Oppenheim's service to the Jewish community derived from his standing in the outside world, which made him (as it traditionally did wealthy Jews) the best representative of Jewish interests in special situations — for instance, when the community wanted to purchase title to a former monastery to serve as the synagogue (see below), and especially in 1806–8, when Napoleon compromised Jewish equality.

42. Philipson, pp. 21ff.; Meyer, *Response to Modernity*, pp. 10ff.; Lowenstein, "The 1840s"; and id., *Berlin Jewish Community*.

43. Suggested prices for several categories of seats are listed in the constitution (Kober, *Cologne*, p. 322), and are largely reflected in the actual record of the sale, which shows 281.50 Reichstaler pledged; *HSTA-D-K*, Königliche Regierung, 3691. Though women's seats were far less expensive than men's, only 8 were purchased, compared to 24 seats for men, 6 of which were on the eastern wall (the most

expensive site). Sixteen members, two less than the number that signed the constitution, bid for seats; the identity of signatories and men who bid is not entirely the same.

44. Signed Joseph Isaac (Isaac Stern), Salomon Oppenheim, and Samuel Benjamin Cohen, 19 Pluviose, An 11; *ANF*, F19-1840. The St. Clarisse monastery had been abolished several months earlier; see Büttner, p. 133.

45. Kober, *Cologne*, pp. 186, 239–40. Cf. Büttner, pp. 368–75, who attributes the failure of Cologne's Jews to purchase secularized church property to the discriminatory policies of Napoleon after 1806. Documents show that French reluctance predated 1806. In correspondence from 1802–3, 1806, and 1810, French officials were adamantly opposed to Jewish purchase of "propriété nationale" for use as a cemetery, first on hygienic grounds and then, they claimed, because the law prohibited Jewish purchase of nationalized property. *HASK*, Französische Verwaltung, 2466, documents 1–12; 2471, documents 1–4.

46. Szajkowski, p. 299.

47. The condemned Jew's crime is not specified. *HASK*, Französische Verwaltung, 2468, documents 4–5.

48. The entire correspondence took place between the 15th of Messidor and the first of Thermidor, an interval of 16 days; see *HASK*, Französische Verwaltung, 2468, documents 6–9. On the history of the *Leibzoll* in French-occupied territories on both sides of the Rhine, see Kober, "French Revolution," pp. 315ff.

49. *HASK*, Französische Verwaltung, 2468, documents 21, 21a, 22, 22a. The police commissioner himself, the Jews said, could attest that the rumor was circulating, since he had business with Jews and had received numerous inquiries about it.

50. Weyden, pp. 282ff.; Brisch, 2: 150ff. Kober is curiously silent about the blood libel. I have been unable to locate court or other records about it.

51. The fullest treatment of the consistorial system is Albert; see also Anchel; Mahler, pp. 53ff.; Schwarzfuchs; Tama; and Maslin.

52. On Alsatian Jewry in this period, see Hyman.

53. Quoted in Maslin, p. 22.

54. Ibid., p. 39.

55. Napoleon's tendency to single Jews out for special treatment while insisting on their complete assimilation is seen in another law passed in 1808, requiring Jews to adopt fixed personal and family names, despite the fact that an 1803 law required this of all French citizens. The Jewish legislation took note of the general law but deviated from it in prohibiting Jews from taking Biblical names or in calling themselves after towns, unless such names had long been in family use, and in mandating deportation in case of infraction. Deportation, of course, is an expedient against aliens. See Maslin, pp. 56ff.; and Anchel, pp. 433ff., 459.

56. Cited in Maslin, p. 5.

57. Anchel, p. 469. On the Sephardim, see Malino; and Hertzberg, pp. 78ff.

58. The decrees establishing the consistorial system and anti-Jewish economic discrimination were both promulgated in 1808, but it is the latter that concerns us most. Unless otherwise specified, "the 1808 decree" refers to this one.

59. Translated from Anchel's paraphrase, p. 267.

60. Ibid., pp. 355–56.

61. On the exemption petitions of Jewish communities, see Anchel, pp. 352–411.

62. Ibid., p. 387. The remarks of the *sous-préfet* dated September 10, 1812, were addressed to the prefect; *HSTA-D*, Französische Abteilung, II Div., 1 Bureau (Juden Patente 1809–1813), no. 1797. The *sous-préfet* endorsed exemption on another occasion, when compiling intelligence on Jewish occupations and their civil and patriotic behavior; see *Recueil des Actes* (1808), pp. 137–38; and *HSTA-D*, Französische Abteilung, II Div., 1 Bureau (Erkundigung über die Juden), no. 1789, Arr. de Cologne. It was not unusual for French departmental officials to endorse Jewish petitions for exemption from the decree, but then most petitions came from departments where Jews thought they had a chance of success; none were filed from Alsace, for instance. See Anchel, pp. 411, 374. See also the endorsement of the mayor of Cologne, who forwarded Oppenheim's petition for exemption; *HASK*, Französische Verwaltung, 2473, letter dated April 25, 1808. The text of the petition is not extant, but we have its supporting documents and information from secondary sources: *HASK*, Französische Verwaltung, 2473; *HSTA-D*, Französische Abteilung, II Div., 1 Bureau, nos. 1789, 1797; Anchel, pp. 369–74, 387–88; and Kober, *Cologne*, p. 189.

63. On the communities that obtained exemption, see Anchel, pp. 371ff.

Chapter Three

1. Cited in Hässlin, p. 208.

2. Residential and, with the important exceptions of the civil service and the army, occupational discrimination were abolished. See in detail Freund; for background and summary, see Lowenstein, *Berlin Jewish Community*, p. 85.

3. Kober, *Cologne*, p. 189.

4. A population survey conducted on June 29, 1820, listed 73 Jewish adults and 149 children in Cologne; *HASK*, Oberbürgermeisteramt, 400, II-13-C-10. Of these adults, 64 were married couples, 56 of whom (28 couples) had children. Thus, the Jewish population consisted overwhelmingly of married couples with resident children (it appears that the surveyors noted not the total number of children born to a couple but only those resident in the household). Wealth (*Wohlstand*) was noted on the survey; as we would expect in a preindustrial population, wealth and family size were directly related. The wealthiest Jewish family in Cologne, the Oppenheims, had the most children of any in the survey: twelve.

An average of 4.6 Jewish households per year were established between 1814 and 1835. Relatively heavy years of immigration were 1825 (13 households), 1832 (9 households), and 1835 (12 households). For a yearly breakdown, see Magnus, "Cologne," Table 3.1, p. 174.

5. Of 83 Jewish households established in Cologne in the first two decades of Prussian rule, 32 drop from the records by 1835, and occasional notations in official records state that long-settled Jews also emigrated. See *HASK*, Oberbürgermeisteramt, 400, II-4-D-1, 1825/26; ibid., II-4-B-2, Sept. 8, 1820; and ibid., II-4-C-1, Council sessions of Feb. 25, 1818, Nov. 28, 1821, Oct. 31, 1823, May 17, 1825, Dec. 3, 1828, Jan. 8, 1829, Dec. 24, 1833, letter of the police director to the mayor, Jan. 16, 1835.

I base my count of Jewish households for this period on *Judenpatente* records, *HASK*, Oberbürgermeisteramt, 400, II-4-C-1 (henceforth to be cited as "*Judenpa-*

tente"; all documents cited by date and signature only come from this collection); on the records of membership dues paid to the consistorial synagogue of Bonn, "Vertheilung der Cultus Kosten der Consistorial Synagogue zu Bonn," in *HASK*, Oberbürgermeisteramt, 400, II-4-D-1, 1825/26–35 (henceforth to be cited as "Cultus Kosten"); and on the city address books, *Adress-Buch oder Verzeichniss der Einwohner der Stadt Köln* of 1822, 1828, and 1835; and on Kober, *Cologne*, pp. 193, 328.

6. Kober, "Aus der Geschichte," p. 79; and von Restorff, p. 220. Kober, *Cologne*, p. 328, reports the Jewish population at 150 in 1816; on p. 193, however, he reports without comment an official statement that the Jewish population of the city had doubled between 1813 and 1817. A number of sources give different population counts. According to the *Mitteilungen*, the Jewish population numbered 150 in 1816, 535 in 1821, 637 in 1825, 351 in 1831, and 454 in 1837, but the extremely high figures for the 1820's are very suspect (cf. Ayçoberry, "Histoire Sociale," 2: 106, Appendix 15). They are also contradicted by other published sources. The *Kölner Statistisches Handbuch* 13 (1958), I: 64, gives a more plausible count of 150 in 1816, 376 in 1820, 343 in 1821, 272 in 1825, 390 in 1828, 362 in 1831, and 436 in 1834, figures similar though not identical to those in Kober, *Cologne*, p. 328. Reports in provincial records of a sharp drop in the Jewish population between 1817 and 1823 led Toury, *Der Eintritt*, p. 216, to speculate that an expulsion took place, but this clearly is not true. Not only is there no mention of this in the sources, but a census showed 42 family heads in 1820. Moreover, some of the most heated debates between the city and Prussian authorities about the Jews took place in these years regarding a resident Jewish population, as well as one likely to immigrate.

7. Silbergleit, Table 6, p. 9. Silbergleit counts 42 such cities, but one is "Köln mit Deutz." Since the two cities were not joined until much later in the century, I omit this entry from my count. The other cities were in old Prussia or Posen. The statistic on Bonn is in Kober, "Aus der Geschichte," p. 79.

8. Ayçoberry, "Histoire Sociale," 1: 4, figures rounded. Cf. the somewhat higher figures in van Eyll, *Wirtschaftsgeschichte*, p. 167, which may include the military presence; see Ayçoberry, "Histoire Sociale," 1: 171.

9. See Ayçoberry, "Histoire Sociale," 1: 6–7.

10. Only 13 Jewish households were established in Cologne between 1816 and 1820 (inclusive) and only 6 between 1828 and 1831, while 30 were established between 1832 and 1835 (out of a total of 83 for the years 1814–35). Calculated from *HASK*, Oberbürgermeisteramt, 400, II-4-D-1, 1825/26, II-4-B-2, Sept. 28, 1821, Oct. 31, 1823, May 27, 1825, Dec. 3, 1828, Jan. 8, 1829, Dec. 24, 1833, letter of the police director to the mayor, Jan. 16, 1835, 400, II-4-C-1, and *Adress-Buch*, 1822, 1828, and 1835. A yearly breakdown is found in Magnus, "Cologne," p. 174, Table 3.1.

11. On the Prussian Rhine, disturbances were reported only in Koblenz and Kreuznach. The Prussians (and the Austrians) repressed outbreaks in their territories. On the so-called Hep-Hep outbreaks, see Sterling, "Der Kampf," p. 293; id., *Judenhass*, pp. 163ff.; and J. Katz, "The Hep-Hep Riots."

12. Jeggle, p. 199. Urbanization of the wealthy characterized German Jewry during the "boom" years after 1850 and was also true of Alsatian Jewry, whose socioeconomic profile is similar to that of Rhenish Jewry, in the first half of the nineteenth century. The findings from Cologne and Alsace show that wealthy Jews

moved to cities even in bad times. See Richarz, ed., *Jüdisches Leben*, pp. 29–30; Barkai, "German Jews," pp. 126, 136; Lowenstein, "Pace of Modernisation," pp. 41–56; Toury, *Soziale und politische Geschichte*, pp. 27–51; Hyman, "Village Jews," pp. 13–26; id., *Emancipation of the Jews of Alsace*, pp. 86ff.

Other behaviors distinguished Jewish from non-Jewish migrants to Cologne. Unlike the non-Jews, the Jews came mostly in families. Jews were endogamous and thus remained an identifiable group, whereas non-Jewish migrants quickly assimilated into the general population through marriage. See Ayçoberry, "Histoire Sociale," 1: 5–8.

13. On economic conditions in this period, see Gothein; Ayçoberry, "Histoire Sociale," 1: 29ff.; van Eyll, "Wirtschaftsgeschichte"; Kellenbenz and van Eyll, eds., *Geschichte*; Diefendorf, pp. 213ff.; Kähler; Schwann, "Grundlagen und Organisation"; Perlitz; and R. Tilly, *Financial Institutions*.

14. Quoted in Hässlin, p. 208. As Ayçoberry writes, "Histoire Sociale," 1: 15, there was only one Cologne merchant who had even been to England in 1828.

15. Ayçoberry, "Histoire Sociale," 1: 39. The causes for economic decline in the Rhineland in the 1820's and 1830's are much debated. In contrast to R. Tilly, *Financial Institutions*, and Koselleck, *Preussen*, Ayçoberry holds Cologne's merchant and banking elites as much or more responsible for Cologne's languor than the Prussians; see especially 1: 527ff. See also Zorn, pp. 552–60.

16. Ayçoberry, "Histoire Sociale," 1: 12. See also pp. 12–15, 39–47. Ayçoberry excoriates the "parasitical nature of the Colonais," p. 45. For a more sympathetic view, see Diefendorf; and van Eyll, "Wirtschaftsgeschichte."

17. For a more favorable assessment of Prussian intent and policy, see Diefendorf, especially pp. 313–56.

18. Perlitz, p. 51.

19. Richarz, ed., *Jüdisches Leben*, p. 33, states that Prussia did not have a policy of coercing occupational change among Jews. While there was nothing to compare with Bavarian legislation, for example, the 1808 law that Prussia retained in its Rhine province was a form of pressure for occupational reform.

20. I am adopting Helga Krohn's classification of lottery collecting as a form of banking and credit; *Die Juden in Hamburg, 1800–1850*, p. 37.

21. In 1828 and 1830, *Judenpatente* were issued to the "trading house of Salomon Oppenheim."

22. The following is based on Stürmer, Teichmann, and Treue; Krüger, pp. 35ff., 65ff.; Perlitz, pp. 134ff., 182ff.; R. Tilly, *Financial Institutions*, pp. 45ff.; 60ff., 72; and Ayçoberry, "Histoire Sociale," 1: 35–36, 45.

23. Diefendorf, p. 328, is incorrect in stating that the Oppenheim bank had not engaged in mercantile activity before specializing in banking. Salomon Oppenheim is described in French-era records more often as "Commissionaire" than "Banquier."

24. During roughly the same years, the percentage of Jews in Hamburg engaged in any banking activities was lower: 8 percent and 6 percent in 1823 and 1839, respectively. These figures, however, probably reflect Jews who practiced (or were recorded as practicing) banking as a sole or primary occupation, while my figures include Jews who practiced money trades as side occupations. See Krohn, *Die Juden in Hamburg*, p. 80.

25. On the origins of Cologne's lottery, see Pohl, pp. 114, 119–20.

26. *Cultus Kosten* lists (*HASK*, Oberbürgermeisteramt, 400, II-4-D-1) record the name of synagogue members and amount of dues assessed; on this source, see below, "Wealth Stratification." I ascertained occupations from *Judenpatent* records or city *Adressbücher*.

27. Isaac Horn appears in the 1835 *Adressbuch* as a "Lotterie Untereinnehmer und Tarator im städtischen Leihhaus"; the latter activity I understand to have been the weighing of coins.

28. Van Eyll, "Wirtschaftsgeschichte," p. 233; Schulte, "Zur gewerblichen Betätigung"; Bohnke-Kollwitz, Eckert, eds., pp. 133–34; Müller, p. 233; and Schoelkens, pp. 506–18.

29. Gothein, p. 187.

30. On the broader phenomenon, see Kober, "Emancipation's Impact"; Toury, "Der Eintritt"; Liebeschutz and Pauker, eds., pp. 210–15; Toury, *Der Eintritt, Eine Dokumentation*, p. 187; Barkai, "German Jews," p. 130; Richarz, ed., *Jüdisches Leben*, pp. 33, 34, 75. Cf. J. Katz, *Out of the Ghetto*, pp. 176ff.

31. We learn from the residence petition of the Jewish saddler, Isaac Bier, who came from Deutz, that "he took instruction from the saddlemaster Werner, who resides here," *Judenpatente*, Nov. 10, 1835. The latter may well have been J. B. Werner, who several years later pioneered the new horse-drawn wagon transportation business in Cologne; see van Eyll, "Wirtschaftsgeschichte," p. 214. Wolfgang Ochs, a native of Cologne, learned goldsmithing from a non-Jew; see an undated document from the mayor, entitled "Zum Stadtrat," following a document of May 22, 1827, on Ochs. City authorities went out of their way to facilitate Bier's request for settlement "since Israelite artisans should be able to count on especially accommodating [treatment] of their settlement requests." Bier was granted settlement permission and later a *Judenpatent* as a saddler. Ochs's petition for a *Judenpatent*, needed so that he might sell what he produced, was also granted.

32. Müller, p. 179.

33. On artisanship as a means to economic improvement for poor Jews, see Richarz, ed., *Jüdisches Leben*, p. 34; id., "Jewish Social Mobility"; and Barkai, "German Jews," p. 130. On the financial status of Jewish artisans in Cologne, see the section in this chapter entitled "Wealth, Stratification, and Mobility."

34. There was a long history of Jews serving as physicians to non-Jews in the Rhineland and even in the city of Cologne in the *Reichsstadt* era; see Kober, "Rheinische Judendoktoren." We do not know where the Jewish doctors of the 1835 records received their training.

35. These were, respectively, H. David, whose petition for settlement (*Judenpatent*, Council session of May 26, 1835) listed him as "Sprachlehrer," and Joseph Alexander, who appears on the 1835 synagogue membership list and whom the *Adressbuch* of that year lists as "Musiklehrer."

36. Elkan (Hermann) Levy had been a religious teacher for the synagogue since 1805. Weyden, p. 287, describes him as "director of the Jewish elementary school" in the period after 1820. Levy changed occupations in 1827, when he declared himself incapable of continuing as an educator; see *Judenpatente*, list of Jews under consideration for patents for 1827. His replacement was Josue Schloss, whom the *Adressbuch*

lists as a teacher, no specialty stated, who nevertheless applied for a *Judenpatent*, necessary only for Jews who engaged in business, in 1835; see *Judenpatente*, mayor to City Council, probable date, Nov. 12, 1835. He appears as a businessman in the *Adressbuch* of 1835. On teachers in the Jewish community, see Kober, *Cologne*, pp. 259ff.; Weyden, 286ff.; and Brisch, 2: 151–52. On Jews as owners and operators of lending libraries, see Toury, "Der Eintritt," p. 187.

37. The *Cultus Kosten* records (*HASK*, Oberbürgermeisteramt, 400, II-4-D-1) are a more inclusive source than *Gewerbesteuer* records (ibid., II-16-1) or *Judenpatent* records (ibid., II-4-C-1), since some Jews were too poor to pay even the minimum *Gewerbesteuer*, and Jews who were not independent businesspeople did not need patents; e.g., professionals, artisans, and employees. I gleaned occupational information about Jews who appear in *Cultus Kosten* lists but not on either of the other two types of records from city *Adressbücher*.

Cultus Kosten were apportioned in a very progressive manner. There were 15 payment categories (brackets) in 1825/26 and 18 in 1835, with most of the gradations in the lowest payment range. Since the number of dues payers increased by 1835, yet the total assessed the Cologne community was lowered by the Bonn consistory from the 1825 level, we may see how fairly the tax reductions were distributed. In absolute terms, the most highly assessed experienced the biggest drop in assessments: the dues assessed Salomon Oppenheim fell from 17 to 13 taler between 1825 and 1835 (paid in the latter year by his widow); a wealthy member of the synagogue board, whose work it was to decide assessments, experienced a drop in dues from 8.20 taler in 1825 to 3 taler in 1835. The percentage of the total amount paid by the wealthiest, however, remained constant over time, and disproportionately high relative to their numbers in the group. In 1825/26, those paying the highest tax were 14 percent of the group, yet they carried 51 percent of the tax burden; in 1835, the highest payers constituted 9 percent of the group and were assessed 35 percent of the total burden, proportionally the same ratio as in 1825/26. The synagogue board of 3 or 4 wealthy members does appear to have underassessed itself.

38. *HASK*, Oberbürgermeisteramt, 400, II-13-C-10, "Nachweisung" of June 20, 1820. The bias of this government source is toward overstating the number of the wealthy, who could then be taxed accordingly.

39. Kober, *Cologne*, p. 212. Prussian provincial authorities refused this request.

40. See Schulte, "Zur gewerblichen Betätigung," p. 125. Since rural Jews practiced trade, this comparison is appropriate.

41. Ayçoberry, "Histoire Sociale," 1: 158.

42. Ibid., 1: 157ff. Because there was no direct tax in Cologne in this period, there is no comparable measure to the *Cultus Kosten* with which to assess non-Jewish wealth.

43. On the need for such methodology, see M. Katz.

44. Occupational information is taken from *Judenpatente* records or the *Adressbuch* of 1835 for Abraham Ochsenstern and Abraham Ochse.

45. The elite of 1825/26 was also composed largely of one family, Gompertz, none of whom were in the high income rankings in 1835. The *Cultus Kosten* list of 1835 shows Salomon Oppenheim's place taken by his widow, Therese (Salomon died in 1828), and the addition of two of their sons, Abraham and Simon.

46. Ayçoberry, "Histoire Sociale," 1: 159.

47. Ibid., 1: 73–74.

48. Using information on Jewish addresses from *Adressbücher* and *Judenpatente* records of 1835, I found ten Jewish households on Schildergasse and five each on Streitzeuggasse, Breitestrasse, and Hohestrasse that were all located very close to the synagogue on Glockengasse. I was able to judge distances within the city by using *HASK*, Pläne, "Köln, gesamt und einzelne Wasser- und Brückenbaugrundanlagen, Plan 1–27, 'Strassenkarte von Köln . . . zur Orientierung ohne Führer,'" of July 1824, which uses a most tangible measure of distance: the number of footsteps between locations.

49. On housing patterns in the city, see Ayçoberry, "Histoire Sociale," 1: 8–11.

50. Schulte, "Zur gewerblichen Betätigung," pp. 137–38.

51. Thus, for example, the Jewish banker S. B. Cohen lived a few doors from one of Cologne's largest non-Jewish bankers, J. D. Herstatt. Until hard times hit in 1826, the wealthy Jewish merchant Heymann Cassel lived next door to another of the city's greatest bankers, Schaafhausen. See ibid., pp. 130–31. Salomon Oppenheim maintained a residence in Budengasse 8, in the city's fourth section. Almost all the Jews assessed the highest synagogue membership fees lived either in the fourth or the first sections. The latter, as Ayçoberry shows ("Histoire Sociale," 2: 110–11, Plan no. 1A), had significant pockets of poverty in its southern zone, but the addresses of the wealthy Jews were in the northern zone, toward the geographic and commercial center of the city. My location of street addresses is per *HASK*, Oberbürgermeisteramt, Pläne, Plan 1-27.

52. On the difficulty Cologne's middle classes had in obtaining credit and the negative impact this had on their chances for upward mobility, see Ayçoberry, "Histoire Sociale," 1: 145, 148.

53. On the concept of a "Jewish economy," see Schofer, "History of European Jewry," pp. 20–22, 34; Barkai, "German Jews," p. 125.

54. We see, for example, wealthy Jews who hired unrelated Jews: Salomon Oppenheim for a time employed Andreas Gottschalk (on whose religious, political, and occupational metamorphoses see Chapters 5 and 6); Samuel B. Cohen employed Alexander Oppenheim; Joseph Stern and later another Jew, Schubach, hired a Meyer Samuel. Salomon Aser Fichtenberg and H. Gompertz formed a partnership; Marcus Lowenstein formed a brief partnership with his father-in-law, J. Schlicher; a Jew named Lowenstein took over the business of another Jew, Alexander Hess. Immigration was also fostered through employment situations, as for example the immigration of a Jewish maid, Mina Moses, through a special dispensation granted her employer, the wealthy Heinrich Cassel.

55. Schulte, "Zur gewerblichen Betätigung," pp. 128–30, 138–39. Cologne's non-Jewish bankers had credit associations with Jews of other nearby cities as well. The houses having deals with each other were those of Salomon Oppenheim, Jr., Joseph Stern, S. B. Cohen, Isaac Ochse, and Philip Gomperts (all Jewish) and the Schaafhausen, J. D. Herstatt, J. H. Stein, and Haan and Leiden companies, some of Cologne's largest non-Jewish firms.

56. Calculated on the basis of figures in Ayçoberry, "Histoire Sociale," 1: 68–69, Appendix 2.

57. See Eliav; Richarz, *Der Eintritt*; id., ed., *Jüdisches Leben*, pp. 89–90; id., "Jewish Social Mobility"; Toury, "Der Eintritt," pp. 174–76.

58. The 1782 Edict of Tolerance of Austria's Joseph II, the first major revision of Jewish legal status in Europe, allowed "tolerated" Jews to send their children to the Christian primary and secondary schools; see the text of the edict in Mendes-Flohr and Reinharz, eds., p. 34.

59. See Richarz, *Der Eintritt*, p. 143.

60. Ibid.

61. See Richarz, ed., *Jüdisches Leben*, p. 42. Cf. Lowenstein, "Pace of Modernisation," p. 43.

62. Among Berlin's Jews, whose tendency to "cultural surrender" Richarz has characterized as "especially crass," 40 percent of Jewish children in 1839 — about the same percentage as in Cologne in 1820 — attended Jewish schools; *Der Eintritt*, p. 145. The source for my information about Cologne is the previously cited population survey of June 29, 1820. This census simply lists the number of children in a family and whether or not ("ja," "nein") children attended "öffentliche" schools. It does not state the ages of children or, in the case of families that used such schools, how many of the children attended them. With eighteen families having children educated in non-Jewish institutions, Weyden's count of fifteen such children is clearly too low; p. 287. Parish schools were officially labeled "public" after 1816; see Gothein, p. 204.

63. See Weyden, p. 287; Brisch, 2: 152; and Lowenthal, p. 161. The non-Jewish educational options in the 1820s were: church-run schools, Catholic or Protestant, in which instruction was by clergy; institutions run by private individuals; or private tutoring. See Gothein, pp. 197–98, 202. Jews made use of all these options. Again, Cologne's Jews were precocious in this regard — compare Lowenstein, "Pace of Modernisation," p. 44: "As early as 1860 Jews made up almost 6% of all secondary school students."

64. See Lowenthal, pp. 161–63. On the initiators of the *Realgymnasium*, its utilization, and social importance, see Ayçoberry, "Histoire Sociale," 1: 68–69, 86–91, 109.

65. Both Josua (Josue) Schloss, who taught in the synagogue school, and Markus Mannheimer, who ran it, sent their sons to the Kreutzgasse *Gymnasium*. See Lowenthal, p. 161.

66. On Jewish educational policies elsewhere in this period, see Lowenstein, "Pace of Modernisation," p. 43. The Prussian provincial government began regulating the education of Jewish children in 1824; see announcement of *Oberpräsident* von Ingersleben of Sept. 13, 1824, *Amtsblatt*, pp. 257–59; and Kastner, ed., 1: 27–29, 37–38.

67. A situation comparable to Berlin, where barely 40 percent of Jewish school-age children attended Jewish schools in 1839. See Richarz, *Der Eintritt*, p. 145.

68. Cited in Weyden, p. 287; cf. Brisch, 1: 152. This same desire, manifest among assimilated Jewish parents in Berlin, led the community director there to lament in 1841, "The Jew so fears his children attending school in the constant company of other Jewish students that — I speak from experience — he even shuns the Christian

schools, because he knows many Jewish students go there." Cited in Richarz, *Der Eintritt*, p. 145.

Jewish apathy in Cologne about establishing a school may have been the legacy of the lack of a preexisting, traditional Jewish community, in which a religious school would have already been established. In Würzburg, also a community newly established (1803) after a seventeenth-century expulsion, pressure for a formal Jewish school also came from the (Bavarian) government, with the Jewish community unenthusiastic; see Gehring-Münzel, pp. 321ff. It would be worth examining whether newness was a factor in the educational policies of German Jewish communities in this period.

69. The statistic on school attendance is cited in Ayçoberry, "Histoire Sociale," 2: 97, Chart 13A. Kober's count of 55 children enrolled in 1831 is an apparent misprint—the year should read 1838; see *Cologne*, p. 262, and cf. Ayçoberry for 1838.

70. Brisch's characterization, 2: 152.

71. The majority of Jews were self-employed and thus already fulfilled a basic criterion of *Bürger* status. On the definition of *Bürger* in Cologne, see Ayçoberry, "Histoire Sociale," 1: 59ff.

Chapter Four

1. Cited in Hansen, *Rheinische Briefe*, 2: 276, n. 1.

2. Mohnen, p. 269.

3. E. M. Arndt, cited in Aubin et. al., eds., 2: 268–69.

4. Krefeld on the left bank and the districts of Duisburg, Essen, and Rees on the right had belonged to Prussia until they were overrun by France. See Diefendorf, pp. 214, 264; and Landsberg, 1: 149.

5. On the territorial negotiations of the allied powers, see Nipperdey, pp. 82ff.; and Artz, p. 110.

6. Schutz, p. 22.

7. References are to Prussia's left Rhine territories unless otherwise indicated. On Rhenish sentiment regarding the French legal and administrative heritage, see Faber, *Die Rheinlande*; and Vierhaus, pp. 152–75.

8. On the *Allgemeines Landrecht*, see Kosseleck, *Preussen*; and id., "Staat und Gesellschaft."

9. On this see especially Faber, *Die Rheinlande*, parts 2 and 3.

10. On Prussian administration in the territory, see Schutz; Gerschler, ed.; and, for a good summary, Diefendorf, pp. 213ff.

11. See Diefendorf, pp. 213ff.; Schwann, "Grundlagen und Organisation"; Kähler, 1: 196–249, 506–60; and Zorn.

12. On the creation of the *Kommission* and its intended functions, see Faber, *Die Rheinlande*, pp. 129ff.; Lademacher, pp. 507ff. Prussia did not concede the ultimate goal of imposing its legal system on the Rhineland; the matter became one of the chief preoccupations of the newly created Rhenish Provincial Diet after 1826.

13. On the democratic convictions of *Kommission* members, see Faber, *Die Rheinlande*, pp. 157–58.

14. The Prussian Ministry of Interior had announced in 1817 that the Jewry legislation in effect in all its recently acquired territories, east and west, would remain in force pending a general revision of Jewish status in the monarchy. While this meant that the "infamous decree" would not be abolished on the left bank, as some representatives of Rhenish Jewry had asked, it left open the possibility that the decree would be allowed to lapse in 1818. See *Reskript* of September 5, 1817, in Freund, 1: 243–44; and Michaelis, ed., p. 11.

15. *HSTA-D-K*, Acta der Immediat Justiz Kommission, no. 7: "Bürgerliche Verhältnisse der Juden in der Rheinprovinz, 1816–1819"; and petitions of the Jewish consistories of Krefeld, March 30, 1818, and Bonn, date unreadable (the petition is on pages 21–23b). The 1815 protest of Heinrich Marx, Jewish *Advocat* from Trier and father of Karl Marx, against the 1808 decree found its way to the *Kommission* and is in this same collection. On this, see Kober, "Karl Marx' Vater." Marx also expressed his opinions on other aspects of Prussian law. See Faber, *Die Rheinlande*, p. 135.

16. Cited in Sterling, "Der Kampf," p. 294; and Schulte, "Die Rechtslage," pp. 96–97. See also, Kastner, 1: 22. Kober, "Aus der Geschichte," p. 80, and *Cologne*, p. 195, says the *Kommission* received only negative reports about the Jews, but this was clearly not the case.

17. "Die deutsche Juden das erwucherte Geld nach Jerusalem schleppten." *HSTA-D-K*, Acta der Immediat Justiz Kommission, no. 7: "Auszug aus dem ersten Stück des Allgemeinen Rheinischen Anzeigers für 1818," document 161–169b.

18. The document is found in *HSTA-D-K*, Acta der Immediat Justiz Kommission, no. 7, pp. 93–132. It is undated, although its archival placement indicates a date in early 1818; the *Kommission*'s report is dated January 30. The document is unsigned and unaddressed, titled merely "Uber Judenthum und die bürgerliche Verbesserung der Juden." This, the fact that the document is a draft (unlike affidavits to the *Kommission*, which are written by professional scribes, the handwriting here is extremely rough and sloppy, with much crossing out), and the statement in the *Kommission*'s report that its own members had made observations about the Jews lead me to conclude that this report was written by a member of the *Kommission*.

19. There are striking similarities between the organization, substance, and language of this report and the anti-emancipation writings of Friedrich Rühs and Jakob Friedrich Fries, both of whom published in 1816. On Rühs and Fries, see Stern-Täubler; Sterling, *Judenhass*; and J. Katz, *From Prejudice to Destruction*, pp. 74ff. This document insists on adherence to Christianity as a prerequisite for citizenship in European states, a prominent argument of Rühs's. In addition to condemning rabbinic tradition, it repeatedly condemns the alleged particularism and mean-spiritedness of the Hebrew Bible, a central feature of Fries's writings. It also employs the phrase "state within a state" regarding the Jews, as does Fries.

20. Numerous official reports noted the stark increase in the region's Jewish population; see Kastner, 1: 13, and documents there, pp. 177–81, 185–87, 189–92, 201–5, 225–33, 237–38, 261, 263–64.

21. *HSTA-D-K*, Acta der Immediat Justiz Kommission, no. 7, p. 123b.

22. "Weil man also diese Nation nicht gänzlich aus Europa entfernen, und sie in ihre alten Wohnsitze verweisen, so bleibt nichts übrig als eine durchgreifende allge-

meine Reform." *HSTA-D-K*, Acta der Immediate Justiz Kommission, no. 7, 122b.

23. *Zentrales Staatsarchiv, Merseburg*, Acta Generalia des Justiz-Ministeriums, 2.5.1, no. 7, 420: betreffend: das Judenwesen in der Rheinprovinz, 1818, "Die Erneuerung der Juden-Ordnung vom 17.3.1808."

24. In 1815, the Congress of Vienna left it to the future Diet of the German Confederation to make an ultimate determination of Jewish status in the states of the Confederation. The Diet, in fact, would never take this step. See Sachar, pp. 100–103; and Mendes-Flohr and Reinharz, eds., p. 129.

25. That decision was announced in Cologne's district through the *Amtsblatt der Königlichen Regierung zu Köln*, no. 11, March 17, 1818, entry 76. On the end of the Prussian reform era, see Nipperdey, pp. 272ff.; Rosenberg, *Bureaucracy, Aristocracy and Autocracy*, pp. 202–28; and W. Simon.

26. On the debate regarding renewal of the decree in France in 1818 and the decision to let it lapse, see Anchel, pp. 412ff.

27. On this, see Freund, 1: 229ff.; and Kastner, 1: 25–26.

28. On the number of ordinances, see Freund, 1: 246; and Dubnow, 9: 35ff. For population statistics for the 1810's and early 1820's, see Silbergleit, Tables 5, 7, and 8, pp. 7, 11, 14; and Richarz, ed., *Jüdisches Leben*, p. 27.

29. Despite this, none of the German historical literature on the *Immediat Justiz Kommission* treats its deliberations on the Jews. There is only the most meager mention of the *Kommission* by Jewish historians. Jost and Freund, both very concerned with legal aspects of the emancipation struggle, do not mention the *Kommission* in their treatments of Prussia's Jewish policies. Brief references in Schulte, "Die Rechtslage," Sterling, "Der Kampf," H. Strauss, "Pre-Emancipation," and Kober, "Aus der Geschichte," p. 80, are all that is available on the subject.

The ability of proponents of liberty and equality to oppose Jewish emancipation has been studied at length by Reinhard Rürup, especially for Baden. This aspect of the *Kommission*'s work is in dire need of study. Of particular interest is the role of Heinrich Gottfried Wilhelm Daniels in drafting the *Kommission*'s report on the Jews. Daniels was a lawyer from Cologne and a staunch patriot of the city and the region who authored several essays advocating Cologne's interests; he served briefly as the city's lobbyist at the Congress of Vienna. Daniels became the dominant influence in the *Kommission* as a whole, in its ministerial committee (which examined the *Kommission*'s reports), and in drafting the *Kommission*'s recommendation to retain French law. See Diefendorf, p. 256. It is inconceivable that he was uninvolved in the *Kommission*'s statement on the Jews.

30. H. Strauss, "Pre-Emancipation," p. 111.

31. On the success and political significance of the *Kommission*'s independent course, see Faber, *Die Rheinlande*, pp. 157–60.

32. Gothein, p. 109.

33. Gothein's paraphrase.

34. Cited in Gothein, p. 110.

35. On these rights, see Diefendorf, pp. 28–29. On the Chamber of Commerce and the economic issues I discuss here, see Diefendorf; Schwann, *Geschichte*; Kellenbenz and van Eyll, eds., *Geschichte*; and Gothein.

36. Diefendorf, pp. 239, 263–64. On the administrative divisions of the territory, see Bär.

37. The *Regierungspräsident* was the functional equivalent of the prefect of the Napoleonic system; on this and the provincial offices in general, see Klausa; Ilgen; Diefendorf, pp. 264–65; and Fann.

38. On the appointment and duties of the *Landrat*, see Erbel, p. 253; on the administrative structure and function of the *Kreis*, see Kosseleck, *Preussen*, p. 448; and Klausa, p. 80.

39. The alternative, which Cologne preferred, was some form of Stein's *Städteordnung*, which gave cities a measure of self-rule. See Faber, *Die Rheinlande*, pp. 186ff.; Erbel; Diefendorf, pp. 256ff.; and Gothein, pp. 122ff.

40. On von Mylius, see Droz, p. 136, n. 12; and Klein, pp. 79–84.

41. On Struensee's loyalties, see Faber, *Die Rheinlande*, pp. 136–37, 141. Berlin was informed that Struensee's appointment "has created much ill will." Cited in Mohnen, p. 270. Struensee hailed from Magdeburg; see Schwann, *Geschichte*, p. 420. On Struensee's autocratic behavior, see Gothein, pp. 220–21.

42. Gothein, pp. 218, 221.

43. On this, see Gothein; Diefendorf; Kellenbenz and van Eyll, eds.; and Schwann, *Geschichte*.

44. Cologne was the only Rhenish city with a full-fledged Chamber of Commerce. Aachen and Krefeld had merchants' committees with functions similar to, but with less authority than, Cologne's Chamber. They were also far less assertive than Cologne's Chamber. See Diefendorf, pp. 135–59.

45. Diefendorf's characterization of the entire organized Rhenish business community, pp. 334–41.

46. Schwann, van Eyll, Kellenbenz and van Eyll, eds., and Diefendorf make no mention of the dispute between the City Council and Prussian provincial authorities over the Jews, in which the Chamber of Commerce played an important role. Gothein knows of the *Judenpatente* records and the city's stance against the Prussians, but he never explores it.

47. Gothein, pp. 312–13.

48. For an evocative treatment of the sensitivity of "home towns" on this issue, see Walker, especially pp. 137ff., 271ff. and 319ff. While Cologne does not fit Walker's definition of a home town, the dynamics of defining and controlling civic membership and the attitudes of the locality and the state bureaucracy that Walker describes are strikingly similar to what we find in Cologne regarding Jews. Walker's analysis deeply informs what follows here.

49. In order to receive a *Judenpatent*, a Jew not only had to fulfill the special requirements of the 1808 law but also to pay the normal business tax (*Gewerbesteuer*) appropriate to the scale of his or her business. The amount of this tax determined if the Jew (or any other merchant) was "class A," with such privileges as the right to vote in elections to the Chamber of Commerce, or was in an inferior category. In either case, Jewishness was no longer the determining factor. On the requirement of Jews granted *Judenpatente* to pay the *Gewerbesteuer* and on the tax itself, see *HASK*, Oberbürgermeisteramt, 400, II-16-1, "Vertheilung der Gewerbesteuer," letter of Royal Police President and Landrath Struensee to mayor's office, Dec. 14,

1822, and documents following; and Ayçoberry, "Histoire Sociale," vol. 2, Appendixes 9 and 10, pp. 47, 57.

50. Proclamation cited in the letter of the Königliche Regierung, Erste Abteilung of Aug. 5, 1817, to Königliche Polizei Präsident and Landrath Struensee, *Judenpatente*. Frederick William III announced Prussia's formal possession of the Rhineland on Apr. 5, 1815. A Royal Cabinet order of March 3, 1817, reiterated that the 1808 decree remained in effect, with particular reference to its immigration control. In Sept. 1817 the Ministry of the Interior confirmed that the Jews of Prussia's newly acquired territories would continue to be governed by the laws in effect there at the time of their takeover. Decree of Sept. 5, 1817; see n. 14, above; cf. citations in the Dec. 12, 1818, session of the Cologne City Council.

51. On von Mylius, see Gothein, p. 133. Müller, p. 50, is incorrect in stating that official Cologne had a "liberal" attitude to Jewish immigration until the crackdown of 1817; see also n. 58. Mayor Wittgenstein was the French appointee; he was particularly concerned with controlling Jewish immigration. His letter is no longer extant, but Hahn, p. 43, describes its contents; I have also deduced them from the response the letter received from the *Kreisdirektor*, dated Aug. 19, 1814; see *HASK*, Oberbürgermeisteramt, 400, II-4-B-1.

52. The law required heads of households—primary providers who were engaged in their own business—to be patented. Household servants and business assistants were not patented. Female family members—usually widows but sometimes daughters—who took over a business were patented. See the section in Chapter 6 entitled Women's Work.

53. Prefectural resolution of July 25, 1808; *Recueil des Actes* (1808).

54. Letter of First Division to Police President Struensee, Apr. 10, 1817. First Division was also responsible for internal security, public order, health, rural police, town administration, military affairs, statistics, censorship, and school and church administration. Its three councillors (*Räte*) worked closely with the *Regierungspräsident* and directly represented him. See Diefendorf, p. 265; and *Die Rheinprovinz der preussischen Monarchie*, p. 103. A Second Division was charged with oversight of government finances, taxes, transport, trade and industry, and official bookkeeping.

55. *Judenpatente*, "Nachweisung Sämmtlicher in Stadtkreis Köln wohnenden Jüdischen Glaubensgenossen," Apr. 19, 1817, signed by Struensee.

56. My calculation, based on Struensee's data. Technically, it was not absurd to demand that a Jew settling in Cologne take up agriculture, since there was cultivation within the city walls in this period. Ayçoberry, "Histoire Sociale," 1: 3–4; van Eyll, "Wirtschaftsgeschichte," pp. 178–79. Practically, however, this was not a real option. The Jews who came to Cologne were businesspeople, while the farmers of the city were a close-knit, guildlike community. The decree specified that migrating Jews should not just own agricultural property but work it and not practice commerce. According to the June 29, 1820, population survey, 6 of 42 male Jewish householders in the city owned *Feldgüter* but none cultivated land themselves.

57. First Division to von Mylius, June 17, 1817; First Division to Struensee, Aug. 5, 1817. The city's sloppiness refutes Gothein's assertion, pp. 312–13, that the city was meticulous in this regard.

58. First Division to von Mylius, June 17, 1817, and Oct. 5, 1818; Council

session of July 7, 1817. Henceforth, Council sessions will be noted by "C.C.," followed by the date.

It was not uncommon for Rhine Province officials in this period to consider deporting Jews who had immigrated illegally. See H. Strauss, "Die Preussische Bürokratie," p. 47. No expulsion of Cologne's illegal immigrants occurred, although First Division repeated its call for this in a letter to Struensee on Oct. 5, 1818. As we shall see, such Jews were processed into the system through judgments on their petitions for *Judenpatente*.

There is no doubting the earnestness with which the Prussian authorities in Cologne began enforcing the 1808 decree from 1817 on. First Division insisted that Jews either have patents or be denied the right to trade (pending possible expulsion), and this demand was enforced. While Struensee gathered intelligence and the City Council deliberated issuance of patent recommendations in the spring of 1817, First Division authorized von Mylius to issue temporary trading permits to Jews who had lived in the city since 1808 and "conducted themselves blamelessly"; First Division to von Mylius, Apr. 18, 1817. This contingency was envisaged in the prefectural ordinance of July 25, 1808. That Salomon Oppenheim, among others, urgently applied for such a permit indicates the stringency of the crackdown; First Division to von Mylius, Apr. 16 and 18, 1817. Oppenheim's request was granted. The requests of other Jews for temporary permits are also preserved. See letters of S. B. Cohen to von Mylius, Aug. 25, 1817; David Hess, Oct. 1, 1817; Salomon Dejonge Jacobs, Oct. 6 and 7, 1817.

The delay in enforcement was not because of any Prussian liberality on the Jewish question but because, apparently, the new provincial government did not have the means to enforce the law until 1817. Cf. Müller, p. 50.

59. C.C. session of Nov. 20, 1817.

60. One of the Jews in question, Alexander Oppenheim, had already been denied the Council's recommendation on other pretexts—he was never accused of usury or other illicit business dealings—and had vigorously appealed this verdict. The Council then devised this reason for denial—which, of course, had broader implications and would have had a crippling effect on Jewish immigration, had it been upheld. On Oppenheim, see report of Police Inspector Werner to von Mylius, Apr. 30, 1817; Oppenheim's petition to Werner, May 1, 1817; C.C. session of May 21, 1817. See also below, "Jewish Responses."

61. Letter of the Interior Ministry, First Division, Berlin, to the Royal Government in Cologne of July 7, 1818, ordering strict application of the 1808 decree "without any limitations or changes," adding, "moreover, there is no doubt [that], instead of the previous division [of the territory] into so-called departments in the [1808] decree, there is now division into government districts." Several months later, First Division conveyed this judgment to Struensee and rejected patent recommendation denials that the Council had based on its interpretation. Article 16, First Division declared, restricted the migration of "alien, that is, foreign Jews," not Jews who possessed French citizenship at the time of the decree's issuance. The Council's rejection of the patent application of several Jews born in Bonn, therefore, could in no way be considered valid. Letter of First Division to Struensee, Oct. 5, 1818.

62. In its session of Oct. 29, 1818, the Council accepted Berlin's ruling.

63. See document signed "Exp W[erne]r," dated Apr. 28, 1817, *Judenpatente*, document no. 7915, to the Police Commission and the Chamber of Commerce; and *Judenpatente*, document no. 756.

64. The letters to the police and Chamber of Commerce had asked for a "confidential report to be given about whether the Jews named on the list have done any kind of usurious businesses or illegal hawking. . . . The City Council . . . however, has expressed the wish above all for precise inquiries about the morality of the Jews."

65. See report of Police Inspector Werner of Apr. 30, 1817, to von Mylius regarding the Jew Alexander Oppenheim, who was about to quit his job as an assistant in another Jew's business to become an (independent) old-clothes dealer, but about whom Werner said, "Notwithstanding the good reputation he enjoys, this type of business does not make him suitable for recommendation." The City Council denied Oppenheim's application, later adding the reasons that he came from Bonn ("foreign" soil) and was previously unpatented. C.C. sessions of May 21, 1817, and May 26, 1819. See also the report of Police Inspector von Othengraven to von Mylius of May 10, 1817, regarding the Jew Joseph Stern. Stern had previously operated a pawnshop and, as we know from French-era sources, had once been wealthy, but he was now a small-wares dealer and therefore not necessarily to be trusted ("Zur Zeit treibt er einen Kramhandel — in wie fern dies im Wucher und einem Juden zu gestatten ist mögen Euer Hochwohlgeboren selbst ermessen"). Stern was granted the Council's testimonial.

66. "Wie uppiges Schlingkraut allenthalten sich festsetzen." Chamber report to von Mylius, May 13, 1817. Stereotypes and fears of Jewish fertility were legion in this period (and in anti-Jewish thinking generally); see Brunschwig, pp. 255, 281.

67. The Chamber did not define here what "rights" it intended, but the very fact that it did not indicates that it was referring to "kaufmännischen Rechten," merchants' rights, in the usual sense. These gave freedom to conduct business, including wholesale trade; more generally, they meant acceptance into the business community. On the contemporary definition of the term "merchant," see Diefendorf, pp. 18–19. On "merchant's rights," see Ayçoberry, "Histoire Sociale," 2:47, 57, Appendixes 9 and 10; and Müller, p. 198, n. 1. More than a decade later, the Chamber said explicitly that its references to the "rights" Jews obtained when they received patents were, in fact, "Kaufmännischen Rechten"; see the Chamber's letter to Mayor Steinberger of May 14, 1828.

68. The first C.C. session to deliberate *Judenpatente* since the Prussian takeover took place on May 21, 1817.

69. As the Council asserted in the minutes of its Apr. 18, 1818, session (as well as in subsequent sessions), "Jews who previously received no patent recommendation are not now to receive one either, since regarding Jews who had previously resided here, the City Council has no grounds to place greater trust in them than at the time the necessary certificate was first denied them; and regarding those Jews who have since immigrated here, they have not demonstrated that they have devoted themselves to agriculture." Cf. the Council's further rationale for this aspect of its policy in its letter to First Division of Dec. 21, 1818.

70. See, for instance, the favorable recommendation of the Chamber of Commerce to the City Council, dated May 8, 1820, of the patent application of Abraham

Ochsenstern, "because he is the son of a patented Jew who has long resided here and enjoys a good reputation."

71. On this exemption, see the letter of First Division to Struensee of Oct. 5, 1818. Several specimens of such exemptions are extant in the Council's records. See, for example, that granted to J. Eschrott (Aschrott) by the Ministry of Interior, Berlin, on Apr. 15, 1820. Eschrott was told that the Ministry is "moved to permit you to reside in Cologne, with exemption from the obligation to devote yourself exclusively to agriculture, to which end the [office of the] Royal Government there is being furnished with instructions." The Council denied Eschrott a patent anyway until forced by the Prussians to relent. See C.C. session of July 20, 1820, and the letter of the Chamber of Commerce to the City of Aug. 11, 1821, lamenting the Prussians' liberal decision. See the C.C. decision on *Judenpatente* of May 19, 1820, among others, for examples of Jews being denied patents merely "because [they] previously possessed no trading patent."

72. This innovation seems to have been the Council's own. See "Nachweisung der im Stadt Kreise Cöln wohnenden Handels—und Gewerbe treibenden Israeliten" of Nov. 28, 1821; see also denials to Moises Cassel, Ezechiel Ritter, and Leib Voss.

73. Thus, when the Chamber or the Council used the terms "the public" or "public opinion," they were always referring to the city's trading community.

74. For this and another, slightly different wording, see the deliberations of the Council of May 21, 1819, and May 19, 1820. Apparently the city got this formulation, as it did other structural elements of its Jewish policy, from the Chamber of Commerce. Two weeks before the Council session in which this formulation appeared, the Chamber had sent the city a letter with its patent recommendations, which contained a virtually identical, though more elaborate and vicious, paragraph on the Jews. See the Chamber's letter to the mayor's office of May 3, 1820.

75. Three of eight Jews whose applications were rejected in May 1820 fit this description; the reason given for their denials was that they had not previously held patents (a fourth "long-timer" who was denied a testimonial had previously held a patent, but was accused of association with thieves). Five of fifteen Jews denied testimonials in 1821 had lived in the city since before 1808—three of them had even held patents. A fourth was denied merely because the Council said it "knew nothing about him"—including any negative information.

76. Letter of the Chamber to the Council of May 3, 1820.

77. C.C. session of July 30, 1822. See the untitled, undated Council document immediately preceding this session, which cites the intelligence of the Chamber on Jews to whom the Council had denied patents. The Jews accused of usury and fraud were Baruch Joseph Cassel, Alexander Oppenheim, and Moises Cassel.

78. Compare letters of First Division to von Mylius of June 17, 1817; First Division to Police President Struensee of Aug. 5, 1817; Police President Struensee to von Mylius of Sept. 27, 1817. On the case of the "bad Jew" M. Pollack, see below.

79. The phrase is Mack Walker's, employed in a different context, with no reference to Cologne, but describing perfectly the behavior of the Prussians, certainly, as this was viewed by the city; see Walker, p. 321.

80. See letter of First Division to von Mylius of Aug. 19, 1818, and the C.C.

session held in response to this letter on Sept. 17, 1818; letter of First Division to von Mylius of Nov. 26, 1818; letter of Police President Struensee to the mayor's office of Aug. 16, 1821; letter of First Division to the mayor's office of May 30, 1822.

81. See letter of First Division to von Mylius of Aug. 19, 1818, and the C.C. session held in response to this letter on Sept. 17, 1818. Despite this, the Council continued to reject this Jew's application for patent endorsement until 1828.

82. See letter of First Division to the mayor's office of July 14, 1820, regarding the Jews Israel Aschrott and Abraham Halinbourg.

83. See the letter of First Division to the mayor of Nov. 26, 1818; letter of Police President Struensee to the mayor's office of May 24, 1820; letter of First Division to the mayor's office of June 14, 1820; and especially the correspondence between First Division, Struensee, and the mayor's office regarding the C.C. session of Nov. 28, 1821, in particular, the letter of First Division of Dec. 19, 1821, to the mayor's office. These and other regulations were spelled out in the "Verordnung und Bekannt-machung der Königlichen Regierung" of Feb. 26, 1820, *Amtsblatt* (1820), no. 65, pp. 58–60.

84. First Division, for instance, utterly rejected the Council's Nov. 28, 1821, session for a host of rules violations. As early as Dec. 1818 the City Council held a special session after First Division refused to accept the minutes of an earlier session held in the absence of a quorum. See C.C. session of Dec. 12, 1818.

85. "Verordnung und Bekanntmachung der Königlichen Regierung" of Feb. 26, 1820, in *Amtsblatt* (1820), no. 65, pp. 58–60. In 1822, First Division charged that Cologne was the only place in the entire *Landkreis* that was not meeting *Judenpatent* deadlines. See its letter to the mayor's office of May 30, 1822.

86. Letter of July 17, 1820.

87. See, for example, letters of Police President Struensee to the mayor's office of June 26, 1821, July 24, 1821, Aug. 18, 1821; letter of First Division to the mayor's office of Aug. 16, 1822; letter of First Division to Mayor Steinberger of Dec. 10, 1824.

88. See Struensee's letters to the mayor's office of July 24, 1821, and Aug. 18, 1821, in which he states that he had been repeatedly ordered by First Division "henceforth to forward [*Judenpatente* documents] immediately, at the latest within fourteen days." "Your Honorable Mayor's Office, I must accordingly beseech you most urgently to put me in a position to meet this deadline" (Ein wohllöbliches Oberbürgermeisteramt, muss ich daher recht dringend ersuchen, mich in den Stand zu setzen diesen Termin inne halten zu können).

89. "Dem so ungebürliche verzögerte Berathschlagung." Letter of Dec. 19, 1821.

90. First Division to the mayor's office, May 30, 1822. On the broader context of this letter, see below.

91. Letter of the mayor's office to First Division, July 18, 1820, and draft of a letter from the mayor's office to First Division, undated, untitled, unnumbered document following immediately the March 4, 1822, letter of Police President Struensee to the mayor's office.

92. The mayor's office, for example, wrote the Chamber on July 26, 1821, with a list of the Jews to be investigated, soliciting the Chamber's negative comments "as soon as possible." The Chamber responded on August 11 with its own request for

information. When, on Oct. 29, the mayor's office had still not received the Chamber's recommendations, it wrote to urge speedier handling. The Council finally held its session on *Judenpatente* on Nov. 28, 1821; we do not know whether it had received the Chamber's recommendations. It was at this point that First Division first condemned the Council's "indecent delay" (letter of First Division of Dec. 19, 1821), a charge subsequently repeated. See First Division to the mayor's office of Mar. 19, 1822.

93. Mayor's office to Struensee, July 26, 1821, and Jan. 19, 1822; mayor's office to First Division, Mar. 22, 1822. As the earlier of the letters to Struensee put it, "In its sessions of yesterday and today, the City Council could not occupy itself very well with investigation of renewal of Jewish patents because of many urgent matters at hand which required consultation."

94. Letters of Jan. 24, 1822, and Mar. 22, 1822.

95. In their July 26, 1821, letter, the deputies informed Struensee that since the Council could not deal with *Judenpatente* it had decided to seek the advice of the Chamber of Commerce. On the pace and substance of the latter's response, see above, n. 92. See, however, the Chamber's response of Sept. 21, 1821.

96. Letter of the mayor's office to the police president of May 26, 1820. The reference to "other communities" in which Jewish affairs were handled by the mayor's office was, apparently, to rural communities in which the office of the mayor and *Landrat* were combined.

97. Letter to the mayor's office of Dec. 19, 1822.

98. Undated, untitled, unnumbered draft of a response to First Division, following immediately the Mar. 4, 1822, letter of Struensee to the mayor's office; minutes of the C.C. session of Mar. 11, 1822; the Council's letters to Struensee of Mar. 18, 1822, and to First Division of Mar. 22, 1822.

99. There were 26 members of the Council and roughly 35 Jewish applicants for patents (910 signatures).

100. Indeed, henceforth the Council dispensed with the "three class" patenting system, granting endorsements simply to those who "have given themselves over neither to usury nor to other illegal business, however, only in the sense that the City Council knows nothing to the contrary"; denying them to those who "have not earned the trust of public opinion that they have refrained from all usurious business" (weder mit Wucher noch mit anderen unerlaubten Gewerbe sich abgegeben habe, doch in dem Sinne dass dem Stadtrath das Gegentheil nicht bekannt geworden; sich in der allgemeinen Meinung das Zutrauen sich allem Wucherhandel zu enthalten, nicht erworben habe). Additional reasons for denial might also be stated, for example, not belonging to the Jewish community or having recently immigrated and not yet having established a "reputation."

101. Letter of First Division to the mayor's office of May 30, 1822.

102. Minutes of the C.C. session of July 30, 1822. See also Magnus, pp. 638–42 (Document A).

103. See the wording of the Council's endorsements, n. 100. The Council insisted on granting a less-than-absolute endorsement, saying that a Jew recommended for patenting was innocent of usury and other illicit trade only insofar as the Council had no information to the contrary. See the undated, untitled C.C. session

following immediately the session of July 30, 1822, which begins with an announcement that the royal government was not satisfied with the Council's deliberations and which discusses the wording of the Council's *Judenpatente* endorsement.

The tactics and language that city authorities and the Prussians used in their fight to control Jewish status are strikingly similar to those used by embattled localities and encroaching state bureaucracies elsewhere in Germany regarding "outsiders." In Hesse and Bavaria, old economic elites fighting state challenges to their exclusivity began insisting on their right to reject newcomers of "bad reputation." The term, legally undefined, generally connoted sexual promiscuity; it was also used to signify laziness or anticipated business failure — including failure caused by the new environment's hostility. In response to this tactic, the state governments of Hesse and Bavaria demanded that "bad reputation" be defined legally "as specific actions, identified and judicially condemned by state courts. What other fair and uniform criteria could there be for an idea like bad reputation?" Yet, as Mack Walker writes, "The hometownsmen knew: a person's reputation is bad when the town council and the community deputies agree that it is." Walker, p. 303, also pp. 276–77, 298–304, 320–21. Compare this with the attempts of the Christian merchant elite of Würzburg in the first half of the nineteenth century to exclude Jews using, in the words of a contemporary, the "pettiest chicanery" to deny Jews' acceptance to the merchant association; see Gerhing-Münzel, pp. 250, 251.

104. See the untitled, undated document immediately following the C.C. session of July 30, 1822, with "Notizen der Handelskammer."

105. First Division to the mayor's office, Aug. 16, 1822.

106. First Division to the mayor's office, Oct. 7, 1822; mayor's office to First Division, Oct. 15, 1822.

107. Letter of Oct. 27, 1822.

108. C.C. session of Nov. 15, 1822; letter of the mayor's office to First Division of May 21, 1822.

109. First Division to the mayor's office, Feb. 1, 1823; and C.C. session of Nov. 27, 1823.

110. Struensee to Mayor Steinberger, Nov. 25, 1823; C.C. session of Nov. 27, 1823; Steinberger to Struensee, Dec. 8, 1823.

111. First Division to Steinberger, Jan. 14, 1824.

112. Since First Division was charged with overseeing the affairs of religious minorities, among other concerns, it was under the aegis of the First Division of the Ministry of Interior. On the Prussian bureaucracy's internal loyalty, see Gillis, pp. 16–17.

113. See draft and final copy of the C.C. session of Dec. 17, 1824. The original count showed eleven Council members in favor of not deliberating patents (that is, of disobeying orders) and nine who counseled the more conservative course. The latter number, however, was switched from "neun" to "zehn" and the following margin notation appended: "Since the Mayor is also a member, twenty-one [rather than twenty members] were present." Thus, while Steinberger was among the more levelheaded on the Council, he also took part in an act of insubordination to provincial Prussian authorities.

114. Letter of First Division to Steinberger of Jan. 15, 1825. None of the authors

who have previously reported on the city's dispute with the Prussians—Kober, Hahn, Müller—treat this document.

115. Ministry of Interior, First Division, to the City Council of Cologne, Feb. 10, 1825.

116. C.C. session of Mar. 29, 1825; "Nachweisung der in Stadtkreise Coeln wohnenden Handels und Gewerbetreibende Israeliten, welche pro 1824/5 Handelspatente verlangen," Oct. 21, 1825. The March Council minutes were signed by all 21 members, including Mayor Steinberger.

117. C.C. session of Mar. 29, 1825. See Magnus, pp. 643–46 (Document B).

118. "Weil der öffentlichen Ruf gegen ihn spricht und der Stadtrath nicht der Überzeugung hat, dass er sich keinen Wucher habe zu schulden kommen lassen." See, for example, the denial to J. B. Cassel, C.C. session of Oct. 21, 1825.

119. I reach this conclusion based on the abundance of material from the local police and the paucity of correspondence with the Chamber of Commerce on the "morality" and patentworthiness of Jews. There is clear indication of the hostility between the City Council and the Chamber of Commerce in the Council's *Judenpatente* records. In May 1828 the Chamber recommended denying a patent to a Jew against whom it had no negative information but whose business was so insignificant he had not even paid the minimum trade tax (*Gewerbesteuer*); the Jew ought to be asked to show proof of having paid this tax before being granted a recommendation, it said. Mayor Steinberger, who was then embroiled in a bitter turf conflict with the Chamber, remarked in his notes to the Council about the case that matters of the trade tax were to be left to the proper authorities—in short, that this was none of the Chamber's business. The Council granted the Jew in question, M. J. Cahen, a patent recommendation.

120. Mayor Steinberger to First Division, May 9, 1828.

121. First Division to Mayor Steinberger, June 3, 1828. The Council held in abeyance its decision on the Jew Mendel Lehman while it solicited the recommendation of authorities of his previous residence. These were obviously satisfactory, since the Council quietly granted the man a patent in November 1828. See the memorandum of Mayor Steinberger to the Council, undated, entitled "Zum Stadtrath," following the letter of the Chamber of Commerce to the mayor of May 14, 1828; the letter of the Council to First Division of June 18, 1828; C.C. session of Nov. 12, 1828; and Steinberger's letter to First Division of Nov. 15, 1828.

122. Reports of the consistory's actions and the number of endorsements it issued appear occasionally in Prussian or city communications. The consistory, for example, issued highly favorable endorsements to two Jews, Moses Pollack and Salomon Lejonge, who were nevertheless denied patents; see letter of the Police President to von Mylius of Sept. 27, 1817. On the strength of the consistory's recommendation, First Division challenged the Council's denial of its testimonial to one Isaac Waller, who had persistently pressed the government for a patent. See C.C. session of Jan. 16, 1818. The Council denied Waller anyway, on the grounds that he had immigrated and had not previously been patented. It seems that left-bank consistories had a history of granting endorsements to all who asked; in its 1818 report, the *Immediat Justiz Kommission* stated that the consistories had an unbroken record of doing so.

123. Some unpatented Jews living in Cologne conducted their business else-where, in places like the right bank of the Rhine, where the lack of a *Judenpatent* was not a problem. See, for example, the petition of Moses Pollack to First Division, Aug. 13, 1818, in which Pollack states that although he had lived in Cologne for years, "I earn my living outside the city through sale of wares [*Waarenverkauf*]." The prohibition of Jews conducting business without a *Judenpatent* on pain of arrest, which the 1808 decree does not specify, is in "Verordnungen und Bekannt-machungen der Königlichen Regierung" of Feb. 26, 1820, in *Amtsblatt* (1820), pp. 58–60. The consequences of being without a patent were sufficient for Jews denied them to seek reversals of the negative judgment. See, for example, First Division's letter to Struensee of Sept. 27, 1817, about M. Pollack and S. Lejonge, who were seeking such reversal in order to trade. Pollack alleged that he had been forbidden to travel because he lacked a patent. See his petition to First Division, Aug. 13, 1818. Salomon Oppenheim himself urgently appealed for a temporary patent in 1817, after the Prussians had begun insisting that Jews possess a *Judenpa-tent* but before the Council had yet deliberated on their issuance. See letter of First Division to von Mylius of Apr. 16, 1817, and von Mylius's note of Apr. 19, 1817.

There are several petitions for patents from Jews who were no longer in business but who needed them in order to collect debts; as we recall, the patents were a prerequisite to Jews using the courts to enforce business contracts. See "Nach-weisung der in hiesigen Stadt Wohnenden Israeliten, welche pro 1826 das Judenpa-tent verlangen" of Dec. 5, 1825, entry number 18 on Simon Cohen; undated docu-ment entitled "Judenpatente pro 1827" (placed immediately before document dated Feb. 3, 1827) regarding David Daniel.

The persistence of Cologne Jews in pursuing patents appears to be in contrast to the behavior of Jews in the French department of the lower Rhine, less than half of whom, according to Moche Catane, got patents because they declined to subject themselves to the patenting procedures; see Catane, p. 262, cited in Hyman, *Eman-cipation*, p. 17. Of course, Alsatian Jews were subjected to the 1808 decree for far less time than Jews of the left bank of the Rhine, and we can only speculate about their behavior had the law remained in force after 1818.

124. As Ayçoberry writes, "Le titre de 'marchand' est . . . porté avec fierté . . . il implique l'honneur en un certain sens de la grandeur, vertus acquises par héritage et formation plus que conférées par une quelconque ordonnance. Etre marchand, c'est inscrire sa vie dans un cours fixé par l'usage"; "Histoire Sociale," 1: 68. It was one of the paradoxes of German Jewish life in the era of emancipation that, in Cologne and the left bank of the Rhine, acceptance into respectable society had to be purchased with a special "Jew" patent.

125. See the original police report by Police Inspector Werner on Oppenheim, on which the original denial was based, dated Apr. 30, 1817, and Oppenheim's instantaneous appeal to Werner, May 1, 1817. In April of 1826 Oppenheim was finally granted a patent for 1824 and 1825, and was regularly granted patents thereaf-ter. He died in 1829, after which his wife was patented in his stead.

126. Letter of A. Oppenheim to Steinberger, Jan. 9, 1826. It is notable that Oppenheim wrote this letter in German, apparently in his own hand, that is, with-out the help of a translator or scribe.

127. Letter of First Division to Oppenheim, copy to von Mylius, of Dec. 26, 1817: "Sie werden daher mit Ihrem Gesuche hierdurch ein für allemal abgewiesen." This was before First Division began examining and challenging the Council's grounds for rejecting Oppenheim's and other Jews' petitions.

128. Mahler, p. 75.

129. The class of patent was determined by the amount of trade tax paid. See Ayçoberry, "Histoire Sociale," 2: 47, 57, Appendixes 9 and 10.

130. Letter received in the mayor's office on Oct. 7, 1817.

131. See Rohrbacher, p. 119.

132. See the original police report on Pollack by Police Inspector Schönig to Mayor von Mylius, May 1, 1817, in which Schönig states that although Pollack denied charges of receiving stolen goods he admitted knowing a man who was under arrest in Bonn on robbery charges.

133. Police Inspector Schönig's report, May 1, 1817.

134. See Struensee's letter to the Council recommending that it reconsider granting Pollack a testimonial, Jan. 9, 1818.

135. Petition of M. Pollack to First Division of Aug. 13, 1818, a copy of which was sent to von Mylius on Aug. 19, 1818.

136. See letter of First Division to von Mylius of Aug. 19, 1818, and the C.C. session of Sept. 17, 1818.

137. Each year his application was denied with a formulaic reference to his (alleged) association with thieves.

138. Letter of Steinberger to First Division of Dec. 31, 1827.

139. Report of Police Inspector Lutter, Jan. 8, 1828.

140. Walker's phrase, p. 276.

141. Ibid., p. 284.

142. See Walker, especially chapters 8, 9, and 10. The right to decide *Bürgeraufnahme* was "the main issue between the communities and state officials during the first half of the nineteenth century"; p. 276.

143. Ibid., pp. 319–20. Jews, whether immigrant or resident, were outsiders by definition. On Jews and resident aliens, see ibid., pp. 207, 219–20, 238–40, 247, 271, 275, 304, 319–21, 341–42. Compare with Toury, "Probleme Jüdischer Gleich-berechtigung"; id., "Types of Jewish Municipal Rights."

144. The Privy Council of Württemberg, for example, commenting on the state government's attempts to open local citizenship and deflect opposition from local elements in the Diet, wrote in 1823, "Proposals for [admission into] the trades and on the civil condition of Jews will come up for discussion in Diet Committees, and they are related to [the question of *Bürgeraufnahme*] in many ways." Cited in Walker, p. 289.

145. This, despite the large number of destitute people in the city and significant strains on the city's poor relief. We know of one early positive statement by von Mylius on the general subject of urban migration, presumably including migration to Cologne; he wanted to restrict immigration only of those incapable of work. Cited in Gothein, p. 132.

146. On the social composition of Cologne's ruling elite, see Ayçoberry, "His-

toire Sociale," 1: 60–62; Kellenbenz and van Eyll, eds., pp. 91–92; and Perlitz, pp. 130ff., 168ff. On the Council in the 1820's, see Gothein, pp. 218ff.

147. On P. H. Merkens, see below. Hermann Löhnis, a leading member of the Chamber for decades, was a Protestant. Johann Philipp Heimann, whose name appears on several of the Chamber's anti-Jewish letters, was a Catholic who had joined the Freemasons. See Diefendorf, pp. 76, 138. On the composition of the Chamber of Commerce and the City Council, see Kellenbenz and van Eyll, eds., pp. 28ff., 49ff., 86ff., 234ff.; Diefendorf, pp. 303ff. On the quick entry of Protestants and other non-Jewish immigrants into the upper reaches of Cologne's economic elite, see Diefendorf, pp. 37–38, 40–41, 56, 69–70, 75, 138, 307; Kellenbenz and van Eyll, eds., p. 73; Gothein, p. 190; and Perlitz, pp. 186–87, 326ff.

148. See Diefendorf, pp. 306–7, 310ff.; Becker-Jákli.

149. On Merkens, see the many references in Gothein; Schwann, *Geschichte*; Kellenbenz and van Eyll, eds.; Diefendorf; Faber, *Die Rheinlande*; Becker-Jákli; Schwank; Hartsough; and Grupe.

150. Diefendorf, pp. 302–3.

151. The Chamber had a general practice of assigning special issues to subcommittees; see Kellenbenz and van Eyll, eds., p. 107. Letters of the Chamber relating to Jewish affairs signed by Merkens are those of June 16, 1819, May 8, 1820, May 30, 1820, Sept. 21, 1821, and May 1, 1828. They are found in the *Judenpatent* collection.

152. Thus Droz, p. 137, speaks of the "liberal milieu" of Cologne's Chamber of Commerce, in which Merkens "was raised," and of Merkens's admiration for French institutions, particularly the civic equality of rural and town dwellers, as indication of his liberalism in the pre-1840's period. On the uses of the word *liberal* in German historiography, see Diefendorf, pp. 4ff. On early German liberalism, see Sheehan, *German Liberalism*, pp. 6–48. On the development of Rhenish liberalism, see Droz; Diefendorf; and Chapter 5.

153. Gothein, p. 222; Ayçoberry, "Histoire Sociale," 1: 60. See, too, Gothein, pp. 158–59.

154. On the 1840's, see Chapter 5. References to Merkens's 1843 position on Jewish rights are in Schwank; Diefendorf, p. 284.

155. Gothein, pp. 172ff.; Ayçoberry, "Histoire Sociale," 1: 29ff.; Kellenbenz and van Eyll, eds., pp. 112ff.

156. Gothein, p. 170.

157. Council document, untitled, undated, and unnumbered, immediately following the C.C. session of July 30, 1822; see especially remarks concerning the Jew Baruch Joseph Cassel. See, too, the minutes of the C.C. session of July 30, 1822, no. 5279.

158. See petition of the Jew Philipp Wolff to the City Council, Oct. 18, 1824.

159. Seven of the nine Jews accused in the aforementioned documents were eventually granted patents as a result of Prussian intervention; two appear to have left the city.

160. Diefendorf, pp. 272, 279, 305–6.

161. Ibid., p. 273. Steinberger was the first of the city's mayor-bureaucrats. He took office acknowledging "with deepest conviction and joy the intimate connec-

tion between the welfare of our great . . . city and that of the merchant community," and he soon turned to business ventures himself; ibid., p. 272. On his involvement in railroad enterprises, see Chapter 5.

162. On the tight membership of the Chamber, see Diefendorf, pp. 303ff.

163. Under French law, which governed Cologne's Chamber until 1831, candidates for membership in the Chamber were notables named by the mayor or the prefect; see Diefendorf, pp. 293, 297. On the "first class" of merchants, see Ayçoberry, "Histoire Sociale," 2: 46–48, Appendix 9. On class distinctions within the merchant class, see ibid., 1: 68. On merchants' voting rights in Chamber of Commerce elections, see Kellenbenz and van Eyll, eds., p. 81.

164. See Schwann, *Geschichte*, pp. 424ff.; Kellenbenz and van Eyll, eds., pp. 87–88; and Diefendorf, pp. 291ff.

165. See Diefendorf, pp. 296ff.; Kellenbenz and van Eyll, eds., pp. 80–81.

166. Paraphrasing Diefendorf, pp. 293, 299.

167. Merkens accepted reelection in 1835 and became the Chamber president. Shortly thereafter the Prussians raised the tax eligibility requirement for the franchise, thereby reducing the number of businessmen with "merchants' rights," although still not restricting it as much as the Chamber had demanded. Kellenbenz and van Eyll, eds., p. 90; Diefendorf, p. 302.

168. A *Judenpatent* was an all-or-nothing business license, while non-Jewish merchants were divided into three categories according to the scale of their business and the *Gewerbesteuer* paid; licenses were granted accordingly. See Ayçoberry, "Histoire Sociale," 2: 47–48, Appendix 9. Although Jews were also required to pay *Gewerbesteuer* and were therefore subject to the same divisions into merchant's categories, the Chamber of Commerce and the City Council, apparently, were irked by the "classlessness" of the *Judenpatent*. This would seem to have been behind the Chamber's manufacture, and the Council's acceptance, of first- and second-class *Judenpatente*. See, too, the letter of the Chamber to the city on May 14, 1828, regarding the Jew M. J. Cahen. On the connection between possession of a *Judenpatent* and payment of the *Gewerbesteuer*, see *HASK*, Oberbürgermeisteramt, 400, II-16-1, "Vertheilung der Gewerbesteuer," especially document no. 2615 (1822).

169. Diefendorf, p. 292.

170. Ibid., pp. 303–5. Diefendorf argues that Prussian policy was not fundamentally inimical to the economic interests of the Rhineland's business community or even to its political self-expression as long as such expression was contained within clear bounds.

171. Those opposing Jewish rights consistently raised the specter of uncontrolled, massive Jewish immigration. See the report of the *Immediat Justiz Kommission* (*HSTA-D-K*, Acta der *IJK*, no. 7); the recommendations of the French-appointed mayor of Cologne shortly after the Prussian takeover (*HASK*, Französische Verwaltung, 4923); and the letter of the *Kreisdirektor*, *Judenpatente*, Aug. 19, 1814; Hahn, p. 43.

172. In 1828, Merkens and two other Chamber of Commerce members recommended denying a *Judenpatent* to a Jew who, by their own admission, had practiced no usury or other illegal commerce, merely because the scale of the Jew's business had not warranted a 30 taler trade-tax assessment. See Chamber of Commerce letter

to the city of May 14, 1828, regarding M. J. Cahen. Such a requirement was highly discriminatory, since only 27 percent of Cologne merchants assessed *Gewerbesteuer* in 1833 paid between 30 and 47 taler; 60 percent paid between 12 and 30 taler. See Ayçoberry, "Histoire Sociale," 2: 51, Appendixes, graph 9E.

173. Diefendorf, p. 307; cf. Müller, pp. 238, 240, 307. Stürmer, Teichmann, and Treue, p. 51, place Oppenheim's election in the context of his growing economic power but make his inclusion in the power elite sound more seamless than it actually was; see below. On Oppenheim's election in 1822 and his reelection in 1825, see *HO*, vol. 50.

Given all this, the Chamber's anti-Jewish policy can hardly be ascribed to fear of "threatening Jewish competition," as Müller, p. 55, says, since it feared and opposed precisely the least economically powerful Jews and elevated the most powerful — Oppenheim — to Chamber membership.

174. Treue, "Das Bankhaus Salomon Oppenheim," p. 399; Schwann, *Geschichte*, p. 42. In 1818, following the Congress of Aachen, Oppenheim's firm was involved in politically sensitive liquidation of French assets. Schnee, "175 Jahre Bankhaus," p. 72.

175. On the city government's assistance to the Prussian authorities against the Chamber of Commerce in the franchise battle, see Diefendorf, pp. 292ff.

176. The Jew in question was Ezechiel Ritter, denied the Council's testimonial on Nov. 28, 1821, and Nov. 3, 1822, and finally granted one after Prussian pressure on Oct. 31, 1823. I deduce Ritter's secure financial standing from his stated address on one of the city's better streets in 1821 (Untergoldschmied 35, listed on the Jewish population list of June 9, 1821), from the relatively high *Cultus Kosten* contribution he was assessed by the Jewish community in 1825–26, and from the fact and nature of the business advertisement Ritter placed in the *Kölnische Zeitung* of Jan. 6, 1821, preserved among the *Judenpatent* records. I thus differ with Müller, p. 48, who says that the Council's decisions on *Judenpatente* were a function of the wealth of the individual applicant.

177. One Jew whose *Judenpatent* application the Chamber of Commerce and City Council opposed was exempted from Article 16 by Berlin and championed by First Division because he "is employed as a commission agent . . . in the copper depot established in Cologne and to this end intends to move his residence to Cologne." Letter of Minister of Interior von Schuckmann to First Division, Nov. 8, 1820. See, too, the letter of Apr. 15, 1820, of the Ministry to the Jew J. Eschrott (Aschrott) informing him of the exemption; the C.C. sessions of May 19, 1820, and July 20, 1820, in which the Council's recommendation was denied him; and the letter of the Chamber of Commerce to the mayor's office of Aug. 11, 1821, ruing the fact that Aschrott had been granted a patent as a result of Prussian action.

178. Letter of von Mylius to First Division of May 7, 1819, found in *HASK*, Oberbürgermeisteramt, 400, II-4-B-5, "Verhältnisse und Aufenthalt der Juden in hies. Stadt, 1819." On the context of this exchange, see below. The material from which von Mylius quoted (uncited) is several journals and pamphlets preserved in the records of the municipality after the minutes of the Oct. 29, 1818, C.C. session. These are entries from the "Haller Litt. Zeitung," May 1817, labeled "Juden"; "Oppositions Blatt," Apr. 2, 1819; and the "Oppositionsblatt oder Weimarische Zeitung," of May 16, 1818.

179. "Regarding the Jewish merchant Hermann Gompertz . . . the latter has conducted himself steadily and blamelessly and we can, therefore, considering his conduct, do no other than grant him a favorable report." Letter from the Chamber to von Mylius, June 16, 1819.

180. Gillis, p. 17.

181. See *HASK*, Oberbürgermeisteramt, 400, II-4-B-2, "Schulden Tilgung-Commission"; and *Amtsblatt* 1819, no. 8, entry 58; no. 6, entry 20; no. 40, entry 314; 1820, no. 20, entry 165; no. 35, entry 255; 1821, no. 31, entry 219; no. 41, entry 284; 1822, no. 37, entry 303; 1823, no. 4, entry 34; no. 5, entry 348; 1824, no. 3, entry 25; 1825, no. 17, entry 125. For the broader context of Prussia's debt policy, see Zorn, p. 555: "Die Schuldenpolitik Preussens zielte auf eine möglichst rasche Rückzahlung auch der provinziellen und Kommunalen Schulden ab."

182. *HASK*, Oberbürgermeisteramt, 400, II-4-B-5, "Verhältnisse und Aufenthalt der Juden in hiesigen Stadt."

183. Von Mylius's major response to First Division is dated May 7, 1819. A second letter was sent on Dec. 11, 1819, in response to an inquiry from the Debt Liquidation Commission.

184. The Division's letter had opened without salutation, simply with the words, "We order you hereby to reply to the following questions as quickly as possible."

185. See, too, Police President Struensee's lengthy letter of Jan. 15, 1829, to Mayor Steinberger in support of the *Judenpatente* applications of several petty Jewish merchants. There was no case when the Prussians denied a patent requested purely for business purposes.

186. Diefendorf, p. 300. See also Ayçoberry, "Histoire Sociale," 2: 47, Appendix 9.

187. See letters of First Division to Struensee of Dec. 15, 1828, and Jan. 8, 1829, regarding Jews whose applications for *Judenpatente* were to be denied because the individuals no longer practiced trade and had requested *Judenpatente* merely in order to enjoy the status and legal benefits the patent bestowed.

188. Letter of May 30, 1822.

189. Letter of First Division to Mayor Steinberger, June 3, 1828.

190. Walker, p. 283.

191. See the case of Mendel Lehmann; letter of Steinberger to First Division, May 9, 1828.

192. The tone of communications coming from the mayor's office after 1825 is markedly different from that of previous years. Applications of "new" Jews for *Judenpatente* recommendations or of "old" Jews long denied patents, or denied them through administrative mistakes, are thoroughly investigated but usually recommended to the Council for positive action. Steinberger was conducting matters very differently than had the deputies or von Mylius, largely following Prussian directives on *Judenpatente*. See, however, the stance Steinberger took on the case cited above, n. 189.

193. Diefendorf, pp. 135–59, emphasizes that Cologne's Chamber of Commerce was, from its founding, far more politically alert, articulate, and aggressive than the businessmen's associations of any other major city on the left bank of the Rhine.

194. On Oppenheim's membership in several Freemason societies in 1806–7, see *HO*, vol. 35. Oppenheim was one of the most highly taxed businessmen in the city in 1820, the two others being the bankers Herstatt and Schaafhausen. They paid, respectively, 165, 171, and 163 taler in patent tax. See Müller, pp. 217, n. 2, 237.

195. Ayçoberry, "Histoire Sociale," 1: 66.

196. Treue, "Bankers Simon and Abraham Oppenheim," p. 57. According to Kaudelka-Hanish (p. 91), the title of Commercial Councillor was the "highest honorary title not connected with office that could be bestowed [by the Prussian state] on merchants, manufacturers and industrialists," normally upon recommendation by prominent individuals, local officials, or bodies such as Chambers of Commerce. Salomon Oppenheim seems to have been one of the earliest Rhenish recipients of the title. See Kaudelka-Hanisch, pp. 91–93, n. 27, 110. The title was not hereditary; Abraham and Simon Oppenheim received their own in 1857–58 and 1865, respectively. See W. Mosse, *Jews in the German Economy*, p. 90. See Mosse's remarks on the nature, acquisition, and importance of this title, ibid., pp. 3, 39–42, 44, 46, 49, 51, 53, 55, 56, 69.

197. Stürmer, Teichmann, and Treue, pp. 31, 35, 39, 40, 41, 59, 60, 62, 63.

198. "Nur kein fressend Möbel!" Ernst Weyden recalls hearing Salomon Oppenheim make these remarks to Weyden's father when Weyden was a child; Weyden, p. 292.

199. Stürmer, Teichmann, and Treue, p. 39.

200. On the proxy marriage, see ibid., p. 41. One of the two witnesses, Heimann was no friend of the Jews (see n. 147), which is more evidence that treatment accorded the Oppenheims cannot be assumed to have had broader implications — the elite treated a wealthy businessman, even a Jew, differently from "nonentities," Jewish or otherwise. On the marriage patterns of Cologne's business and financial elite and the consolidation of wealth and power thereby, see Perlitz, pp. 168ff.; Ayçoberry, "Histoire Sociale," 1: 65–66; van Eyll, "Wirtschaftsgeschichte," p. 239.

201. Salomon Oppenheim died in 1828. At the time of his death, three of eleven children were married, all to Jews: Helena to the banker Benoit Fould of Paris, Charlotte to the banker Adolf Ratisbonne of Strasbourg, and Betty to the businessman Heinrich David Hertz in Hamburg (Hertz later converted); *HO*, vol. 43, "Offenkundigkeitsakt" of Feb. 5, 1829. All but one of the later matches of Salomon and Therese Oppenheim's children were also endogamous; a daughter, Eva, converted and married a Prussian army officer and nobleman in 1831. One son, David (Dagobert), who converted in 1839 for professional reasons, never married (on these two, see Chapter 6). Simon and Abraham Oppenheim, who ran the firm after Salomon's death, were married to Jews and remained Jewish; they were ennobled late in life, Abraham by the Prussian state, Simon by the Austrian. Two of Simon's four children converted, one to Protestantism, one to Catholicism. Abraham was childless but he and his wife adopted a niece of hers who later converted and married a non-Jew, on which, see Chapter 6. See Schnee, "175 Jahre Bankhaus"; Stürmer, Teichmann, and Treue, pp. 41, 59, 65, 69–71; Treue, "Dagobert Oppenheim," pp. 145–75; and Chapters 5 (especially n. 28) and 6. As Schnee, "175 Jahre Bankhaus," p. 73, notes, "While the earliest [Oppenheim] generations were connected to families of well-known court factors such as the houses of Obermayer,

Kusel, Beyfuss, Hertz, von Haber, von Kaskel, von Rothschild, Fould, [and] the Pereire brothers, after ennoblement, marriage connections ensued with numerous recognized noble families of the old aristocracy."

All this contrasts with the assertion of one of Simon Oppenheim's grandsons that the Oppenheims, in contrast to the Rothschilds, had no preference for their children marrying Jews; see the memoir of Max von Oppenheim, *HO*, vol. 40, hand-lettered p. 6. This is an apparent retrojection of later family attitudes. The prenuptial agreement of Simon Oppenheim and Henriette Obermayer even stipulates (undoubtedly at her family's behest) that the bride be freed from the obligation under Jewish law (which presumably, might otherwise have been followed) to marry one of her brothers-in-law should the marriage be childless when her husband died; *HO*, vol. 35, "Ehe Beredung," Aug. 1830. Many thanks to Roger Kohn for help in clarifying this document.

202. Cf. Diefendorf, p. 307. Müller, pp. 65, 238, speculates that the markedly diminished role of the Chamber of Commerce in the Council's *Judenpatente* deliberations in the mid-1820's was the result of Oppenheim's election to the Chamber in 1822, but cites no evidence to support this. Since there is evidence (see n. 172) that the Chamber remained hostile to the Jews as late as 1828 (Oppenheim was reelected in 1825), I link the Chamber's lessened role to Steinberger's accession to the mayor's chair and the extreme tension between him and the Council, on the one hand, and the Chamber, on the other, during these years; see n. 119.

Similarly, I would not overrate the significance for the history of Jewish emancipation in Cologne of the accession of Simon Oppenheim, Salomon's son, to the presidency of the Chamber of Commerce for a short interval in 1833–34. Oppenheim was elected by default at a time of extreme turmoil in the Chamber's internal affairs. He was quickly replaced by a Chamber veteran and shortly thereafter by Merkens, who had previously served as president of the body. See Kellenbenz and van Eyll, eds., pp. 89–93 (who give different dates for the exact tenure of Oppenheim's presidency; cf. pp. 92 and 93); and below, Chapter 5. Other Jews elsewhere in Germany also served on Chambers of Commerce, whose attitudes, according to Jacob Toury, were far more favorable to Jewish economic contributions than those of Cologne's Chamber. See Toury, "Der Eintritt," p. 166; id., *Der Eintritt*, p. 223.

Chapter Five

1. On the *Kölnische Zeitung*, see Buchheim.

2. On the term *emancipation* to designate the struggle for Jewish rights, see J. Katz, "The Term 'Jewish Emancipation'"; id., *Out of the Ghetto*, pp. 191ff.; and Baron, "Civil versus Political Emancipation." See also Toury, "The 'Jewish Question.'"

3. As Rürup notes, it was only in modernity that the Jewish position in society began to be seen as anomalous or disturbing; see "Jewish Emancipation," p. 69.

4. See Rürup, "Emanzipation der Juden in Baden"; id., "Jewish Emancipation"; id., "German Liberalism"; id., *Emanzipation und Antisemitismus*; id., "Emancipa-

tion and Crisis"; id., "Emanzipation und Krise"; id., "Emanzipation und Anti-semitismus"; and id., "Tortuous and Thorny Path."

5. See Henderson, p. 95; Kitchen, p. 32; Gothein, pp. 275ff.; Diefendorf, pp. 323ff.; and van Eyll, "Wirtschaftsgeschichte," pp. 200, 203, 216.

6. Ayçoberry, "Histoire Sociale," 1: 186, 190; Gothein, pp. 351–52, 355, 363–64, 372; van Eyll, "Wirtschaftsgeschichte," pp. 200–201, 203–6, 211.

7. Ayçoberry, "Histoire Sociale," 1: 363.

8. Calculated from van Eyll, "Wirtschaftsgeschichte," p. 218, Table 12. See also Looz-Corswarem; Hamerow, p. 9; and Gothein, 280ff. On the rarity of joint stock ventures in this period, see R. Tilly, *Financial Institutions*, pp. 11, 92, 94, 111–17, 135–37; and Landes, *Unbound Prometheus*, pp. 156, 167, 197–98, 206, 222, 227.

9. On Cologne's increasing importance as a tourist spot and the growth of innkeeping in the city, see van Eyll, "Wirtschaftsgeschichte," pp. 212, 218; and id., *In Kölner Adressbüchern geblättert*, pp. 11–18. On developments in local transport, see van Eyll, "Wirtschaftsgeschichte," pp. 214–15, 226.

10. See Ayçoberry, "Histoire Sociale," 1: 276–77; van Eyll, "Wirtschaftsge-schichte," pp. 166–67; and Chapter 6, this volume.

11. Ayçoberry, "Histoire Sociale," 1: 278.

12. On the Protestant immigrant elite of Cologne in this period, see Hashagen, p. 62; Gothein, p. 356; Ayçoberry, "Histoire Sociale," 1: 191–95, 276–82; van Eyll, "Wirtschaftsgeschichte," pp. 238–39; Becker-Jákli, pp. 177–83; and Becker-Jákli and Müller, eds. On Camphausen and Mevissen, see Kellenbenz and van Eyll, eds., pp. 95–99; Hartsough; Schwann, *Ludolf Camphausen*; Hansen, *Gustav von Mevissen*; and Zunkel, *Der Rheinisch-Westfälische Unternehmer*, pp. 13–33.

13. Ayçoberry, "Histoire Sociale," 1: 194.

14. Trevor-Roper, pp. 1–45. Cf. Ayçoberry, "Histoire Sociale," 1: 192–93.

15. Jacob Toury has noted the significance of the emergence of new business classes, composed especially of immigrants who, like Jews, were outsiders to the local *Stammbürgertum* and were thus more open to Jews; see "Der Eintritt," p. 236.

16. See Henderson; R. Tilly, *Financial Institutions*; Diefendorf; Tipton; H. Henning; and Brose.

17. Quoted in Hühne, p. 34.

18. See Hühne; Henderson, pp. 150ff., 163; Clapham, pp. 46ff.; Schnabel, 3: 371ff.; and von Waltershausen, pp. 77ff.

19. See Kumpmann, pp. 40–65; van Eyll, "Wirtschaftsgeschichte," p. 222; Gothein, pp. 306–7; Ayçoberry, "Histoire Sociale," 1: 187–88; Schwann, *Ludolf Camphausen*, 1: 53, n. 1.

20. Eberhard Gothein, cited in Henderson, p. 156.

21. Cited in Kumpmann, pp. 208–9. See also Kellenbenz, "Die Wirtschaft," p. 337.

22. In contrast to its response to some other railroad ventures. See Henderson, pp. 150ff.; and R. Tilly, *Financial Institutions*, pp. 96–97.

23. See Deeters, p. 141.

24. See Kumpmann, pp. 104ff., 208; R. Tilly, *Financial Institutions*, pp. 101–2, 109; Krüger, p. 174; and Treue, "Abraham Oppenheim," pp. 6–7.

25. See Steitz; Treue, "Abraham Oppenheim," pp. 9–10; and van Eyll, "Kölner Banken," part 1, p. 256.

26. Treue, "Abraham Oppenheim," p. 10. Dagobert became the railroad's president in 1867.

27. Quoted in R. Tilly, *Financial Institutions*, p. 64.

28. One document in the Oppenheim archive states the marriage strategy explicitly: "Founding of the banking house Fould and Fould-Oppenheim through the [proxy] marriage of Salomon Oppenheim's oldest daughter, Helene, with Benoit Fould, 1 January 1814" (the day Prussian occupation forces crossed the Rhine!); *HO*, vol. 105. On the Oppenheim marriage ties and their financial uses, see Schulte, "Zur gewerblichen Betätigung," pp. 128, 132; Treue, "Einige Kapitel," p. 142; Stürmer, Teichmann, and Treue, pp. 41, 59, 69, 70, 71; and the family memoir of Max von Oppenheim, *HO*, vol. 40. On the status of the Haber house in the period when the Oppenheim link was made, see Toury, "Der Eintritt," pp. 166, 210. Benoit Fould of Paris was the brother of the French finance minister; see Prinz, *Juden im Deutschen Wirtschaftsleben*, p. 47, n. 49. The Bischoffsheims were very active in railroad funding; see ibid., p. 48. On the Oppenheim children, see Schulte, *Bonner Juden*, pp. 405–7; *HASK*, Französische Verwaltung, 2468, 2470, 2479; Schnee, "174 Jahre Bankhaus"; Krüger, p. 68, n. 1; above, Chapter 4, n. 201.

29. R. Tilly, *Financial Institutions*, p. 100; *HO*, vol. 93. Abundant material on Oppenheim business dealings with the Rothschild, Fould, Bischoffsheim, Mendelssohn, Haber, and Bleichröder houses is found in *HO*, vols. 23, 24, 25.

30. This was Eduard Herstatt, as reported in Schwann, *Ludolf Camphausen*, 1: 256.

31. Cited in Max von Oppenheim's memoir, *HO*, vol. 40, hand-lettered p. 10.

32. On the importance of networks, kinship ties, and "internationalism" to German Jewish banking firms, see W. E. Mosse, *Jews in the German Economy*, p. 382. The following draws on R. Tilly, *Financial Institutions*, pp. 100–103, 118–19; and Kumpmann, pp. 65–66, 107, 123–24.

33. Treue, "Abraham Oppenheim," p. 6; Kumpmann, pp. 96, 104, 107; *HO*, vol. 159a.

34. This amounted to some 3,000 out of 12,000 shares sold; see Deeters, pp. 116, 118–34, 141; van Eyll, "Kölner Banken," p. 256; Treue, "Abraham Oppenheim," p. 6; Kumpmann, pp. 105, 164, n. 1, 201ff.

35. R. Tilly, *Financial Institutions*, p. 101. See also Landes, "Bleichröders and Rothschilds," pp. 95–114, especially pp. 98–99.

36. R. Tilly, *Financial Institutions*, p. 106. See also Friedrich-Wilhelm Henning, "Der Beitrag Kölner Unternehmer zur Entwicklung des Ruhrkohlebergbaus in der Mitte des 19. Jahrhunderts," in *Kölner Unternehmer*, p. 180. The Oppenheims also invested heavily in iron and steel manufacturing; see Feldenkirchen.

37. Treue, "Abraham Oppenheim," p. 11; and Perlitz, p. 241.

38. Perlitz, pp. 226–27.

39. Treue, "Abraham Oppenheim," p. 12; Krüger, p. 149; and R. Tilly, *Financial Institutions*, p. 123.

40. F. Stern, *Gold and Iron*, p. 9.

41. I have focused only on examples of the Oppenheims using their connections to raise capital. Richard Tilly's *Financial Institutions* abounds with examples of the Oppenheims manipulating the market through their associations.

42. Van Eyll, "Wirtschaftsgeschichte," pp. 232, 233. See Treue, "Einige Kapitel," p. 143; and Prinz, *Juden im Deutschen Wirtschaftsleben*, p. 47.

43. R. Tilly, *Financial Institutions*, pp. 106ff. On p. 107 he writes, "There was scarcely a Rhenish joint-stock company between 1830 and 1870 which did not have at least one banker in a key managerial position . . . and some, like the Rhenish or Cologne-Minden Railway, had five or six. [Moreover,] bankers very often used their voting power and influence to obtain the appointment of friends (or businessmen who were dependent on them) to managerial positions either in addition to, or in lieu of, their own appointment." See also Eichholtz, pp. 18ff., especially p. 31, n. 68.

44. "In cases like these," Richard Tilly writes, "bankers rewarded themselves with the credit and payments business attached to such transactions. This business . . . swelled a banker's turnover without reducing his liquidity." See *Financial Institutions*, pp. 90, 98, 106–8, 177, n. 45.

45. Ibid., p. 40.

46. R. Tilly, *Financial Institutions*, p. 171, n. 6. Cf. Eichholtz, pp. 138ff. On the general subject of bourgeois business morals, see also R. Tilly, "Moral Standards."

47. Treue, "Einige Kapitel," p. 143.

48. Schwann, *Ludolf Camphausen*, 1: 55. Cf. Perlitz, pp. 226–27. In this last undertaking an Oppenheim bid was accepted and then refused, a situation that could have led to a "downright unpleasant" dispute, in Schwann's words, had the Oppenheims chosen to press their claim.

49. See Schwann, *Ludolf Camphausen*, 1: 51–53, 63–78, 87, 91–93, 120–21, and 2: 443. Schwann gives a disturbingly stereotyped explanation for the Oppenheims' "unsatiated pushiness," 1: 51, approvingly noting its alleged taming with time, 1: 53. Cf. Gothein, pp. 307–15.

50. See Chapter 4; and Schwann, *Ludolf Camphausen*, 1: 26ff. Treue's depiction of this election, "Einige Kapitel," p. 142, does not mention its context and conveys too rosy a sense of Oppenheim acceptance; the same is true of his depiction of Abraham Oppenheim's founding activity in the Cologne-Antwerp railroad, p. 143.

51. Schwann, *Ludolf Camphausen*, 1: 26–31, 51.

52. See Camphausen's letter to Deichmann of March 25, 1839, in which Deichmann is addressed with the familiar "Du"; Schwann, *Ludolf Camphausen*, 2: 442–44. See also ibid., 1: 461–64; Kumpmann, pp. 156–60; R. Tilly, *Financial Institutions*, p. 107; and Krüger, p. 57. Abundant material on Oppenheim dealings regarding the railroad, with Hansemann and others, is in *HO*, vols. 160, 161.

53. "Wegbeissung durch seinen Schützling Oppenheim." Cited in Eichholtz, p. 21. On Hansemann's departure from the Rhenish Railway, see Hansen, *Gustav von Mevissen*, 1: 309ff.; and Bergengrün, pp. 253–55.

54. R. Tilly, *Financial Institutions*, pp. 104, 173, n. 48.

55. Schwann, *Ludolf Camphausen*, 1: 442; and Kumpmann, p. 226. See also Bergengrün, p. 258, n. 1.

56. On Mevissen, see Hansen, *Gustav von Mevissen*; Rohr, pp. 139ff.; Hömig;

Droz, pp. 247ff.; and Köster, pp. 34ff. Mevissen's papers are in *HASK*, 1073, and contain correspondence of various members of the Oppenheim family, some very familiar in tone. See also *HO*, vol. 101b. As Abraham Oppenheim prepared to go to Berlin to lobby for Jewish rights in 1847, he asked Mevissen ("dear friend") to arrange accommodations for himself and his wife that would suit both their personal comfort (details cited) and his need for suitable working space; see *HASK*, 1073, letter of Apr. 28, 1847.

57. On the *Rheinische Zeitung*, see Köster, pp. 42ff.; Droz, pp. 252ff.; Klutentreter; and Asmus. On Dagobert Oppenheim and the paper, see below, Chapter 6.

58. Camphausen's seething comments about both Mevissen and Oppenheim are cited in Hansen, ed., *Rheinische Briefe*, 1: 725–26, n. 3. On the events themselves, see Hansen, *Gustav von Mevissen*, 1: 284–86, 309–28, 341–42, 620–24; Bergengrün, pp. 157ff.; Gothein, pp. 322–23; Treue, "Abraham Oppenheim," p. 12, and R. Tilly, *Financial Institutions*, pp. 105, 108–9, 123.

59. On Mevissen-Oppenheim collaboration in the 1840's, see Hansen, *Gustav von Mevissen*, 1: 284–86, 341–42, 620–24; Treue, "Abraham Oppenheim," p. 12; and Tilly, *Financial Institutions*, pp. 105, 108–9, 123.

60. Brisch, 2: 156.

61. Barthold, p. 167.

62. Sterling, *Judenhass*, p. 192, n. 7.

63. See Bergengrün, pp. 210ff., 248–56.

64. A Bavarian deputy asked his colleagues, "How many of you . . . have been entrusted by your electors with the mandate to vote for emancipation? I can go further and ask: who among you has had the courage of informing your voters of the mere possibility of such a step without causing them to raise their voices in loud protest?" Paraphrased and quoted by Rürup, "German Liberalism," p. 62, n. 11, 66, n. 25; see also p. 65.

65. Tal; and J. Katz, *From Prejudice*, especially pp. 129–38, 147–58, 203–9. See also the controversial work of Arendt; and Hertzberg.

66. Holeczek, "Jews and the German Liberals," pp. 87–88.

67. See Sheehan, *German Liberalism*, pp. 7–18; Snell, pp. 22–76; Nipperdey, pp. 286–300; and Schieder, "Probleme einer Sozialgeschichte," pp. 18–19.

68. Cited in Kastner, 1: 47. On Rhenish liberalism, see Hansen, "Das Politische Leben"; Droz; Buchheim; Rohr, pp. 91–102, 139–47; and Hömig.

69. On popular disturbances against Jews in the Rhineland, see Sterling, "Der Kampf," pp. 302–3; id., *Judenhass*, p. 79; Kober, "Aus der Geschichte," p. 80; and H. Strauss, "Die preussische Bürokratie," pp. 27–55.

70. Kastner, 1: 53, 2: 617, 969; Sterling, "Der Kampf," p. 299; Barthold, pp. 245–46, n. 4. Sterling dates the inclusion of Jews in the councils of these cities to the beginning of the decade, but the Christian exclusivity of Cologne's Council was breached only in 1846. Cf. Wenzel; and Toury, "Der Anteil der Juden."

71. From a study by Heinrich Oppenheim, quoted in Sterling, *Judenhass*, p. 77.

72. Sterling, *Judenhass*, p. 78; and id., "Der Kampf," p. 297.

73. Hsia, p. 61.

74. Ibid., p. 65; see also Israel, pp. 5–34; and Wenninger.

75. Wenninger, p. 262.

76. Hsia; Langmuir, *Toward a Definition*; id., *History, Religion, and Antisemitism*; and J. Cohen.

77. Hsia, pp. 155, 203, 228.

78. On "neutral" ground between Jews and non-Jews, see J. Katz, *Tradition and Crisis*, pp. 245ff.; and id., *Out of the Ghetto*, pp. 42ff. The quote here is found in Sterling, "Der Kampf," p. 300.

79. On the relationship between Camphausen and Merkens, see Schwann, *Ludolf Camphausen*, 1: 43–45.

80. As Heinz Holeczek notes, "the change of middle-class consciousness" toward a positive valuation of commercial occupations, which he dates to around 1830, has not yet received full study. See Holeczek, "The Jews," p. 81 and n. 13. Cf. Toury, "Der Eintritt," pp. 222ff., 235.

81. Sperber, pp. 35–36.

82. Droz, p. 366. According to Buchheim, pp. 62, 66–68, Hansemann, a Protestant, was "a true child of the Enlightenment, religiously rationalist"; Camphausen, a Catholic, was "no zealous church-goer"; Mevissen, a Catholic, was "thoroughly reared in the principles of confessional indifference . . . [and] suffused with a purely subjective, unchurched religiosity"; and Beckerath was a believer but a Mennonite committed to religious tolerance. Van der Heydt was the only liberal who was a believing, loyal member of his (Reformed) church — and he did not long remain in the liberal camp. See also, Droz, pp. 228, 250, 275, 293, n. 4, 394; and Köster, pp. 34ff. On van der Heydt's support for Jewish rights in his liberal phase, see Bergengrün, pp. 89–90.

83. Sterling, "Der Kampf," p. 300. On Lensing, see Hansen, *Rheinische Briefe*, 1: 564, n. 6; on Rhenish liberals' opposition to the Christian state and to church-state relations in general, see Buchheim, pp. 60–82, 339–72.

84. These statistics are cited in Eduard Simons, 2: 215.

85. On Hansemann, see Droz, p. 394; and Hansen, *Rheinische Briefe*, 1: 151–52. On Rhenish Protestants, see Eduard Simons; and Hashagen. On the Protestant minority in Cologne before the French, see Becker-Jákli, pp. 1–92.

86. Ayçoberry's characterization, "Histoire Sociale," 1: 386.

87. Dohm, pp. 55, 56–58. I have translated the German title differently than Lederer to convey the dual program of Jewish and state reform that Dohm advocated.

88. Dohm, pp. 61–64.

89. Articles of Sept. 24, 1842, and Oct. 28, 1843, cited in Droz, pp. 241, 242.

90. The words of David Hansemann, cited in Fehrenbach, p. 289. Considering the social and symbolic importance of the railroad, in addition to its obvious profit potential for developers, we can only speculate about the symbolic significance of Oppenheim involvement to the Rhenish entrepreneurs, especially given their extreme dependence on the Oppenheim bank. Although Jewish banking houses were deeply involved in railroad financing in France, Belgium, Russia, Austria, as well as Prussia after 1850, railroads there were wholly or partly state-owned and operated, while in the Rhineland they were private. Alliances forged elsewhere between Jewish bankers and statesmen were forged in the Rhineland between Jewish bankers

and railroad mavericks, many of whom had political aspirations but did not yet exercise power — causing them perhaps to resent their dependence on the Oppenheims all the more. On Jewish banks and European railroad building, see Grunwald, "Europe's Railways"; id., " 'Windsor-Cassel' "; Jenks; Prinz, *Juden*, pp. 44–54, 132–34, 180–84; Greenberg, 1: 173–74; and especially F. Stern, *Gold and Iron*.

Werner E. Mosse notes that German Jewish banks were especially prominent in financing railway construction, in part because they were positioned for capital formation, in part because of a "special Jewish interest in matters of transportation" deriving from Jewish experience "in having to move sometimes heavy loads over considerable distances." He concludes that some Jewish bankers, like Salomon Oppenheim, may also have been "economic visionar[ies]" who "may have foreseen a 'railway age' "; see W. Mosse, *Jews in the German Economy*, pp. 383–84.

91. See Puppke; and Köster.

92. "Uber das Geld," 1839; cited in Schwann, *Ludolf Camphausen*, 2: 218–22.

93. Cited in Diefendorf, p. 333.

94. Cited in Bergengrün, p. 35.

95. Cited in Haym, p. 339.

96. Quoted in Sterling, "Der Kampf," p. 297.

97. Letter of Aug. 3, 1844, *HO*, vol. 104.

98. See above, Chapter 4; Heffter, pp. 207–31; and Hansen, Introduction, *Rheinische Briefe*, 1: 10–62.

99. On the "Cologne troubles," see Franz Schnabel, *Deutsche Geschichte*, 4: 106–64; Holborn, *History of Modern Germany, 1648–1840*, pp. 504–6; and Hansen, *Rheinische Briefe*, 1: 48–50.

100. Quoted in Gothein, p. 466. See Mevissen's letter to Rudolf Haym of Aug. 29, 1847, in Hansen, *Rheinische Briefe*, 2: 329–31; and Droz, pp. 252ff., 368ff. On the financial backing many major Cologne banks and enterprises gave the *Rheinische Zeitung*, see Cervelli.

101. Buchheim, p. 75.

102. On this important distinction, see Wolfgang Schieder, "Probleme einer Sozialgeschichte," p. 20; Fehrenbach, p. 280; and Cervelli, pp. 322, 333.

103. See Hansen, "Politische Leben," pp. 675ff. On the split between Cologne's moderates, who tended to be businessmen, and radicals, who tended to be from the *Bildungsbürgertum* — jurists and doctors — see the report of *Regierungspräsident* Raumer to the Minister of Interior, Jan. 16, 1846, cited in Hansen, *Rheinische Briefe*, 2: 3–8.

104. Thus Rürup is not altogether accurate in stating that pre-1848 Prussia had "no institutionalized basis for parliamentary debates on the subject" of Jewish emancipation. See Rürup, "German Liberalism," p. 61, n. 7. Cf. Barthold, p. 7; Freund, 1: 241–53; and Jost, pp. 271–317.

105. See Kastner, 1: 41ff.; G. Croon, pp. 112–13; H. Strauss, "Pre-Emancipation"; Barthold, pp. 13–15; and Schulte, "Die Rechtslage."

106. The other, from 1826–33, was Georg Heinrich Koch, a ranking member of Cologne's Chamber of Commerce since 1813, including the years when the body took a negative position on Jewish rights. Koch also sat in the City Council for a

time. See Kellenbenz and van Eyll, p. 92; and G. Croon, p. 351.

107. As Merkens put it in 1831, "The persistence of French institutions during the last thirty years has given to Rhinelanders the sense of equality of rights on which their entire social organization rests," and "Rhinelanders appreciate not only the complete equality of all their citizens in administration and justice . . . [but] the simplicity of communal organization which accelerates the rhythm of affairs and prevents friction between people." Cited in Droz, p. 138.

108. Description by G. Croon, p. 111. Ayçoberry echoes the descriptions of Merkens as a liberal; "Histoire Sociale," 1: 60, 74–75, 104, 183.

109. There were eight votes in favor of emancipation at the fifth *Landtag*; see G. Croon, p. 113.

110. See H. Strauss, "Pre-Emancipation"; id., "Liberalism and Conservatism"; and Rürup, "Tortuous and Thorny Path."

111. On the notion of a German Christian state and its relation to the Jewish situation, see Tal, pp. 120–59; and Katz, *From Prejudice*, pp. 195–202.

112. Frederick William to the Ministry of State, Charlottenburg, Dec. 13, 1841; a copy is in CAHJP.

113. H. Strauss, "Pre-Emancipation," p. 111.

114. Von Rochow/Regierung, Apr. 1, 1842, CAHJP. On the inquiry in the Rhine Province, see Kastner, 1: 51–52.

115. The Royal Government in Cologne to Steinberger, May 2, 1842, and Steinberger's response of Aug. 1, 1842, both in *HASK*, Oberbürgermeisteramt, 400, II-4-B-13, "Die von der hies. Regierung verlangten Aufschlüsse zur allgemeinen Regulirung [sic] des Judenwesens betr." See the response, similar in tone and content, of the mayor of Bonn, June 18, 1842, in Kastner, 1: 392–94; and Toury, *Der Eintritt*, pp. 405–7; and the excerpts of the letter of the *Regierungsrat* of Cologne, Freiherr von Munch, to the Minister of Interior, von Arnim, of Nov. 9, 1842, in Toury, *Der Eintritt*, pp. 409–10.

116. On this case, see Chapter 6.

117. On Jewish reactions to the king's 1841 cabinet order, see Chapter 6. See also Kastner, 1: 44ff.; Dubnow, 9: 43ff.; Schorsch, *Heinrich Graetz*, pp. 1–63.

118. Cited in Droz, p. 367, n. 1. On Hansemann's views on religion and the state, see Bergengrün, pp. 274–75.

119. See Buchheim, pp. 1–24, for a survey of the paper's history in the 1830's and 1840's; see also Droz, pp. 252ff.; Gothein, pp. 44ff.; Ayçoberry, "Histoire Sociale," 1: 363–65; Bunyan; and Kastner, 1: 47ff., who also reproduces leading newspaper articles on the debate.

120. On the *Rheinische Zeitung*'s stand on Jewish rights, see König; Hirsch, "Karl Marx und die Bittschriften"; and Bunyan. The paper joined the debate on the king's proposed legislation almost as soon as it went into print in January 1842, commenting with increasing frequency; see nos. 22, 74, 141, 149, 208, 217, 221, 222, 226, and 231, and the *Beiblatt* to nos. 142, 144, and 167. Despite all this, Asmus does not make any mention of the paper's position on the Jewish question.

121. *Kölnische Zeitung*, July 6, no. 187; see also Buchheim, pp. 176–79, 370–71.

122. Buchheim, pp. 8–9, 114ff. Bunyan argues that the *Kölnische Zeitung*'s sup-

port of Jewish rights was primarily political — "a stick [with which] to beat the government and prop up the liberals at the provincial and . . . the [United] Diet[s]" — and that its reversal on the Jewish question was motivated by a need to keep up with Rhenish public opinion and remain economically viable. This is vivid commentary on the strength of support for Jewish rights by this time. See Bunyan, pp. 42, 50. Cf. Ayçoberry, "Histoire Sociale," 1: 297.

123. Nos. 82/83, 23/24, March 1845. Andree's successor was Ernst Weyden, who later wrote the solid (and very sympathetic) history of Cologne's Jewish community that we have often cited; see Kastner, 1: 47.

124. See Droz, pp. 236–45; for the growing importance of the press in pre-1848 Germany and the Rhineland, see Snell, pp. 37–38 and the literature cited there; Faber, *Die Rheinlande*, pp. 406–31; Ayçoberry, "Histoire Sociale," 1: 91–93, 356–63. Hansemann was elected a substitute deputy to the Diet in 1843; the first Diet in which he participated was the eighth, in 1845. Hansen, *Rheinische Briefe*, 2: 92; and G. Croon, p. 353.

125. With a circulation of 9,000 in 1847, the *Kölnische Zeitung* had by far the greatest readership of the Rhenish newspapers: the *Aachener Zeitung* had 1,200; the *Rhein- und Mosel Zeitung* had 1,000; and the *Trierische Zeitung* had 900. The government mouthpiece, the *Rheinisches Beobachter*, had the smallest of all: 700. These statistics are cited in Buchheim, pp. 8, n. 4, and 23.

126. *Kölnische Zeitung* no. 25 of Jan. 25, 1845. The tactic was successful: 170 names appeared on the 1843 petition, 420 on that of 1845; these statistics are cited in Kastner, 1: 59. It is no accident that all the Rhenish petitions on behalf of Jewish rights came from cities with a liberal press; see Kastner, 1: 53.

127. See Hirsch, "Karl Marx und die Bittschriften," pp. 237–39, 241–43.

128. On the increasing popularity of petition writing after 1840, see Ayçoberry, "Histoire Sociale," 1: 370. Cf. Harris on the very different circumstances, and negative content, of petitions about Jewish rights in Bavaria in 1849–50.

129. Droz, p. 300.

130. The Oppenheims' 1841 *Immediate Eingabe* to Frederick William IV is intended; see Chapter 6.

131. L. Camphausen to O. Camphausen, in Hansen, *Rheinische Briefe*, 1: 527.

132. Ibid., p. 720.

133. See Mevissen's letter to his brother-in-law, W. Koenigs, Feb. 16, 1845, ibid., pp. 755–57.

134. Cited in ibid., pp. 755–56, n. 4.

135. Cited in ibid., pp. 755–57. See ibid., pp. 718–19, n. 2. Cf. the letter of liberal delegate J. Wergifosse to Mevissen, Feb. 16, 1845, ibid., p. 756.

136. Ibid., p. 848, n. 3, 755–56, 742–43.

137. As noted in a letter of the *Regierungspräsident* to the *Oberpräsident* of the Rhine Province, Mar. 4 and 5, 1831, ibid., p. 90. See also p. 91.

138. Ibid., p. 822.

139. Abraham Oppenheim did not confine his lobbying to Cologne's Diet delegates. When the Royal Prorogation (*Landtagsabschied*) of 1843 failed to affirm the Diet's call for emancipation, he wrote to Joseph Wergifosse, delegate from Düren, "In the matter of the Jews, by all means we must not stay idle; on the contrary, the

next Diet must continue to pursue the honorable path already begun, for only through persistence will the beautiful objective dangling before us be attained." Letter of Aug. 3, 1844, *HO*, vol. 104. See, too, his letter to G. Mallinckrodt of May 12, 1847, ibid.

140. Bauer expressed his views on Jewish rights in his famous essay of 1843, "Die Judenfrage." See B. Bauer.

141. On Brüggemann, see Buchheim, pp. 12–22, 114, 117, 339–71; and Rohr, 98ff.

142. Quoted in Buchheim, p. 372, n. 3.

143. *Kölnische Zeitung*, no. 94 (1847), signed "*** Köln," Brüggemann's signature. Cited in Buchheim, p. 372.

144. See the *Judenpatent* letter from Minister of Interior von Arnim and Finance Minister Flotwell to the Royal Government in Trier, June 21, 1845; copy sent to Mayor Steinberger on July 23, 1845, who sent it to his police director.

145. Despite an unimpeachable public record on Jewish rights, Hansemann felt a mix of admiration and mistrust toward Jews. In an address to the United Diet in which he opposed the government's plan to exclude Jews from eligibility to serve as Diet delegates, Hansemann conceded a major point to the Jews' detractors: their alleged materialism and lack of civic sense. "Even the argument that . . . ambition would drive them to become members of the Diet is one which sets me on granting them [such rights]. Indeed, that is precisely the intention, that we want to arouse in them a nobler ambition, that we want to encourage the sentiment in them [not] to regard Mammon as the highest objective, rather, that a more noble ambition than being rich might permeate their character"; cited in Bergengrün, pp. 373–74. During the eighth Rhenish Provincial Diet, Hansemann had turned the tables in a similar fashion on an opponent of Jewish rights who feared that civic rights would lead to Christian-Jewish intermarriages, applauding the prospect that emancipation would facilitate the "absorption of this alien spot into German blood"; cited and paraphrased in Bergengrün, pp. 373–74, 321. Even when they supported Jewish rights, German liberals throughout the nineteenth century made it clear they expected Jews to cease maintaining a separate, Jewish identity. On this see Tal; and J. Katz, *From Prejudice*. Bunyan, p. 51, aptly terms this "the conformist demands of German liberalism."

146. Cited in Bergengrün, p. 374.

147. Speech of May 19, 1847; cited in Haym, pp. 300–303.

148. Cited in Kastner, 1: 63.

149. Cited in Hansen, *Gustav von Mevissen*, 2: 246. Although Mevissen had lived in Cologne since 1841, peculiarities of the election code made him run for the Diet from his home town of Dulken, which elected him a delegate in 1846; see id., *Rheinische Briefe*, 2: 96.

150. Speech of June 17, 1847, to the Assembly of the Third Estate, cited in Hansen, *Gustav von Mevissen*, 2: 311–15.

151. Speech of June 14, 1847; ibid., pp. 308–11.

152. Letter of May 20, 1847; ibid., p. 281.

153. Letter of May 24, 1847; ibid., pp. 282–83.

154. "The *Landtag* was . . . presented with the following five proposals: 1) Jewry

law (no emancipation, rather a regulation of their relations to the state). . . ." Letter of Apr. 6, 1847, Berlin, in Hansen, *Rheinische Briefe*, 2: 198.

In this instance, the *Kölnische Zeitung* was acting as a political arm of the Rhenish liberal bloc, a role it had been playing for several years in order to circumvent government restrictions on dissemination of news from the Provincial Diet and the United Diet. Delegates would report to the editorial staff on assembly proceedings and government maneuvers; these would then be printed in the paper.

155. Letter of Apr. 26, 1847, in Hansen, *Gustav von Mevissen*, 2: 246. On the behavior of Cologne's community and its connections to Abraham Oppenheim's mission in Berlin, see Chapter 6.

156. See his letters of June 17, 19, and 20, ibid., p. 315.

157. Letter of June 17, 1847, ibid., p. 315.

158. *Gemeindeordnung für die Rheinprovinz, erlassen zu Berlin am 23 Juli 1845* (Aachen, 1845). Under the king's new Jewry law, Oppenheim, of course, could not have been elected. On his election, see Chapter 6.

159. For the text of the petition, see Hansen, *Rheinische Briefe*, 2: 183–88. Only three members of the City Council refused to sign this memorandum; see Ayçoberry, "Histoire Sociale," 1: 375–76.

Chapter Six

1. See Steinberg; and Kellenbenz, "Grundzüge," pp. 126ff.

2. See Kollmann; H. Croon, pp. 88–90; and W. Hoffmann, pp. 60ff.

3. Sterling, "Der Kampf," p. 307, n. 42. Sterling miscalculates the earlier year's figure; cf. statistics in *Beiträge zur Statistik*; *Statistik und Hand-Adressbuch*; and Kober, "Aus der Geschichte," pp. 79, 86. See aso Kastner, 1: 31 and the documents cited there.

4. See Arnold, pp. 90ff.; and Schulte.

5. Jacob Toury has shown that the internal migration of German Jewry in these years was not entirely directed to cities. Jews also moved away from urban centers to villages and small towns, some with no prior record of Jewish settlement. Such migration was especially pronounced in largely rural Posen but also occurred elsewhere, including the relatively urbanized Rhineland. Toury, *Soziale und Politische Geschichte*, pp. 38ff.; cf. Lowenstein, "Pace of Modernisation," pp. 51–53; Barkai, "German-Jewish Migrations"; and Kastner, 1: 27ff.

6. These calculations are based on statistics in Sterling, "Der Kampf," p. 307, n. 42; and Köllmann, pp. 12, 22. See also Kastner, 1: 29ff.

7. This calculation is based on statistics cited by Kober, *Cologne*, pp. 328–29; see my Table 11. There are no data on a reflux of immigrants or on Jewish emigration, but some such movement can be assumed.

8. Compare the lists of September 1845 and September 1848 in *HASK*, Oberbürgermeisteramt, 400, II-4-D-1, "Vertheilung der Cultus Kosten der Consistorial Synagoge zu Bonn."

9. Ayçoberry, "Histoire Sociale," 1: 276–77.

10. Ibid., 1: 276.

11. Between the years 1841 and 1849, the average rate of natural increase in the

city was 1.1 percent (some 5,600 live births); between 1840 and 1850, it was 5 percent for Jews (277 live births). Absolute numbers, percentages, and averages are calculated from material in Ayçoberry, "Histoire Sociale," 2: 9, Table 3A; and Kober, *Cologne*, p. 329, Appendix B. See Magnus, "Cologne," p. 505, Table 6.4.

12. See Toury, *Soziale und Politische Geschichte*, pp. 27ff.; Schofer, "Emancipation"; Barkai, "German Jews," pp. 123–49; Bennathan; Richarz, ed., *Jüdisches Leben*, pp. 11–69; id., "Jewish Social Mobility"; Lowenstein, "Rural Community"; and Posener. Cf., on France, Albert; and Hyman. For a broad perspective on the causes and contexts of internal migrations, see Kosinsky and Prothero, eds.

13. On the settlement request of Amalia Bier, see the letters of the mayor of Cologne to the mayor of Barmen, Aug. 15, 1839; mayor of Barmen to the mayor of Cologne, Aug. 20, 1839; Police Director Heister to the mayor of Cologne, Mar. 23, 1844; memo of Beigeordneter Bürgermeister und Justizrath Schenk of Mar. 29, 1844, and letter of the mayor to the royal government of Apr. 23, 1844; settlement request of Moses Horn, Mar. 16, 1842.

14. Salomon Oppenheim from Bonn, "banker" in "Oppenheim, Salomon Joseph and Co.," was recorded on the list of Jews requiring *Judenpatente* for 1842. The other was Salomon Oppenheim, Jr.'s, son-in-law M. S. H. de la Parra from Amsterdam; see a letter of the police director to the mayor of May 4, 1839.

15. See Anderson, pp. 63, 74. See the settlement requests of the brothers Hermann and Heimann Goldschmidt, C.C. session of July 12, 1839, and the brothers Abraham and Samuel Bielefeld, C.C. session of Jan. 7, 1840.

16. See Richarz, ed. *Jüdisches Leben*, p. 30; id., *Der Eintritt*, pp. 83ff.; and Toury, *Soziale und Politische Geschichte*, pp. 163ff.

17. See C.C. session regarding Abraham Jacob of Aug. 23, 1838.

18. Toury, "Die rheinischen Jahre," pp. 183–85.

19. Memo to the C.C. of Sept. 8, 1839, regarding the brothers Hermann and Heimann Goldschmidt; C.C. session of July 28, 1837, on the settlement petition of Abraham Salomon; C.C. session of Jan. 12, 1836, on the settlement petition of Lehman Meyerstein; memo to the C.C. of Aug. 9, 1842, on the settlement petition of Simon David Bier; memo of the mayor regarding Jews wanting *Judenpatente* for 1841, Dec. 1840, notation about Isaac Thuringer.

20. See Gothein, pp. 264ff.

21. On native fears of an invasion of indigent immigrants, see Ayçoberry, "Histoire Sociale," 1: 277–78. For an example of this fear expressed about a Jew, see C.C. session of Oct. 20, 1836, regarding Veronica van Geldern.

22. C.C. session of Mar. 31, 1836, on the application of David Herz.

23. C.C. session of Aug. 9, 1842, regarding Gustav Lessing.

24. See the letter of the royal government to the mayor of Dec. 6, 1839, regarding "die Juden Gebrüder Goldschmidt."

25. Letter of the royal government to the mayor, Dec. 30, 1842, and C.C. session of Jan. 12, 1843, regarding Bernard Horn. Additional cases are those of Cosman Coppel, who had in his previous residence paid 18 taler of *Gewerbesteuer* (a relatively high assessment) in two occupational categories, stated in the C.C. session of Aug. 31, 1841, and Andreas Frank, "a very wealthy man," mentioned in a letter of the mayor to the police commissioner of Nov. 18, 1843. Regarding another Jew, who

declared his wish to establish an ironware business, the Council noted, "and he has the means to do this"; see communications of the mayor of June 25, 1842, and Aug. 19, 1842, and unspecified summer date, 1842.

26. C.C. session of Oct. 20, 1836, and an undated document immediately following it regarding Veronica van Geldern. See also the case of Carl Philipp Kaufmann, in the C.C. sessions of July 4 and 6, 1844, and the mayor's communication of July 20, 1844; and of Isaac Wolff de Jonge, in the C.C. sessions of July 28, 1837, and May 15, 1838.

27. Kober, *Cologne*, pp. 293, 381.

28. Although the mayor then suggested that immigration control was, therefore, as much a Jewish as a general concern and that the opinion of the synagogue board be consulted about prospective Jewish immigrants, there is no evidence that the initiative for this emanated from the Jewish community, as Müller, p. 50, suggests. Nor is there evidence in City Council records that such collaboration ever actually occurred.

29. *HASK*, Oberbürgermeisteramt, 400, II-4-D-1, Jewish population lists of Jan. 19, 1844, Sept. 1, 1845, Sept. 2, 1846 (1ten Bezirk), Sept. 2, 1846 (2ten Bezirk), Sept. 4, 1846 (4ten Bezirk) and Sept. 4, 1846 (5ten Bezirk). The 1844 survey showed 190 Jewish households totaling 731 persons, 442 of whom were children; 97 married couples with children and 11 without; 57 single males and 2 females; 12 widowers with children and 1 without, 6 widows with children and 4 without, and 1 male living with a sibling. See Magnus, p. 508, Table 6.7.

30. Ayçoberry, "Histoire Sociale," 1: 281.

31. The 1845 law established special controls for peddlers of any religion; these, rather than any specifically Jewish licenses, now bound Jewish peddlers. *Judenpatent* records in Cologne cease in the fall of 1845. On the 1845 law, see Bechtel, pp. 214ff.; Wurm, pp. 35ff.; Kosseleck, *Preussen*, pp. 597ff.; and Hamerow, pp. 29, 31. On the attitude of Cologne's business class to the law, see Gothein, pp. 402ff. On the emancipating effects of this law for Cologne's Jews, see Kober, *Cologne*, p. 206 and especially p. 373, n. 70. On the continued applicability of the 1808 decree to Jewish peddlers, see the letter of the ministers of interior and of finance to the royal government in Trier of June 21, 1845; letters of the royal government in Cologne to Mayor Steinberger of July 23, 1845, and to Police Director Heister of Cologne of Sept. 2, 1845.

32. Barkai, "German Jews," pp. 129ff.

33. On the distinction between occupational structure and occupational mobility, see M. Katz. On the relationship between occupational structure and mobility, see Thernstrom, pp. 94–96.

34. Werner Sombart, quoted in Prinz, *Juden im Deutschen Wirtschaftsleben*, p. 29, n. 59.

35. On Cologne's savings and loan, see Schoelkens. Joseph Stern, the first Jew to settle in Cologne, ran it. He later took a son-in-law, Abraham Ochse-Stern, into the business. Ochse-Stern succeeded him in 1845, serving until 1851, when he fled the city under charges of embezzlement. See Müller, p. 233; and Schulte, "Gewerblichen Betätigung," pp. 133–34.

36. See Ayçoberry, "Der Strukturwandel."

37. See Barkai, "German Jews," p. 130; and Richarz, "Jewish Social Mobility," pp. 75–76.

38. C.C. session of July 28, 1837, case of Abraham Salomon.

39. See Richarz, "Jewish Social Mobility," p. 75; Barkai, "German Jews," pp. 129ff.; and Toury, "Der Eintritt," pp. 212ff. Toury stresses guild impediments as a hindrance to Jewish entry into crafts. This was less of a factor in the Rhineland, where guilds had lost their corporate privileges.

40. M. S. H. de la Parra, an Oppenheim son-in-law. See *HASK*, Oberbürgermeisteramt, 400, II-4-D-1, "Nachweisung der im Bezirke der Stadt Cöln wohnenden Juden," Jan. 19, 1844; the population surveys of Jan. 30, 1844, and Sept. 22, 1846; and de la Parra's listing on the *Verzeichniss der Meistbeerbten*.

41. See Silbergleit, pp. 75–76, Table 29; and Toury, "Der Eintritt," p. 232, Table 18.

42. Rürup, "Emanzipation und Krise"; W. Mosse, "Juden in Wirtschaft"; Nipperdey, pp. 250–53; Prinz, *Juden im Deutschen Wirtschaftsleben*; and Silbergleit, pp. 106–21.

43. Van Eyll, "Wirtschaftsgeschichte," p. 179.

44. Gothein, pp. 346–52; van Eyll, "Wirtschaftsgeschichte," p. 238; Becker-Jákli, p. 183; Toury, "Der Eintritt," pp. 200ff.

45. On land speculation in Cologne during these years, see Ayçoberry, "Histoire Sociale," 1: 282ff. The Oppenheims had not been involved in speculation in real property nationalized during the French years, either; ibid., 1: 26; and Stürmer, Teichmann, and Treue, p. 77.

46. Ayçoberry, "Histoire Sociale," 2: 220–21.

47. See the cases of Moritz Morel and Isaac Kahn, C.C. session of Aug. 23, 1838, and undated memo to the C.C., probably in July 1842; on the metal trade in Cologne, see Ayçoberry, "Histoire Sociale," 1: 221. On David Levy-Elkan, see Kober, *Cologne*, pp. 249, 283, 306–8; van Eyll, "Wirtschaftsgeschichte," p. 198; and Gothein, p. 397. On lithography and the tourist industry, see Ayçoberry, "Histoire Sociale," 1: 396.

48. See letter of Mayor Steinberger, dated Nov. 17, 1838, and below.

49. The Council discussed Jewish eligibility for settlement and *Judenpatente* on 17 occasions in 1838 and 24 in 1839.

50. On Schnoog, see the C.C. sessions of Apr. 26, 1838; on Johan and Josua Schloss, see the letter of Police Director Heister to the mayor of Nov. 11, 1842, and C.C. sessions of Jan. 20, 1843, and Mar. 13, 1844.

51. See the letter from Police Director Heister to the mayor of Feb. 10, 1843, regarding Maximilian Hirschbach; C.C. session of Jan. 20, 1843, and letter to Hirschbach of June 13, 1843; and Hirschbach's appeal to the mayor and Council of June 27, 1843.

52. See the case of the merchant Isaac Mayer, C.C. session of Mar. 13, 1844, and *Judenpatent* list of Oct. 3, 1844.

53. Thernstrom, pp. 83–84, 255, n. 4.

54. On the low equivalency between actual standing and occupational title in commerce, see M. Katz, p. 71.

55. On Koppel and Katz, see C.C. sessions of May 12 and June 16, 1843; for other instances of business as well as business and marriage partnerships, see the cases of Jacob Werner, C.C. sessions of June 17 and June 22, 1844; Nathan Horn, C.C. session of Mar. 13, 1844; and Isaac Levy, C.C. session of Dec. 14, 1843.

56. Listed for the first time in the *Judenpatent* record of Dec. 11, 1835.

57. On the bourgeois doctrine of female domesticity, see Smith, *Ladies of the Leisure Class*; id., *Changing Lives*; and Lown. On this phenomenon in the German Jewish context, see Kaplan, *Making of the Jewish Middle Class*; and id., "Priestess and Hausfrau."

58. See the mayor's notes to the list of Jews requesting *Judenpatente* for 1841, dated Dec. 1840, and the C.C. session of Jan. 12, 1841. The three daughters are not mentioned by name in the settlement petition and do not appear on *Judenpatente* lists (under the name Bielefeld, at least).

59. See the mayor's letter to the mayor of Barmen, Aug. 15, 1839; the latter's reply of Aug. 20, 1839; the mayor's letter to the police director of Sept. 28, 1839; and the royal government's letter to Bier of Oct. 21, 1839.

60. See the C.C. session of Aug. 23, 1838, regarding Gudula Cassel.

61. Müller, p. 233, n. 1.

62. On the value of Jewish women's income, domestic labor, and dowries, see Kaplan, *Making of the Jewish Middle Class*; and Toury, *Soziale und Politische Geschichte*, pp. 112, 113. On women's work in Cologne, see Ayçoberry, "Histoire Sociale," 1: 290, 320, 329; and van Eyll, "Wirtschaftsgeschichte," pp. 245–46.

63. Lowenthal, p. 161. A small number of the Jewish children attending the school came from such neighboring towns as Deutz and Nippes.

64. Ayçoberry, "Histoire Sociale," 1: 342.

65. Kober, *Cologne*, pp. 308ff., n. 102. See also below.

66. The banker Louis Eltzbacher moved to Cologne shortly after the population survey that is the basis for the analysis here, but even were he included, the overall occupational profile of immigrants would not be altered. On the Eltzbacher family, see *HO*, vol. 35.

67. See the settlement permission request of Moses Horn, Mar. 16, 1842. On the controls on importing meat into Cologne, see Ayçoberry, "Histoire Sociale," 2: 24, Appendix 6E.

68. It is unclear how economically attractive butchering was. Synagogue tax records indicate that butchers were not generally wealthy, yet some Jews on the *Meistbeerbten* list were in the meat trade. Ayçoberry says that butchers were generally well off but also that meat consumption declined continually during this period; "Histoire Sociale," 1: 444, 331. Van Eyll describes butchers as an economically troubled group; "Wirtschaftsgeschichte," p. 184. Gothein describes them as relatively secure; p. 406.

69. In addition to previously cited literature, see Ayçoberry, "Probleme der Sozialschichtung."

70. See Ayçoberry, "Histoire Sociale," 1: 302–55; id., "Strukturwandel," 78–98; and Gothein, pp. 400ff.

71. H. Croon, "Rheinische Städte," pp. 94–95; and id., "Das Vordringen," p. 21.

72. As I have noted, the list did not specify religion. I did not rely on names to identify Jews except when such evidence was incontrovertible (Cohen, Levi), since there were many ambiguous cases (Jacob Kaufmann, Joseph Baum). When no corroborating evidence was available from *Judenpatent* or Jewish settlement records, I discounted the cases. Since both these types of records cease in 1845, I was most likely to exclude Jews who came to Cologne between that year and the date of the

list's compilation, which were years of particularly heavy Jewish immigration. This method would also exclude native-born Jews who came to their majority, or to independent economic status, after 1844 and thus did not have *Judenpatente* in the last years of the system's existence. On my method of calculating Jewish wealth, see Appendix B.

73. Cf. Müller, pp. 218–21, who shows a higher percentage of the Jewish than the non-Jewish population paying *Gewerbesteuer*. Müller's analysis of the *Meistbeerbten* list gives figures somewhat different from mine; our conclusions about relative Jewish wealth are the same.

74. Toury, *Soziale und Politische Geschichte*, p. 100, Table 42.

75. Ibid., p. 108, Table 49, based on Krohn, *Die Juden in Hamburg, 1800–1850*, pp. 49–50.

76. Stern to the royal government in Cologne, Oct. 4, 1841.

77. See the many letters and memos to, from, and/or about Nathan Stern, Moses Mathias, Amschel de Jonge, and Heimann Jacobson, not all dated or filed in chronological order, beginning in Aug. 1838 and continuing through Dec. 1, 1841; a detailed listing may be found in Magnus, pp. 490–91, n. 107.

78. See "Der Strukturwandel"; "Histoire Sociale," 1: 302ff.

79. *HASK*, Französische Verwaltung, 4884; Kober, *Namensregister*.

80. Ayçoberry, "Histoire Sociale," 1: 312–14; see also id., "Der Strukturwandel," pp. 89–90.

81. See Prinz, *Juden im Deutschen Wirtschaftsleben*, pp. 55–62; Toury, *Soziale und Politische Geschichte*, pp. 89–90; and Reissner, "Histories."

82. Van Eyll, *In Kölner Adressbüchern*, pp. 51, 52, 53, 54.

83. On the definition of acculturation, see Gordon.

84. *HASK*, Oberbürgermeisteramt, 400, II-4-D-1, 3758/3, no. 2756, "Verzeichniss der in 3 Bezirk wohnenden israelitischen Familien," Sept. 1, 1845; "Verzeichniss der in der 1. Section von Cöln wohnenden Israeliten," Sept. 1846.

85. The city was divided into six sections after 1840.

86. On occupation and residence patterns, see Ayçoberry, "Histoire Sociale," 1: 291ff.

87. On a similar dynamic in late-nineteenth-century Vienna, see Rozenblit, pp. 71ff. Rozenblit argues that the residential concentration of Viennese Jews was deliberate.

88. On Hersch, see Toury, "Rheinischen Jahre," pp. 186, 193; statistics on the number of converts are cited in Müller, p. 82, Table 3.

89. Honigmann, "Jewish Conversion," p. 8; see also id., *Austritte*; and Lowenstein, *Berlin Jewish Community*, pp. 120–33.

90. Menes; Honigmann, "Jewish Conversion"; Hertz, "Seductive Conversion," and Lowenstein, *Berlin Jewish Community*, pp. 121–26.

91. Honigmann, "Jewish Conversion," p. 24.

92. Toury, *Soziale und Politische Geschichte*, p. 53, Table 29a.

93. Cologne population statistics may be found in Ayçoberry, "Histoire Sociale," 2: 106, Appendix 15; Catholic conversion statistics may be found in Becker-Jákli, p. 253, n. 10.

94. Becker-Jákli, p. 253, n. 10.

95. Conversion statistics for Germany are found in Toury, *Soziale und Politische Geschichte*, p. 52, Table 28.

96. See Hertz, "Seductive Conversion"; id., *Jewish High Society*; id., "Intermarriage"; id., "Women at the Edge"; and Lowenstein, *Berlin Jewish Community*, pp. 165–70.

97. Hertz, "Seductive Conversion," pp. 73, 66. Strictly speaking, there was no "intermarriage" in Prussia, because only same-faith partners could marry: hence the need for Jews to convert in order to marry Christians. (Sometimes, though rarely, conversions were to Judaism.)

98. Hertz, "Seductive Conversion," p. 71.

99. On the Oppenheim-Kusserow connections, see *HO*, vol. 35, "Aus dem Trauregister der evangelischen Kirchengemeinde zu St. Moritz in Halle," 1831, a twelve-page, typed, untitled, unsigned manuscript beginning "Ein Artikel," and a typed, one-page document, "Betr. Taufschein." See also the memoirs of Max von Oppenheim, *HO*, vol. 40, p. 7, who reports that a Kusserow daughter married David Hansemann (actually, it was Adolph, David's son; my thanks to Gabriele Teichmann for clarifying this). On social patterns of intermarried families, see Hertz, *Jewish High Society*, p. 66; and Lowenstein, *Berlin Jewish Community*, p. 129.

100. Almost half of the 107 Jewish students from the Rhineland and Westphalia who attended the University of Bonn between 1819 and 1848 studied medicine; see Herzig, "Andreas Gottschalk"; and id., "Politische Zielvorstellungen," p. 277. Gottschalk applied for (and was denied) a *Judenpatent* in 1831; see memo of the Royal Government, Interior Division, Feb. 8, 1831. It is not clear why he applied for the patent, which was needed to operate a legally recognized business, enforce business contracts, or establish a "reputation" in the business world. Gottschalk appeared on the synagogue tax list as late as 1844. See *HASK*, Oberbürgermeisteramt, 400, II-4-D-1, list dated Jan. 30, 1844.

101. Herzig, "Andreas Gottschalk," p. 178. On Gottschalk's political career, see also Dowe; Ayçoberry, "Histoire Sociale," 1: 404–9, 412, 419, 427, 433–34, 445–46, 451–52; and Gothein, pp. 477–83.

102. The "Jews" referred to here are male; female Jews, like female non-Jews, were barred from educational and professional opportunities by gender discrimination. On the legal disabilities of Prussian Jews, see Freund; Horst Fischer; Hamburger, *Juden in öffentlichen*; Brammer; and Richarz, *Der Eintritt*. See also the summaries in Kastner, 1: 20ff.; Kampe and Schmiedebach; and Meyer, *Origins*, pp. 178–79. The complaint about being barred from jury service was expressed in the 1841 Oppenheim petition to Frederick William.

103. See Toury, *Soziale und Politische Geschichte*, pp. 52ff.; Kisch, *Judentaufen*; Reissner, "Rebellious Dilemma"; Sterling, "Jewish Reactions"; C. Cohen; and Lowenstein, *Berlin Jewish Community*, p. 126. I would note in this context the eventual conversion of Jacob (later Jacques) Offenbach, son of the cantor of the Cologne synagogue, whose conversion was preceded by thorough acculturation, abetted by his father. The boy was taught European music and at the age of eleven taken along with two siblings to entertain in various Cologne pubs; see Kober, *Cologne*, pp. 309–10. No cantor behaving this way would have retained his position in a premodern community.

104. Treue, "Einige Kapitel," p. 142. See also id., "Dagobert Oppenheim." On Dagobert's conversion to Protestantism, specifically, see *HO*, vol. 40, memoir of Max von Oppenheim, p. 6. On the extremely close association between legal training and state service in Prussia, see John. Technically, lawyers in the Rhineland could have purely private practices but this would not hold much potential.

105. Letter of Jan. 24, 1838.

106. On Hess, see Berlin, pp. 213–51; Wistrich, pp. 35–44; Avineri, *Making of Modern Zionism*, pp. 36–46; id., *Moses Hess*; Frankel, pp. 6–28; and Rotenstreich, *Jews and German Philosophy*.

107. Hess, pp. 64–65.

108. Avineri, *Moses Hess*, p. 10.

109. Ibid.; and Hirsch, "Moses Hess und Köln," p. 166. Avineri's description of this group is based on a partial publication of Hess's diary by Mönke.

110. Avineri, *Moses Hess*, pp. 11–12.

111. Cf. Lowenstein, "Rural Community," especially p. 235.

112. Cited by Hirsch, "Moses Hess und Köln," p. 174, n. 15.

113. See Avineri, *Moses Hess*, pp. 5–6; and Baeck. On generational conflict in this era, see Sterling, "Jewish Reactions," p. 106.

114. Herzig, "Politische Zielvorstellungen"; Toury, *Politischen Orientierungen*, p. 53, n. 29; Liebeschutz, "German Radicalism"; and Figes.

115. Kober, *Cologne*, pp. 203–4; first names are taken from *Judenpatent* and synagogue tax records. Morel and Ochse-Stern sat on the synagogue executive board in the late 1840's; see Brisch, 2: 155. Cohn, Hellwitz, and Morel were on a government list of the city's wealthiest Jews, eligible to serve as Consistory notables; see *HASK*, Oberbürgermeisteramt, 400, II-4-B-15, memo of Mar. 26, 1846. On the large number of Jews as guarantors, shareholders, editorial staff, and contributors to the paper, see Klutentreter, pp. 20–21.

116. Cited in Gothein, p. 465, who makes his own anti-Jewish characterization of Moses Hess.

117. Avineri, "Marx and Jewish Emancipation," p. 448. See also Prinz, "New Perspectives"; Stepelevich, p. 155; Rotenstreich, "For and Against Emancipation"; Berlin, pp. 252–86, especially pp. 276ff.

118. See Hirsch, "Karl Marx und die Bittschriften," p. 231; id., *Marx und Moses*, p. 98; and J. Carlebach, especially p. 28. The *Rheinische Zeitung* published its pro-emancipation pieces between March and August of 1842; Marx became editor only in October of that year. Cf. Silberner, p. 17; Hirsch, *Marx und Moses*, p. 98; id., "Karl Marx und die Bittschriften," p. 230.

119. Marx, pp. 1–40.

120. Quoted in Silberner, p. 18, and Hirsch, *Marx und Moses*, p. 100. We do not know the identity of the "leader" referred to.

121. Toury, *Politischen Orientierungen*, pp. 16ff., especially p. 27. See also Holeczek, "Jews and the German Liberals," pp. 77–91.

122. Toury, *Politischen Orientierungen*, pp. 47ff.; and Kober, "Jews in the Revolution."

123. Toury, *Politischen Orientierungen*, p. 98.

124. Ibid., p. 53, n. 29; and Kober, "Jews in the Revolution," pp. 152–53.

125. Gothein, p. 507. The paper's announcement is dated Oct. 26, 1846. The election took place on Dec. 19; see Kober, *Cologne*, p. 304.

126. See Toury, *Politischen Orientierungen*, pp. 16, 17; and F. Stern, *Gold and Iron*, p. 473.

127. Treue, "Einige Kapitel," p. 144.

128. Letter cited in Hansen, ed., *Rheinische Briefe*, 2: 210–11. Dagobert implored Mevissen to keep news of the *Landtag* coming to the group "so that we can see to further dissemination . . . [of it]."

129. On the *Gemeindeordnung*, see Ayçoberry, "Histoire Sociale," 1: 296ff.; Gothein, pp. 236–39; Heffter, pp. 227–29; and Karl-Georg Faber, "Die Kommunale," pp. 132–51.

130. Ayçoberry, "Histoire Sociale," 1: 296–300.

131. Treue, "Abraham Oppenheim," p. 29. The record of City Council sessions shows Abraham Oppenheim present at several Council meetings (Dec. 29, 1846; Apr. 23, 1847). The roll call for the Council meeting of Apr. 30, 1847 notes that Oppenheim was "excused" (*entschuldigt*); in fact, he had left for Berlin to participate in the lobbying campaign against the king's proposed Jewry law.

132. Toury, *Soziale und Politische Geschichte*, pp. 125–26.

133. Ibid., 121–22.

134. On popular outbreaks against the Jews during the revolution, see Toury, *Turmoil and Confusion*; Rürup, "European Revolutions of 1848"; and Sterling, *Judenhass*, pp. 132ff.

135. On the development of anti-Jewish expression in the workers' movement in Cologne, see Herzig, "Andreas Gottschalk," and the literature cited there. On Marx in Cologne during the revolution and the power struggle with Gottschalk, see G. Becker. On the artisan antisemitism, see Volkov, *Rise of Popular Antimodernism in Germany*, pp. 215–36.

136. See J. Katz, *Out of the Ghetto*, p. 44. On "Junge Deutschland" in Cologne, see Hansen, ed., *Rheinische Briefe*, 1: 280, 293–94, n. 2, 295; and id., *Gustav von Mevissen* 1: 245, 257ff.

137. Hansen, ed., *Rheinische Briefe*, 1: 296–305, 311, 315–16, 317, 319, 321–24, 329–32, 347–49; 2: 271–72, 292, 329–31.

138. Letter of Feb. 16, 1845, to his brother-in-law, cited in ibid., 1: 756.

139. On the Oppenheims' purchase of rural property in Klettenberg in 1839 and Türmchen in 1845, as well as earlier purchases, see transcriptions of notarial acts in *HO*, vol. 45.

140. Ayçoberry, "Histoire Sociale," 1: 226–27.

141. On Oppenheim support for the Cathedral building project, see below, Chapter 7 and n. 90 there; van Eyll, *In Kölner Adressbüchern*, pp. 68–70; and Treue, "Einige Kapitel," pp. 144. See also Ayçoberry, "Histoire Sociale," 1: 393–95.

142. Cf. Eichholtz, p. 21, n. 32.

143. Report of the executive board of the Jewish community to Mayor Steinberger, May 18, 1843, *HASK*, Oberbürgermeisteramt, 400, II-4-B-8. A slightly different version of this document appears in Weyden, pp. 288–89, and in Brisch, 2: 153–55.

144. On the Reform rabbinical conferences of the 1840's, see Philipson; and

Meyer, *Response to Modernity*. In 1843, the community of Breslau was wracked over the Geiger-Tiktin controversy (see below) while disputes over the reissuance of a reformed prayerbook were raging in Hamburg. See also Lowenstein, "The 1840s."

145. On the rabbis Auerbach, see Kober, *Cologne*, pp. 211–14, 225–26; A. Carlebach, pp. 11–12; and below, Chapter 7. Material on the friction between Cologne's community leadership and Rabbi Aron Auerbach in 1843 is in *SA*, Bonn, PR 4881.

146. This according to the version reported in Weyden, p. 289, and Brisch, 2: 154, which seems to be an earlier draft of the document. The document extant in the city archives leaves out the commentary, stating only that "according to Article 23 of the regulation, collection, however, can be compulsory." This document has a margin notation in an official hand saying that Herr Cohen, a member of the synagogue executive and one of the document's signatories, had stated that the power to coerce contributions was both desirable and granted in other jurisdictions.

147. Kober, *Cologne*, pp. 213–14.

148. On the distinction between "old" and "modern" rabbis, which began to emerge only in the 1840's, see Schorsch, "Emancipation"; Lowenstein, "The 1840s"; and M. Gruenwald. The rabbinical student, Isaacsohn, then studying in Bonn (presumably at the university), eventually became *Ober-Rabbiner* in Rotterdam; see Brisch, 2: 154.

149. Kober, *Cologne*, p. 214.

150. See Schorsch, "Emancipation," p. 245, Appendix 6. Not surprisingly, Auerbach did not attend the Reform rabbinical conferences of the 1840's. See Lowenstein, "The 1840s," p. 276; and Kober, *Cologne*, p. 252.

151. This would account for the "consistorial" (presumably, Rabbi Auerbach's) opposition to the young Bible preacher; see Kober, *Cologne*, p. 262. Such a man was objectionable not for religious or ideological but professional reasons. As Schorsch, "Emancipation," p. 228, notes, attempts in German Jewish communities to introduce "preachers" into congregations already served by rabbis was "a manoeuvre to outflank the . . . rabbinate."

152. The writers may also have been directing their remarks to their audience. By the 1840's, the Prussian Minister of Religion had decided that Judaism would wither more quickly if it did not appropriate Christian religious forms (and respectability); rabbis, for instance, were forbidden to don pastor's robes. See Schorsch, "Emancipation," pp. 236–37.

153. See Brandenburg; Kober, *Cologne*, pp. 261–63, n. 93; and the 1843 report of the synagogue executive board, *HASK*, Oberbürgermeisteramt, 400, II-4-B-8. See also *HASK*, Oberbürgermeisteramt, 402-C-161, regarding the Jewish teachers.

154. See Toury, *Soziale und Politische Geschichte*, p. 169, Table 54; data and comments on Cologne are in Brandenburg, pp. 4, 6. For a comprehensive study of Jewish educational policy in Bavaria during the era of emancipation, see Prestel.

155. The remaining hours were spent on arithmetic (six per week), geography (one), and German history (one).

156. The remaining hours were devoted to drawing and natural history (one each) and geography (two). Girls, like boys, had 39 weekly classroom hours. By 1847, boys had an after-hours option of French language study. Kober, *Cologne*, p. 382, n. 93.

157. Even schools for girls run by the *maskilim*, the "enlighteners," who made reform of Jewish education and schools for girls a priority, taught relatively little Hebrew and Bible, because girls were assumed to need little formal Jewish knowledge. On this and education for girls in this era, see Eliav, pp. 271–79; on teaching Jewish girls French, see ibid., pp. 169, 271ff.; *Memoirs of Glückel of Hameln*, pp. 11–12.

158. *Unterthänigste Immediat-Eingabe*, Jan. 5, 1841.

159. Kastner, 1: 44. Dagobert Oppenheim was very active on behalf of Jewish emancipation well after his conversion, lobbying at the Eighth Rhenish Diet, where he was involved in the petition campaign, for instance: see *HO*, vol. 104; and Kastner, 1: 59. It is unclear why the Oppenheims would have anguished about Dagobert's conversion and not, apparently, about Eve's, especially since, according to the memoirs of one of Simon's grandchildren, Simon Oppenheim and his (Jewish) wife raised their five children without religion so that they might become Christians, leaving the choice of church to them "when they reached majority or married [Christians]"; *HO*, vol. 40, pp. 12, 21. Perhaps the Oppenheims viewed the conversion of a woman in order to improve social standing as acceptable, or even desirable, but experienced the need for a man to convert in order to pursue his profession as dishonorable and degrading.

The Oppenheims circulated the *Immediat-Eingabe* to other government officials (at least one of whom was sympathetic), as well as to business associates; see *HO*, vol. 104, especially letters from Geheime Postrat Schmuckler of Dec. 1840 and Aug. 1842.

160. Cited in the printed manuscript of the Oppenheim petition.

161. See Brisch, 2: 155–56.

162. See Mevissen's letter of Apr. 22 and 26, 1847, cited in Hansen, *Gustav von Mevissen*, 2: 245–46; and Brisch, 2: 155–56.

163. Brisch, 2: 155–56. See also Robert Liberles, "Was There a Jewish Movement." On the organized reaction of Prussian Jewry to the 1847 law, see Horst Fischer, pp. 158ff., who notes on page 160 a Jewish movement in the Rhineland and Westphalia against an 1841 cabinet order that was the precursor of the 1847 law; the movement was supported by "the large communities of the Rhine Province in Krefeld, Koblenz, Cologne, Düsseldorf, Cleves."

164. Rürup, "Jewish Emancipation," p. 84.

Chapter Seven

1. Letter of the *Vorsteher* and *Repräsentanten* of the Synagogue Community of Cologne to *Oberpräsident* von Kleist-Retzow, June 14, 1852, *HSTA-D-K*, Königliche Regierung zu Köln, II Abteilung, Kirchenwesen, Specialia, 3689.

2. On the settlement patterns of nineteenth-century German Jewry, see Toury, *Soziale und Politische Geschichte*, pp. 9ff.; Schofer, "Emancipation," pp. 63–89; Lowenstein, "Pace of Modernisation"; and id., "Rural Community."

3. These statistics are taken from Keyser, ed., *Rheinisches Städtebuch*, p. 41; and id., *Städtebuch Rheinland-Pfalz und Saarland*, p. 210.

4. On economic developments in Cologne during these years, see Gothein, pp. 576–674; and Ayçoberry, "Histoire Sociale," 2: 453–556.

5. Characterization by Rürup, "Tortuous and Thorny Path," p. 26. The text of the law is in Freund, 2: 501–20.

6. On forces working against assimilation in German Jewry, see Volkov, "Dynamics of Dissimilation." Cf. on French Jewry, Graetz.

7. Kober, *Cologne*, pp. 214ff.

8. *Soziale und Politische Geschichte*, p. 151; also id., "Revolution von 1848."

9. See Toury's categorization of the post-1848 policies of the German states, *Soziale und Politische Geschichte*, p. 307. As he says, only five of the German states (Prussia not among them), with a combined population of 12,000 Jews, upheld the emancipation granted during the 1848 revolution.

10. See Baron, "Aspects," p. 127.

11. See Rürup, "Tortuous and Thorny Path"; Lamberti, "Prussian Government"; Wilhelm; Schorsch, "Emancipation"; and Auerbach.

12. See Schorsch, *Jewish Reactions*, pp. 2–5.

13. Schorsch, "Emancipation," pp. 236ff.; and Auerbach as paraphrased in Schorsch, *Jewish Reactions*, p. 75.

14. See Liberles, "Emancipation," pp. 52, 63.

15. Schorsch, "Emancipation," p. 237; cf. Liberles, *Religious Conflict*, pp. 76ff.; and Lowenstein, "The 1840s," p. 258. Cf. for Bavaria, Gehring-Münzel, p. 307.

16. See Schorsch, *Jewish Reactions*, pp. 17ff., 118ff.

17. The phrase is from Schorsch, "Emancipation," p. 237.

18. See Toury, "Revolution von 1848"; and id., *Soziale und Politische Geschichte*, pp. 119ff.

19. Letter of the *Oberpräsident* of the Rhine Province to the Israelite Consistories of Trier, Bonn, and Krefeld of June 2, 1848; *SA, PR* 59.

20. Cited in Toury, "Revolution von 1848," p. 374.

21. See Baron, "Aspects," pp. 135ff.; and Toury, *Soziale und Politische Geschichte*, pp. 237ff.

22. Baron, "Aspects," p. 139.

23. Toury, *Soziale und Politische Geschichte*, p. 236.

24. The *Zirkulär* appears in the *AZdJ*, no. 47, Nov. 18, 1850.

25. Private correspondence dated Mar. 3, 1851, in *AZdJ*, no. 15, Mar. 10, 1851.

26. They were, in addition to Cologne, Aachen, Trier, Kreuznach, Essen, Siegburg, Deutz, Mülheim, Remagen, Frechen, Bergheim, Soest, Paderborn, and Neukirchen.

27. Hahn, pp. 107–11.

28. Reported in a private communication of Feb. 5, 1850, to *AZdJ*, no. 8, Feb. 17, 1850.

29. Communication of June 26, 1851, reproduced in *AZdJ*, no. 35, Aug. 25, 1851.

30. In addition to the articles cited, see those dated Nov. 18, 1850; Dec. 9, 1850; Feb. 17, 24, 1851; Mar. 10, 1851; Aug. 25, 1851.

31. No. 47, Nov. 18, 1850.

32. See the Feb. 17, 1850, petition of the synagogue executive to the Ministry of the Interior and the Ministry of Religious, Educational, and Health Affairs for corporate rights *in vermögensrechtlicher Beziehung*, and the letter of Police Director

Geiger to the Royal Government, Division of the Interior, supporting the request, May 17, 1850, in *HSTA-D-K*, Königliche Regierung zu Köln, II Abteilung, Kirchenwesen, Specialia, 3689. See also the paraphrase of a government report of Mar. 19, 1851, in Brisch, 2: 157–58.

33. Cologne shared in a growing predicament for many German Jewish communities at this time. As Baron notes, an influx of immigrants into urban communities made it essential "for the larger communities to find equitable means of absorbing new members and imposing on them their due share of communal burdens." See "Aspects," p. 48.

34. See the letter of *Vorsteher* of Feb. 17, 1850, in *HSTA-D-K*, Königliche Regierung zu Köln, II Abteilung, Kirchenwesen, Specialia, 3689.

35. Decree of the Minister of the Interior to the Royal Government in Cologne of July 22, 1850, cited by Hahn, p. 111, n. 1; and paraphrased in detail by Kober, *Cologne*, pp. 215–16.

36. According to the petition of the synagogue administration to the *Oberpräsident* of June 14, 1852, the community appointed a commission to draft a constitution "immediately" after promulgation of the 1847 law, and "this [body] went about its work without delay." See letter cited in note 1, above.

37. The Minister's letter is dated July 22, 1850; the communal assembly first met on Aug. 4, 1850, according to the *Statuten der Israelitischen Religions-Gemeinde zu Köln*, 1850, *HSTA-D-K*, Königliche Regierung zu Köln, II Abteilung, Kirchenwesen, Specialia, 3689.

38. See the letter of the synagogue administration to the *Oberpräsident* of June 14, 1852, cited in note 1, above.

39. Kober, *Cologne*, p. 219.

40. See Toury, *Soziale und Politische Geschichte*, pp. 237ff.; id., "Revolution von 1848"; and Schorsch, "Emancipation," pp. 228ff. Cf. for French Jewry, Albert, pp. 283ff.

41. Letter of the *Vorsteher*, cited in note 1, above.

42. Community leaders had reason to fear troublemaking by the rabbi. Two communities notably absent from the Congress of the Cities were Bonn and Krefeld, both consistorial seats. Krefeld's Consistory and its *Oberrabbiner* Bodenheimer strongly opposed the Cologne initiative. Having urged communities in their jurisdiction not to sign the petition to the government that Cologne's executive had circulated, they also petitioned the government against it. The reason for the opposition is obvious. In the words of a "private correspondent" from Berlin to the *AZdJ*, "We know that in the Rhine Province . . . a hierarchical body, the shadow of a previous age, the Consistory of Krefeld, works against [Cologne's request of a general grant of corporate rights to Prussian communities]. Why? Because it still wants to preserve its pretend existence [*Scheinexistenz*]. . . . No matter. Since this Consistory has no legal basis anymore, sooner or later people will realize even more than now that it just—exists in illusion." *AZdJ*, no. 9, Feb. 24, 1851, p. 101. See also, in the same issue, pp. 100, 124–25.

Not all rabbis opposed Cologne's initiative. The *Oberrabbiner* of Saar responded favorably, circulating a letter of support in his region, saying he considered it his "holy duty" to urge communities to participate in the conference. Failure to do so would be a "great sin against the holy spirit of our religion. It is time to act for the sake of God. Now is the most important time to do our outmost for God and our holy religion in order to stave off the threatening decay of our religion [*Kultus*] and the total dissolution of our communities." Rabbi Kahn also suggested means by which the best men of each region could be elected and the costs of the journey to Cologne be defrayed. Private correspondence from the Saar dated Nov. 25, 1850, *AZdJ*, vol. 14, no. 50, Dec. 9, 1850.

43. There is no basis in the extant documents for Alexander Carlebach's portrayal of Auerbach's stance as religious orthodoxy versus reforming trends; see *Adass Yeshurun*, pp. 11–12.

44. There is only apparent similarity between this and the proposed compromise several years earlier in Breslau, which would have made the traditional, veteran rabbi of the community responsible for ritual functions and charged the new preacher, Reform leader Abraham Geiger, with spiritual guidance. There, the preacher would in reality be the rabbi, discharging all the functions the synagogue board chose to delegate to him.

Synagogue leaders in Cologne did not needlessly antagonize Auerbach; they continued to contribute to his salary and customary "emoluments," for instance, rejecting a call a few years earlier from "several large communities to join in open resistance against" him. There was communal strife around Auerbach in his home community of Bonn as well as in the 1840's and 1870's; see *SA*, PR 4881 and 69.

45. A. Carlebach, *Adass Yeshurun*, p. 12.

46. See Kober, *Cologne*, pp. 217–23, 239–41; and *HO*, vol. 54, 35 (eulogy for Abraham Oppenheim, Oct. 10, 1878, by Dr. Frank, then rabbi of Cologne).

47. See Schwarz's letter to the city *Schulkommission*, Nov. 4, 1857; in *HASK*, Oberbürgermeisteramt, 400, 40-44-112.

48. Kober, *Cologne*, p. 265; A. Carlebach, *Adass Yeshurun*, p. 13; see also Schwarz, *Glaube und Pflicht*. In contrast to earlier changes, the apparent desire of some members for Schwarz to participate in the Leipzig synod and for an organ in the synagogue do represent a trend toward Reform. It is significant, however, that neither proposal came to pass. Cologne's rabbi and synagogue remained Orthodox, provisions against ritual change written into its constitutions of 1864 and 1887. Writing in 1867/68, Schwarz insisted that services were carried out "in the strictly prescribed ritual manner [Der Gottesdienst wird . . . in streng rituelle Weise vollzogen]"; see Schwarz, "Skizzen," p. 61. Indeed, Schwarz's words were published in *Jeschurun*, the journal of neo-Orthodox leader Samson Raphael Hirsch. *Jeschurun* surely would not have published an article by a rabbi whose Orthodox credentials it felt were compromised.

Still, according to Alexander Carlebach, some 30 "strictly Orthodox" members of the synagogue opposed to abolition of *Kol Nidre* and *piyyutim* broke away and formed their own prayer group in 1863; see A. Carlebach, *Adass Yeshurun*, pp. 13–14. Carlebach clearly models his portrayal of this group (and of the group that supported Rabbi Auerbach in the early 1850's) on hagiographical depictions of the emergence of secessionist Orthodoxy in Frankfurt am Main, where S. R. Hirsch established his base. On the myth of the heroic Orthodox minority in Frankfurt, see Liberles, *Religious Conflict*. Unfortunately, the original sources for reformist trends and secessionist Orthodoxy in Cologne are missing. Rabbi Schwarz, "Skizzen," says nothing about reformist strivings or a right-wing secession, a notable omission. We have only Carlebach's partisan account.

49. Kober, *Cologne*, p. 223.

50. Schulte, *Dokumentation zur Geschichte*, p. 13; and Ernst Simons, pp. 30, 28.

51. Auerbach, pp. 252–55; and Rürup, "Tortuous and Thorny Path," p. 30.

52. Schorsch, "Emancipation," pp. 234ff.; and Lamberti, pp. 6, 8.

53. *HASK*, Oberbürgermeisteramt, 400, 40-44-112.

54. Brisch, 2: 161; and Brandenberg, pp. 9ff.

55. Provisions on the education of Jewish children are in paragraphs 60–67. The establishment of special Jewish schools did not necessarily contradict the state's aim of fostering collective Jewish disappearance, since the curricular content of "public schools" was subject to outside control, and limits could thus be set to the number of hours and the content of religious instruction (Bible rather than Talmud, for example). German was the mandated language of instruction, according to paragraph 67 of the law, so the schools would at least function as agents of acculturation. De facto, of course, separate schooling powerfully reinforces minority group identity.

56. Brandenberg, p. 7; and Brisch, 2: 161.

57. Brandenberg, p. 7. Brandenberg supported the Jewish case and the principle of equal treatment in educational subsidies to the various denominations.

58. Assembly sessions of Feb. 17, 1853; May 31, 1860; May 22, 1862 (recorded in two parts); Jan. 5, 1865; Nov. 7, 1867; Dec. 5, 1867; Mar. 5, 1868; Oct. 1, 22, 1868; and Sept. 24, 1868. Relevant information is also found in the "Budget der Elementarschulen für 1867." Records of the Municipal Assembly's deliberations are also in *Verhandlungen des Gemeinderaths der Stadt Köln.*

The Jews won on another, albeit less loaded, issue: getting city funding for a Jewish cemetery. Although some of the same kinds of objections were raised to this — contesting the need or the right of Jews to a separate cemetery, particularly at city expense — the Municipal Assembly granted the community's request fairly quickly in 1860. The party and personality alignments on this issue were the same as on the Jewish school question. See assembly sessions of May 31 and June 8, 1860, in *Verhandlungen*. Difficulties establishing an actual site were created by opposition of authorities in charge of city fortifications; see Schwarz, "Skizzen," p. 61.

59. Padtberg, *Rheinischer Liberalismus in Köln*; see also Sperber, pp. 99–100. The following relies for context on Gothein, pp. 497–520; Ayçoberry, "Histoire Sociale," 2: 695ff.; and Padtberg, *Rheinischer Liberalismus in Köln*, especially pp. 82–159, 265–68. None of these works mentions the two-decade-long wrangling in the assembly over funding the Jewish school, which even Padtberg does not see as an issue for liberalism in the city.

60. These characterizations are by Gothein, p. 506. On the rise of the Catholics as an opposition party in the assembly, see Padtberg, *Rheinischer Liberalismus in Köln*, pp. 155–56.

61. On religious developments in Cologne during these years, see Gothein, pp. 519ff.; and Ayçoberry, "Histoire Sociale," 2: 707ff. For broader background on the Rhenish Catholic revival of these years, see Sperber. In 1857, a Jew, Dr.

M. Joseph Goldschmidt, opened a private secondary school and advertised in the *Kölnische Zeitung* for enrollment. The city School Commission (on which Dr. Broix, a cleric and a member of the Municipal Assembly, sat) and the "politically intransigent, ultramontanist" (in Sperber's characterization, p. 97) Archbishop Geissel (through his General-Vicariat) strongly challenged the right of a Jew to run an educational institution in which Christian children would be educated, even if the school offered separate Protestant and Catholic religious instruction by qualified religious instructors, as this one did. Although local Prussian authorities supported Goldschmidt and were annoyed by the machinations of the School Commission, Berlin, at the latter's prompting, ruled against Goldschmidt in 1863. He was given permission to continue running the school as a private institution for Jewish children only, but this never materialized. *HASK*, Oberbürgermeisteramt, 403, Abteilung 12, Unterabteilung 1, no. 745.

62. Session of May 22, 1862, Schluss. Toward the end of the period studied here, the assembly did vote in favor of making city elementary schools nondenominational. The government rejected the proposal, but the attempt indicates the seriousness of the secular threat to Catholic interests. See Kober, *Cologne*, p. 266.

63. Thus as Sperber, p. 125, notes, in the 1860's, Rhenish Catholic leaders were even willing to make political deals with Progressives on the provincial level in return for Progressive support of Catholic opposition to three policies that mortified the church: secular education, civil marriage, and a "small German" approach to German unification (that is, one that would leave Catholic Austria out of a unified Germany, which would make Germany predominantly Protestant). Catholic fear of Progressive opposition to confessional education, and of secular education, is seen in the following lament in a Catholic paper in 1861: "If the program of the [Progressive] party is ever carried out . . . if the school is separated from the church and turned into a state institution in which Christians, Jews and sectarians are taught and religious education [is] excluded . . . then we will be on the edge of that abyss against which the watchman on the throne of Peter has warned us time and again." Cited in Sperber, p. 151.

64. Session of May 22, 1862, Schluss.

65. Session of May 22, 1862.

66. See his response to the prejudiced remarks of *Advocat* Böcker against the Jewish claim in the May 22, 1862, session, in which Claessen restricts himself to legal technicalities and never addresses, much less challenges, Böcker's Judeophobia.

67. Session of May 22, 1862.

68. The tax figures were presented in the session of Nov. 7, 1867. Jews, 2.2 percent of the population, paid a more nearly proportionate 3 percent (1,065 of 35,703 taler) of the land and building tax, a sign that Jewish wealth was concentrated in movable rather than real goods.

69. Assemblyman Schneider, "Budget," *Verhandlungen*.

70. Assemblyman Liessin, session of Feb. 17, 1853.

71. Session of May 22, 1862.

72. See the calculations in the session of Nov. 7, 1867, and the comments of Assemblyman Kohlhaas in "Budget," *Verhandlungen*.

73. It is also possible that the more traditional parents sent their children to

private institutions that were segregated by sex, rather than to the Jewish school where, for cost and space, not ideological reasons, they were not. See Assemblyman Hospelt's remarks, session of Dec. 5, 1867. In 1881, after school enrollment had increased sufficiently to warrant it, sex-segregated instruction was instituted. See Kober, *Cologne*, p. 369.

74. Kober, *Cologne*, p. 382, n. 95.

75. See, for example, the remarks of Assemblyman Kohlhaas, "Budget," *Verhandlungen*, and the remarks of Classen supporting the Jewish request, session of Dec. 5, 1867.

76. See sessions of Mar. 5, 1868, and Oct. 22, 1868.

77. See Brandenberg, pp. 10ff.; and Kober, *Cologne*, p. 382, n. 95.

78. Assemblyman Fischer, in session of Dec. 5, 1867.

79. Session of Dec. 5, 1867.

80. A sentiment Baudri strongly seconded; see session of Dec. 6, 1867.

81. Session of Dec. 5, 1867. The issue of local control of the Jewish question was also raised briefly at this session after Assemblyman Mühlens, hostile to Jewish claims, had suggested that if the Jews were not satisfied with the city subsidy they should appeal to Berlin. Assemblyman Schneider, favorable to the Jews, objected. The Municipal Assembly was quite capable of deciding the issue itself, he said, and "it would be a wretched consolation to refer anyone to the higher authorities when one is in the position himself to arrive at the correct decision."

82. Assemblyman Hospelt, session of Dec. 5, 1867. Hospelt felt strongly that the Jewish claim was justified, which was all the more reason to resolve the seemingly endless debate over it.

83. Assemblyman Fischer, ibid.

84. Statistic on the number subsidized in Brandenberg, pp. 6, 8–9; the enrollment statistic is in Schwarz, "Skizzen," p. 60.

85. Kober, *Cologne*, p. 264.

86. Brandenberg, p. 13; and Kober, *Cologne*, p. 269. By 1889, Jewish parents overwhelmingly preferred the Jewish elementary school to others: 398 Jewish children attended it, while 102 attended other elementary schools. Kober, *Cologne*, p. 383, n. 102.

87. This is in sharp contrast to the situation in Alsace, where the leaders of the Jewish community sought to use the Guizot Law of 1833, which "facilitated establishment of [Jewish] primary schools by mandating local government subsidies for salaries" in order "to [seek] the acculturation of the Jews"; see Hyman, *Emancipation of the Jews of Alsace*, p. 103. On the curriculum reform in Cologne, see Kober, *Cologne*, pp. 267–69; and Brandenberg, pp. 8–13.

88. Kober, *Cologne*, pp. 275–76.

89. Surmised from Kober, *Cologne*, p. 230; the communal documents no longer exist.

90. On Cologne as an architectural center, see Ayçoberry, "Histoire Sociale," 1: 393.

91. Brisch, 2: 160; Weyden, p. 291; and Schwarz, "Skizzen," p. 60.

92. The Oppenheims contributed their own money to completion of the cathe-

dral and also helped raise money from others, hosting fund-raising events. Simon bequeathed money in several wills, pointedly saying each time that he was doing so "as a Jew [who had] always been one of the chief promoters" of the cathedral's completion. Abraham's widow, Simon and his wife, and Dagobert also dedicated windows in the cathedral in commemoration of Oppenheim family events. Nothing could better express how the cathedral had come to represent Cologne, or Germany, as opposed to just Catholicism — or the Oppenheims' stubborn pride in their Jewish identity, for all their distance from traditional Judaism. Details in *HO*, vol. 55; see also a letter of Abraham Oppenheim to Mevissen of Dec. 9, 1859, in *HO*, vol. 101b. That pride, and the fact that the Oppenheims viewed their success not just in personal but in Jewish terms, is clearly expressed in a letter Abraham Oppenheim wrote to Gerson Bleichröder, Bismarck's Jewish banker, in 1868, after Abraham had been ennobled by the Prussian King: "The King [has] been pleased to raise me to the ranks of the nobility. . . . It is a triumph for all of our faith." Cited in Treue, "Bankers Simon and Abraham Oppenheim," p. 69.

93. Brisch, 2: 160; Weyden, p. 291; Asaria, pp. 190–92; Kober, *Cologne*, pp. 240–41; and *Adressbuch*, 1863, p. 3, "Chronik für 1861."

94. Benjamin Disraeli's *Wondrous Tale of Alroy* appeared in 1833; in 1841, Eugène Delacroix depicted a Jewish wedding in a Middle Eastern setting. Cited in Wischnitzer, p. 200.

95. This thought is suggested by Krinsky, pp. 80–81. Cf. the analysis by Schorsch, "Myth of Sephardic Supremacy," pp. 56–57; however, I do not see any evidence, in original or secondary sources, of a desire in Cologne to emulate Sephardic culture.

96. Krinsky, pp. 78, 82.

97. Ayçoberry, "Histoire Sociale," 1: 394.

98. Wischnitzer, p. 201. On the sense that Moorish style was most appropriate for synagogues, see also Hammer-Schenck, 2: 251–301.

99. Krinsky, p. 84.

100. Ibid., p. 83. Hennelore Künzl argues the same point, noting that the synagogue built in Dresden in 1838–40 used Islamic style for the interior but not the exterior "because the Jewish community did not want an Oriental-looking building. . . . As the municipality of Dresden took an extremely obstructive attitude toward the . . . community and the construction of the building, they were not encouraged to build a synagogue with any unusual character. On the contrary: the building was to express the will to integration." The first Jewish architect to build a synagogue in Germany, in Leipzig, "was courageous enough to erect a building in an Islamic style" despite the "opposition of the municipality and the bad location of the piece of land the town sold the community"; Künzl, p. 74.

Thus it would seem that Toury missed an essential point in noting the marked increase in synagogue building in Germany after 1848 but attributing it to conspicuous compensation ("eine gewisse ostentative Betriebsamkeit") for the putative decline in any deeper commitment to Jewish communal life in those years; *Soziale und Politische Geschichte*, p. 151. Cf. the discussion in Gehring-Münzel, pp. 307, 309.

101. Kober, *Cologne*, p. 224.

Conclusion

1. Berlin, according to Steven M. Lowenstein, was a "new city," with "little of the entrenched urban patriciate so typical of the imperial free cities . . . with their proud traditions of independence and their unwillingness to accept 'new men.' In Berlin, almost everyone was new to the city. The elites were much more open to admitting new groups than the more established cities"; *Berlin Jewish Community*, p. 19. Jacob Toury has noted the significance for Jews of the emergence of new classes, often with a heavy immigrant composition; "Der Eintritt," p. 236.

2. The evidence from Cologne and the Rhineland would thus seem to contradict Shulamit Volkov's conclusion, drawn apparently from the situation elsewhere in Prussia, that "as the ghetto walls . . . were beginning to crumble, the primary target for *Annäherung* for Jews with ambition and talent was the *Bildungsbürgertum*. . . . The old *Stadtbürgertum* was traditionally closed to the Jews; the emerging commercial bourgeoisie was socially dependent on the aristocracy and its standards of entry were very stiff"; " 'Verbürgerlichung' of the Jews," p. 372.

3. George L. Mosse, in particular, has stressed this; *German Jews Beyond Judaism*. Elsewhere he writes that "Jewish emancipation was a cultural emancipation (its motto was 'culture first')"; "Deutsch-jüdische Bildungsbürgertum," p. 170. While stressing the indispensability of wealth to Jewish efforts for acceptance, Shulamit Volkov has also argued that wealth "was definitely not enough. . . . The only door that was not entirely closed to newcomers [to civil society], Jews included, was that which led to the *Bildungsbürgertum*"; " 'Verbürgerlichung' of the Jews," pp. 371, 372.

4. Presented for his services on behalf of Jewish emancipation in 1847. The goblet is in the Oppenheim archive, as is the "proclamation of thanks from the Consistories and Israelites of the Rhine Province" of July 1847, addressed to Oppenheim (129 of 531 signatures were from Cologne); *HO*, vol. 104.

5. On the twinned backlash against modernity and Jews in Germany, see F. Stern, *Politics of Cultural Despair*; id., *Failure of Illiberalism*, pp. 3–73; id., *Gold and Iron*; N. Cohen, *Warrant for Genocide*, pp. 23–24, 164–79; Volkov, "Popular Anti-Modernism"; id., "Social and Political Function"; and id., *Rise of Popular Anti-modernism*. On the economic and cultural crisis of the 1870's, see Rosenberg, *Grosse Depression*. Paula Hyman, *Emancipation of the Jews of Alsace*, p. 27, notes that the climate for bourgeois French Jews, too, improved markedly in the commercial and industrial expansion of the middle decades of the century.

6. Hyman, *Emancipation of the Jews of Alsace*, pp. 93–94; for the same situation in Germany, see Lowenstein, "Rural Community"; and id., "Pace of Modernisation."

7. I agree with Hyman, who calls for greater study of the "role of the state throughout Europe in the adaptation of the Jews to the conditions of modernity"; see *Emancipation of the Jews of Alsace*, p. 157.

8. Some of Ginzberg's (also known as Ahad Ha-Am) scathing assessments of emancipation and emancipated Jews may be found in English in Ginzberg, *Selected Essays of Ahad Ha-'Am*. Those of Hannah Arendt may be found in Arendt, especially pp. 23–25, 54. Those of Gerschom Scholem may be found in Scholem, *On Jews and Judaism*; and id., *From Berlin to Jerusalem*.

9. More case studies of German Jewish emancipation might well uncover other instances of such assertiveness and revise the image of German Jews as unable to organize even against antisemitism until the century's end. On organized German Jewish defense both of rights and Jewish identity from the 1890's on, see Schorsch, *Jewish Reactions*; and Lamberti, *Jewish Activism*.

10. Cited in Mendes-Flohr and Reinharz, eds., pp. 14–15.

11. Cited in Rürup, "Tortuous and Thorny Path," p. 33.

Bibliography

Archival Sources

Archives of the Jewish Theological Seminary of America, New York (JTSA)
  History Mic. 8600; Consistorial Correspondence, Box II, 1814.
Archives of the Leo Baeck Institute, New York (LBINY)
  Adolf Kober Collection, Boxes 2, 6, 7, 8, 9, 10, 11, 23, 24.
The Central Archives for the History of the Jewish People, Jerusalem (CAHJP)
  Nachlass Freund: RP2b, Geheime Staatsarchiv Ministerium des Innern, Rep. 77,
  XXX, No. 85, "Entwerfung einer allgemeine Judenordnung für die Preussischen
  Monarchie, 1822–1847," vol. 3, 25B.
France: Archives Nationales (ANF)
  F19-1840.
Hauptstaatsarchiv Düsseldorf (HSTA-D)
  Französische Abteilung, II Div., 1 Bureau, nos. 1788, 1789, 1790, 1791, 1792,
  1793, 1794, 1795, 1796, 1797, 1798, 1799 I, 1799 II, 1800 II, 1801 I.
Hauptstaatsarchiv Düsseldorf, Zweigarchiv Schloss Kalkum (HSTA-D-K)
  Acta der Immediat Justiz Kommission, no. 7.
  Oberpräsidium Köln, Abteilung 401, nos. 38, 44, 763, 764, 765, 781, 878, 916,
  1141, 1144, 1594.
  Königliche Regierung zu Köln, II Abteilung, Kirchenwesen, 7381, 7383, 7384;
  Specialia, 3688, 3689, 3690, 3691, 3692, 3693, 3695, 3696, 3697, 3698.
Hausarchiv Oppenheim, Cologne (HO)
  Vols. 2, 16–20, 23–27, 28–30, 35, 38, 40, 42–45, 47, 50–55, 58, 64–65a, 68, 70,
  72–74, 81–84, 92–95, 100–5, 117–20, 131a, b, 159a, b, 160–64, 182–88, 236, 276,
  277a, 278.
Historisches Archiv der Stadt Köln (HASK)
  Französische Verwaltung, 2466, 2467, 2468, 2469, 2470, 2471, 2472, 2473, 2474,
  2475, 2476, 2477, 2478, 2479, 2480, 2481, 2793, 4293, 4884, 4888, 4923.
  Oberbürgermeisteramt, 400, II-4-B-1, 2, 3, 5, 8, 13, 15, 17; II-4-C-1, vols. 1–3;
  II-4-D-1; II-13-C-10; II-16-1.
    40-44-112, 402-C-161, 403-XII.1.
    403, Abteilung 11, Caps 23, Band III; 12, Unterabteilung 1, nos. 636, 745.
    1023/C21.
    Pläne, 1–27.

1073, Nachlass, Gustav Mevissen
    Chroniken und Darstellungen, Fuchs, "Chronik der Stadt Köln, 1816–1854."
Staatsarchiv, Koblenz
    Bestand 403, nos. 935, 10219, 15227.
Stadtarchiv, Bonn (*SA*)
    PR 59, 62, 69, 1980, 1981, 1983, 3372, 4881, 4916, 4922, 5172.
Zentrales Staatsarchiv, Merseburg
    Acta Generalia des Justiz-Ministeriums, 2.5.1., no. 7 420.

Printed Primary Sources

Adress-Buch oder Verzeichniss der Einwohner der Stadt Cöln. 1822–73.
Amtsblatt der Königlichen Regierung zu Köln. 1818, 1820, 1824, 1830, 1846, 1850.
Beiträge zur Statistik der königlichen preussischen Rheinlande aus amtlichen Nachrichten zusammengestellt. Aachen, 1829.
Dohm, Christian Wilhelm. *Concerning the Amelioration of the Civil Status of the Jews*. Helen Lederer, trans. Cincinnati, Ohio, 1957.
Dorsch, Anton Josef. *Statistique du département de la Roer*. Cologne, 1804.
Haym, Rudolf. *Reden und Redner der ersten Vereinigten Preussischen Landtags*. Berlin, 1847.
Michaelis, Alfred, ed. *Die Rechtsverhältnisse der Juden in Preussen seit dem Beginne des 19. Jahrhunderts*. Berlin, 1910.
Mitteilungen des königlichen-preussischen Statistischen Büros in Berlin, vol. 2. Berlin, 1849.
Oppenheim, Abraham, and Simon Oppenheim. *Unterthänigste Immediat-Eingabe der zu Cöln wohnenden Banquiers Abraham und Simon Oppenheim die Rechtsverhältnisse der Juden in der Monarchie, insbesondere in den Rheinprovinzen betreffend*. January 5, 1841.
Recueil des Actes de la Préfecture du Département de la Roer. 1803–13.
Restorff, F. von. *Topographisch-Statistisch Beschreibung der Königlichen Preussischen Rheinprovinzen*. Berlin, 1830.
Rheinprovinz der preussischen Monarchie, Die. Düsseldorf, 1833.
Rönne, Ludwig von, and Heinrich Simon. *Die früheren and gegenwärtigen Verhältnisse der Juden in sämmtlichen Landesteilen des preussischen Staates*. Breslau, 1843.
Schwarz, Israel. *Glaube und Pflicht*. Cologne, 1864.
———. "Skizzen zu einer Geschichte der Juden in Köln." *Jeschurun* 13 (1866/67): 18–25; 14 (1867/68): 43–61.
Statistik und Hand-Adressbuch der Rheinprovinz für das Jahr 1842. Koblenz, 1842.
Tama, Diogene. *Transactions of the Parisian Sanhedrin*. F. D. Dirwan, trans. London, 1807.
Verhandlungen des Gemeinderaths der Stadt Köln (1846–69).
Verzeichniss der Meistbeerbten der Stadt Köln. 1849.
Vollständige Verhandlungen des ersten Vereinigten Landtages über die Emanzipationsfrage der Juden. Berlin, 1847.

Newspapers

Allgemeine Zeitung des Judentums (*AZdJ*). 1850, 1851.
Kölnische Zeitung. 1842–45.
Rheinische Zeitung. 1842.

Secondary Sources

"Abraham Freiherr von Oppenheim (1804–1878)." *Mitteilungsblatt der Industrie- und Handelskammer zu Köln 5*, no. 19 (Oct. 1, 1950): 297–300.
Albert, Phillis Cohen. *The Modernization of French Jewry*. Hanover, N.H., 1977.
Allen, William Sheridan. *The Nazi Seizure of Power: The Experience of a Single German Town, 1930–1935*. Chicago, 1965.
Altmann, Alexander. *Moses Mendelssohn: A Biographical Study*. Philadelphia, 1973.
Anchel, Robert. *Napoléon et les Juifs*. Paris, 1928.
Anderson, M. "The Study of Family Structure." In E. A. Wrigley, ed., *Nineteenth-Century Society: Essays in the Use of Quantitative Methods for the Study of Social Data*, pp. 47–81. Cambridge, Eng., 1972.
Arendt, Hannah. *The Origins of Totalitarianism*. 2nd ed. New York, 1958.
———. "Privileged Jews." *Jewish Social Studies* 8 (1946): 3–30.
Arnold, Hermann. *Von den Juden in der Pfalz*. Speyer, 1967.
Aronius, Julius. *Regesten zur Geschichte der Juden im frankischen und deutschen Reiche bis zum Jahre 1273*. 2nd ed. Hildesheim, 1970.
Artz, Frederick. *Revolution and Reaction, 1814–1837*. New York, 1943.
Asaria, Zvi. *Die Juden in Köln von den ältesten Zeiten bis zur Gegenwart*. Cologne, 1959.
Asmus, Helmut. "Die 'Rheinische Zeitung' und die Genesis des rheinpreussischen Bourgeoisliberalismus." In Helmut Bleiber, ed., *Bourgeoisie und Bürgerliche Umwalzung*, pp. 135–67. Berlin, 1977.
Aubin, H., et al. *Geschichte des Rheinlandes von der ältesten Zeit bis zur Gegenwart*. 2 vols. Essen an der Ruhr, 1922.
Auerbach, Leopold. *Das Judenthum und seine Bekenner in Preussen und in den anderen deutschen Bundesstaaten*. Berlin, 1890.
Avineri, Shlomo. *The Making of Modern Zionism: The Intellectual Origins of the Jewish State*. New York, 1981.
———. "Marx and Jewish Emancipation." *Journal of the History of Ideas* 25 (July–Sept., 1964): 445–50.
———. *Moses Hess: Prophet of Communism and Zionism*. New York and London, 1985.
Ayçoberry, Pierre. *Cologne entre Napoléon et Bismarck: la croissance d'une ville rhénane*. Paris, 1981.
———. "Histoire Sociale de la Ville de Cologne (1815–1875)." 2 vols. Ph.D. diss., Université de Paris I, 1977.
———. "Probleme der Sozialschichtung in Köln im Zeitalter der Frühindustrialisierung." In Wolfram Fischer, ed., *Wirtschafts- und Sozialgeschichtliche Probleme der Früheren Industrialisierung*, pp. 512–28. Berlin, 1968.

——. "Der Strukturwandel im Kölner Mittelstand, 1820–1850." *Geschichte und Gesellschaft* 1 (1975): 78–98.

Bachrach, Bernard. *Early Medieval Jewish Policy in Western Europe*. Minneapolis, Minn., 1977.

Baeck, Leo. "Excerpts from Baeck's Writings." *Leo Baeck Institute Yearbook* 2 (1957): 35–44.

Bär, Max. *Die Behördenverfassung der Rheinprovinz seit 1815*. Bonn, 1919.

Barkai, Avraham. "German-Jewish Migrations in the Nineteenth Century, 1830–1910." *Leo Baeck Institute Yearbook* 30 (1985): 301–18.

——. "The German Jews at the Start of Industrialisation — Structural Change and Mobility, 1835–1860." In Werner E. Mosse et al., eds., *Revolution and Evolution: 1848 in German-Jewish History*. Tübingen, 1981.

Baron, Salo. "Aspects of the Jewish Communal Crisis in 1848." *Jewish Social Studies*, 14 (April, 1952): 99–144.

——. "Civil versus Political Emancipation." In Siegfried Stein and Raphael Loewe, eds., *Studies in Jewish Religious and Intellectual History*, pp. 29–49. University, Ala., 1979.

——. "Ghetto and Emancipation." *Menorah Journal* 14, no. 6 (1928): 515–26.

——. "Medieval Nationalism and Jewish Serfdom." In Salo Baron, ed., *Essays in Ancient and Medieval Jewish History*, pp. 308–22. New Brunswick, N.J., 1972.

——. "Newer Approaches to Jewish Emancipation." *Diogenes* 29 (Spring 1960): 56–81.

——. "'Plenitude of Apostolic Powers' and Medieval Jewish Serfdom." In Salo Baron, ed., *Essays in Ancient and Medieval Jewish History*, pp. 284–307. New Brunswick, N.J., 1972.

——. *A Social and Religious History of the Jews*. 17 vols. New York, 1952–80.

Barthold, Erich. "Die Preussische Judenemanzipation und die öffentliche Meinung, 1824–1845." Diss., Westfälischen Wilhelms–Universität zu Münster, 1924.

Bauer, Bruno. *The Jewish Problem*. Helen Lederer, trans. Cincinnati, Ohio, 1958.

Bauer, Kurt. *Judenrecht in Köln bis zum Jahre 1424*. Cologne, 1964.

Bechtel, Heinrich. *Wirtschaftsgeschichte Deutschlands im 19. und 20. Jahrhundert*. Munich, 1956.

Becker, Gerhard. *Karl Marx und Friedrich Engels in Köln, 1848–1849*. East Berlin, 1963.

Becker-Jákli, Barbara. *Die Protestanten in Köln*. Cologne, 1983.

Becker-Jákli, Barbara, and Alwin Müller. "Zur Religionsgehörigkeit Kölner Unternehmer (1810 bis 1870)." In Klara van Eyll, ed., *Kölner Unternehmer und die Frühindustrialisierung im Rheinland und in Westfalen (1835–1871)*, pp. 217–31. Cologne, 1984.

Bennathan, Esra. "The German Jews at the Start of Industrialisation, A Comment." In Werner E. Mosse et al., eds., *Revolution and Evolution: 1848 in German-Jewish History*, pp. 151–56. Tübingen, 1981.

Ben-Sasson, H. H., ed. *A History of the Jewish People*. Cambridge, Mass., 1976.

Bergengrün, Alexander. *David Hansemann*. Berlin, 1901.

——. *Staatsminister August Freiherr von der Heydt*. Leipzig, 1908.

Bergman, Rudolf. *Geschichte des rheinischen Versicherungswesens bis zur Mitte des 19. Jahrhunderts*. Essen, 1928.

Berlin, Isaiah. *Against the Current: Essays in the History of Ideas*. London, 1979.

Biro, Sidney Seymour. *The German Policy of Revolutionary France: A Study in French Diplomacy During the War of the First Coalition, 1792–1797*. 2 vols. Cambridge, Mass., 1957.

Blackbourne, David, and Geoff Eley. *The Peculiarities of German History: Bourgeois Society and Politics in Nineteenth-Century Germany*. Oxford and New York, 1984.

Blackbourne, David, and Richard J. Evans. *The German Bourgeoisie: Essays on the Social History of the German Middle Class from the Late Eighteenth to the Early Twentieth Century*. London and New York, 1991.

Blau, Bruno, "Die Entwicklung der jüdischen Bevölkerung in Deutschland von 1800 bis 1945." Manuscript, 1950.

Bleiber, Helmut. *Bourgeoisie und bürgerliche Umwalzung in Deutschland, 1789–1871*. Berlin, 1977.

Bohnke-Kollwitz, Jutta, Willehad Paul Eckert, et al., eds. *Köln und das rheinische Judentum*. Cologne, 1984.

Bonn, Ursula. "Einblicke in die Geschichte der Juden in Deutschland vom 13. bis 19. Jahrhundert." In *Juden in Deutschland: Zur Geschichte einer Hoffnung*, pp. 51–68. Berlin, 1980.

Brammer, Annegret H. *Judenpolitik und Judengesetzgebung in Preussen, 1812 bis 1847. Mit einem Ausblick auf das Gleichberechtigungsgesetz des Norddeutschen Bundes von 1869*. Berlin, 1987.

Brandenberg, Paul. *Beiträge zur Geschichte der Elementarschulen, A: Israelitische Schule in Köln-Altstadt*. Cologne, 1894.

Braubach, Max. *Die Vier Letzten Kurfürsten von Köln*. Bonn and Cologne, 1931.

——. *Maria Theresias jüngster Sohn, Max Franz*. Vienna and Munich, 1961.

Breuer, Mordechai. *Jüdische Orthodoxie im deutschen Reich, 1871–1918*. Frankfurt am Main, 1986.

Brilling, Bernhard. "Die Intervention des Kurfürsten und Erzbischofs von Köln zugunsten der Prager und böhmischen Juden im Jahre 1745." *Annalen des Historischen Vereins für den Niederrhein* 174 (1977): 122–37.

Brincken, Anna-Dorothee von den. "Das Rechtfertigungsschreiben der Stadt Köln wegen Ausweisung der Juden im Jahre 1424. Zur Motivierung spättmittelalterlicher Judenvertreibungen in West- und Mitteleuropa." In Hugo Stehkämper, ed., *Köln, Das Reich und Europa. Mitteilungen aus dem Stadtarchiv von Köln*, pp. 305–39. Cologne, 1971.

Brisch, Carl. *Geschichte der Juden in Cöln und Umgebung aus ältester Zeit bis auf die Gegenwart*. 2 vols. in one. Mülheim am Rhein, 1879.

Brose, Eric Dorn. *The Politics of Technological Change in Prussia*. Princeton, N.J., 1993.

Brunschwig, Henri. *Enlightenment and Romanticism in Eighteenth-Century Prussia*. Frank Jelinek, trans. Chicago, 1974.

Buchheim, Karl. *Die Stellung der kölnischen Zeitung im vormärzlichen rheinischen Liberalismus*. Leipzig, 1914.

Bunyan, Anita. "Rhenish Liberalism and the Jewish Question in the Vormärz: The

Case of the *Kölnische Zeitung*, 1841–1847." *Leo Baeck Institute Yearbook* 39 (1994): 31–51.

Büttner, Richard. *Die Säkularisation der Kölner Geistlichen Institutionen.* Cologne, 1971.

Cahnman, Werner. "A Regional Approach to German Jewish History." *Jewish Social Studies* 5 (1943): 211–24.

Carlebach, Alexander. *Adass Yeshurun of Cologne.* Belfast, 1964.

Carlebach, Julius. "The Problem of Moses Hess' Influence on the Young Marx." *Leo Baeck Institute Yearbook* 28 (1973): 27–39.

Caron, Vicki. *Between France and Germany. The Jews of Alsace-Lorraine, 1871–1918.* Stanford, Calif., 1988.

Carsten, F. L. "The Court Jews, A Prelude to Emancipation." *Leo Baeck Institute Yearbook* 3 (1958): 140–56.

Cassis, Youssef. "Businessmen and the Bourgeoisie in Western Europe." In Jürgen Kocka and Allan Mitchell, eds., *Bourgeois Society in Nineteenth-Century Europe*, pp. 103–24. Oxford, 1993.

Catane, Moche. "Les Juifs du Bas-Rhin sous Napoléon I: leur situation démographique et économique." Ph.D. diss., Université de Strasbourg, 1967.

Cervelli, Innocenzo. "Deutsche Liberale im Vormärz: Profil einer politischen Elite (1833–1847)." In Wolfgang Schieder, ed., *Liberalismus in der Gesellschaft des deutschen Vormärz*, pp. 312–40. Göttingen, 1983.

Chazan, Robert. *Church, State and Jew in the Middle Ages.* New York, 1980.

Clapham, J. H. *The Economic Development of France and Germany, 1815–1914.* Montreal, 1978.

Cohen, Carl. "The Road to Conversion." *Leo Baeck Institute Yearbook* 6 (1961): 259–79.

Cohen, Jeremy. *The Friars and the Jews: The Evolution of Medieval Anti-Judaism.* Ithaca, N.Y., 1982.

Cohen, Norman. *Warrant for Genocide. The Myth of the Jewish World Conspiracy and the Protocols of the Elders of Zion.* London, 1967.

Conze, Werner, and Jürgen Kocka, eds. *Bildungsbürgertum im neunzehnten Jahrhundert*, vol. 1, *Bildungssystem und Professionalisierung in internationalen Vergleichen.* Göttingen, 1985.

Croon, Gustav. *Der Rheinische Provinziallandtag bis zum Jahre 1874.* Düsseldorf, 1974.

Croon, Helmut. "Rheinische Städte." In Walter Först, ed., *Das Rheinland in Preussischer Zeit*, pp. 87–108. Cologne, 1965.

———. "Das Vordringen der politischen Parteien im Bereich der Kommunalen Selbstverwaltung." In *Kommunale Selbstverwaltung im Zeitalter der Industrialisierung*, pp. 15–58. Stuttgart and Berlin, 1971.

Däbritz, Walter. "David Hansemann." In *Rheinisch-Westfälische Wirtschaftsbiographien*, vol. 7, pp. 1–24. Münster, 1960.

Deeters, Joachim. "Die Aktionäre der Rheinischen Eisenbahn-Gesellschaft im Gründungsjahr 1837." In Klara van Eyll, ed., *Kölner Unternehmer und die Frühindustrialisierung im Rheinland und in Westfalen (1835–1871)*, pp. 116–46. Cologne, 1984.

Diederich, Toni. "Bürgermeister und Rat der Stadt Köln von 12. bis zum 20. Jahrhundert." In Peter Fuchs, ed., *Das Rathhaus zu Köln*, pp. 41–69. Cologne, 1973.

Diefendorf, Jeffry M. *Businessmen and Politics in the Rhineland, 1789–1834*. Princeton, N.J., 1980.

Dowe, Dieter. *Aktion und Organization*. Hannover, 1970.

Droz, Jacques. *Le Libéralisme Rhénan*. Paris, 1940.

Dubnow, Simon. *Weltgeschichte des jüdischen Volkes*. Vols. 8, 9. Berlin, 1928, 1929.

Eckert, Willehad. "Das Verhältnis von Christen und Juden im Mittelalter und Humanismus." In Konrad Schilling, ed., *Monumenta Judaica*, pp. 131–98. Cologne, 1963.

Ehrlich, Ernst Ludwig. "Geschichte und Kultur der Juden in den rheinishen Territorialstaaten vom Beginn der Neuzeit bis zum Absolutismus." In Konrad Schilling, ed., *Monumenta Judaica*, pp. 242–82. Cologne, 1963.

Eichholz, Dietrich. *Junker und Bourgeoisie vor 1848 in der Preussischen Eisenbahngeschichte*. East Berlin, 1962.

Eidelberg, Shlomo, ed. *The Jews and the Crusaders*. Madison, Wis., 1977.

Elbogen, Ismar, and Eleonore Sterling. *Die Geschichte der Juden in Deutschland*. Frankfurt am Main, 1966.

Eliav, Mordechai. *Jewish Education in Germany in the Period of Enlightenment and Emancipation* [Hebrew]. Jerusalem, 1960.

Encyclopaedia Judaica. 16 vols. Jerusalem, 1972.

Endelman, Todd. *The Jews of Georgian England, 1714–1830*. Philadelphia, 1979.

Engelhardt, Ulrich. *"Bildungsbürgertum." Begriffs- und Dogmengeschichte eines Etiketts*. Stuttgart, 1986.

Ennen, Edith. "Die jüdische Gemeinde in Bonn." *Bonner Geschichtsblätter* 29 (1977): 81–94.

———. "Köln als politisches, wirtschaftliches und kulturelles Zentrum im Mittelalter." In Institut für Geschichtliche Landeskunde der Rheinlande an der Universität Bonn, ed., *Die Stadt Köln: Gestalt und Wirkung*. Bonn, 1970, pp. 11–19.

Erbel, Arno. "Von der Munizipalverfassung zur Rheinischen Gemeindeordnung von 1845." In *150 Jahre Regierungsbezirk Köln*, pp. 250–58. West Berlin, 1966.

Ehrlich, Ernst Ludwig. "Geschichte und Kultur der Juden in den rheinischen Territorialstaaten." In Konrad Schilling, ed., *Monumenta Judaica*, Handbuch, pp. 242–81. Cologne, 1964.

Eyck, Franz. "Liberalismus und Katholizismus in der Zeit des deutschen Vormärz." In Wolfgang Schieder, ed., *Liberalismus in der Gesellschaft des deutschen Vormärz*, pp. 133–46. Göttingen, 1983.

Faber, Karl-Georg. "Die Kommunale Selbstverwaltung in der Rheinprovinz im 19. Jahrhundert." *Rheinische Vierteljahrsblätter* 30 (1965): 132–51.

———. *Die Rheinlande zwischen Restauration und Revolution*. Wiesbaden, 1966.

Fann, Willerd R. "The Rise of the Prussian Ministry, 1806–1827." In Hans-Ulrich Wehler, ed., *Sozialgeschichte Heute*, pp. 119–29. Göttingen, 1974.

Fehrenbach, Elisabeth. "Rheinischer Liberalismus und gesellschaftliche Verfassung." In Wolfgang Schieder, ed., *Liberalismus in der Gesellschaft des deutschen Vormärz*, pp. 272–94. Göttingen, 1983.

Feldenkirchen, Wilfried. "Kölner Unternehmer und die Entwicklung der Eisen- und Stahlindustrie des Ruhrgebietes bis 1871." In Klara van Eyll, ed. *Kölner Unternehmer und die Frühindustrialisierung im Rheinland und in Westfalen (1835–1871)*, pp. 184–92. Cologne, 1984.

Figes, Orlando. "Ludwig Börne and the Formation of a Radical Critique of Judaism." *Leo Baeck Institute Yearbook* 29 (1984): 351–82.

Fischer, Herbert. *Die Verfassungsrechtliche Stellung der Juden in den deutschen Städten während des 13. Jahrhunderts*. Breslau, 1931.

Fischer, Horst. *Judentum, Staat und Heer im frühen 19. Jahrhundert*. Tübingen, 1968.

Först, Walter. *Raum und Politik*. Cologne and Berlin, 1977.

———. *Rheinisch-Westfälische Rückblende*. Cologne and Berlin, 1967.

———, ed. *Das Rheinland in Preussischer Zeit*. Cologne and Berlin, 1965.

Frankel, Jonathan. *Prophecy and Politics: Socialism, Nationalism, and the Russian Jews, 1862–1917*. Cambridge, Eng., 1981.

Freund, Ismar. *Die Emanzipation der Juden in Preussen*. 2 vols. Berlin, 1912.

———. *Die Rechtsstellung der Juden im Preussischen Volksschulrecht*. Berlin, 1908.

Gall, Lothar. *Bürgertum in Deutschland*. Berlin, 1989.

———. "Liberalismus und Bürgerliche Gesellschaft." *Historische Zeitschrift* 220 (1975): 324–56.

Gehring-Münzel, Ursula. *Vom Schutzjuden zum Staatsbürger. Die Gesellschaftliche Integration der Würzburger Juden, 1803–1871*. Würzburg, 1992.

Gerschler, Walter, ed. *Das preussische Oberpräsidium der Provinz Jülich-Kleve-Berg in Köln, 1816–1822*. Cologne and Berlin, 1967.

Gillis, John. *The Prussian Bureaucracy in Crisis*. Stanford, Calif., 1988.

Ginzberg, Asher. *Selected Essays of Ahad Ha-'Am*. Leon Simon, ed. and trans. New York, 1970.

Glanz, Rudolf. *Geschichte des niederen jüdischen Volkes in Deutschland*. New York, 1968.

Glückel of Hameln. *The Memoirs of Glückel of Hameln*. Marvin Lowenthal, trans. New York, 1977.

Gordon, Milton. *Assimilation in American Life*. New York, 1964.

Gothein, Eberhard. *Verfassungs- und Wirtschaftsgeschichte der Stadt Cöln vom Untergange der Reichsfreiheit bis zur Errichtung des Deutschen Reiches*. Cologne, 1916.

Grab, Walter, and Julius Schoeps, eds. *Juden im Vormärz und in der Revolution von 1848*. Stuttgart, 1983.

Graetz, Michael. *From Periphery to Center* [Hebrew]. Jerusalem, 1982.

Grayzel, Solomon. *The Church and the Jews in the Thirteenth Century*. New York, 1966.

Greenberg, Louis. *The Jews in Russia: The Struggle for Emancipation*. New York, 1976.

"Grodno." *Encyclopaedia Judaica*, pp. 924–28. Jerusalem, 1972.

Grunwald, Kurt. "Europe's Railways and Jewish Enterprise." *Leo Baeck Institute Yearbook* 12 (1967): 163–209.

———. " 'Windsor-Cassel' — The Last Court Jew: Prolegomena to a Biography of Sir Ernst Cassel." *Leo Baeck Institute Yearbook* 14 (1969): 119–61.

Grupe, Heinz. "Heinrich Merkens." In *Rheinisch-Westfälische Wirtschaftsbiographien*, vol. 5, pp. 1–26. Münster, 1953.

"Hamburg." *Encyclopaedia Judaica*, pp. 1225–29. Jerusalem, 1972.

Hahn, Rolf. "Das 'schändliche Dekret' vom 17.3.1808 und seine Auswirking auf die rechtliche Stellung der Kölner Juden." Ph.D. diss., University of Cologne, 1967.

Hamburger, Ernest. *Juden im öffentlichen Leben Deutschlands: Regierungsmitglieder, Beamte und Parliamentarier in der monarchischen Zeit, 1848–1918.* Tübingen, 1968.

———. "One Hundred Years of Emancipation." *Leo Baeck Institute Yearbook* 14 (1969): 3–66.

Hamerow, Theodore S. *Restoration, Revolution, Reaction: Economics and Politics in Germany, 1815–1871.* Princeton, N.J., 1972.

Hammer-Schenck, Harold. *Synagogen in Deutschland. Geschichte einer Baugattung im neunzehnten und zwanzigsten Jahrhundert.* 2 vols. Hamburg, 1981.

Hansen, Joseph. *Gustav von Mevissen, Ein rheinisches Lebensbild.* 2 vols. Berlin, 1909.

———. "Das Politische Leben." In Joseph Hansen, ed., *Die Rheinprovinz,* 1: 610–861. Bonn, 1917.

Hansen, Joseph, ed. *Die Rheinprovinz, 1815–1915.* 2 vols. Bonn, 1917.

———, ed. *Rheinische Briefe und Akten zur Geschichte der politischen Bewegung, 1830–1845.* 2 vols. Osnabrück, 1967.

Harris, James F. "Public Opinion and the Proposed Emancipation of the Jews in Bavaria, 1849–1850." *Leo Baeck Institute Yearbook* 34 (1989): 67–79.

Hartsough, Mildred. "Business Leaders in Cologne in the Nineteenth Century." *Journal of Economic and Business History* 2 (1929–30): 332–52.

Hashagen, Justus. *Der rheinische Protestantismus und die Entwicklung der rheinischen Kultur.* Essen an der Ruhr, 1924.

Hässlin, Johann Jakob. *Köln, Die Stadt und ihre Bürger.* Stuttgart, 1964.

Haym, Rudolf. *Reden und Redner des ersten Vereinigten Preussischen Landtags.* Berlin, 1847.

Heffter, Heinrich. *Die Deutsche Selbstverwaltung im 19. Jahrhundert.* Stuttgart, 1950.

Hegel, Eduard. *Das Erzbistum Köln zwischen Barock und Aufklärung, 1688–1814.* Cologne, 1979.

Hegel, K. *Verfassungsgeschichte von Cöln im Mittelalter.* Leipzig, 1877.

Heimann, F. C. "Die Alte Synagoge in Deutz." *Mitteilungen der Rheinischer Verein für Denkmalpflege und Heimatschutz* 8 (1914): 108–81.

Henderson, W. O. *The State and the Industrial Revolution in Prussia, 1740–1870.* Liverpool, Eng., 1958.

Henning, Friedrich-Wilhelm. "Der Beitrag Kölner Unternehmer zur Entwicklung der Ruhrkohlebergbaus in der Mitte des 19. Jahrhunderts." In Klara van Eyll, ed., *Kölner Unternehmer und die Frühindustrialisierung im Rheinland und in Westfalen (1835–1871)*, pp. 171–83. Cologne, 1984.

Henning, Hansjoachim. "Preussische Sozialpolitik im Vormärz?" *Vierteljahrsschrift für Sozial- und Wirtschaftsgeschichte* 52 (1965): 485–539.

Herborn, Wolfgang. "Bürgerliches Selbstverständnis in spätmittelalterlichen Köln." In Werner Besch et al., eds., *Die Stadt in der Europäischen Geschichte*, pp. 490–520. Bonn, 1827.

Hertz, Deborah. "Intermarriage in the Berlin Salons." *Central European History* 16 (Dec., 1983): 303–34.

———. *Jewish High Society in Old Regime Berlin.* New Haven, Conn., 1988.

———. "Seductive Conversion in Berlin, 1770–1809." In Todd M. Endelman, ed., *Jewish Apostasy in the Modern World*, pp. 48–82. New York, 1987.

———. "Women at the Edge of Judaism: Female Converts in Germany, 1600–1750." In Menachem Mor, ed., *Jewish Assimilation, Acculturation and Accommodation*, pp. 87–109. Lanham, N.Y., 1992.

Hertzberg, Arthur. *The French Enlightenment and the Jews*. New York, 1968.

Herzig, Arno. "Andreas Gottschalk und der Kölner Arbeiterverein." In Jutta Bohnke-Kollwitz, Willehad Paul Eckert, et al., eds., *Köln und das rheinische Judentum*, pp. 177–82. Cologne, 1984.

———. *Judentum und Emanzipation in Westfalen*. Münster, 1973.

———. "Die Jüdische Minderheit Rheinland-Westfalens im Assimilationsprozess (1780–1860)." *Rheinland-Westfalens im Industriezeitalter* 2 (1984): 72–85.

———. "Politische Zielvorstellungen jüdischer Intellektueller aus dem Rheinland und aus Westfalen im Vormärz und in der Revolution von 1848." In Walter Grab and Julius H. Schoeps, eds., *Juden im Vormärz und in der Revolution von 1848*, pp. 272–311. Stuttgart and Bonn, 1983.

Hess, Moses. *Rome and Jerusalem*. Meyer Waxman, trans. New York, 1943.

Hirsch, Helmut. "Karl Marx und die Bittschriften für die Gleichberechtigung der Juden." *Archiv für Sozialgeschichte* 8 (1968): 229–45.

———. "Karl Marx 'Zur Judenfrage' und zu Juden—Eine weiterführende Metakritik?" In Walter Grab and Julius H. Schoeps, eds., *Juden im Vormärz und in der Revolution von 1848*, pp. 199–213. Stuttgart and Bonn, 1983.

———. *Marx und Moses: Karl Marx zur 'Judenfrage' und zu Juden*. Frankfurt am Main, Bern, Cirencester, 1980.

———. "Moses Hess und Köln—bis zur Emigration im Jahre 1842." In Jutta Bohnke-Kollwitz, Willehad Paul Eckert, et al., eds., *Köln und das rheinische Judentum*. Cologne, 1984.

Hoffmann, Georg. "Die Juden im Erzstift Köln im 18. Jahrhundert." Ph.D. diss., Ludwig-Maximilian-Universität, Munich, 1927.

———. *Die Juden im Erzstift Köln im 18. Jahrhundert*. Aachen, 1928.

Hoffmann, Wolfgang. "Oberbürgermeister und Stadtverweiterungen." In *Kommunale Selbstverwaltung im Zeitalter der Industrialisierung*, pp. 59–90. Stuttgart and Berlin, 1971.

Holborn, Hajo. *A History of Modern Germany, 1648–1840*. New York, 1969.

———. *A History of Modern Germany, 1840–1945*. New York, 1969.

Holeczek, Heinz. "The Jews and the German Liberals." *Leo Baeck Institute Yearbook* 28 (1983): 77–91.

———. "Die Judenemanizapation in Preussen." In Bernd Martin and Ernst Schulin, eds., *Die Juden als Minderheit in der Geschichte*, pp. 131–60. Munich, 1981.

Hömig, Herbert. *Rheinische Katholiken und Liberale in den Auseinandersetzungen um die preussischen Verfassung unter besonderer Berücksichtigung der Kölner Presse*. Cologne, 1971.

Honigmann, Peter. *Die Austritte aus der Jüdischen Gemeinde Berlin, 1873–1841*. Frankfurt am Main, 1988.

———. "Jewish Conversion—A Measure of Assimilation? A Discussion of the Berlin Secession Statistics of 1770–1941." *Leo Baeck Institute Yearbook* 34 (1989): 3–39.

Hsia, R. Po-Chia. *The Myth of Ritual Murder: Jews and Magic in Reformation Germany*. New Haven, Conn., 1988.

Hubatsch, Walter. *Grundriss zur deutschen Verwaltungsgeschichte, 1815–1945*. Vol. 7, *Rheinland*. Aachen, 1978.

Hühne, Werner. "Aus der Westdeutsche Eisenbahngeschichte." In Walter Först, ed., *Raum und Politik*, pp. 33–58. Cologne and Berlin, 1977.

Hundertfünfzig Jahre Regierungsbezirk Köln. West Berlin, 1966.

Hyman, Paula. *The Emancipation of the Jews of Alsace: Acculturation and Tradition in the Nineteenth Century*. New Haven, Conn., 1991.

———. "Village Jews and Jewish Modernity: The Case of Alsace in the Nineteenth Century." In Ronald Dotterer, Deborah Dash Moore, and Steven M. Cohen, eds., *Jewish Settlement and Community in the Modern Western World*, pp. 13–26. Selinsgrove, Penn., 1991.

Ilgen, Theodore. "Organisation der Staatlichen Verwaltung und der Selbstverwaltung." In Joseph Hansen, ed., *Die Rheinprovinz, 1815–1915*, 1: 92–114. Bonn, 1917.

Israel, Jonathan I. *European Jewry in the Age of Mercantilism, 1550–1750*. 2nd ed. New York, 1989.

Jeggle, Utz. *Judendörfer in Württemberg*. Tübingen, 1966.

Jenks, William A. "The Jews in the Habsburg Empire, 1879–1918." *Leo Baeck Institute Yearbook* 16 (1971): 155–62.

John, Michael. "Between Estate and Profession: Lawyers and the Development of the Legal Profession in Nineteenth Century Germany." In David Blackbourne and Richard J. Evans, eds., *The German Bourgeoisie*, pp. 162–97. London and New York, 1991.

Jost, Isaac M. *Neuere Geschichte der Israeliten*. Berlin, 1846.

Kähler, Wilhelm. "Handel, Bankwesen, Versicherungswesen." In Joseph Hansen, ed., *Die Rheinprovinz*, 1: 196–249, 506–60. Bonn, 1917.

Kampe, Norbert, and Heinz-Peter Schmiedebach. "Robert Remak (1815–1865) — A Case Study of Jewish Emancipation in the Mid-Nineteenth-Century German Scientific Community." *Leo Baeck Institute Yearbook* 34 (1989): 95–129.

Kaplan, Marion A. *The Making of the Jewish Middle Class: Women, Family and Identity in Imperial Germany*. New York, 1991.

———. "Priestess and Hausfrau: Women and Tradition in the German-Jewish Family." In Steven M. Cohen and Paula E. Hyman, eds., *The Jewish Family*, pp. 62–81. New York, 1986.

Kaschuba, Wolfgang. "German Bürgerlichkeit after 1800: Culture as Symbolic Practice." In Jürgen Kocka and Allan Mitchell, eds., *Bourgeois Society in Nineteenth-Century Europe*, pp. 392–421. Oxford, 1993.

Kastner, Dieter, ed. *Der Rheinische Provinziallandtag und die Emanzipation der Juden im Rheinland, 1825–1845*. 2 vols. Cologne, 1989.

Katz, Jacob. "The Hep-Hep Riots in Germany in 1819: The Historical Background" [Hebrew]. *Zion* 38 (1973): 62–115.

———. *From Prejudice to Destruction*. Cambridge, Mass., 1980.

———. *Out of the Ghetto*. New York, 1978.

———. "The Term 'Jewish Emancipation': Its Origin and Historical Impact." In

Alexander Altmann, ed., *Studies in Nineteenth-Century Jewish Intellectual History*, pp. 1–25. Cambridge, Mass., 1964.

———. *Tradition and Crisis*. New York, 1971.

Katz, Michael. "Occupational Classification in History." *Journal of Interdisciplinary History* 3 (Summer, 1972): 63–88.

Kaudelka-Hanisch, Karin. "The Titled Businessman: Prussian Commercial Councillors in the Rhineland and Westphalia During the Nineteenth Century." In David Blackbourne and Richard J. Evans, eds., *The German Bourgeoisie*, pp. 87–114. London and New York, 1991.

Kellenbenz, Hermann. "Der Aufstieg Kölns zur Mittelalterlichen Handelsmetropole." *Jahrbuch des Kölnisches Geschichtsvereins* 41 (1967): 1–30.

———. "Grundzüge der Wirtschaftsgeschichte." In Walter Först, ed., *Das Rheinland in Preussischer Zeit*, pp. 125–44. Cologne and Berlin, 1965.

———. "Die Juden in der Wirtschaftsgeschichte des rheinischen Raumes von der Spätantike bis zum Jahre 1648." In Konrad Schilling, ed., *Monumenta Judaica*, pp. 199–241. Cologne, 1963.

———. *Sephardim an der unteren Elbe*. Wiesbaden, 1958.

———. "Die Wirtschaft in Regierungsbezirk Köln, 1816–1945." In *150 Jahre Regierungsbezirk Köln*, pp. 321–40. West Berlin, 1966.

Kellenbenz, Hermann, and Klara van Eyll. *Die Geschichte der Unternehmerische Selbstverwaltung in Köln, 1797–1914*. Cologne, 1972.

Keyser, Erich, ed. *Bayerisches Städtebuch*. 2 vols. Stuttgart, 1971, 1974.

———. *Hessisches Städtebuch*. Stuttgart, 1957.

———. *Rheinisches Städtebuch*. Stuttgart, 1956.

———. *Städtebuch Rheinland-Pfalz und Saarland*. Stuttgart, 1964.

Kisch, Guido. *The Jews in Medieval Germany*. New York, 1970.

———. *Judentaufen*. Berlin, 1973.

———. "The Yellow Badge in History." *Historia Judaica* 4 (1942): 95–144.

Kitchen, Martin. *The Political Economy of Germany, 1815–1914*. London, 1978.

Klausa, Udo. "Die Verwaltung der Provinz." In Walter Först, ed., *Das Rheinland in Preussischer Zeit*, pp. 71–86. Cologne and Berlin, 1965.

Klein, August. *Die Personalpolitik der Hohenzollernmonarchie bei der Kölner Regierung*. Düsseldorf, 1967.

Klersch, Joseph. *Volkstum und Volksleben in Köln*. Cologne, 1968.

Klutentreter, Wilhelm. *Die Rheinische Zeitung von 1842/43 in der Politischen und Geistigen Bewegung des Vormärz*. Dortmund, 1966.

Knemeyer, Franz-Ludwig. *Regierungs- und Verwaltungsreformen in Deutschland zur Beginn des 19. Jahrhunderts*. Berlin and Cologne, 1976.

Kober, Adolf. "Aus der Geschichte der Juden im Rheinland." *Rheinische Verein für Denkmalpflege und Heimatschutz* 1 (1931): 11–98.

———. *Cologne*. Philadelphia, 1940.

———. "Emancipation's Impact on German Jewry." *Jewish Social Studies* 16, no. 1 (1951): 3–32, no. 2 (1951): 151–69.

———. "The French Revolution and the Jews in Germany." *Jewish Social Studies* 3 (1945): 291–322.

——. "Jewish Communities in Germany from the Age of Enlightenment to Destruction by the Nazis." *Jewish Social Studies* 9 (1947): 195–238.

——. "Jews in the Revolution of 1848 in Germany." *Jewish Social Studies* 10 (1948): 135–64.

——. "Karl Marx' Vater und das Napoleonische Ausnahmegesetz Gegen die Juden 1808." *Jahrbuch des Kölnischen Geschichtsvereins* 14 (1932): 111–25.

——. *Das Namensregister der Kölner Juden von 1808. Sonderdruck aus den Mitteilungen des Gesamtarchivs der deutschen Juden*. Berlin, 1926.

——. "Die Reichsstadt Köln und die Juden in den Jahren 1685–1715." *Monatsschrift für Geschichte und Wissenschaft des Judentums* 75 (1931): 412–28.

——. "Rheinische Judendoktoren, vornehmlich des 17. und 18. Jahrhunderts." In *Festschrift zum 75 jährigen Bestehen des jüdisch Theologischen Seminars*, pp. 173–236. Breslau, 1929.

Koch, H. W. *A History of Prussia*. London, 1978.

Kocka, Jürgen. "The European Pattern and the German Case." In Kocka and Allan Mitchell, eds., *Bourgeois Society in Nineteenth-Century Europe*. Oxford, 1993, pp. 3–39.

——, ed. *Bürger und Bürgerlichkeit im neunzehnten Jahrhundert*. Göttingen, 1987.

Kocka, Jürgen, and Allan Mitchell, eds. *Bourgeois Society in Nineteenth-Century Europe*. Oxford, 1993.

Koebner, Richard. *Die Anfänge des Gemeindewesens der Stadt Köln*. Bonn, 1922.

Kohler, Max. "Jewish Rights at the Congresses of Vienna (1814–1815) and Aix-la-Chapelle (1818). *Publications of the American Jewish Historical Society* 26 (1918): 33–125.

Köllmann, Wolfgang. "Bevölkerungsentwicklung im Industriezeitalter." In Walter Först, ed., *Raum und Politik*, pp. 11–30. Cologne and Berlin, 1977.

Kölner Statistisches Handbuch 13. Cologne, 1958.

König, Hermann. *Die Rheinische Zeitung von 1842–43 in ihrer Einstellung zur Kulturpolitik des Preussischen Staates*. Münster, 1927.

Kopp, August. *Die Dorfjuden in der Nordpfalz*. Meisenheim am Glan, 1968.

Kosseleck, Reinhart. *Preussen zwischen Reform und Revolution*. Stuttgart, 1967.

——. "Staat und Gesellschaft in Preussen, 1815–1848." In Werner Conze, ed., *Staat und Gesellschaft im deutschen Vormärz, 1815–1848*, pp. 79–112. Stuttgart, 1962.

Kosseleck, Reinhart, ed. *Bildungsbürgertum im neunzehnten Jahrhundert*, vol. 2, *Bildungsgüter und Bildungswesen*. Stuttgart, 1990.

Kosinsky, Leszek A., and R. M. Prothero, eds. *People on the Move: Studies on Internal Migration*. London, 1975.

Köster, Johanna. *Der rheinische Frühliberalismus und die soziale Frage*. Berlin, 1938.

Kracauer, Isidor. *Geschichte der Juden in Frankfurt am Main*. Frankfurt, 1925.

Krinsky, Carol Herselle. *Synagogues of Europe*. Cambridge, Mass., 1985.

Krohn, Helga. *Die Juden in Hamburg, 1800–1850*. Frankfurt am Main, 1967.

——. *Die Juden in Hamburg, 1848–1918*. Hamburg, 1974.

Krüger, Alfred. *Das Kölner Bankiergewerbe*. Essen, 1925.

Kumpmann, Karl. *Die Entstehung der Rheinischen Eisenbahn Gesellschaft, 1830–1844*. Essen an der Ruhr, 1910.

Künzl, Hennelore. "Nineteenth-Century Synagogues in the Neo-Islamic Style." In *Proceedings of the Eighth World Congress of Jewish Studies*, pp. 71–78. Jerusalem, 1982.

Lademacher, Horst. "Die nördlichen Rheinlande von der Rheinprovinz bis zur Bildung des Landschaftsverbandes Rheinland (1815–1953)." In Franz Petri and Georg Droege, eds., *Rheinische Geschichte*, 2: 473–912. Düsseldorf, 1976.

Lamberti, Marjorie. *Jewish Activism in Imperial Germany*. New Haven, Conn., 1978.

———. "The Prussian Government and the Jews: Official Behavior and Policy-Making in the Wilhelminian Era." *Leo Baeck Institute Yearbook* 17 (1972): 5–17.

Landes, David S. "Bleichröders and Rothschilds: The Problem of Continuity in the Family Firm." In Charles E. Rosenberg, ed., *The Family in History*, pp. 95–114. Philadelphia, 1975.

———. *The Unbound Prometheus: Technological Change and Industrial Development in Western Europe from 1750 to the Present*. Cambridge, Mass., 1972.

Landsberg, Ernst. *Die Gutachten der Rheinischen Immediat-Justiz-Kommission und der Kampf um die Rheinische Rechts- und Gerichtsverfassung, 1814–1819*. Bonn, 1914.

———. "Das rheinische Recht und die rheinische Gerichtsverfassung." In Joseph Hansen, ed., *Die Rheinprovinz, 1815–1819*, 1: 149–95. Bonn, 1917.

Langewiesche, Dieter. "Liberalism and the Middle Classes in Europe." In Jürgen Kocka and Allan Mitchell, eds., *Bourgeois Society in Nineteenth-Century Europe*, pp. 40–69. Oxford, 1993.

Langmuir, Gavin. *History, Religion, and Antisemitism*. Berkeley, Calif., 1990.

———. *Toward a Definition of Antisemitism*. Berkeley, Calif., 1990.

Lau, Friedrich. *Entwicklung der Kommunalen Verfassung und Verwaltung der Stadt Köln bis zum Jahre 1396*. Amsterdam, 1969.

Lepsius, M. Rainer. "Das Bildungsbürgertum als ständische Vergesellschaftung." In M. Rainer Lepsius, ed., *Bildungsbürgertum im neunzehnten Jahrhundert*, pt. 3, *Lebensführung und Ständische Vergesellschaftung*, pp. 8–18. Stuttgart, 1992.

Liberles, Robert. "Emancipation and the Structure of the Jewish Community in the Nineteenth Century." *Leo Baeck Institute Yearbook* 31 (1986): 51–67.

———. *Religious Conflict in Social Context: The Resurgence of Orthodox Judaism in Frankfurt am Main, 1838–1877*. Westport, Conn., 1985.

———. "Was There a Jewish Movement for Emancipation in Germany?" *Leo Baeck Institute Yearbook* 31 (1986): 35–49.

Liebeschutz, Hans. "German Radicalism and the Formation of Jewish Political Attitudes During the Early Part of the Nineteenth Century." In Alexander Altmann, ed., *Studies in Nineteenth-Century Jewish Intellectual History*, pp. 141–70. Cambridge, Mass., 1969.

———. "The Relevance of the Middle Ages for the Understanding of Contemporary Jewish History." *Leo Baeck Institute Yearbook* 18 (1973): 3–25.

Liebeschutz, Hans, and Arnold Paucker, eds. *Das Judentum in der Deutschen Umwelt, 1800–1850*. Tübingen, 1977.

Littmann, Ellen. *Studien zur Wiederaufnahme der Juden nach dem Schwarzen Tod*. Breslau, 1928.

Lojewski, Günter Von. *Bayerns Weg nach Köln*. Bonn, 1962.

Looz-Corswarem, Clemens von. "Die Anfänge der Preussisch-Rheinischen Dampfschifffahrts-Gesellschaft." In Klara van Eyll, ed., *Kölner Unternehmer und die Frühindustrialisierung im Rheinland und in Westfalen (1835–1871)*, pp. 96–115. Cologne, 1984.

Lowenstein, Steven M. *The Berlin Jewish Community, Enlightenment, Family, and Crisis, 1770–1830*. New York, 1994.

——. "The 1840s and the Creation of the German-Jewish Religious Reform Movement." In Werner E. Mosse et al., eds., *Revolution and Evolution*, pp. 255–97. Tübingen, 1981.

——. "The Pace of Modernisation of German Jewry in the Nineteenth Century." *Leo Baeck Institute Yearbook* 21 (1976): 41–56.

——. "The Rural Community and the Urbanization of German Jewry." *Central European History* 13 (1980): 218–36.

Lowenthal, Ernst G. "Jüdische 'höhere Bürgerschüler' in Köln, Eine Skizze aus den Jahren 1828 bis 1858." In Jutta Bohnke-Kollwitz, Willehad Paul Eckert, et al., eds. *Köln und das rheinische Judentum*, pp. 159–64. Cologne, 1984.

Lown, Judy. *Women and Industrialization: Gender at Work in Nineteenth-Century England*. Cambridge, Eng., 1990.

Magnus, Shulamit S. "Cologne: Jewish Emancipation in a German City, 1798–1871." Ph.D. diss., Columbia University, 1988.

Mahler, Raphael. *A History of Modern Jewry, 1780–1815*. London, 1971.

Malino, Frances. *The Sephardic Jews of Bordeaux*. University, Ala., 1978.

Marcus, Jacob R. *The Jew in the Medieval World*. New York, 1969.

Marx, Karl. *Karl Marx, Early Writings*. T. B. Bottomore, trans. New York, 1963.

Maslin, Simeon J. *An Analysis of Selected Documents of Napoleonic Jewry*. Cincinnati, Ohio, 1957.

Mendelssohn, Ezra. *The Jews of East Central Europe Between the World Wars*. Bloomington, Ind., 1983.

Mendes-Flohr, Paul R., and Jehuda Reinharz, eds. *The Jew in the Modern World*. New York, 1980.

Menes, Abraham. "The Conversion Movement in Prussia During the First Half of the Nineteenth Century." *YIVO Annual of Jewish Social Science* 6 (1951): 187–205.

Meyer, Michael A. "Jews as Jews versus Jews as Germans: Two Historical Perspectives." *Leo Baeck Institute Yearbook* 36 (1991): xv–xxii.

——. *The Origins of the Modern Jew: Jewish Identity and European Culture in Germany, 1749–1824*. Detroit, 1977.

——. "Reform Jewish Thinkers and Their German Intellectual Context." In Jehuda Reinharz and Walter Schatzberg, eds., *The Jewish Response to German Culture*, pp. 64–84. Hanover, N.H., 1985.

——. *Response to Modernity. A History of the Reform Movement in Judaism*. New York, 1988.

Mohnen, Heinz. "Die Stadt Köln, 1815–1965." In *150 Jahre Regierungsbezirk Köln*, pp. 269–95. West Berlin, 1966.

Mönke, Wolfgang. "Neue Quellen zur Hess Forschung." *Abhandlungen der deutschen Akademie der Wissenschaften zu Berlin* 1 (1964): 39–41.

Mosse, George L. *The Crisis of German Ideology*. New York, 1964.

――. "Das Deutsch-jüdische Bildungsbürgertum." In Reinhart Kosseleck, ed., *Bildungsbürgertum im neunzehnten Jahrhundert*, pt. 2, *Bildungsgüter und Bildungswesen*, pp. 168–80. Stuttgart, 1990.

――. *German Jews Beyond Judaism*. Bloomington, Ind., 1985.

――. *Germans and Jews*. New York, 1970.

――. "Jewish Emancipation: Between Bildung and Respectability." In Jehuda Reinharz and Walter Schatzberg, eds., *The Jewish Response to German Culture*, pp. 1–16. Hanover, N.H., 1985.

Mosse, Werner E. *Jews in the German Economy: The German-Jewish Economic Elite, 1820–1935*. Oxford, 1987.

――. "Die Juden in Wirtschaft und Gesellschaft." In Werner E. Mosse and Arnold Paucker, eds., *Juden in Wilhelminischen Deutschland, 1890–1914*, pp. 57–113. Tübingen, 1976.

Mosse, Werner E., and Arnold Paucker, eds. *Juden im Wilhelminischen Deutschland, 1890–1914*. Tübingen, 1976.

Mosse, Werner E., et al., eds. *Revolution and Evolution: 1848 in German-Jewish History*. Tübingen, 1981.

Müller, Alwin. *Die Geschichte der Juden in Köln von der Wiederzulassung 1798 bis zum 1850*. Cologne, 1984.

Niethammer, Lutz, ed. *Bürgerliche Gesellschaft in Deutschland: Historische Einblicke, Fragen, Perspektiven*. Frankfurt am Main, 1990.

Niewyk, Donald. *The Jews in Weimar Germany*. Baton Rouge, La., 1980.

Nipperdey, Thomas. *Deutsche Geschichte, 1800–1866: Bürgerwelt und starker Staat*. Munich, 1984.

Padover, Saul K. "The Baptism of Karl Marx's Family." *Midstream* 34 (June/July, 1978): 36–44.

Padtberg, Beate-Carola. "Kölner Unternehmer und die preussische Politik—Vom Vormärz zum Verfassungskonflikt." In Klara van Eyll, ed., *Kölner Unternehmer*, pp. 232–49. Cologne, 1984.

――. *Rheinischer Liberalismus in Köln während der politischen Reaktion in Preussen nach 1848/49*. Cologne, 1985.

Parkes, James. *The Jew in the Medieval Community*. 2nd ed. New York, 1969.

Perlitz, Uwe. *Das Geld-, Bank- und Versicherungswesen in Köln, 1700–1815*. Berlin, 1976.

Petri, Franz. "Preussen und das Rheinland." In Walter Först, ed., *Das Rheinland in Preussischer Zeit*, pp. 37–70. Cologne and Berlin, 1965.

Petri, Franz, et al., eds. *Handbuch der Historischen Stätten Deutschlands*, vol. 3, *Nordrhein-Westfalen*. Stuttgart, 1970.

Petri, Franz, and Georg Droege, eds. *Rheinische Geschichte*, vol. 2. Düsseldorf, 1976.

Philipson, David. *The Reform Movement in Judaism*. New York, 1931.

Pohl, Hans. "Wirtschaftsgeschichte Kölns im 18. und beginnenden 19. Jahrhundert." In Hermann Kellenbenz, ed., *Zwei Jahrtausende Kölner Wirtschaft*, 2: 9–62. Cologne, 1975.

Poliakov, Leon. *The History of Anti-Semitism from the Time of Christ to the Court Jews*. New York, 1974.

Pollack, Hermann. *Jewish Folkways in Germanic Lands, 1648–1806*. Cambridge, Mass., 1971.

Posener, S. "The Immediate Economic and Social Effects of the Emancipation of the Jews in France." *Jewish Social Studies* 1 (1939): 271–326.

Prestel, Claudia. *Jüdisches Schul- und Erziehungswesen in Bayern, 1804–1933.* Göttingen, 1989.

Priebatsch, Felix. *Die Judenpolitik des fürstlichen Absolutismus im 17. und 18. Jahrhundert.* Jena, 1915.

Prinz, Arthur. *Juden im Deutschen Wirtschaftsleben, 1850–1914.* Tübingen, 1948.

———. "New Perspectives on Marx as a Jew." *Leo Baeck Institute Yearbook* 15 (1970): 107–24.

Puppke, Ludwig. *Sozialpolitik und Soziale Anschauungen frühindustrieller Unternehmer.* Cologne, 1966.

Reinharz, Jehuda, and Walter Schatzberg, eds. *The Jewish Response to German Culture: From the Enlightenment to the Second World War.* Hanover, N.H., 1985.

Reissner, H. G. "The Histories of 'Kaufhaus N. Israel' and of Wilfrid Israel." *Leo Baeck Institute Yearbook* 3 (1958): 227–56.

———. "Rebellious Dilemma: The Case Histories of Eduard Gans and Some of His Partisans." *Leo Baeck Institute Yearbook* 2 (1957): 179–93.

Richarz, Monika. *Der Eintritt der Juden in die Akademischen Berufe.* Tübingen, 1974.

———. "Emancipation and Continuity—German Jews in the Rural Economy." In Werner E. Mosse et al., eds., *Revolution and Evolution: 1848 in German-Jewish History*, pp. 95–115. Tübingen, 1981.

———. "Jewish Social Mobility in Germany During the Time of Emancipation (1790–1871)." *Leo Baeck Institute Yearbook* 20 (1975): 69–77.

Richarz, Monika, ed. *Jüdisches Leben in Deutschland, 1780–1871.* New York, 1976.

Ritterband, Paul, ed. *Modern Jewish Fertility.* Leiden, 1981.

Robertson, Priscilla. *An Experience of Women: Pattern and Change in Nineteenth-Century Europe.* Philadelphia, 1982.

Rohr, Donald G. *The Origins of Social Liberalism in Germany.* Chicago, 1963.

Rohrbacher, Stefan. "Räuberbanden, Gaunertum und Bettelwesen." In Jutta Bohnke-Kollwitz et al., eds., *Köln und das rheinische Judentum*, pp. 117–24. Cologne, 1984.

Rosenberg, Hans. *Bureaucracy, Aristocracy and Autocracy: The Prussian Experience.* Cambridge, Mass., 1958.

———. *Grosse Depression und Bismarckzeit.* Berlin, 1967.

Rotenstreich, Nathan. "For and Against Emancipation: The Bruno Bauer Controversy." *Leo Baeck Institute Yearbook* 4 (1959): 3–36.

———. *Jews and German Philosophy.* New York, 1984.

Roth, Ernst. "Die Geschichte der jüdischen Gemeinden am Rhein im Mittelalter: Von der Epoche der Kreuzzüge bis zur Auflösung der Grossgemeinden im 15. Jahrhundert." In Konrad Schilling, ed., *Monumenta Judaica*, pp. 60–120.

Rozenblit, Marsha L. *The Jews of Vienna, 1867–1914: Assimilation and Identity.* Albany, N.Y., 1983.

Rürup, Reinhard. "An Appraisal of German-Jewish Historiography." *Leo Baeck Institute Yearbook* 35 (1990): xv–xxiv.

———. *Deutschland im 19. Jahrhundert, 1815–1871.* Göttingen, 1984.

———. "Emancipation and Crisis." *Leo Baeck Institute Yearbook* 20 (1975): 13–25.

———. "Emanzipation der Juden in Baden, 1782–1862." *Zeitschrift für die Geschichte des Oberrheins* 114 (1966): 225–38.

———. *Emanzipation und Antisemitismus.* Göttingen, 1975.

———. "Emanzipation und Antisemitismus: Historische Verbindungslinien." In Herbert A. Strauss and Norbert Kampe, eds., *Antisemitismus: Von der Judenfeindschaft zum Holocaust*, pp. 88–98. Bonn, 1984.

———. "Emanzipation und Krise: Zur Geschichte der 'Judenfrage' in Deutschland vor 1890." In Werner E. Mosse and Arnold Paucker, eds., *Juden in Wilhelminischen Deutschland*, pp. 1–56. Tübingen, 1976.

———. "The European Revolutions of 1848 and Jewish Emancipation." In Werner E. Mosse, Arnold Paucker, and Reinhold Rürup, eds., *Revolution and Evolution*, pp. 1–62. Tübingen, 1981.

———. "German Liberalism and the Emancipation of the Jews." *Leo Baeck Institute Yearbook* 20 (1975): 59–68.

———. "Jewish Emancipation and Bourgeois Society." *Leo Baeck Institute Yearbook* 14 (1969): 67–91.

———. "Kontinuität und Diskontinuität der 'Judenfrage' im 19. Jahrhundert. Zur Entstehung des modernen Antisemitismus." In Hans-Ulrich Wehler, ed., *Sozialgeschichte Heute*, pp. 388–415. Göttingen, 1971.

———. "The Tortuous and Thorny Path to Legal Equality — 'Jew Laws' and Emancipatory Legislation in Germany from the Late Eighteenth Century." *Leo Baeck Institute Yearbook* 31 (1986): 3–33.

Sachar, Howard Morley. *The Course of Modern Jewish History.* New York, 1977.

Schieder, Wolfgang. "Probleme einer Sozialgeschichte des frühen Liberalismus in Deutschland." In Wolfgang Schieder, ed., *Liberalismus in der Gesellschaft des deutschen Vormärz.* Göttingen, 1983, pp. 9–21.

———, ed. *Liberalismus in der Gesellschaft des deutschen Vormärz.* Göttingen, 1983.

Schilling, Konrad, ed. *Monumenta Judaica, Handbuch.* Cologne, 1963.

Schnabel, Franz. *Deutsche Geschichte im Neunzehnten Jahrhundert*, vols. 2, 3, and 4. Freiburg im Breisgau, 1934, 1949, 1951.

Schnee, Heinrich. "175 Jahre Bankhaus Salomon Oppenheim Jr. Bonn/Köln." *Bonner Geschichtsblätter* 18 (1964): 66–79.

———. *Die Hoffinanz und der Moderne Staat*, vol. 3. Berlin, 1955.

———. "Studien zur Institution des Hofjudentums in Kürköln." *Annalen des Historischen Vereins für den Niederrhein insbesondere das alte Erzbistum Köln* 151/152 (1952): 221–56.

Schoelkens, Josef. "Die Soziale Fürsorge." In *Die Stadt Cöln im ersten Jahrhundert unter Preussischer Herrschaft, 1815–1915*, 2: 506–18. Cologne, 1915.

Schofer, Lawrence. "Emancipation and Population Change." In Werner E. Mosse et al., eds., *Revolution and Evolution: 1848 in German-Jewish History*, pp. 63–89. Tübingen, 1981.

———. "The History of European Jewry — Search for a Method." *Leo Baeck Institute Yearbook* 24 (1979): 17–36.

Scholem, Gershom. *From Berlin to Jerusalem.* New York, 1980.

———. *On Jews and Judaism in Crisis.* New York, 1976.

Schorsch, Ismar. "Emancipation and the Crisis of Religious Authority: The Emergence of the Modern Rabbinate." In Werner E. Mosse et al., eds., *Revolution and Evolution: 1848 in German-Jewish History*, pp. 205–47. Tübingen, 1981.

——. "German Antisemitism in the Light of Post-war Historiography." *Leo Baeck Institute Yearbook* 19 (1974): 257–71.

——. *Heinrich Graetz: The Structure of Jewish History*. New York, 1975.

——. *Jewish Reactions to German Anti-Semitism, 1870–1914*. New York and London, 1972.

——. "The Myth of Sephardic Supremacy." *Leo Baeck Institute Yearbook* 34 (1989): 47–66.

Schulte, Klaus H. S. *Bonner Juden und ihre Nachkommen bis um 1930*. Bonn, 1976.

——. *Dokumentation zur Geschichte der Juden am linken Niederrhein seit dem 17. Jahrhundert*. Düsseldorf, 1972.

——. "Die Rechtslage der Juden in Köln und am Niederrhein, 1815–1847." In Jutta Bohnke-Kollwitz et al., eds., *Köln und das rheinische Judentum*, pp. 95–101. Cologne, 1984.

——. "Zur gewerblichen Betätigung der Juden in Köln und im ländlichen Rheinland." In Jutta Bohnke-Kollwitz et al., eds., *Köln und das rheinische Judentum*, pp. 125–40. Cologne, 1984.

Schultheis, Constantin. *Erläuterungen zum Geschichtlichen Atlas der Rheinprovinz*, vol. 1. Bonn, 1895.

Schutz, Rüdiger. *Preussen und die Rheinlande: Studien zur preussischen Integrationspolitik im Vormärz*. Wiesbaden, 1979.

Schwank, Klaus. "Peter Heinrich Merkens." In Nachrichtenamt der Stadt Köln, ed., *Kölner Biographien*, vol. 2. Cologne, 1973.

Schwann, Mathieu. *Geschichte der Kölner Handelskammer*. Cologne, 1906.

——. "Grundlagen und Organisation des Wirtschaftslebens." In Joseph Hansen, ed., *Die Rheinprovinz, 1815–1915*, 1: 196–249. Bonn, 1917.

——. *Ludolf Camphausen*. 3 vols. Essen an der Ruhr, 1915.

Schwarzfuchs, Simon. *Napoleon, the Jews and the Sanhedrin*. London, 1979.

Schwering, Leo. "Die Auswanderung protestantischer Kaufleute aus Köln nach Mülheim am Rhein im Jahre 1714." *Westdeutsche Zeitschrift* 26 (1907): 194–250.

Sheehan, James J. *German History, 1770–1866*. Oxford, 1989.

——. *German Liberalism in the Nineteenth Century*. Chicago and London, 1983.

——. "Liberalism and Society in Germany, 1815–48." *Journal of Modern History* 45 (1973): 583–604.

——. "Liberalism and the City in Nineteenth-Century Germany." *Past and Present* 51 (1971): 116–37.

——. "Partei, Volk and Staat: Some Reflections on the Relationship Between Liberal Thought and Action in Vormärz." In Hans-Ulrich Wehler, ed., *Sozialgeschichte Heute*, pp. 162–74. Göttingen, 1971.

Shorter, Edward. *The Making of the Modern Family*. New York, 1975.

Silbergleit, Heinrich. *Die Bevölkerungs- und Berufsverhältnisse der Juden im deutschen Reich*. Berlin, 1930.

Silberner, Edmund. "Was Marx an Anti-Semite?" *Historia Judaica* 11 (1949): 3–52.

Simon, W. *The Failure of the Prussian Reform Movement, 1807–1819*. New York, 1971.

Simons, Eduard. "Die Evangelische Kirche." In Joseph Hansen, ed., *Die Rheinprovinz, 1815–1915*, 2: 197–216. Bonn, 1917.

Simons, Ernst. *Geschichte der Judischen Gemeinden in Bonner Raum*. Bonn, 1959.

Smith, Bonnie. *Changing Lives: Women in European History Since 1700*. Lexington, Mass., 1989.

———. *Ladies of the Leisure Class: The Bourgeoises of Northern France in the Nineteenth Century*. Princeton, N.J., 1981.

Snell, John L. *The German Democratic Movement in Germany, 1789–1914*. Chapel Hill, N.C., 1976.

Soliday, Gerald. *A Community in Conflict: Frankfurt Society in the Seventeenth and Early Eighteenth Centuries*. Hanover, N.H., 1974.

Sorkin, David. "The Invisible Community: Emancipation, Secular Culture, and Jewish Identity in the Writings of Berthold Auerbach." In Jehuda Reinharz and Walter Schatzberg, eds., *The Jewish Response to German Culture*, pp. 100–119. Hanover, N.H., 1985.

———. *The Transformation of German Jewry, 1780–1840*. New York, 1987.

Sperber, Jonathan. *Popular Catholicism in Nineteenth-Century Germany*. Princeton, 1984.

Stanislawski, Michael. *Tsar Nicholas I and the Jews: The Transformation of Jewish Society in Russia, 1825–1855*. Philadelphia, 1983.

Steffens, Wilhelm. "Die linksrheinischen Provinzen Preussens unter Französischer Herrschaft." *Rheinischer Vierteljahresblätter* 19 (1954): 402–65.

Stehkämper, Hugo. "Über die rechtliche Absicherung der Stadt Köln gegen eine erzbischöfliche Landesherrschaft vor 1288." In Werner Besch et al., eds., *Die Stadt Köln in Europäischen Geschichte*, pp. 343–77. Bonn, 1972.

Steimel, Robert. *Kölner Köpfer*. Cologne, 1958.

Steinberg, Heinz Günter. "Phasen der Bevölkerungsentwicklung." In Walter Först, ed., *Das Rheinland in Preussischer Zeit*, pp. 109–24. Cologne and Berlin, 1965.

Steitz, Walter. *Die Entstehung der Köln-Mindener Eisenbahngesellschaft*. Cologne, 1974.

Stepelevich, Lawrence S. "Marx and the Jews." *Judaism* 23, no. 2 (Spring, 1974): 150–60.

Sterling, Eleonore. "Jewish Reactions to Jew-Hatred in the First Half of the 19th Century." *Leo Baeck Institute Yearbook* 3 (1958): 103–21.

———. *Judenhass: Die Anfänge des politischen Antisemitismus in Deutschland (1815–1850)*. Frankfurt am Main, 1969.

———. "Der Kampf um die Emanzipation der Juden im Rheinland." In Konrad Schilling, ed., *Monumenta Judaica*, pp. 282–308. Cologne, 1963.

Stern, Fritz. *The Failure of Illiberalism: Essays on the Political Culture of Modern Germany*. New York, 1972.

———. *Gold and Iron: Bismarck, Bleichröder and the Building of the German Empire*. New York, 1977.

———. *The Politics of Cultural Despair: A Study in the Rise of the Germanic Ideology*. Berkeley, 1974.

Stern, Selma. *The Court Jew: A Contribution to the History of Absolutism in Europe.* Philadelphia, 1950.

———. *Die Preussische Staat und die Juden,* 8 vols. Tübingen, 1962.

Stern-Täubler, Selma. "Der literarische Kampf um die Emanzipation in den Jahren 1816–1820 und seine ideologischen und soziologischen Voraussetzungen." *Hebrew Union College Annual* 23 (1950–51): 171–96.

Strait, Paul. *Cologne in the Twelfth Century.* Gainesville, Fla., 1974.

Straus, Raphael. "The Jews in the Economic Evolution of Central Europe." *Jewish Social Studies* 3 (1941): 15–40.

———. *Die Juden in Wirtschaft und Gesellschaft.* Frankfurt am Main, 1964.

Strauss, Herbert. "Liberalism and Conservatism in Prussian Legislation for Jewish Affairs, 1815–1847." In Herbert Strauss and Hanns G. Reissner, eds., *Jubilee Volume Dedicated to Curt C. Silberman,* pp. 114–32. New York, 1969.

———. "Pre-Emancipation Prussian Policies Towards the Jews, 1815–1847." *Leo Baeck Institute Yearbook* 11 (1966): 107–36.

———. "Die Preussische Bürokratie und die anti-jüdischen Unruhen im Jahre 1834." In Herbert Strauss and Kurt Grossman, eds., *Gegenwart im Rückblick,* pp. 27–55. Heidelberg, 1970.

Stürmer, Michael, Gabriele Teichmann, and Wilhelm Treue. *Wägen und Wagen: Sal. Oppenheim jr. & Cie. Geschichte einer Bank und einer Familie.* Munich, 1989.

Szajkowski, Zosa. "Jewish Participation in the Sale of National Property During the French Revolution." *Jewish Social Studies* 14 (1952): 291–316.

Tal, Uriel. *Christians and Jews in Germany: Religion, Politics and Ideology in the Second Reich, 1870–1914.* Ithaca, N.Y., 1975.

Thamer, Hans-Ulrich. "Emanzipation und Tradition: Zur Ideen- und Sozialgeschichte von Liberalismus und Handwerk in der ersten Hälfte des neunzehnten Jahrhunderts." In Wolfgang Schieder, ed., *Liberalismus in der Gesellschaft des deutschen Vormärz,* pp. 55–73. Göttingen, 1983.

Thernstrom, Stephan. *Poverty and Progress: Social Mobility in a Nineteenth-Century City.* Cambridge, Mass., 1964.

Tilly, Louise, and Joan Scott. *Women, Work and Family.* New York, 1978.

Tilly, Richard. *Financial Institutions and Industrialization in the Rhineland, 1815–1870.* Madison, Wis., 1966.

———. "Finanzielle Aspekte der preussischen Industrialisierung, 1815–1870." In Wolfram Fischer, ed., *Wirtschaft- und Sozialgeschichtliche Probleme der frühen Industrialisierung,* pp. 476–90. Berlin, 1968.

———. "Moral Standards and Business Behavior in Nineteenth-Century Germany and Britain." In Jürgen Kocka and Allan Mitchell, eds., *Bourgeois Society in Nineteenth-Century Europe,* pp. 179–206. Oxford, 1993.

Tipton, Frank B. "The National Consensus in German Economic History." *Central European History* 3 (Sept. 1974): 195–224.

———. *Regional Variations in the Economic Development of Germany During the Nineteenth Century.* Middletown, Conn., 1976.

Toury, Jacob. "Der Anteil der Juden an der Städtischen Selbstverwaltung im Vormärzlichen Deutschland." *Bulletin des Leo Baecks Instituts* 6, no. 23 (1963): 265–86.

———. "Der Eintritt der Juden ins deutsche Bürgertum." In Hans Liebeschutz and Arnold Paucker, eds., *Das Judentum in der Deutschen Umwelt, 1800–1850*, pp. 139–242. Tübingen, 1977.

———. *Der Eintritt der Juden ins Deutsche Bürgertum, Eine Dokumentation.* Tel Aviv, 1972.

———. "The 'Jewish Question,' A Semantic Approach." *Leo Baeck Institute Yearbook* 11 (1966): 85–106.

———. *Die politischen Orientierungen der Juden in Deutschland.* Tübingen, 1966.

———. "Probleme Jüdischer Gleichberechtigung auf Lokalbürgerliche Ebene." *Jahrbuch des Instituts für Deutsche Geschichte* 2 (1973): 267–86.

———. "Die Revolution von 1848 als innerjüdischer Wendepunkt." In Hans Liebeschutz and Arnold Paucker, eds., *Das Judentum in der Deutschen Umwelt, 1800–1850*, pp. 359–76. Tübingen, 1977.

———. "Der rheinischen Jahre des Schriftstellers Hermann Hersch." In Jutta Bohnke-Kollwitz et al., eds., *Köln und das rheinische Judentum*, pp. 183–96. Cologne, 1984.

———. *Soziale und Politische Geschichte der Juden in Deutschland, 1847–1871.* Düsseldorf, 1977.

———. *Turmoil and Confusion in the Revolution of 1848* [Hebrew]. Tel Aviv, 1968.

———. "Types of Jewish Municipal Rights in German Townships." *Leo Baeck Institute Yearbook* 22 (1977): 55–80.

Treitschke, Heinrich von. *Deutsche Geschichte im neunzehnten Jahrhundert*, vols. 4 and 5. Leipzig, 1889, 1894.

Treue, Wilhelm. "Abraham Oppenheim, 1804–1878." *Rheinische-Westfälische Wirtschaftsbiographien* 8 (1962): 1–31.

———. "The Bankers Simon and Abraham Oppenheim, 1812–1880. The Private Background to the Professional Activity, Their Role in Politics and Ennoblement." In *German Yearbook on Business History*, pp. 41–76. Berlin and Heidelberg, 1987.

———. "Das Bankhaus Salomon Oppenheim Jr. und Cie und der öffentlich Kredit." In *150 Jahre Regierungsbezirk Köln*, pp. 398–404. West Berlin, 1966.

———. "Dagobert Oppenheim." *Tradition* 9 (Aug. 1969): 145–96.

———. "Einige Kapitel aus der Geschichte der Kölner Bankiersfamilie Oppenheim." In Jutta Bohnke-Kollwitz, Willehad Paul Eckert, et al., eds. *Köln und das rheinische Judentum*, pp. 141–58. Cologne, 1984.

———. "Die Juden in der Wirtschaft des rheinischen Raumes, 1648 bis 1945." In Konrad Schilling, ed., *Monumenta Judaica*, pp. 419–65. Cologne, 1963.

———. "Die Kölner Banken, 1835 bis 1871." In Klara van Eyll, ed., *Kölner Unternehmer*, pp. 85–95. Cologne, 1984.

———. "Das Verhältnis von Fürst, Staat und Unternehmer in der Zeit des Merkantilismus." *Vierteljahrsschrift für Sozial- und Wirtschaftsgeschichte* 44 (1957): 26–56.

Trevor-Roper, Hugh. "Religion, the Reformation and Social Change." In Hugh Trevor-Roper, *The European Witch Craze of the Sixteenth and Seventeenth Centuries and Other Essays*, pp. 1–45. New York, 1967.

Ulrich, Herbert. "Von der 'Reichskristallnacht' zum Holocaust." In Lutz Niethammer, ed., *Bürgerliche Gesellschaft in Deutschland: Historische Einblicke, Fragen, Perspektiven*, pp. 489–504. Frankfurt am Main, 1990.

van Eyll, Klara. *In Kölner Adressbüchern geblättert*. Cologne, 1978.

———. "Kölner Banken im 19. Jahrhundert und ihr Einfluss auf die Industrialisierung in der Rheinprovinz." 2 parts. *Mitteilungen der Industrie- und Handelskammer* 1 (1955): 250–58; 2 (1956): 274–80.

———, ed. *Kölner Unternehmer und die Frühindustrialisierung im Rheinland und in Westfalen (1835–1871)*. Cologne, 1984.

———. "Wirtschaftsgeschichte Kölns vom Beginn der Preussischen Zeit bis zur Reichsgründung." In Hermann Kellenbenz, ed., *Zwei Jahrtausende Kölner Wirtschaft*, 2: 163–266. Cologne, 1975.

Vierhaus, Rudolf. "Preussen und die Rheinlande 1815–1915." *Rheinische Vierteljahrsblätter* 30 (1965): 152–75.

Volkov, Shulamit. "Antisemitism as a Cultural Code: Reflections on the Historiography of Antisemitism in Imperial Germany." *Leo Baeck Institute Yearbook* 23 (1978): 25–46.

———. "The Dynamics of Dissimilation: Ostjuden and German Jews." In Jehuda Reinharz and Walter Schatzberg, eds., *The Jewish Response to German Culture*, pp. 195–211. Hanover, N. H., 1985.

———. *Die Juden in Deutschland, 1780–1918*. Munich, 1994.

———. *Jüdisches Leben und Antisemitismus im 19. und 20. Jahrhundert*. Munich, 1990.

———. *The Rise of Popular Antimodernism in Germany: The Urban Master Artisans, 1873–1896*. Princeton, N.J., 1978.

———. "The Social and Political Function of Late-Nineteenth-Century Antisemitism: The Case of the Small Handicraft Masters." In Hans-Ulrich Wehler, ed., *Sozialgeschichte Heute*, pp. 416–31. Göttingen, 1971.

———. "The 'Verbürgerlichung' of the Jews as a Paradigm." In Jürgen Kocka and Allan Mitchell, eds., *Bourgeois Society in Nineteenth-Century Europe*, pp. 367–91. Oxford, 1993.

Walker, Mack. *German Home Towns: Community, State, and General Estate, 1648–1871*. Ithaca, N.Y., 1971.

Waltershausen, A. Sartorius von. *Deutsche Wirtschaftsgeschichte, 1815–1914*. Jena, 1923.

Wehler, Hans-Ulrich, ed. *Moderne deutsche Sozialgeschichte*. Cologne and Berlin, 1966.

Weinryb, Bernard. *The Jews in Poland: A Social and Economic History of the Jewish Community in Poland from 1100–1800*. Philadelphia, 1972.

———. "Prolegomena to an Economic History of the Jews in Modern Times." *Leo Baeck Institute Yearbook* 1 (1956): 279–306.

Wenninger, Markus. *Man Bedarf Keiner Juden Mehr. Ursachen und Hintegründe ihrer Vertreibung aus deutschen Reichsstädten im 15. Jahrhundert*. Vienna, Cologne, and Graz, 1981.

Wenzel, Stefi Jersch. *Jüdische Bürger und Kommunale Selbstverwaltung in Preussischen Städten, 1808–1848*. Berlin, 1967.

———. "Die Lage von Minderheiten als Indiz für den Stand der Emanzipation einer Gesellschaft." In Hans-Ulrich Wehler, ed., *Sozialgeschichte Heute*, pp. 365–87. Göttingen, 1971.

Weyden, Ernst. *Geschichte der Juden in Köln am Rhein von den Römerzeiten bis auf die Gegenwart.* Cologne, 1867.

———. *Köln am Rhein vor fünfzig Jahren.* Cologne, 1862.

Wilhelm, Kurt. "The Jewish Community in the Post-Emancipation Period." *Leo Baeck Institute Yearbook* 2 (1957): 47–75.

Winter, David. *Geschichte der jüdischen Gemeinde in Moisling/Lübeck.* Lübeck, 1968.

Wischnitzer, Rachel. *The Architecture of the Synagogue.* Philadelphia, 1964.

Wistrich, Robert S. *Socialism and the Jews: The Dilemmas of Assimilation in Germany and Austria-Hungary.* East Brunswick, N.Y., 1982.

Wolf, G. *Zur Geschichte der Juden in Worms und des deutschen Städtewesens.* Breslau, 1862.

Wurm, Franz F. *Wirtschaft und Gesellschaft in Deutschland, 1848–1948.* Opladen, 1969.

Zimmerman, Mosche. "Jewish History and Jewish Historiography." *Leo Baeck Institute Yearbook* 35 (1990): 35–52.

Zorn, Wolfgang. "Preussischer Staat und rheinische Wirtschaft, 1815–1830." In Georg Droege et al., eds., *Landschaft und Geschichte*, pp. 552–60. Bonn, 1970.

Zunkel, Friedrich. "Kolner Unternehmer im Zeitalter der Frühindustrialisierung — zur Unternehmertypologie." In Klara van Eyll, ed., *Kölner Unternehmer*, pp. 208–16. Cologne, 1984.

———. *Der Rheinisch-Westfälische Unternehmer, 1834–1879.* Cologne and Opladen, 1962.

———. "Das Verhältnis des Unternehmertums zum Bildungsbürgertum zwischen Vormärz und Ersten Weltkrieg." In M. Rainer Lepsius, ed., *Bildungsbürgertum im neunzehnten Jahrhundert*, pt. 3, *Lebensführung und Ständische Vergesellschaftung*, pp. 82–101. Stuttgart, 1992.

Index

In this index "f" after a number indicates a separate reference on the next page, and "ff" indicates separate references on the next two pages. A continuous discussion over two or more pages is indicated by a span of page numbers. *Passim* is used for a cluster of references in close but not consecutive sequence.

Library of Congress Cataloging-in-Publication Data

Magnus, Shulamit S.
   Jewish emancipation in a German city : Cologne, 1798–1871 /
Shulamit S. Magnus.
      p.   cm. — (Stanford studies in Jewish history and culture)
Includes bibliographical references and index.
ISBN 0-8047-2644-2 (cloth : alk. paper)
1. Jews — Germany — Cologne — History — 19th century.   2. Jews —
Emancipation — Germany — Cologne.   3. Cologne (Germany) — Ethnic
relations.   I. Title.   II. Series.
DS135.G4C684   1997
943'.5514004924 — dc20   96-25758
                                                              CIP

⊛ This book is printed on acid-free, recycled paper.

Original printing 1997
Last figure below indicates year of this printing:
06 05 04 03 02 01 00 99 98 97